Henrietta Drake-Brockman
Australia's best-known author:
Her writing career began in
stationed with her husband, then Commissioner for the
North-West, in Broome. She wrote lively articles based
on her extensive travels in the region, which appeared
in the *West Australian* under the pseudonym "Henry
Drake". However, it was not long before her own name
became a force in Australian literature.

Drake-Brockman's first novel, *Blue North* (1934), was
followed by *Sheba Lane* (1936), *Younger Sons* (1937),
The Fatal Days (1947) and *The Wicked and the Fair*
(1957). Well-known for her short stories, she published
a collection, *Sydney or the Bush*, in 1948, and edited the
anthologies *Australian Short Stories* (with Walter
Murdoch, 1951), *Australian Legendary Tales* (with K.
Langloh Parker, 1953) and *West Coast Stories* (1959).

She was an accomplished playwright and in 1938 won
the Sesqui-Centenary Celebration Prize for best full-
length Australian play—*Men Without Wives*.

Drake-Brockman was active in the foundation and
running of the Fellowship of Australian Writers (W.A.),
and was granted Honorary Life Membership in 1967.
She was generous with her time, and is remembered
as having given much encouragement and advice to
young writers.

Paradoxically, although Drake-Brockman considered
herself first and foremost a creative writer, *Voyage to
Disaster* is her greatest work. It was a project that
consumed more than ten years of her life and marked
a major achievement in historical research and writing.

Henrietta Drake-Brockman died in 1968, at the age
of sixty-six.

Ongeluckige Voyagie,
Van't
SCHIP BATAVIA,
Nae
OOST-INDIEN.

Uytgevaren onder de E. *François Pelsaert.*

Ghebleven op de Abrolhos van Frederick Houtman, **op de hooch-**
te van 28; graden/ bp Zupden de Linie Æquinoctiael.

Vervattende 't verongelucken des Schips, en de grouwelijcke
Moorderyen onder 't Scheeps-volck, op 't Eylandt *Batavies Kerck-hoff;*
nevens de straffe der handtdadighers in de Jaren
1628 en 1629.

**Hier achter is by-gevoeght eenige discoursen der Oost-Indi-
sche Zee-vaert/ als mede de gantsche gelegentheydt der Koop-
manschappen dienen in Indien doet.**

t'AMSTERDAM,

Voor Joost Hartgers, **Boeck-verkooper in de Gasthups-steegh / besyden het
Stadt-huys / in de Boeck-winckel,** Anno 1648.

Title page of the Joost Hartgers 1648 edition of *Ongeluckige Voyagie van't Schip Batavia.* The two ships can be taken to represent the *Batavia* and the smaller *Sardam.* The overhanging "gallery" aft shows clearly in the larger vessel.

HENRIETTA DRAKE-BROCKMAN

VOYAGE TO DISASTER

University of Western Australia Press

To
JOHANNA
BARONESS VAN LYNDEN–DE CLERCQ

This edition published in 1995 by
University of Western Australia Press
Nedlands, 6907 Western Australia
Reprinted 2000

First published by Angus & Robertson Publishers, Australia, 1963,
and in Australian Classics edition, 1982

This book is copyright. Apart from any fair dealing for the purposes of private study, research, criticism or review, as permitted under the Copyright Act 1968, no part may be reproduced by any process without written permission. Enquiries should be made to the publisher.

© Copyright translation Kitty I. T. Drok, Estate of H. Drake-Brockman 1963
© Copyright this selection, Estate of H. Drake-Brockman 1963
© Copyright introduction F. Broeze 1995

National Library of Australia
Cataloguing-in-publication data

Drake-Brockman, H. (Henrietta), 1901–1968.
   Voyage to disaster.

   New ed.
   Bibliography
   ISBN 1 875560 32 7

1. Pelsaert, Francisco, D. 1630. 2. Batavia (Ship). 3. Shipwrecks—Western Australia. 4. Merchant seamen—Netherlands—Biography. I. Pelsaert, Francisco, d. 1630. II. Drok, E. D. (Evert D.). III. Title.

919.413

Cover illustration: *Wreck of the Batavia* by Arthur Wakefield Bassett, reproduced with kind permission of Max Cramer.

Produced by Benchmark Publications Management, Melbourne
Printed by Scott Print Perth

FOREWORD

STORIES of ships and the sea, of islands and coral reefs are to me irresistibly compelling. Perhaps the reason for this is that my father sailed from London to the Tonga Isles long before I was born. To a small child his stories of blue-water sailing ships and those who manned them opened a thrilling world of danger and courage, of endurance, of adventure. And of all sea-stories the wrecking of the Dutch ship *Batavia* on the Abrolhos Islands off the coast of Western Australia, in 1629, has caught and held my attention most.

I first learnt of this world-famous disaster at the age of twelve, when I became a friend of the Broadhurst family. The father of my playmates, Mr Florance Broadhurst, was no longer living, but he had been one of the pioneers of the Abrolhos guano industry. Becoming interested in the history of the islands, he had acquired a copy of *Ongeluckige Voyagie van't Schip Batavia*, printed at Amsterdam in 1647; also in his library was a novel by W. J. Gordon, published in London in 1888, named *The Captain General*. This latter we youngsters read. Even at that age, delighted as I was by the drama of the wreck, I felt that the inaccuracy of the historical background and more particularly the ingenuousness of the human story (though hardly realized in those terms) were unworthy of such a tragedy. Possibly then and there I determined to discover the real facts—I cannot remember—but for a time the island story conditioned our games and coloured my dreams. Here was a coral islet close at hand, haunted, beckoning.

Five years later I visited Geraldton to stay at the Residency, then the home of Mr Raymond Gee. From the veranda I stared out to sea: just over the horizon lay the Abrolhos Islands. I listened eagerly to all (not many) who had been there; but fishing and fun called up neither ghosts nor a background to legend. When soon I married, yearly passing up and down to the North-West, the Abrolhos continued to tantalize, never visible, still just over my horizon.

By then I had read William Siebenhaar's translation of the 1647 *Ongeluckige Voyagie*; I had also begun to write. About this time I consciously made up my mind that some day I would search out the details of the *Batavia* wreck. Books by other writers were published; but no one had been able to afford time for full research, an intimidating task when most material was in Old Dutch, in Holland. Nor was I able to think seriously about the subject until 1938. Then Mr Justice Ferguson, of Sydney, kindly wrote to Djakarta on my behalf; but before any progress was made, war intervened.

Ten more years passed before I was able to return to my intention. Even then the difficulties of communication with Holland and Java were great. The Hon. T. D. Mutch offered encouragement and help, introducing me to Pelsaert's Indian life, and so to Professor Pieter Geyl of Utrecht, who with extraordinary kindness sent me one of his own copies of *Jahangir's India*, an English translation of Pelsaert's own Indian Report.

It was first of all necessary to find someone able and willing to translate Old Dutch. My friend the Baroness van Lynden–de Clercq arranged for me to meet Mr E. D. Drok; and with great generosity he engaged in an undertaking that, I must admit, we would neither of us have considered had we realized the years of toil involved.

At first, after I had located Pelsaert's Journals at the Algemeen Rijksarchief, The Hague, we thought it might hasten matters to have a free translation into modern Dutch made on the spot. This was done at my expense by Dr G. J. W. de Jongh, and duly rendered into English by Mr Drok, reading aloud from the typescript. For fiction, originally in my mind, this would have sufficed; but the more facts we uncovered (from other sources as well), the more the historical aspect appealed to me. Also, modern science, as well as new equipment at the State Library, Perth, came to our aid, enabling me to have the original Journals, as well as other documents, microfilmed at The Hague and in Amsterdam, to be read here. In addition, by the courtesy of Mr K. Wallace-Crabbe, of Melbourne, who had long been interested in the *Batavia* story, many important passages of the Journals were enlarged from the microfilm into handsome prints nearly twice the size of the original pages—a most valuable assistance. Throughout this time I remained torn between fiction and fact. As I am a novelist, the former won. But no sooner was a novel—*The Wicked and the Fair*—completed, than I began to sort, sift, and more accurately examine the enormous amount of factual material accumulated; it seemed unreasonable not to publish in full various documents of social and historical importance to Australia. Moreover, it was surely more than ungracious not to give proper recognition to Mr Drok's exacting and scholarly work in thus translating Pelsaert's Journals and many other documents from the original Old Dutch.

All renderings from Dutch and Old Dutch used in this work have been made by Mr Drok, reading aloud from microfilm, photostat, or the printed page, for me to take down by hand and later transcribe to typescript for study and selection; but he is not responsible for either the presentation or the notes and explanations appearing throughout. My own researches into the life of Francisco Pelsaert, the history of the wrecked *Batavia* and the probable site of the wreck ended in 1961.

Now, in 1963, the discovery of the remains of the wreck, submerged on the reefs of the Wallabi Group of the Abrolhos Islands rather more than a mile from where my researches led me to believe she must lie, is a gratifying proof of sound reasoning. In 1955 and 1956 I published, respectively, an article in *Walkabout* and the text of a paper read before the Western Australian Historical Society, both stating that I considered that the *Batavia* had been wrecked in the vicinity of Noon Reef. Discovery shows that she lies slightly more to the east, on Morning Reef.

In 1960 Mr Hugh Edwards, whose notable adventures in skin-diving have been recorded in his book, *Gods and Little Fishes*, discussed with me the probable site of the wreck. Soon after, as part of a plan concerned with the discovery of Dutch wrecks on the Western Australian coast, a decision was made, in view of my theories, to search for the *Batavia* on the southern reefs of the Wallabi Group.

Considerably later Mr David Johnson, a crayfisherman of Beacon Island and Geraldton, who also knew of my theories, spotted the remains of an unknown wreck on Morning Reef. When this year he heard that Mr Max Cramer, President of the Geraldton Skin-divers Club, in association with Mr Edwards was planning an expedition to the Wallabi Reefs, Mr Johnson sent word of his find. Mr Cramer at once visited the islands. On 4th June, three hundred and thirty-four years to the day after the disaster, Mr Cramer inspected the remains of this ship and found many surrounding guns lying encrusted on the sea floor. One was immediately raised. It is marked with the cipher of the Dutch East India Company and also a large A, signifying that it belonged to the Chamber of Amsterdam (as did the *Batavia*). Skeletons bearing marks of violent death, and other relics since found on Beacon Island, notably a brass lamp-base marked with the date 1627 (the year the new ship would have been fitted), make it certain that this island must have been the principal one inhabited by the castaways.

Originally my own choice of wreck site had been Morning Reef in preference to Noon Reef. However, it was not possible for me to visit Beacon Island in 1952. I had perforce to depend on fishermen's statements that there was no beach (a necessity for *Batavia's*

Graveyard) on that island. But in fact there is a small beach, sufficient to meet the requirements.

These discoveries have therefore led to the removal of two chapters from the main text of this volume; one dealing with the wreck site, the other with the subsequent landings on the continent. These chapters have now been incorporated as appendixes, in order that readers who are interested may follow in full the reasoning that led to my contention that the wreck took place where it did, on the Wallabi reefs, and not, as hitherto so frequently maintained, in the Pelsart Group. The landing sites on the mainland still remain an open question; but I am encouraged to hope that my reckonings in that respect are equally near the mark.

It is not possible to acknowledge individually the innumerable people who assisted research. My grateful thanks are due to the Hon. W. McMahon, M.P., whose permission as Minister for Air enabled me to fly on a routine exercise covering the islands and the neighbouring coast; and to the R.A.A.F. personnel at Pearce who made me welcome. I would like also to thank the fishermen who took me in their boats to both the Pelsart and Wallabi groups of the Abrolhos and readily contributed the benefit of their local knowledge.

I am greatly indebted, for help and encouragement, to the Baroness van Lynden–de Clercq, Perth; to the Hon. Paul Hasluck, M.P. and his wife, Alexandra Hasluck, Perth; to Professor Pieter Geyl, Utrecht; to Dr F. R. J. Verhoeven, Amsterdam; to Dr Terpstra, Hilversum; to the late Professor Neville Burkitt, Sydney; to Commander A. H. Cooper, R.A.N., Sydney; to the late Dr W. Arriens, of the Netherlands Consulate, Perth; to Mr C. de Heer, Perth, and Mr J. Bouwes, Amsterdam; to Mr E. M. Barker, and Mr F. H. Goldsmith, Perth; to Mr David Elder, Melbourne; to Dr Ross McWhae and Mr Murray Johnstone, Perth; and to Mr Frank Forman, Dr D. L. Serventy, Captain E. J. Courthope, and the late Mr L. Glauert, Perth.

I am especially grateful for the untiring assistance given by the librarians, archivists, and staffs of many libraries and state offices both in Australia and overseas. In particular I wish to acknowledge the help of Miss P. Mander-Jones, former Librarian of the Mitchell Library, Sydney, and members of her staff, particularly Mr J. Penbroek; Miss M. Lukis, Librarian of the J. S. Battye Library and State Archives, Perth, and the members of her staff; Mr A. van der Poest Clement and Mrs. M. A. P. Meilink-Roelofsz, of the Algemeen Rijksarchief, The Hague; Mr C. L. Drake, of the Library Board of Western Australia; Miss M. E. Wood, former Librarian of the University of Western Australia;

Mr R. Price, Mr R. Wright, and other officers of the State Library, Perth; Mr G. A. Cox, Director of the Scheepvaart Museum, Amsterdam, and officers of the British Museum, London, and of the Hydrographic Department of the Admiralty, London; also the officers of the Commonwealth Bureau of Mineral Resources and of the Lands and Surveys Department, Perth; the late Mr H. S. Spigl, formerly Government Astronomer, Perth, and Mr B. J. Harris of his staff; Mr S. Wirjowinoto, of Arsip Negara, Djakarta; Professor F. Blockmans, of the Stadsarchief, Antwerp; Dr G. H. Kurtz, of the Archief der Gemeente Haarlem; Mr W. F. H. Oldewelt and Dr I. H. van Eeghen, Gemeentelijke Archiefdienst of Amsterdam; Dr R. van Roijen, Gemeente-Archief of Leyden; Mrs A. N. Zadoks-Josephus Jitta, of the Royal Coin Cabinet, The Hague, and Miss D. Miner, of the Walters Art Gallery, Baltimore, U.S.A.

Lastly, I wish to express my deep appreciation to Dr W. Ph. Coolhaas, Professor of Colonial History at the University of Utrecht, for so graciously and carefully reading this work in manuscript and offering expert advice on the correction or elucidation of a number of points, and to Dr I. Schöffer, formerly of the University of Western Australia, for generously giving his time for yet another reading of the manuscript.

The care and patience of Mrs Marjorie Rees in typing this, the worst of many manuscripts she has handled for me, cannot be sufficiently acknowledged; nor my husband's constant and sympathetic support to an undertaking he must frequently have found tedious.

It is to be hoped that those who study the Journals of Francisco Pelsaert and the other documents included in this book will agree with the words of Mr T. D. Mutch, who wrote to me in 1947:

> There is manuscript material in the Rijksarchief . . . which should be dug out and translated by a competent scholar . . . for the wreck of the *Batavia* provides the greatest dramatic tragedy in Australian history, beside which the Mutiny on the *Bounty* is an anaemic tale.

Perth, W.A.
1963   H. DRAKE-BROCKMAN

CONTENTS

Introduction to New Edition by Frank Broeze		xvii

THE LIFE AND TIMES OF FRANCISCO PELSAERT

I.	Pelsaert and the East India Company	3
II.	Report From India	21
III.	Distinction, Disaster, and Death	35
IV.	The Skipper of the *Batavia*, and Others	61
V.	Trade Jewels	84
VI.	The Journals, and Some Legal Aspects	94

THE JOURNALS OF FRANCISCO PELSAERT

Officers, Crew and Others Aboard the *Batavia* who are mentioned in the Journals	107
Diary of Events following the Wreck of the *Batavia*, 1629	112
Text of the Journals	122

APPENDIXES

I.	J. P. Coen's Order to Pelsaert	257
II.	Last Letter of Francisco Pelsaert	259
III.	The Dagh Register Report of 22nd March 1636	262
IV.	The Letter of Gijsbert Bastiaensz, Predikant	263
V.	Final Sentences on Men Already Examined and Sentenced Aboard *Sardam*	270
VI.	Letter From Rubens to Peiresc	272
VII.	The White Angel	273
VIII.	Moreland's Assessment of Pelsaert	274
IX.	The Site of the Wreck	275
X.	The Landings in Australia	295
XI.	Henrietta Drake-Brockman's Account of the Wreck Expedition	305

BIBLIOGRAPHY	311
INDEX	317

ILLUSTRATIONS

Title page of the Joost Hartgers 1648 edition of *Ongeluckige Voyagie van't Schip Batavia*. *Frontispiece*
The Trustees, Mitchell Library, Sydney

Section of V.O.C. map compiled after the 1642 and 1644 voyages of Abel Janszoon Tasman. The whole map shows all that was known of Australia and New Guinea in 1644. 46
The Trustees, Mitchell Library, Sydney; The Library Board of Western Australia

View of Amsterdam by C. Janszoon Visscher, dated 1614. 47
Rijksmuseum, Amsterdam

Francisco Pelsaert, a reputed portrait from a copy of an etching or engraving supposedly made in India about 1625. It was presented by E. Das Gupta in Lahore in 1945 to K. Wallace-Crabbe Esq. of Melbourne, who gave it to the author. 78

The Emperor Jahangir (Selim Ghe-hangier Shah), from a contemporary drawing reproduced in *Purchas His Pilgrimes*. 79
Library Board of Western Australia

Hendrick Brouwer (brother-in-law to Pelsaert), Governor-General for the V.O.C. at Batavia 1632-6. From *Vies des Gouverneurs-Généraux*, Du Bois, 1763. 94
Library Board of Western Australia

Antonio van Diemen, Governor-General for the V.O.C. at Batavia 1636-45. From *Vies des Gouverneurs-Généraux*, Du Bois, 1763. 94
Library Board of Western Australia

Jan Pieterszoon Coen, from a seventeenth-century portrait. 94
Rijksmuseum, Amsterdam

The Old Church, Amsterdam, towards the end of the sixteenth century. 95
Rijksmuseum, Amsterdam

A view of Batavia about 1625. From *Vies des Gouverneurs-Généraux*, Du Bois, 1763. 95
Library Board of Western Australia

No. 113 The Nieuwendijk, Amsterdam, in 1960, known in the seventeenth century as The White Angel. 142
Photo by Henk Postma, The Jack Studios, Amsterdam

The first page of the Predikant's letter about the wreck and mutiny, from the Lucas de Vries 1649 edition of *Ongeluckige Voyagie*. 143
The Trustees, Mitchell Library, Sydney

The Great Cameo of Gaspar Boudaen. It was once in the hands of the mutineers on the Abrolhos Islands. 158
Royal Coin Cabinet, The Hague

An engraving of the Great Cameo by Paulus Pontius, after a drawing by Peter Paul Rubens. 158
Royal Coin Cabinet, The Hague

The Rubens Vase. This exquisite gem, cut from a single agate in the Byzantine period, once belonged to the great artist.   159
Walters Art Gallery, Baltimore, U.S.A.

The wreck and the two small islands, from an illustration in the Jan Jansz 1647 edition of *Ongeluckige Voyagie*.   182
Library Board of Western Australia

Detail of the Houtman Rocks and the coast.   182
Reproduced from British Admiralty Chart No. 1056 with the permission of the Controller of H.M. Stationery Office and of the Hydrographer of the Navy

The murders on *Batavia's* Graveyard, from an illustration in the Jan Jansz 1647 edition of *Ongeluckige Voyagie*.   183
Library Board of Western Australia

The hangings on Seals Island as illustrated in the Lucas de Vries 1649 edition of *Ongeluckige Voyagie*.   222
The Trustees, Mitchell Library, Sydney

A page from Pelsaert's Journal, showing part of the declaration to the truth of the evidence set down at the trial of Mattijs Beer.   223
Algemeen Rijksarchief, The Hague

Resolution by the Ship's Council of the *Sardam* to punish the mutineers, dated 28th September 1629.   238
Algemeen Rijksarchief, The Hague

Instructions handed to Wouter Loos and Jan Pelgrom de Bye when they were marooned on the mainland of Australia.   239
Algemeen Rijksarchief, The Hague

Author's map of the Wallabi Group of the Houtman Rocks.   276

Author's map of the part of the Western Australian coast along which Pelsaert sailed.   296

ABBREVIATIONS

VOC	Vereenigde Oost-Indische Compagnie (United East India Company)
ARAKA	Algemeen Rijksarchief, Kolonial Archief, The Hague
GAA	Gemeente-Archief, Amsterdam
AND	Arsip Negara, Djakarta
MLS	Mitchell Library, Sydney
BLWA	J. S. Battye Library of West Australian History, Perth
LSDWA	Lands and Surveys Department, Western Australia

INTRODUCTION TO NEW EDITION

THE PUBLICATION in 1963 of Henrietta Drake-Brockman's *Voyage to Disaster* was a milestone in the historiography of early European contact with Western Australia.[1] The well-illustrated book resulted from many years of intensive research in the archives of the Dutch United East India Company (Vereenigde Oost-Indische Compagnie, V.O.C.) at The Hague, in the Netherlands. It contained the first detailed scholarly account of both the terrible shipwreck and mutiny of the V.O.C. ship *Batavia* in 1629 on the Houtman Abrolhos, an island group off the Western Australian coast, and the career of Francisco Pelsaert, the highest authority aboard, who, after a remarkable return voyage to Batavia, brought the mutiny to an end.[2] The book also included an excellent and complete English translation of Pelsaert's personal diary, written in Old Dutch, made by E. D. Drok. For many people in Australia and the English-language world, the *Batavia* story was transformed from myth into vivid reality. Drake-Brockman, moreover, was a creative author with a high profile in the Western Australian intelligentsia and her engaging style of writing made the book an immediate success with a wide public in Western Australia and elsewhere.[3]

When Drake-Brockman wrote, a new wave of studies dealing with the Dutch East India Company, increasingly free from colonialist ideology and interests, was just beginning to appear.[4] In these years of decolonization, when the last remaining Dutch were forcibly ejected from Indonesia and the challenge of reorientation and reinterpretation could no longer be postponed,

[1] Henrietta Drake-Brockman, *Voyage to Disaster. The Batavia Mutiny*. With translations of the Journals of Francisco Pelsaert by E. D. Drok (Sydney, Angus & Robertson, 1963), xvi + 318 pp. Reprinted in 1982 in the "Australian Classics" series.

[2] Significantly, in view of the double-barrelled theme of the book, the subtitle on the title page differs from that on the dust cover: *The Life of Francisco Pelsaert*. The dust jacket of the 1982 edition has no subtitle.

[3] On Drake-Brockman's importance for Western Australian literature see John Hay, "Literature and Society 1829–1979", in C. T. Stannage, ed., *A New History of Western Australia* (Nedlands, UWA Press, 1981), pp. 614–634, *passim*.

[4] M. A. P. Meilink-Roelofsz, coincidentally herself the widow of a member of the "old guard", was the first major Dutch revisionist with her *Asian Trade and European Influence in the Indonesian Archipelago between 1500 and about 1630* (The Hague, 1962).

the old guard of "imperial historians"[5] was being replaced by historians from the Netherlands itself and overseas, mostly the former colonial areas (Indonesia, India and Sri Lanka) which had recently gained their independence.[6] Drake-Brockman's book on the *Batavia* and Pelsaert was also very much part of that process of rejuvenation and innovation.

These new studies provided incisive reassessments of the views of previous generations and investigated many new aspects of the fascinating and diverse history of the V.O.C.—for a long time the largest multinational corporation in the world—in both the Netherlands and the many regions of Asia and Australia where it operated or explored. As a result, the broader historical matrix within which we must understand the *Batavia* voyage and Pelsaert's life has emerged in much sharper relief. We now have a far clearer view of the overall shipping movements of the V.O.C., its personnel and mutinies, its administration and financial operations, the dynamics of its expansion into many areas of Asian trade, and its relations with indigenous traders and rulers.[7]

Of direct relevance to the stories of Pelsaert and the *Batavia*, two volumes later appeared under the aegis of the Linschoten Vereniging, a society which since the beginning of the century has been dedicated to the publication of books containing original travel accounts and other archival sources dealing with voyages and other themes from the rich maritime history of the Netherlands. These sources are presented with the appropriate annotation as well as a scholarly introduction. One of these volumes

---

[5] The most prominent included H. T. Colenbrander, C. Gerretson, H. Terpstra, and W. Ph. Coolhaas; for the "discovery" of Australia by the Dutch the classical studies are J. E. Heeres, *The Part Borne by the Dutch in the Discovery of Australia, 1606–1765* (Leiden, 1899), and F. W. Stapel, *De Oostindische Compagnie en Australië* (Amsterdam, 1937).

[6] See, for example, S. Arasaratnam, *Dutch Power in Ceylon 1658–1687* (Amsterdam, 1958); T. Raychauduri, *Jan Company in Coromandel 1605–1690* (The Hague, 1962); J. E. Wills Jr, *Pepper, Guns, and Parleys: The Dutch East India Company and China 1662–1681* (Cambridge Mass., 1974); and several other contributors to M. A. P. Meilink-Roelofsz, ed., *De V.O.C. in Azië* (Bussum, 1976).

[7] See, for example, G. Schilder, *Australia Unveiled. The Share of Dutch Navigators in the Discovery of Australia* (Amsterdam, 1976); J. P. Sigmond and L. Zuiderbaan, *Dutch Discoveries of Australia. Shipwrecks, Treasures and Early Voyages off the West Coast* (Adelaide, 1979); J. R. Bruijn, F. Gaastra and I. Schöffer, eds, *Dutch Asiatic Shipping* (3 vols, The Hague, 1979–87); J. R. Bruijn and E. S. van Eyck van Heslinga, *Muiterij. Oproer en berechting op de schepen van de V.O.C.* [Mutiny. Insurrection and the Law on the Ships of the V.O.C.] (Haarlem, 1980); F. S. Gaastra, *De geschiedenis van de V.O.C.* (Haarlem, 1982); H. W. van Santen, *De Verenigde Oost-Indische Compagnie in Gujarat en Hindustan* (Meppel, 1982).

threw further light on Pelsaert's Indian career.[8] The other analysed the development of the *Batavia* story in the print media of the Dutch Republic in the seventeenth century.[9] Its author convincingly showed that the first full-length account, the *Ongeluckige Voyagie, van 't Schip Batavia*, published in 1647 in Amsterdam by Jan Jansz, was written by Isaac Commelin, one of the most active professional travel writers of the day.[10] The most remarkable achievement of *Voyage to Disaster* is that, despite the explosion of V.O.C. literature and despite the fact that Drake-Brockman did her research largely through correspondence with the archives in the Netherlands and the yeoman translation effort of E. D. Drok, her book has passed the test of time with full colours. By resting her story on the complete manuscript journal of Francisco Pelsaert, which included the accounts of the legal proceedings against all mutineers, as well as on many other documents from the V.O.C. archives, it covered its subject so comprehensively that subsequent publications have not been able to add much of significance.[11] This does not mean that *Voyage to Disaster* cannot be criticized. It concentrates too much on Pelsaert and his career at the expense of the other personalities and circumstances involved. The "Great Cameo" and the other jewels which Pelsaert, on behalf of the famous painter Rubens and others, carried for private sale in India too much overshadow the

[8] D. H. A. Kolff and H. W. van Santen, eds, *De Geschriften van Francisco Pelsaert over Mughal Indië, 1627. Kroniek en Remonstratie* (Linschoten Vereniging, vol. 81, Zutphen, 1979).

[9] V. D. Roeper, ed., *De schipbreuk van de Batavia 1629* (Linschoten Vereniging, vol. 92, Zutphen, 1993). It was this account that in 1897 was translated by Willem Siebenhaar and published in English in the Perth newspaper the *Western Mail*. See below, note 17.

[10] The book actually contained two stories apart from that of the *Batavia*. Its full title related to all three stories; the relevant part was *Ongeluckige Voyagie, Van 't Schip Batavia, Nae de Oost-Indien. Gebleven op de Abrolhos van Frederick Houtman, op de hooghte van 28 1/3 graet, by-Zuyden de Linie Æquinoctiael. Uytgevaren onder den E. Francoys Pelsert*.

[11] Stimulated by the building in recent years of a replica of the *Batavia* in Lelystad, Netherlands, three books appeared in Dutch, besides Roeper's documentary study: J. Fabricius, *Het beest uit de zee. De ondergang van de Oostindiëvaarder "Batavia"* (The Hague, 1986); E. Leijenaar, *De Batavia, het gruwelijke, waar gebeurde verhaal over de trotse Oostindiëvaarder* (Amsterdam, 1989); and G. C. Molewijk, *Pelsaerts journaal van de ongelukkige reis van het schip Batavia* (Weesp, 1989). On the building of the replica ship see R. Parthesius, ed., *Herbouw van een Oostindiëvaarder. Batavia Cahiers* (3 vols, Lelystad, 1990–93). In Australia interest was rekindled by the facsimile edition *The Voyage of the Batavia, by Francois Pelsaert* (Sydney, Hordern House, 1993); and Philippe Godard, *The First and Last Voyage of the Batavia* (Perth, Abrolhos Press, 1993); for a critical review of the latter two books see the *Sydney Morning Herald*, 29 January 1994, "Spectrum", p. 10A.

silver coins and routine cargo of the V.O.C. and also the *Batavia* itself and its crew. The leader of the mutiny, Jeronimus Cornelisz, receives perhaps less attention than his demonic behaviour warranted. On both these points, later studies have provided some further insights,[12] but one can only marvel at the lasting quality and value of Drake-Brockman's book.

Voyage to Disaster was pivotal to the historiography of the *Batavia* story and the V.O.C., but the total impact and importance of its publication were far greater: it stood at the beginning and the heart of a series of events which created Maritime Archaeology as a scientific profession in Australia, caused progressive and exemplary Historic Shipwrecks legislation to be adopted at State and Commonwealth levels, revolutionized the Western Australian Museum, created the Fremantle and Western Australian Maritime Museums, and by introducing Maritime History as a scholarly discipline significantly expanded the frontiers of Australia's general history. All these developments, in turn, were part of the remarkable transformation of Perth (including, of course, Fremantle), from a relatively isolated and provincial centre to a cosmopolitan city of cultural sophistication, that occurred after 1965.

Voyage to Disaster appeared at a most propitious time. In 1963 the wrecks of both the *Batavia* and another V.O.C. ship, the *Vergulde Draeck* (*Gilt Dragon*), were discovered by divers. In fact, many other old shipwrecks had already been found previously. Diving was becoming an increasingly popular sport and, with Australia's involvement in the Vietnam War and the development of both the fisheries and oil and gas exploration on the North West Shelf, a specialist profession. The rapid expansion of the crayfishing industry on the Abrolhos[13] and the fortuitous location of one of the fishers' seasonal settlements on Beacon Island in the Wallabi group had already led to the discovery of a skeleton and some artefacts relating to the *Batavia* mutiny. All of this was bound to result in the discovery of many more historical shipwrecks on the Western Australian coast. But discovery in itself, however exciting the idea of "treasure ships" may have been, was only the very first stage of momentous developments.

[12] Philip Tyler, "The Batavia Mutineers", *Westerly*, December 1970, pp. 33-45; Stan Wilson, *Doits to Ducatons. The Coins of the Dutch East India Company Ship "Batavia" Lost on the Western Australian Coast 1629* (Perth, WA Museum, 1989).

[13] The full name, Houtman Abrolhos, has gone out of currency. Abrolhos or also Abrolhos Islands is commonly used, although the latter, strictly speaking, is a pleonasm as "Abrolhos" (which in Portuguese means "Open your eyes") denotes a group of low islands.

Elsewhere, especially in the Mediterranean, maritime archaeology was emerging as a powerful tool for scientific excavation and historical interpretation.[14] The discovery of a diverse range of wrecks and the raising of innumerable and often unique artefacts had begun to open up exciting new sources of knowledge and insights into the maritime history of the world since antiquity. History departments of Australian universities in the 1960s experienced their greatest spurt ever of expansion and diversification, and the availability of ample funds enabled them to increase dramatically the number and range of subjects taught and researched. Maritime history became an established discipline with great popular appeal.[15] Community awareness of history and heritage matters was also developing strongly and close to reaching a "critical mass" which governments and museums could no longer afford to overlook. Of particular significance in this context was that several of the most active divers, including Hugh Edwards and James Henderson, were journalists who brought maritime archaeology into the living rooms of all Western Australians—and beyond.[16] Their enthusiasm was contagious and was captured by editors of West Australian Newspapers, publishers of the *Daily News* and the *West Australian*. Through their cordial relations with the Liberal–Country Party Government of Sir David Brand, they in turn were able to interest State politicians in the subject. Maritime archaeology, in all its ramifications, became democratized and a priority on Western Australia's cultural and political agenda. Later, this would lead to the systematic excavation of the *Batavia* and the conservation and restoration of the artefacts raised from the wrecksite, and the creation of a world-class exhibition in the Western Australian Maritime Museum at Fremantle.

Drake-Brockman had been interested, and had stimulated the interest of others, in the *Batavia* story for a long time before she published *Voyage to Disaster*. Significantly, her immediate connection with the Abrolhos was, as that of Willem Siebenhaar, through friendship with the Broadhurst family, who had been the proprietors

[14] George Bass, *Archaeology Underwater* (London, 1966), and ed., *A History of Seafaring, Based on Underwater Archaeology* (London, 1972). The first head and all British staff members of the Maritime Archaeology department of the Western Australian Museum (as well as Hugh Edwards) gained their first experience in the Mediterranean.

[15] As evidenced by the great and continued popularity of Geoffrey Blainey, *The Tyranny of Distance* (Melbourne, 1966).

[16] Hugh Edwards's highly successful book *Islands of Angry Ghosts* was published by Hodder and Stoughton in London (1966) and received rave reviews in papers such as the *Chicago Tribune* and the *Los Angeles Times*; in 1973 it was published in paperback by Angus & Robertson, Sydney.

of the guano works on the islands.[17] An earlier article in *Walkabout* (1955) and the novel *The Wicked and the Fair* (1957) were already based on her investigations in the V.O.C. archives.[18] In these early publications, Drake-Brockman had pushed her theory that the *Batavia* was not wrecked on the Southern (or Pelsaert) group of the Abrolhos but instead on a reef in the Northern or Wallabi group. She also gave lectures on the subject and there can be little doubt that her forceful personality[19] and membership of Perth's social and literary élite helped to enhance her influence. Evidence as to the true location of the *Batavia*'s wrecksite and mutiny had already come to light in 1960 when a crayfisherman found a skeleton and a bronze lamp base with an inscription carrying the year 1627 on Beacon Island, strongly suggesting that "Batavia's Graveyard" had to be located there. A large anchor was also sighted at least as early as 1960 but was as yet not associated with the *Batavia*. When *Voyage to Disaster* appeared in 1963, a first expedition had already visited the Wallabi group to investigate these finds.[20]

In hindsight, it is incontestable that the discovery of the *Batavia* would have occurred even if Drake-Brockman had not shown the way through her determined research efforts. And, although she remained highly interested in developments until her sudden death in 1968, other forces and persons now moved to centre stage. Events moved very fast in 1963. Indeed, the pace of divers to and from the wrecks was so furious that, somewhat surprisingly, after thirty years the problems of that time were still capable of generating considerable public controversy, as the establishment, in 1992 and 1993, of two Western Australian parliamentary Select Committees into Historic Shipwrecks demonstrated. The discovery of the *Batavia* (4 June) had in fact been preceded by that of the *Gilt Dragon* (14 April). These two potentially rich wrecks joined two other V.O.C. ships: the *Zuytdorp*, smashed at the foot of high cliffs just north of the Murchison River in 1712,[21] and the *Zeewyk*, found in 1966 on the Half Moon Reef in the Pelsaert group of

---

[17] Willem Siebenhaar made a translation of the *Batavia* story of 1647 in the *Daily Mail*, Christmas edition 1897 ("The Abrolhos Tragedy: The First Complete Translation in English"). On the Broadhursts see Mike McCarthy, "Failure and Success. The Broadhursts and the Abrolhos Guano Industry", in Frank Broeze, ed., *Private Enterprise, Government & Society* (Nedlands, 1992), pp. 10-23.

[18] Henrietta Drake-Brockman, "The Wreck of the Batavia", *Walkabout*, 1955, no. 1, pp. 33-39; *The Wicked and the Fair* (Sydney, 1957).

[19] Hugh Edwards described her as having "a mind of her own" and said that she "could be either charming or formidable as it suited her" (*Islands of Angry Ghosts* [Angus & Robertson, Sydney, 1973], p. 101).

[20] This expedition was described in detail in Edwards's *Islands of Angry Ghosts*.

[21] P. E. Playford, "The Wreck of the *Zuytdorp*", *Journal of the Royal Western Australian Historical Society*, vol. 5, no. 5 (1959), pp. 5-41.

the Abrolhos.[22] A few years later, in 1969, the wreck of the English Eastindiaman *Trial* (or *Tryall*) was discovered on Ritchie's Reef near the Montebello Islands.[23]

Once the location of the *Gilt Dragon* and *Batavia* sites was known, there was no way to stop divers from visiting the wrecks and taking away artefacts. No protective legislation existed apart from the salvage clauses of the British Merchant Shipping Act of 1894, which in a quaint survival of imperial ties still applied in Australia, and the 1921 Navigation Act. Divers who raised artefacts and coins from the sites could do so at will and, after declaring their finds to the Receiver of Wrecks, could legitimately expect to be able to claim salvage rights. As the ships were known to have carried large sums in silver coin and many other valuable items, they were very likely to attract treasure hunters.[24] Indeed, although the wrecksites were located away from centres of population as well as from the watchful eyes of the police, their relatively easy accessibility led to serious and justifiable concern about their security from looters and vandals. Even if Western Australia had not been a State with a flourishing mining industry, explosives were simple to get. Within a few months, evidence of blasting was indisputably established.

Drake-Brockman in the meantime had joined forces with crayfisherman Dave Johnson, the Cramer brothers of Geraldton, and above all Perth journalist Hugh Edwards, who had already been involved in the search for the *Batavia*.[25] They gained support from West Australian Newspapers, the Royal Australian Navy, business interests and the Western Australian Museum for the sending of a major expedition to the Abrolhos. This mixed private and public venture was remarkably successful in raising bronze guns, an astrolabe and other navigational instruments, silver coins and many other invaluable items. Fragile iron anchors, which it was feared would rapidly deteriorate once taken out of their marine environment, were left on the site. Soon, the largest of these became known as "Henrietta's anchor".

[22] Hugh Edwards, *The Wreck on the Half Moon Reef* (Adelaide, 1970).

[23] Jeremy Green, *Australia's Oldest Wreck: The Loss of the Trial, 1622* (Oxford, British Archaeological Reports, Supplementary Series, 1977). Graeme Henderson, *Maritime Archaeology in Australia* (Nedlands, UWA Press, 1986), chs 3 and 6, and *Unfinished Voyages. Western Australian Shipwrecks 1622–1850* (Nedlands, UWA Press, 1980), provides useful discussions of all pre-colonial wrecksites. Note: the term "Eastindiaman" is generally used to describe a ship which was specifically built for the trade with the East Indies.

[24] For two sharply contrasting and fiercely partisan accounts of these issues see Alan Robinson, *In Australia TREASURE is not for the Finder* (Perth, 1980), and James Henderson, *The Phantoms of the Tryall* (Perth, 1993).

[25] Drake-Brockman's previously unpublished account of the expedition is included in this edition as Appendix XI.

The very success of the expedition made it imperative that measures be taken to protect the wrecksite and manage the material which had been raised. Discoverers of the *Gilt Dragon*, including Graeme Henderson and his father James, had established a strong precedent by persuading the Western Australian Museum, through a "Deed of Assignment", to take on the legal custodianship of shipwreck relics—the decisive step in their campaign to have the State adopt protective legislation for the wrecksites. A large part of the *Batavia* artefacts was now also deposited with the museum, obviously the only institution in the State capable of such cultural custodianship. Drake-Brockman supported those like the Hendersons and Edwards who argued that the capacity of divers to remove artefacts from the wrecks had to be limited and that the museum must accept the full responsibility which in this way was thrown into its lap. But, in order to enable the museum to play that role, new legislation was required to override the existing legal situation with regard to salvage rights. Two crucial points, which linked all these issues together and were to remain at the centre of all controversies, had also to be considered: rewards and security.

First, a system would have to be established for the rewards to be given to the discoverers of such historical shipwrecks. On the one hand, finders of shipwrecks would have to be compensated for their loss of salvage rights; and, on the other, they had to be encouraged to report their discoveries and to hand over the artefacts they raised from the sites. In view of the extreme difficulties of policing the long coastline of Western Australia, such a policy could, moreover, be seen as an incentive to divers to comply with the law. To reward good behaviour, in principle, must be cheaper and more effective than large-scale policing and the penalization of transgressors. Right from the beginning, however, it had to be recognized that any reward system would also create immense new problems. Quite apart from relatively technical problems relating to potentially great differences in, for example, the scrap metal, historical or antique market value of artefacts, some questions would always remain: what was discovery and who could claim to be the discoverer of a particular wrecksite? And if somehow through the murk of time discoverers could still be identified, how long after their find should they still legitimately be able to claim a reward?

Second, as soon as the State, through the Western Australian Museum, took over responsibility for the wrecksites, their protection against looters and other potentially damaging visitors had to be ensured. Moreover, as the most effective way of showing the cultural importance of the wrecksites would be systematic excavation, the Western Australian Museum would have to expand from its natural sciences-cum-history base and make a major commitment to maritime archaeology and, inevitably in tandem with it, conservation and restoration of water-logged material. Exhibiting the wealth of material resulting from these programmes would ultimately also necessitate the opening of the Fremantle Museum, in December 1970, and later the Western Australian Maritime Museum in the old Commissariat, in Cliff Street, Fremantle.

The first step on the road to all these exciting developments was the "very bold and far-sighted"[26] decision by the State Government of Premier Sir David Brand, in 1964, to pass the Museum Act Amendment Act. In this legislation the Western Australian Museum was given the responsibility of taking charge of all historical shipwrecks in the State's territorial waters. It would be the repository of all material recovered from historical shipwrecks, a term mainly intended to relate to the vessels of the V.O.C. and the as yet unfound *Trial* of the English East India Company, but also including other ships wrecked up to 1900. The museum was responsible, too, for inspecting all newly discovered wrecksites and administering a system of rewards for finders. In principle, a maximum of £1,000 applied, but in the case of coins or bullion, a sum equivalent to that of the value of the silver and gold could be paid or, alternatively, the specie could be transferred to the finders. Persons who did not report their finds would be penalized, as would divers who interfered with registered historical wrecks. A very real problem existed in that a wreck could have no treasure aboard but still be of immeasurably greater value than the maximum reward. And the government specifically decided not to extend retrospectivity to the reward system. Individuals who had discovered wrecks before the legislation was passed, in consequence, went away empty-handed. It was especially this failure of the Act which, understandably, caused much resentment and which, as late as 1992 and 1993, led to the creation of the parliamentary Select Committees.

The Museum Act Amendment Act was easily passed, but critics had pointed out that, as it dealt with territorial waters, the Commonwealth might have been the better authority to enact the legislation. At that time, however, Australia had just entered an energetic phase of off-shore oil and gas exploration. It was argued that, as an agreement between State and Federal Governments on the general issue of the control over territorial waters was still far off and the matter was of great urgency, State legislation had to be accepted. This issue was, in fact, not solved until 1976, after

[26] Henderson, *Maritime Archaeology*, p. 72.

one diver, Alan Robinson, had successfully challenged Western Australia's State legislation in the High Court and the Federal Government accepted the necessity of taking over control through its own Historic Shipwrecks Act.[27]

With its 1964 Act, Western Australia established, in principle, a commitment to cultural heritage protection and management that was unprecedented worldwide. A coalescence of circumstances had suddenly propelled historical shipwrecks and maritime archaeology to such a position of public prominence and awareness that the large majority of Western Australians accepted that artefacts raised from the sea bottom belonged to the community at large. Although a few persons continued to see this as a lamentable blow to their natural rights, this signified a major triumph of the concept of common heritage—an achievement which was all the more remarkable in view of the strong private enterprise ideology of the day and the lack of government support for cultural affairs. With its pioneering legislation, Western Australia had shown the way to the Commonwealth and the world.

But the lack of sustained interest on the part of the State Government became visible again once the 1964 Act had been passed. Although the Western Australian Museum had a large agenda, no funds were made available for even the most modest programme of excavation. Watch-keeping, the minimum required to keep looters away and protect the wrecksites, was patently ineffective and no facilities existed to handle the artefacts already raised. While it can be said that the government was faced with a situation for which no precedents could be found elsewhere and that the museum itself was hesitant in pushing for the establishment of a full programme of expansion, the fact remains that the State failed to provide finance and leadership. A full-scale maritime archaeological programme would certainly not have been cheap but the rapidly increasing fiscal revenues of the State would have allowed the necessary expenditure. (Overall, the Western Australian Maritime Museum over the last twenty-five years has not cost significantly more than the expenses involved in the building of the replica of James Cook's ship *Endeavour*, around $15.5 million up to January 1994.) But prevarication was no longer possible after the discovery of the *Trial* (1969), and an expedition from The University of Western Australia had observed serious damage on the *Batavia* site. If the purpose of the 1964 Act was to be achieved, the museum had to be galvanized into action.

The final breakthrough came in 1970, at the same time as the

[27] Ibid., ch. 5.

Western Australian Government, the Federal Government in Canberra, and the Government of the Netherlands, as the legal successors to the V.O.C., concluded a tripartite agreement in which the future distribution of all artefacts raised from the Dutch wrecks was arranged. The major items and all unique pieces were to remain in Western Australia, while two "representative collections" were to be made available to a future National Museum of Australia and the Netherlands Ministry of Culture, respectively. This agreement underwrote the intent of the 1964 Museum Act Amendment Act and, with the results of earlier inactivity only too visible, forced the State Government and the Western Australian Museum to act. Fortunately, the nickel boom provided the government with the means to pay for both the necessary expansion of the museum and the restoration of the splendid Fremantle Museum which was to house the maritime archaeology exhibition; a decade later, the former Commissariat, close to Fremantle's waterfront, became the home for the Western Australian Maritime Museum. In 1973 the Museum Act Amendment Act was replaced by the Maritime Archaeology Act in order to provide more effectively for the resource management aspects of the museum's work.

While the museum adopted a high public profile and established the departments of Maritime Archaeology, and Materials Conservation and Restoration, the intervention of The University of Western Australia had in 1970 led to the creation of what soon was called the Maritime Archaeology Advisory Committee. Comprising representatives of the museum, the university sector, the State archives, and the professional and amateur diving fraternities, this committee advised the Director of the Museum on all aspects of its maritime archaeology programme. Especially important were the declaration of historic shipwrecks under the successive State and Federal Acts, the determination of proper rewards, and in general the relationship between the museum and the community at large.[28]

It cannot be said that the setting up of the advisory committee solved all outstanding problems. Although it was active in pushing often unwilling bureaucracies to adopt—and pay!—rewards, there always remained tensions with divers who refused to accept the moral legitimacy of the new system or who felt no inclination to declare potentially rich wrecksites or hand over valuable artefacts. As late as 1993–94 an amnesty yielded considerable and valuable

---

[28] After the Western Australian Maritime Museum became autonomous, in 1994, the Maritime Archaeology Advisory Committee became part of its organizational structure.

material to the museum, including some which is closely related to the *Batavia*, but many artefacts and especially coins may not have been registered.

The intervention of The University of Western Australia had a second result which was to be of long-term consequence. A young historian was hired from the Netherlands to teach Dutch maritime history. This initiative was intended to help provide the historical context for the museum's archaeological work and at the same time to stress that a new chapter had been added to the story of early European contact with Australia. Some even argued that Australian history as such had been expanded, but in view of the minimal interaction between Dutch sailors and Aborigines that opinion was, at least in my thinking, exaggerated.[29] The history of the Dutch wrecks remained very largely that of the V.O.C. But as the museum increasingly became interested in post-1800 wrecks and Australia's own maritime history, a major push of developing maritime archaeology and history went in that direction. During the second half of the 1970s, both the Australian Institute of Maritime Archaeology and the Australian Association for Maritime History were founded.

Ultimately, only the effective commitment of the Western Australian Museum through the undertaking of substantial archaeological work could establish the moral legitimacy of the 1964 Act (which in 1973 was refined in the Maritime Archaeology Act). Between 1972 and 1976, the *Gilt Dragon*, which had suffered most from looters, and the *Batavia* were systematically excavated.[30] Four expeditions were made to the latter ship, whose tragic history had been told so effectively by Drake-Brockman. It must remain a matter of sadness that she did not live to see the wonderful results of that programme of civic, public and individual commitment to shipwreck excavation which she had helped to launch; she had died in 1968. Apart from "Henrietta's anchor", her name lives on in that of the museum workboat, *Henrietta*, which for twenty years or so—in its way not unlike the historical role of its name-giver—has lifted to the surface virtually all heavy items excavated by the museum's archaeologists.

---

[29] For a highly stimulating speculation about the possibility and consequences of contact between the shipwrecked crew and passengers of the *Zuytdorp* and Aborigines see R. Gerritsen, *And their Ghosts may be Heard* (Fremantle, Fremantle Arts Centre Press, 1994).

[30] Jeremy Green, *The V.O.C. Jacht "Vergulde Draeck" Wrecked Western Australia 1656* (Oxford, British Archaeological Reports, 1977), and *The Retourschip Batavia, Wrecked Western Australia 1629* (Oxford, British Archaeological Reports, 1989).

INTRODUCTION   xxix

The Western Australian Maritime Museum has become one of the world's acclaimed museums. Its collection of shipwreck artefacts, covering not just the Dutch wrecks but a myriad of later craft as well, is rich and varied. The centrepiece of its exhibition is the restored section of the *Batavia*'s hull and the portico for the fortress of Batavia, the headquarters of the V.O.C. in Asia. The timbers of the hull were raised during the 1975-76 season and painstakingly preserved and reassembled over the next fifteen years.[31] None of this could or would have been achieved without the protective legislation of 1964, the establishment of the necessary museum departments and facilities, and the dedicated work of specialist staff. The Maritime Museum has also become involved in nineteenth and twentieth century shipwrecks, including the American China-trader *Rapid*,[32] the former slave-ship *James Matthews*, and the early steamship *Xantho*.[33] Maritime museums are "fashionable" nowadays and the Australian National Maritime Museum opened its doors in 1991—further signs of the cultural "arrival" of maritime history and archaeology in Australia—but the Western Australian Maritime Museum has set high standards for anyone to match. Moreover, its experience and strength have enabled it, in cooperation with Perth's university sector, to establish postgraduate courses in Maritime Archaeology and to export its expertise through excavations and consultancies elsewhere in Australia and overseas.[34]

[31] Ian D. MacLeod, "Conservation of Waterlogged Timbers from the *Batavia* 1629", *Bulletin of the Australian Institute for Maritime Archaeology* [henceforth *BAIMA*], vol. 14, no. 2 (1990), pp. 1-8.

[32] Graeme Henderson, "The American China Trader *Rapid* (1811)", *The Great Circle. Journal of the Australian Association for Maritime History*, vol. 3, no. 2 (1981), pp. 125-131.

[33] Mike McCarthy, "SS *Xantho*: The Pre-disturbance, Assessment, Excavation and Management of an Iron Steam Shipwreck off the Coast of Western Australia", *International Journal of Nautical Archaeology*, vol. 17 (1988), pp. 339-347.

[34] See, for example, Jeremy Green and Rosemary Harper, *The Excavation of the Pattaya Wreck Site and Survey of Three Other Sites, Thailand 1982* (Australian Institute for Maritime Archaeology [henceforth AIMA], special publication, no. 1, Fremantle, 1983); Jeremy Green, Rosemary Harper, and Vidya Intakosi, *The Ko Si Chang Three Shipwreck Excavation* (AIMA, special publication, no. 4, Fremantle, 1987); Jeremy Green, "Two Early Shipwreck Sites in Korea", *BAIMA*, vol. 11, no. 2 (1987), pp. 50-51; Graeme Henderson and Myra Stanbury, *The Sirius. Past and Present* (Sydney, 1988); Peter Gesner, "The *Pandora* Project: Reviewing Genesis and Rationale", *BAIMA*, vol. 12, no. 1 (1988), pp. 27-36, and "Interim Report: HMS *Pandora*", *BAIMA*, vol. 14, no. 2 (1990), pp. 41-46; and Dena Garratt, "Sri Lankan Fishing Technology", *BAIMA*, vol. 13, no. 1 (1989), pp. 1-8. Graeme Henderson, Director of the Western Australian Maritime Museum, is a member of several international organizations and committees concerned with underwater cultural heritage.

The latter development, although intrinsically welcome, was also partly due to a perhaps quite natural saturation within Western Australia. After so many years of public commitment and glamour for maritime archaeology, other parts of the Western Australian Museum claimed funds from continually shrinking budgets. To a certain extent, also, the excavation programme on the Dutch wrecks appeared to be close to completion. Other factors also played a role in these changing circumstances; some of these related to maritime archaeology itself, some to issues which ever since 1963–64 remained unsolved. Maritime history, inevitably, became a priority besides maritime archaeology.[35] For many seasons there was an annual programme of inspection and excavation; without such programmes there could indeed have been no museums. The choice of what wrecksite was to be "done" depended as much on its potential value as on the extent to which it was at risk. But only a very small number of all identified sites could ever be excavated and the emphasis shifted towards leaving artefacts in their original "togetherness", as the integrated time capsule that shipwrecks, through their sudden stopping of time, can be imagined to be. Recreational and educational factors became important considerations besides the scientific concern for archaeological and historical research, and an ever larger number of wreck trails offered a fascinating cultural novelty to the submarine tourist.[36]

But also for researchers the undisturbed wrecksite is often more valuable than when it is excavated and, inevitably, fragmented. This is especially so if a national perspective is adopted which aims at understanding all Australia's shipwrecks as parts of one huge underwater "heritage bank". The latter development was the logical culmination of the 1976 Commonwealth Historic Shipwrecks Act, the spreading of maritime archaeology to all States and territories, the increased emphasis on comprehensive registration and the building up of national databases.[37] Interestingly, amongst the institutions to which the Federal Government delegated its responsibilities were only three museums and otherwise a variety of cultural, environmental and heritage instrumentalities. Maritime archaeologists to a certain extent

[35] See, for example, Frank Broeze and Graeme Henderson, *Western Australians and the Sea. Our Maritime Heritage* (Perth, WA Museum, 1987).

[36] The first one was created around Rottnest Island; others followed at Mandurah, Hamelin Bay, Geraldton and Albany. They are very much the brainchild of museum curator Mike McCarthy.

[37] Jeremy Green and Tom Vosmer, "The Australian Shipwreck Database; An Interim Report", *BAIMA*, vol. 17, no. 1 (1993), pp. 33–38. Bill Jeffery, of Adelaide, is leading the move towards establishing a national maritime archaeology research policy.

became land-based "maritime heritage resource" managers; I doubt, however, that they would stay ashore should another "treasure" ship be discovered!

Yet it was the very disposal of such treasure which remained a matter of dispute in Western Australia. Besides the question of private holdings, a major problem arose in finding a way of delineating the legitimate rights of towns outside Fremantle in sharing the material housed in the Western Australian Maritime Museum. In Geraldton, the gateway to the Abrolhos and the home town of some of the early divers on the *Batavia* wreck, a campaign was initiated to have a larger number of *Batavia* artefacts assigned to its museum and, especially, to acquire the portico and perhaps even the reconstructed hull section of the *Batavia*. Agreement over smaller items was not difficult to achieve, but with regard to the latter two major artefacts a considerable controversy arose. The gap between the Geraldton activists and the more numerous supporters of the status quo was large. The latter—amongst whom were international historians and museum experts—argued, above all, that the splendid hull and portico should never be separated. Exhibited together in the superbly balanced Batavia gallery, they were the "natural" centrepiece of what must remain the premier maritime museum of the State. With, moreover, millions of dollars invested in their recovery, conservation, preservation and exhibition and the continuous need to monitor their condition, it appeared at the least risky and at the most negligent to remove them from their present location. After a parliamentary Select Committee had investigated the situation, the State Government made some, although by no means watertight, promises to Geraldton to help finance the building of a suitable top-class museum at that town. These promises were perhaps better understood as a political gesture to a town which, electorally, was a notorious "swinging seat" rather than as a deliberate policy of cultural decentralization. In the meantime, the *Batavia*'s hull and the portico remained in their world-class display at Fremantle.

Drake-Brockman was not to know of all the excitement, achievement, controversy and expansion which took place in the years after 1968. With her dedicated research and publications, she had been a major force in the events which led to the discovery of the wreck of the *Batavia*. This, in turn, enabled others to set the beacons for governments, museums, archaeologists, conservators, historians, journalists, divers and all those who together created the now fundamental and irreversible commitment to preserve Australia's maritime heritage. But *Voyage to Disaster* still stands at the heart of the *Batavia* story and the history of the ship and its infamous mutiny. Its first edition, published by Angus & Robertson, was rapidly sold out and, although in 1982 a reprint appeared in the "Australian Classics" series, it is nowadays well-nigh impossible to obtain a copy. It is therefore most welcome that the University of Western Australia Press has undertaken to reprint the book, in soft cover, and thus to make its dramatic, fascinating and important story once again available to the wide readership that it still so fully deserves.

FRANK BROEZE
Department of History
The University of Western Australia

THE LIFE AND TIMES OF FRANCISCO PELSAERT

I

PELSAERT AND THE EAST INDIA COMPANY

THE NAME of Francisco Pelsaert is written on the map of the world, yet is little known in Holland. To become a figure of fame and legend in a far-off continent and remain a forgotten man in the land of one's allegiance is surely a perverse fate. In Australia, poets and schoolboys, artists and historians, have been inspired for half a century by the tragedy of an ancient shipwreck, a disaster that piled horror upon horror yet revealed so much of human fortitude as to invite comparison with the epic tales of Greece.

There exists a vast literature on the loss of the ship *Batavia*. Yet the strange fact remains that the full story of the famous wreck and its aftermath, written from day to day by Francisco Pelsaert in his Journals, has never until now been published; nor has the story of his life been adequately recorded in one volume. It has certainly not been recognized that the terrible tragedy wrecked also a notable career. In the English-speaking world, owing to misunderstanding of the title *Commandeur* as used by the United East India Company of the Netherlands in the seventeenth century, legend has embalmed Pelsaert as a *commander* who by ill-chance lost his ship. Even reputable historians have been content to accept a myth that turned this distinguished merchant, writer, and Councillor of India into a rough sea-dog, courageous and worthy enough, but scarcely a man of intellect capable of writing the *Remonstrantie*, or Report, which he forwarded to the Directors when stationed at Agra as Uppermerchant in charge of Company affairs. This record left for posterity a glittering account of Indian life at the time of the Emperor Jahangir, son of Akbar the Great Mogul.

On 4th June 1629, within three years of his writing the *Remonstrantie*, the ship *Batavia*, in which Pelsaert was returning from a visit to Amsterdam, perished on the reefs of Houtman's Abrolhos, now shown on British Admiralty charts as The Houtman Rocks, a scattered archipelago lying off the coast of Western Australia between $28°\ 15\frac{1}{2}'$ and $29°\ 00\frac{1}{2}'$, Southern Latitude. On that same date (the Gregorian Calendar was already in use on the Continent) the painter Rubens, voyaging on a diplomatic mission from Spain to the Court of Charles I of England, lay storm-tossed in the English Channel. It would seem improbable that any link should exist between the illustrious Ambassador from the Spanish Netherlands and the doomed ship in unknown seas on the other side of the world, but in fact Pelsaert had in his care a Great Cameo, dispatched for sale at the Mogul Court. Rubens had recently made a drawing of the gem; there are reasons for believing that it belonged to him. Pelsaert sent it immediately, along with the women and children, to a miserable speck of land that was no more than a mushroom of rock rising from furrows of surf. The cameo has survived to this day. But Pelsaert died the following year, in Java.

His Journals, covering the wreck and its calamitous results, were buried in the Company's files in the Netherlands. Twenty years later he became indeed the hero of a popular Dutch horror tale that ran to many editions. Transposed into the third person and considerably rearranged, *Ongeluckige Voyagie van't Schip Batavia*[1] purported to be "Compiled by a Dilettante from Various Writings"; but, with the exception of one small passage, the first edition of 1647 was lifted piecemeal from Pelsaert's Journals. In 1663 the French historian Thévenot translated into French not only parts of the Journals that dealt with the *Batavia* wreck, but also long passages from the *Remonstrantie*.[2]

[1] *Ongeluckige Voyagie van't Schip Batavia* was first published in 1647 at Amsterdam by Jan Jansz. In 1648 another edition was published by Joost Hartgers, also of Amsterdam, which Jansz considered to be pirated. The Hartgers edition has a picture of two ships on the title-page and includes a letter by the predikant Gijsbert Bastiaensz. Jan Jansz immediately republished in the same year, 1648, prefacing the new edition with an indignant letter to Hartgers. Hartgerts (adding a "t" to his name) also published another edition that year, but without the predikant's letter. In 1649 a third bookseller, Lucas de Vries of Utrecht, published an edition which included the letter of G. Bastiaensz (at times erroneously named Sebastiaensz in the Jansz editions as also in Jansz's letter), as well as a list of the rewards made to men who remained loyal to the Netherlands East India Company. In 1652 and 1653 Joost Hartgers and Lucas de Vries respectively republished; an eighth undated edition by Gilles Joosten Saeghman, which appears to be a reprint of Hartgers, was published in the 1660s. This version was also included in a bound volume of collected journeys by sea and land that Saeghman published, probably in 1665.

Information given by the Algemeen Rijksarchief, The Hague, notes that the first published reference to the journal of the *Batavia's* wreck is made in the Journal of Seyger van Rechteren, which appeared in 1635: the author mentions that such a journal is known to him. It is probable that this reference is to Pelsaert's original Journals, now in the Algemeen Rijksarchief, and that the Jan Jansz 1647 edition of *Ongeluckige Voyagie* was the first version to appear publicly. All editions of *Ongeluckige Voyagie* are narrated in the third person.

[2] M. Thévenot, *Relations de divers voyages curieux* (Paris, 1663), part 1, pp. 50-56.

Yet since that faraway date even parts of the *Remonstrantie* and the Journals do not appear to have been published in one volume; nor, for the matter of that, have many historians noted the connection between the Uppermerchant of Agra and the Commandeur of the Abrolhos. Three hundred years had to pass before, in 1925, W. H. Moreland, himself a distinguished officer of the Indian Civil Service, was so caught by the colour and wisdom of Pelsaert's *Remonstrantie* as to translate it from the Old Dutch, with the assistance of Professor Pieter Geyl, a noted Dutch scholar, into English.[3]

Ongeluckige Voyagie van't Schip Batavia came earlier to British eyes. One copy of the first edition by Jan Jansz, an ancient vellum-bound book illustrated with fine copper-plate engravings and printed on hand-made paper of good quality, found its way to Western Australia. The late Mr William Siebenhaar, a Dutchman living in Perth, pored over the difficult black-lettered type and eventually made an excellent English translation. This went no further than the pages of a local weekly,[4] but it excited an interest that eventually spread across Australia and has never completely faded, despite the fact that knowledge is now largely hearsay.

Thus today, more than three centuries after his death, Francisco Pelsaert remains a figure of romance dressed in the motley garments accorded him by scores of writers, not one suit cut to his full measure[5] other than the slim volume of *Jahangir's India*, as his translators named their English rendering of his *Remonstrantie*. Yet with the publication of this work the Uppermerchant and Commandeur of the V.O.C.[6] became also an accredited historian.

The title of Commandeur, which Pelsaert bore at the time of the *Batavia* wreck, has frequently been assumed by British and Australian writers to be equivalent to the British "commodore". But in seventeenth-century records of the V.O.C. the term carried no maritime significance. Commandeur was in fact no more than a courtesy title accorded in certain situations to a competent officer of the Company, generally one of the Uppermerchants, when given charge of a voyage or of one of the smaller districts. A Commandeur might, of course, once have been a seaman, but not necessarily so; by 1618, when Pelsaert joined the Company, a

---

[3] *Jahangir's India. The Remonstrantie of Francisco Pelsaert*, translated from the Dutch by W. H. Moreland, C.S.I., C.I.E., and P. Geyl, Litt. D. (Cambridge, 1925).

[4] BLWA: *Western Mail*, Christmas Number 1897, pp. 3-10.

[5] In fiction, my novel *The Wicked and the Fair* (1957) has attempted to remedy this.

[6] Vereenigde Oost-Indische Compagnie (United East India Company). The cipher VOC was used on the Company's flags, and the initials in general reference.

ship's master was rarely in over-all charge. By then the Directors at Amsterdam had devised a system of control and procedure far more complex and infinitely more advantageous than that of the haphazard and ill-informed first voyages to India, when skippers sailed where they liked and the merchants traded at random.

It is not possible to build the career and character of Pelsaert from the few official records available, or to understand his Journals, especially the evidence of the Abrolhos trials, without some knowledge of his times and of the administration and activities of the United East India Company of the Netherlands.

In many ways the beginning of the seventeenth century is comparable with the present time. In Europe it was a period of transition and expansion, of economic change and uneasy peace following devastating wars, of tremendous energy and rapid scientific improvement. The galvanizing force of the Renaissance was still alive, pushing men to new ideas and new methods, to a widespread quickening of techniques, in much the same way that nuclear energy and the creation of earth satellites push thought and activity today. Yet the population of England and Wales together numbered no more than four and a half millions, the Dutch Republic well under three.

Nevertheless the small Republic, composed of seven United Provinces—by no means what would be considered a republic today; rather, a loosely tied federation of States acknowledging a sovereign Prince as *stadhouder*[7]—was ahead of England in many branches of organization. While they fought for freedom from Spain, the Dutch had never ceased the pursuit of maritime trade. They were the carriers of Europe, their merchant shipping the best managed in the world; their insurance rates lower than the English, so that English ships were often insured at Amsterdam. It has been written, "However obscure the employment, if it demands ingenuity, in the seventeenth century we are not surprised if we find a Dutchman in it."[8] In the Netherlands, people still refer to this period as the Golden Age.

The greatest names belong to the world: Grotius, Huygens, Rubens, Rembrandt, and a dozen more. Hendrick Brouwer, famous officer of the V.O.C. who first discovered that the outward

---

[7] "Rather than go to the trouble of explaining to the natives [of the East Indies] the complicated system of government that existed in the Low Countries, the staunch Dutch Republicans, for business reasons, promoted their stadhouder, Maurice, Prince of Orange, to the royal rank." Bernard H. M. Vlekke, *Nusantara* (London, 1945), p. 99.

[8] G. N. Clark, *The Seventeenth Century* (Oxford, 1931), p. 16.

voyage to Java could be greatly accelerated if the route were altered to take advantage of the Trade Winds, and Jan Pieterszoon Coen, true founder of the Dutch colonial empire and a dominant figure in the history of the East Indies, were the two great contemporaries whose careers most closely touched the life of Francisco Pelsaert. The year before Pelsaert joined the Company, Brouwer became his brother-in-law. Coen became Governor-General for the V.O.C. in the Indies the year Pelsaert reached Java.

Studying the matter-of-fact Day Books of the Company, noting the recorded come and go of shipping, the tables of prices, the discussions regarding trade, it is difficult to feel far distant from the ways of thinking of those days. It is possible to understand the business methods of the time, to admire the craftsmanship of artists still supreme in the world, the architecture, the jewellery, the tapestries, velvets and laces, to applaud the first arguments of international law as set forth by Grotius, as well as the works of philosophers and poets (Shakespeare died in 1616, when Pelsaert was a young man), and conclude that we differ little from the people of that period. Actually, it is more difficult to assess their emotions and reactions than to list their achievements. They relied on magic, on omens, on astrology; they feared the supernatural. "Until late in the century it was believed that comets not only portended great calamity in human history, but were also without natural causes in the ordinary sense."[9] The frequent burning of witches was "one of the foulest blots on the age".[10] Religious discussion, especially in the Netherlands, raged fiercely, so widespread that it would have been impossible in that country to find even a group of fishermen or peasants who did not naturally enter into profound arguments regarding the doctrines of Predestination or Freewill. The sense of sin was ever present. Good and evil, God and the Devil, were never far absent from men's minds or lips. Throughout the entire Christian world there was nothing but merit in subduing, often ferociously, the heretic, the heathen and the infidel.

The single factor that most altered the life of Europeans in this century was the enormous development of mercantile trade with India and the Far East. Europe was growing richer, but the majority of people continued to believe with Bacon that "the increase of any estate must be upon the foreigner (for whatsoever is somewhere gotten is somewhere lost)".[11] Therefore jealousy of trade remained the rule, and the great trading companies that

[9] Ibid., p. 245.   [10] Ibid., p. 246.   [11] Ibid., p. 25.

fought and subdued the natives of the East and West Indies, at the same time fought one another. The home governments were never in a hurry to take over the merchants' quarrels, but they readily gave under-cover assistance with munitions and diplomatic support while they discussed what they still thought more vital, the forming of alliances and enmities in Europe. It was not until the second half of the century that economic and colonizing quarrels took a part in promoting European wars.

From the outset the V.O.C. was a State concern in a way the English East India Company never was. Until the Reformation cancelled the Papal Bull of 1493 dividing the globe into zones of trading, east and west, exclusively allotted to the Portuguese and the Spanish who had first discovered the sea-routes, the Dutch had perforce contented themselves with distributing from Lisbon the vast quantities of spices and other merchandise brought from the East by the Portuguese. Undoubtedly they would before long have rounded the Cape of Good Hope, but the union of Portugal with Spain in 1580 "closed" the port of Lisbon. Many sailors from other lands had joined the Portuguese expeditions; in 1595 Linschoten, a native of Enkhuisen who had voyaged to Portuguese Goa, published an account of the Indian route. Immediately a group of Dutch merchants in Amsterdam formed a trading company to venture to the East. Four ships set out under Cornelis de Houtman, a brother of that Frederik de Houtman after whom the Western Australian Abrolhos are named; they returned in 1597 after many adventures, with cargoes sufficient to stir the wildest hopes. From then on expedition followed expedition as merchants in town after town of the United Provinces found money to build and outfit ships. But it soon became obvious to the shrewd Netherlanders that separate voyages were wasteful; and in 1602 the various groups united to form the V.O.C.[12]

Meanwhile, Drake's voyage round the world had excited the imagination and cupidity of the English. After the defeat of the Armada, Elizabeth I granted leave for direct trade with the East Indies. The English East India Company was formed in 1600, two

[12] The constitution of the company's managing body formed in 1602 was complex. Of the many descriptions, Moreland's in *From Akbar to Aurangzeb*, p. 310 *et seq.*, is chosen: "The different organizations which had united to form the Company retained their individuality, in so far that there were several distinct 'Chambers', one located at each of the principal seaports. Each chamber consisted of a number of directors (*bewinthebber*), who were in the first instance nominated; subsequent vacancies were filled by the provincial government on the nomination of the existing directors. The central management consisted of a 'College' of seventeen, representing the chambers in fixed proportions: its members were often

years before the V.O.C.; from then onwards the Dutch and the English were sometimes friendly, sometimes bitter, rivals.

When Pelsaert joined the Company in 1618, the V.O.C., despite its two-years handicap, was already far advanced in administration, in numbers of ships and staff, in wealth and general efficiency.

spoken of as 'the Seventeen'. The college framed the policy of the Company, which was executed by the chambers, each acting for its own seaport. Thus the size and equipment of the annual fleet was determined by the college, which allotted ships to each chamber: the chamber sent out the ships allotted to it, and marketed the goods brought back in its ships. In practice, then, the business of the Company was entirely in the hands of an oligarchical body, maintaining its continuity by nominating to vacancies. The charter [from the States General, the governing body of the Republic] provided that serious disputes in the college should be referred to the Central Government (the States General), but the historian of the Company is justified in the statement that the directors were practically autocrats, in no way responsible to the shareholders, and only nominally responsible to the State. The accounts of the Company were not published, there were no meetings of members or shareholders corresponding to the General Courts of the English Company, and it is said that no minutes were kept of the proceedings of the college.... The early profits of the Dutch Company were high. The figures given by different writers are discordant, but the average dividend from 1605 to 1609 was certainly 35 per cent annually, and perhaps much more. From 1610 to 1619 the resources of the Company were devoted largely to the struggle for monopoly in the Spice Islands, and in these years the distribution averaged about 21, or, according to another account, 28 per cent. The dividends for the five decades from 1620 to 1669 averaged 12, 20¾, 29, 18 and 14¾ per cent annually, payments being made in most years, but the amounts varying within wide limits.... An important point to realise regarding this Company is what may be regarded as its national aspect."

At this point Moreland gives the following footnote: "The power of the Dutch Company appears very clearly in the records of the negotiations carried on from time to time in London and in Holland. In 1627, for instance, when the English Company was considering the abandonment of its undertaking, a 'mixed court' recorded the opinion that there was very little hope of redress for the losses caused by the Dutch, [fighting in the East] since 'the Government of the Low Countries is so intermixed with Bewinthebbers that in a trial they will be both parties and judges' (*Court Minutes*, July 20, 1627)."

Moreland continues (*From Akbar to Aurangzeb*, pp. 311-12): "... authority was given to it [the Governing Body of the Company] to enter into agreements with foreign Powers in the name of the Dutch Government, and when the first Governor General [of the East Indies] was appointed in 1609, the position assigned to him was very nearly that of an officer of State, with practically a free hand in matters of Asiatic policy. The protracted negotiations between the English and Dutch Governments indicate a great difference in the position held by the two Companies. The impression left . . . by a perusal of the Calendars of State Papers is that, while James I regarded the protection of the Eastern trade as important but not vital, the States General and the Dutch Company acted practically as a single body, ready to stake everything for the attainment of the objects of the latter. . . . The national position enjoyed by the Dutch Company was a material factor in its commercial success, but does not by itself explain its marked superiority over its English rival."

During the initial stages all transactions had been carried on from ships anchored in the roadsteads of various ports. This fluctuating and precarious trade soon gave way to bases, or factories as they were called, established on shore after the ceding of concessions by local native rulers. Thereafter some merchants remained in charge on shore, some continued to travel aboard ship in charge of cargoes for the purpose of conducting trade at the various ports and directing ships' activities. No longer did skippers say where a ship should sail, but merely when, how, and in what manner, according to the rules of good seamanship.

Each ship carried a skipper, an uppersteersman (first mate), two or more understeersmen, and a high (or chief) boatswain, as well as many petty officers. The larger vessels had a constable, or chief gunnery officer, since all ships sailed armed against pirates or the privateers of other nations; also a provost or officer of the law—still maintaining the title used on land, and calling forth the watches as in the cities of the Netherlands. To do this he would strike his mace three times on the mainmast and at the same time he frequently cried aloud his order in rhyme.[13] The barbers were also the surgeons; and if there was no predikant (minister), religious succour was given by a lay brother appointed for that purpose and called a Sick-consoler.

It soon became obvious that on-the-spot co-ordination of overseas activities was a first necessity. From 1619 onwards the Governor-General, now resident at the Company stronghold in Java, named by the Dutch Batavia, presided over an executive committee known as the Council of India.[14] This body controlled V.O.C.

---

[13] One such verse was sent to me by Mr G. A. Cox, Director of the Scheepvaart Museum at Amsterdam, and translated by C. de Heer of Perth as follows:

Hark, men, hark, whether you belong to the watch or the street,
Or the provost will reap money from your forfeits!
Let none drink himself drunk on beer or wine!
Tonight it will be the Prince quarter!*
Prince quarter, keep good watch!
God, send us a good night!
A good night and good peace!
Luck, and a safe voyage with it!
Above, those on watch! To bunks, whose turn it is!
Ring the bell!
Change the man at the helm and the lookout!

> * "Prince quarter" refers to a particular watch; the various watches were given names, generally after well-known men, and slept in the same part of the ship, or "quarters".

[14] The council was known both as the Council of India and the Council of the Indies. I have preferred to use the former term as being more comprehensive.

defence and transport, administration and trade, throughout the Indies.

Continuing expansion made further delegation imperative. Soon the huge area over which the Dutch company traded was divided into zones. The Governor-General and his Council administered directly the Spice Islands, which became known as the Eastern Quarters; Japan and the adjacent lands were called the Northern Quarters; the west coast of India, Persia, etc., became the Western Quarters, with headquarters at Surat on the Indian mainland, where a Director was stationed in charge. From time to time members of the Council of India or other high officers whose duties somewhat resembled those of present-day head-office bank inspectors, travelled with considerable state from port to port, sometimes coming from Amsterdam for that purpose. Below these august officials there followed in order of precedence the Uppermerchants, the Merchants, the Undermerchants, the assistants and the junior assistants; the last two groups included clerks and ledger-keepers.

The Dutch were the first people to devise the modern practice of administration by committees or, as they were then called, councils. In the free Netherlands, from the States-General down, everything was run by councils. On board ship likewise. The senior merchant, no matter to which of the above ranks he belonged, was always chairman of the ship's council. Next in importance came the skipper, next the second merchant, then the uppersteersman, and, as fifth man, the high boatswain. A man's status can readily be assumed from the order in which his signature appears on ships' councils' documents. These councils were convened mainly for the purpose of discipline or when urgent necessity arose, because sailing directions (standing orders) and article-briefs (particular commissions) were invariably issued for each voyage. For matters concerning the soldiers aboard (sometimes quite a large number) there was a separate council consisting of merchant, skipper, sergeant, corporal, and *lanspassaet*, the last being equivalent to a lance-corporal. There were no organized navies in those days; the "fleets" were composed of armed merchant ships or transports, sometimes accompanied by vessels called ships of war, rather better equipped for fighting. These latter also belonged to the Company. When ships sailed in convoy, as was usual, especially on the long voyages from and to the Fatherland, one of the senior merchants was designated Fleet President and would be called either the President or the Commandeur. This officer was empowered to call and preside over a Broad Council, which was composed of merchants and skippers, according to the class of ship (merchant or war), drawn from the vessels in the fleet. The exact form of this council was set forth in the article-brief for the particular voyage.[15]

When the ill-fated *Batavia* left the shelter of the Texel on 29th October 1628, she sailed in company with six other ships. Francisco Pelsaert was not only senior merchant aboard that vessel he had also been designated Fleet President, an office entitling him to be called Commandeur. Moreover, he was shortly to be appointed a Councillor Extraordinary of India, that is to say an extra member of Governor-General Jan Pieterszoon Coen's Council at Batavia. Thus, as Fleet President, Pelsaert was indeed a commodore in our understanding of the term when applied to the command of ships sailing in convoy during World War II; but, unlike those officers, he was not required to be a navigator and was in no way responsible for the nautical management of the *Batavia*, beyond the giving of general advice according to the sailing directions and article-brief laid down for the voyage. That he should so often have been presented as a seafaring man is entirely without foundation in fact. His short but notable career, in which he rose from assistant to Councillor of India in ten years, belonged to the market place, the counting-house, the Mogul Court, and the council tables of the great Company. His claim to a place in history is based on more than the fact that his name on the map of the world commemorates a terrible shipwreck, that he behaved zealously in the dreadful aftermath, or that he later marooned on the continent of the unknown Southland the first Europeans ever to live in Australia, at the same time instructing them in humane behaviour towards the natives. To his further credit can be added the descriptions he has left of life, trade, and custom in the India of his time; and, in addition, a suggested method of trading that, had he lived and come to greater power, might well have led the V.O.C. to oust the English company from the mainland of India (as Jan Pieterszoon Coen succeeded in doing from the islands) and thus open the way to an empire more vast and real than any that great Governor-General saw in dreams.

In the contemporary official records of the V.O.C. the name Pelsaert is generally given this spelling. On de l'Isle's map of the world, 1740,[16] which indicates the route taken by him after the wreck, from "Nouvelle Hollande" to Java in 1629, it is spelt Pelsart—as it remains today on the Admiralty Charts of The Houtman Rocks. The man himself invariably signed "FranC⁰ Pelsartt"; at least there is no variation from that signature on the

---

[15] Nicolaus Witsen, *Aeloude en Hedendaegsche Scheepsbouw en Bestier.* Amsterdam, 1671.

[16] Guillaume de l'Isle, Map of the World, 1740. MLS 1/79.

existing documents that deal with the wreck and its aftermath, although in the text there are variations. In editing the *Remonstrantie* Moreland has preferred to use Pelsaert, a precedent followed in these pages. In fact, as was natural to the times, the deviations were many. In the unpublished notes of the Heeren XVII, or the High and Mighty Seventeen of the Company's Directors, dated 1st September 1635, there is mention of "The brother-in-law of our Hendrik Brouwer: Francoys Pelsaert, also spelt Persaert, Pelsert, Pelser".[17] The occasional French spelling of the Christian name, as here, was adopted consistently by Thévenot in 1663, and thereafter became widely used; Francoys and Pelsert were the forms earlier chosen by the "Dilettante" author of *Ongeluckige Voyagie*. No authentic portrait of Pelsaert is known to exist in Holland. Surprisingly, recent inquiries in India unearthed a copy of what was said to be a print from an etching made during his term at Agra.[18] This portrays a thoughtful, youngish man, with high forehead and Shakespearian beard, wearing what is obviously a good suit with a plain high linen collar. A medallion on a chain hangs round his neck. The print is crudely signed "Franc⁰ Pelsaert". The formation of the letters (apart from the different spelling of the surname) does not tally well with the flowing authentic signature, written so frequently in 1629 on the documents assembled in the Journals. Similar (and genuine) portraits of various European celebrities resident in India at the time do in fact exist. But considerable investigation would be necessary to remove the doubt that surrounds this sketch and the very questionable signature.

Uncertainty attaches also to Pelsaert's age and birthplace. In 1901 H. F. Macco published a history and genealogy of the Pelsaert family.[19] From this it appears that in 1605 Eberhard Pelzer [*sic*] bought a property named Grasleen, between Eupen (near Aachen) and Neureth; he was married to Maria Raye; he died in 1631. Eberhard and Maria had six named children, of whom Agnes [*sic*], shown as being married to the Dutch "Admiral Hendrich Gisbert Brouwer", was the third daughter. The name Francisco does not appear at all; but innumerable documents attest that Francisco Pelsaert was the brother-in-law of Hendrick Brouwer. That Brouwer's wife was born in 1589 is revealed by the marriage

[17] J. E. Heeres, "De Gouverneur-Generaal Hendrik Brouwer", *Oud-Holland*, ed. A. Bredius and E. W. Moes, pp. 237-8, footnote 4. Amsterdam, 1907.
[18] This was given to Mr K. Wallace-Crabbe of Melbourne in 1945 by the Indian historian Das Gupta, of Lahore.
[19] H. F. Macco, *Geschichte und Genealogie der Familien Peltzer*, p. 323.

notice[20] of March 1617 which states that his bride, Agniete Pelser [*sic*], was twenty-eight. Agniete's birth was followed by that of a son named Nikolaus who died without issue; a fourth daughter came next, finally a second son named Leonard. Leonard was "invested" with the property of Grasleen in 1631, presumably on the death of his father. He married, had a family, and held several public offices in the district. Leonard's inheritance suggests that the elder Nikolaus died before the father in 1631. Francisco Pelsaert died in 1630. From Macco's list of Eberhard's children, it must be assumed either that Francisco was not registered along with the rest of the family, or else that he was in fact Nikolaus, who had for some reason changed his name.

Eupen is cited as the home town of Agniete on the marriage notice. But the following year, when Francisco joined the Company as an assistant, the lowest commercial grade but one, he is described as being "of Antwerp".[21] However, no record of his birth has been traced at Antwerp, and recent inquiries at Eupen brought no response. Speculation suggests that unless Nikolaus and Francisco were indeed one and the same, Francisco was the youngest child and may not have been born at Eupen. It is of course possible that he was older than his sister Agniete, but hardly probable, considering the junior capacity in which he entered the service. Brouwer, thirty-five at the time of his marriage, was already famous and a highly placed officer of the V.O.C. If Francisco were in fact older than Agniete, it can scarcely have been by more than a year or so. It is reasonable to regard him as being a man of less than forty when disaster overtook him in 1629, twelve years after the marriage of his sister.

The *Remonstrantie* supports this theory. Written in 1626, it has many descriptions of scenes and customs that suggest a man young enough to take a vigorous interest in life, apart from the mere recording. Pelsaert shows himself fascinated by the strange existence led by the ladies of the zenanas, or *mahals*, as he calls them, and depicts it so well that his words appear to have the ring of first-hand knowledge rather than of hearsay:

> These wretched women wear, indeed, the most expensive clothes, eat the daintiest food, and enjoy all worldly pleasures except one, and for that one they grieve, saying they would willingly give everything in exchange for a beggar's poverty.
>
> The ladies of our country should be able to realise from this description the good fortune of their birth, and the extent of their freedom when compared with the position of ladies like them in

[20] *Oud-Holland*, 1907, p. 237.
[21] *Jahangir's India*, p. ix (Introduction).

other lands; but this topic lies outside the scope of my task, and I shall now speak of the houses which are built here.²²

Pelsaert's interest and sympathy with the "dainty" Moslem women is, as he declares, perceptibly greater than necessary to a trade report. That he was not married can be deduced from the fact that nowhere appears any mention of a wife, and that after his death his mother applied to the Company on her own behalf in 1632 and again in 1634, through her son-in-law Hendrick Brouwer, to wind up her son's estate in her favour.²³ Both applications were refused.

It may be presumed, then, that Francisco Pelsaert first sailed from the Netherlands while still in his twenties. A report from Java in 1620 notes his reappointment:

> Francisco Pelsaert, of Antwerp, sailing out as assistant in the *Wapen van Zeelant* anno 1618 at f. 24²⁴ per month, and now serving in the capacity of undermerchant, whose time will have expired in December 1621, was again appointed to the Company for the time of three years after the expiring of the above-mentioned, his first appointment, to serve on land in the capacity of undermerchant, with the enjoyment from this time until [return to] the Fatherland, of fifty-five guilders per month.²⁵

Pelsaert arrived at the very moment that Coen, newly appointed as Governor-General, was setting his will to consolidate Dutch supremacy in the Indies. It would appear that at first Pelsaert was sent to learn conditions by travelling from port to port: the wording of the reappointment suggests this. Also, in his *Remonstrantie*, Pelsaert writes with the ease of knowledge about the trade in spices and the V.O.C. control of "the whole produce of the trees"²⁶ in the Moluccas and Banda. Almost from the beginning the idea of possessing a spice monopoly had been a fixed policy with the Company. Pieter Both, the first Governor-General, had been instructed that, "The commerce of the Moluccas, Amboyna and Banda should belong to the Company, and that no other nation in the world should have the least part."²⁷ They considered that they had wrested from the Portuguese the right of government in the Spice Islands. The English asserted an earlier claim, the arrival of Drake in 1579. They denied that isolated coastal forts meant effec-

---

²² Ibid., p. 66.
²³ ARAKA, VOC: 185 Resolutions Lords XVII, Chamber of Amsterdam, dated 19th March 1632 and notice of refusal dated 31st August 1635.
²⁴ Twenty-four florins (f.), equal in value to guilders.
²⁵ ARAKA, VOC: 983 (1621¹), 16th July 1620.
²⁶ *Jahangir's India*, p. 21.
²⁷ Sir William Wilson Hunter, *A History of British India*, vol. i, p. 341.

C

tive occupation, and considered themselves possessed of equal rights in the making of treaties with native rulers. English records of the period note that the Hollanders claimed a monopoly on amber, birds' nests, cassia lignum, sapanwood, cloths, camphor, benzoni, cloves, diamonds, gold, opium, pepper, mace, mother-o'-pearl, nutmegs, sago, slaves, tin, tortoiseshell, and wax.[28] But eventually pepper became the most desired of all exports from the Indies.

Shortly after his reappointment to a land post, Pelsaert was directed to Surat, far up on the west Indian coast. By this time indigo was also much in demand. In Europe the ancient woad used in the dyeing of woollen goods was running short and indigo was eagerly sought to take its place. Agra, the site of the Mogul Court, was discovered to be the chief centre of the indigo trade and, in addition, an excellent market for spices. Moreover, concessions were to be gained only from the reigning monarch. Thus Agra became important to both the Dutch and the English companies, busily building the new trade. Surat was the port closest to the imperial city and its rich surrounding districts. The Emperor Akbar had tacitly acknowledged the possession of sea power by granting licences for ships trading in the Red Sea, but in fact the Mogul emperors had no navies; before the arrival of Dutch and English ships, the Portuguese had been the real masters of local seas. Thus it suited the two companies to combine in India against the Portuguese however much they continued to skirmish amongst the islands.

The Dutch had preceded the English at Surat. As early as 1606 a Dutch agency was in existence there, but its operations ended abruptly when the solitary merchant in charge committed suicide owing to the intrigues and persecution of the Portuguese, already well established. The English next gained permission to start a factory at Surat, a concession granted by the Emperor Jahangir to Captain William Hawkins, who married "a white mayden out of his palace".[29] The Portuguese managed to have this grant revoked. Hawkins left in disgust. Some years later English ships in the vicinity defeated Portuguese vessels in impressive battles and exploded Mogul belief in the supremacy of Portuguese sea power. By 1615 both companies again had resident merchants living in considerable style, not to say luxury, at Surat. The English also sent an Ambassador, Sir Thomas Roe, to the Court of Jahangir at Agra, where he had a measure of success and gained sufficient

[28] Ibid., p. 343, footnote.
[29] Ibid., p. 296.

concessions to make a rapid increase in the trade between Surat and London.

Soon the Dutch Governor-General decided, against the advice of his merchants on the Coromandel (or east) coast of India, that direct trade must be firmly established and the hazardous overland contacts between Masulipatam, as well as indirect buying through rapacious Indian merchants, considerably reduced. Accordingly, in 1616 Pieter van den Broecke was dispatched with a number of ships, and a V.O.C. factory duly opened at Surat. This did not become really important until 1620 when van den Broecke himself returned, to remain as resident Director of the Western Quarters. He began immediately to push the Dutch trade with energy and success. From then on the Dutch and English traded side by side in this region. Neither company had any possessions, such as the fortresses on the Coromandel coast, and their officers lived in the cities merely as foreign merchants, however magnificently, on the strength of the terms they could obtain from the Imperial Court. The English were already sending north to Agra for more and more indigo. As soon as the Dutch were firmly established at Surat they did likewise, and almost at once took a leading part.

At Surat there was also a Mogul mint. Practically all foreign coin, as well as bullion, was sent there to be re-issued as rupees or other Indian currency. A great deal of cash and bullion arrived from Europe—every ship carried a number of money chests—because at this period the export trade from India to Europe far exceeded the import. ". . . Sir Thomas Roe's epigram that Europe 'bleedeth to enrich Asia' undoubtedly represented the contemporary Western view."[30] The Indian producers were eager to sell their wares and there were no restrictions on exports, but the mass of the population was too poor to buy imported goods, and the wealthy had little interest in anything but coin or "toys". This aristocratic Indian "toy trade" was destined to have a direct bearing on the wreck of the *Batavia*.

There was in fact a narrow list to imports: Europe supplied few of the commodities in request. Some quicksilver from Lisbon came via the Red Sea; lead came from Europe, and also Mediterranean coral and a superior woollen cloth known as *laken*. Silks, velvets, wines and spirits, glass and mirrors practically completed the list. The bulk of all imports came from Asia. From the outset, European merchants were faced with the difficulty of providing remunerative outward cargoes to Surat.

It was Coen's determination to balance this by buying cotton

[30] W. H. Moreland, *From Akbar to Aurungzeb*, p. 53.

goods wanted in Java in order to create local funds in the East Indies for the payment for pepper, spices, etc. Sir Thomas Roe also saw that the English would never "drive the trade" in India by means of the cargoes they sent out; he suggested trade in the Red Sea.[31] These facts explain why the merchants who came to buy for Europe spent so much time carrying from one Asiatic port to another, dealing in articles not destined for Europe. This practice carried the germ of the "colonial system" and if Coen had been heeded by the V.O.C. Directors, that system would have been fully developed by the Dutch almost from the beginning. The establishment of a local Director at Surat was an early step forward.

Pelsaert arrived at Surat to assist van den Broecke in December 1620, travelling overland from Masulipatam.[32] He was almost at once posted to Agra, and left Surat in January 1621 with his senior officer, van Heuten, and several assistants.

He describes Surat in the *Remonstrantie*:[33]

> Surat (latitude 21¼ degrees[34]) is, owing to its situation, the chief seaport belonging to the King [Jahangir], though the city is 7 kos, or about 4 [Holland] miles,[35] up the river, and all goods, both imports and exports, must be shipped and landed by boat. Three kos, or two miles, further eastwards, the English have found a convenient anchorage named Swally, where there is a sandbank, which is exposed at low water, and gives shelter at high tide, so that it is a desirable place for loading and unloading goods . . . .
> The city is fairly well built, and is about two [Holland] miles in circumference. It has no walls, but ditches have been dug round it, provided with four gates on the land side. On the water front is a castle built of white coral rock, small in circuit, but well-provided with guns and equipment; it is considered locally to be practically impregnable, but it could not withstand a determined siege for long.[36]

[31] Ibid., p. 63.
[32] *Jahangir's India*, p. ix (Introduction).
[33] A recent letter from Dr W. Ph. Coolhaas, who is working on van den Broecke's papers in the Algemeen Rijksarchief, informs me that he has now found a report from van den Broecke to the V.O.C. Directors, dated January 1620, which suggests that this account of Surat was in fact an extract made by Pelsaert. This substantiates Moreland's opinion that some collaboration existed between the two men (see *Jahangir's India*, p. xv). As the object was to report faithfully to the Directors, this seems a natural proceeding.
[34] In the *Mercantile Marine Atlas*, 14th ed., the position of Surat is given as 21° 10′ N.
[35] Pelsaert's own explanation of this measurement appears in an earlier description of Agra, quoted later in this book. Here the square brackets were inserted by Moreland.
[36] *Jahangir's India*, pp. 38-9.

This passage has two points worthy of close attention in regard to the *Batavia* wreck: the noting of the latitude of the city and the definition of the length of the Indian *kos* by comparison with the "Holland mile". In the first instance, there is an error of five minutes in the position of the port, one that must have been checked often enough by various skippers: this suggests that there was either a general inaccuracy or that Pelsaert must have been wrongly informed by whomever he asked. Secondly, the term "Holland mile" was used by Pelsaert in an earlier description of Agra, and thereafter always bracketed into the text of the *Remonstrantie* by Moreland in order to avoid misapprehension. Moreland attaches a significant footnote to Pelsaert's first use of the term in the Agra description:

> The "Holland mile" was nearly 3 English miles, making the kos equal to about 1¾ of the latter. Further on the Holland mile is equated to 1½ kos, making the kos about two English miles.[37]

This discrepancy shows a degree of uncertainty in Pelsaert regarding Indian measurements. But it also allows one to suppose that three years later, in 1629, when writing the *Batavia* Journals for Dutch eyes and with no need for comparisons, he meant a distance of approximately three English miles—his "Holland mile"—whenever he used the word "mile". Both the inaccuracy of the latitudinal postion and the assessment of his reckonings in terms of the "Holland mile" assume considerable importance in determining the site of the *Batavia* wreck, as well as the various points at which people landed in the subsequent voyage up the western coast of Australia.

His own Journals make it quite clear that Pelsaert's "mile" did not at all approximate to a minute, as does the English nautical mile. Moreover, in Coen's dispatches it is clear that he also used "mile" to denote a measurement similar to that intended by Pelsaert.

Moreland's reckoning of Pelsaert's mile as being equal to less than three English miles has been accepted here on the grounds that Moreland was an accurate scholar and historian and therefore was probably at some pains to check the matter; he had greater facilities for researching the correct measurement in Europe. It is, however, possible that the "Holland mile" under discussion was the Snellius mile, which began to be used in the Netherlands after 1617. If that were so, the distance would then be equal to approximately 3.85 British nautical miles; but even this increase would not

[37] Ibid., p. 2, footnote 2.

grossly alter Pelsaert's approximation of distance over comparatively short lengths of measurement. And in any case the evidence offered by the Journals shows that a greater degree of accuracy in Pelsaert's reckoning follows the use of Moreland's assessment.

Surat became in due course the scene of a fateful quarrel between Pelsaert and one of the V.O.C. ships' officers named Ariaen Jacobsz, who was later to be appointed skipper of the *Batavia*: a quarrel so bitter and far-reaching that from then onwards the whole ensuing disaster appears to assume the inevitable character of a Greek tragedy.

II

REPORT FROM INDIA

WITHIN THREE YEARS of being sent with van Heuten to pioneer the V.O.C. district trade at Agra, Pelsaert found himself in command of that important outpost. Van Heuten died. There does not appear to be any record of the new appointment other than an English letter of that period[1] which mentions Pelsaert as being the probable successor to van Heuten; but when a few years later Pelsaert wrote his *Remonstrantie*, or Report, it is obvious that he had been in command for some time.[2]

Historically, this report is significant. Written originally for the Directors of the Company as an assessment of the trade conditions then prevailing, it gives not only an accurate summary of the economic scene and advice as to improved methods of trade, but also the best contemporary account[3] by a European of life at the Mogul Court under the Emperor Jahangir and in the many towns Pelsaert visited.

He is a lively writer with a quite notable flair for words. Moreland considers that sometimes he was carried near to incoherence when wishing to be especially effective in description or comment; but this seems a minor fault to set against the vigorous clarity of

---

[1] *The English Factories in India, 1622-1623*, by William Foster, p. 281: "The broker Jadodas . . . in his letters mentioneth not the death of Walter Hooten, the Dutch Agent, but the cossett [letter carrier] affeirmeth yt and the Dutch have advice also thereof, the Commander [van den Broecke] beinge in doubtfull resolution whom to ordaine to suceed him, butt thinketh Francisco the fittest, if hee will stay; some times sayinge he will goe himselfe. . . ." This letter appears under the heading (p. 279): "Joseph Hopkinson at Surat to President Rastell, October 17, 1623 (*Factory Records, Surat*, vol. cii, p. 411)".

[2] A letter from Dr W. Ph. Coolhaas, who is engaged in editing the diaries of van den Broecke (in the University of Leyden library) gives the following confirmation from the text of an entry dated 22nd March 1624: "The same day I sent the uppermerchant F. Pelsert as leader of a caravan of spices to Agra in order to manage there the business in place of the deceased merchant Wouter Heute [*sic*]" (translated from the Old Dutch by E. D. Drok). Earlier in the same diary (entry dated 28th October 1623) van den Broecke notes that Pelsaert had arrived at Surat (probably from Ahamadabad) with an incoming caravan consisting of 146 packs of cloth, 15 packs of indigo, and three female slaves.

[3] The English Ambassador, Sir Thomas Roe, and the traveller Thomas Coryat also described the Court ten years earlier: *Purchas His Pilgrimes*, vol. iv, p. 323 *et seq.*, and p. 473 *et seq.* See also Appendix VIII.

the whole. There can be no doubt that Pelsaert both enjoyed writing and thought of himself as a writer. In the *Remonstrantie* he refers to a history of the Mogul Empire which he wrote.[4] Although no such work has ever been found, Moreland is of the opinion that "there are some grounds for inferring that it may have been incorporated in the 'fragment of Indian History', which John de Laet printed in *De Imperio Magni Mogolis*."[5] De Laet states that the Dutch version of the Fragment was sent to him by van den Broecke. This fragment was probably part, if not all, of a chronicle of the Moguls from the time of Humayun, containing (as van den Broecke wrote in 1627 to the Directors[6]) everything that he had been able to put together on the subject. It is unlikely that two separate chronicles were made in the same period. Moreland presumes that van den Broecke would naturally seek assistance from Pelsaert, at Agra, and thinks it highly probable that considering "the intimate relations" that existed between Pelsaert and his superior officer, collaboration would be natural.

Pelsaert opens his report with a short preamble:

REMONSTRANTIE

Of the things, and part of the trade of this country, that have been gained by me, Francisco Pelsaert, Upper-Merchant, by serious inquiry and certain experience in that time of 7 years in which the United East India Company has had its trade in the Factory at *Agraa* as well as in other places, under the direction of the Commandeur *Pieter van Broeke*, and have written it in short, as follows . . . .[7]

Pelsaert then launches into a detailed description of the Mogul capital:[8]

Firstly, of the city of Agra, which is situated in 28° 45′ latitude.[9]

[4] *Jahangir's India. The Remonstrantie of Francisco Pelsaert*, p. 38.
[5] Ibid., p. xv (Introduction).
[6] ARAKA, VOC: 1004 (1628II), letter v.d. Broecke to the Directors dated 16th December 1627.
[7] Literal translation by E. D. Drok from photostat copy, VOC 4464, v18. Algemeen Rijksarchief, The Hague.
[8] This quotation from the *Remonstrantie* (pp. 1-2) and all others that follow are from the translation by W. H. Moreland and P. Geyl in *Jahangir's India*.
[9] The *Mercantile Marine Atlas* gives the present position as 27°13′, so this is an even greater error than that made about Surat (see Chapter I, note 34). The centre of the city may well have moved, of course; also, not so many seamen or navigators would have endeavoured to fix the position. Attention is drawn to these discrepancies in latitudes merely to stress the fact that inaccuracy was prevalent because of lack of precise instruments, therefore an error in fixing the site of the *Batavia* wreck would not be astonishing.

The city is exceedingly large, but decayed, open, and unwalled. The streets and houses are built without any regular plan. There are, indeed, many palaces belonging to great princes and lords, but they are hidden away in alleys and corners. This is due to the sudden growth of the city, which was a mere village until King Akbar chose it for his residence in the year 1566, and built the magnificent fort on the Jumna . . . . The luxuriance of the groves all round makes it resemble a royal park rather than a city, and everyone acquired and purchased the plot of land which suited or pleased him best. Consequently there are no remarkable market-places, or bazaars, as there are in . . . other cities, but the whole place is closely built over and inhabited, Hindus mingled with Moslems, the rich with the poor. . . .

The breadth of the city is by no means so great as the length, because everyone has tried to be close to the river bank, and consequently the waterfront is occupied by the costly palaces of all the famous lords, which make it appear very gay and magnificent, and extend for a distance of 6 kos or 3½ Holland miles.[10]

He passes on to the royal bastion of the Fort, "the walls of which are of red cut stone . . . in appearance, as well as in cost, it surpasses many of the most famous structures in the world."[11] He describes its situation and pleasant prospect, adding ". . . it is magnificently adorned with stone lattice work and gilded windows, and here the King was accustomed to sit when he made his elephants fight."[12]

Pelsaert mentions the many "princely edifices" as well as the *mahals*, or private palaces of the queen and other ladies, and says that internally the fort "is built over like a city with streets and shops, and has very little resemblance to a fortress, but from outside anyone would regard it as impregnable".[13]

He continues with a description of the city outside the Fort, and comments on the merchant town of Sikandra on the opposite side of the river, giving a list of merchandise. Duties on all goods were collected there by the Queen's officers (the first hint of her power and influence later explicitly condemned) before anything

[10] This is Pelsaert's own use of the term "Holland miles". It clearly establishes the distance he means when he writes "mile". This is very important to remember in reading the *Batavia* Journals, for he is scarcely likely to have any other definition in mind at most three years later. Moreland's footnote 2 on page 2 of *Jahangir's India* states: "The Holland mile was nearly 3 English miles." This estimate is the one I have accepted in my own later estimations in regard to the wreck. (See Appendix IX.) I have myself checked the script in a photostat copy of the first page of the *Remonstrantie*. It is perfectly clear: *Hollants mijl*.
[11] *Jahangir's India*, p. 3.
[12] Ibid., p. 3.
[13] Ibid., p. 4.

could be ferried across the river to the Court. He is obviously attracted by the beauty of much that he sees:

> ... the city is most pleasantly adorned ... the great lords far surpass ours in magnificence, for their gardens serve for their enjoyment while they are alive, and after death for their tombs, which during their lifetime they build with great magnificence in the middle of the garden. The number of these is consequently so great that I shall abandon the attempt to describe them in detail, and turn to the trade of the country and the city.[14]

The passage on trade opens with sharp criticism in striking contrast to the glowing pictures of the city of Agra:

> Commerce flourished here in the time of Akbar, and also in the beginning of the present reign, while Jahangir still possessed a vigorous intellect, but since this King devoted his life to enjoyment, violence has taken the place of justice. Whereas each governor ought to protect the people under him, they have in fact by subtle means drained the people dry ... consequently the country is impoverished, and the citizens have lost heart, for, as the old people say, the city has now nothing left of the colour and splendour which formerly shone throughout the whole world. The survival of a certain amount of commerce is due to the situation of the city at the junction of all the roads from distant countries.[15]

Throughout the *Remonstrantie* Pelsaert's sympathies are plainly with the Indian people, whom he considers scandalously oppressed. He gives many instances of bad government and cruel practice, displaying himself as a man of humane and civilized outlook. The Rajputs alone command his respect. "They are a bold and courageous people, determined and loyal."[16] He describes in detail the immolation of a young Rajput widow:

> When a Rajput dies, his wives (or rather his wife, for they marry only one if there is genuine love) allow themselves to be burnt alive .... It is not a very pleasant spectacle, but I witnessed it out of curiosity, when a woman who lived near our house declared to her friends, immediately on her husband's death, that she would be *sati*, which means that she would accompany him where he had gone,[17] making the announcement with little lamentation, and as if her heart was sealed with grief.

[14] Ibid., p. 5.
[15] Ibid., p. 6.
[16] Ibid., p. 78.
[17] Ibid., pp. 78-9. Moreland gives a footnote on *sati* as explained by Pelsaert: "This bit of popular etymology seems to have prevailed widely in India at this period."

She was "a handsome young woman of about 18 years of age".[18] Pelsaert emphasizes the fact that she acted voluntarily, despite dissuasion, and concludes:

> Surely this is as great a love as the women of our country bear to their husbands, for the deed was done not under compulsion but out of sheer love. At the same time there are hundreds, or even thousands, who do not do it, and there is no such reproach as is asserted by many, who write that those who neglect it incur the reproach of their caste.[19]

A long section is devoted to the indigo trade, and a description of the three grades of indigo, *ziarie*, *nauti* and *katel*, is worth quoting for its vivid efficiency:

> The *ziarie* indigo is superior in quality to the *nauti*, giving a violet infusion. Its quality can be easily judged . . . for it is much lighter in the hand than the *nauti*. In order to judge indigo with certainty, it should be looked at before midday in the sunshine; if it is pure, it will glisten and show various colours, like a rainbow, so that owing to the variations no opinion of the colour can be formed. If it contains sand or dirt, the adulterations cannot be overlooked in sunlight . . . .
> *Katel* is of extremely bad quantity, hard, dull, without gloss or colour, almost like charcoal . . . .
> The best comparison I can give to illustrate these three kinds of indigo is that the *nauti* is like a growing lad who has still to come to his prime and vigour; the *ziarie* is like a man in his vigorous prime; the *katel* is like an old, decrepit man, who in the course of his journey has had to cross many valleys of sadness and many mountains of misery, not only changed and wrinkled in the face, but falling gradually into helpless senility.[20]

As well as displaying Pelsaert's flair for words and delight in accurate description (much of which has been omitted), this passage is a fairly good pointer to his age: if in his own estimation he had not still been in "his vigorous prime" it is safe to assume it would not have been written. There is also a certain gaiety of expression that precludes any assessment of character that might suggest a pompous or domineering nature.[21] It is in addition a

---

[18] Ibid., p. 79.
[19] Ibid., p. 80.
[20] Ibid., pp. 11-12.
[21] It is in fact on record that Pelsaert together with several men and women were reported to the President of the Church Council at Batavia for "some irregularities", and on 3rd January 1630 a resolution was passed to the effect that they must be warned "to refrain from such untimely and altogether familiar conversation" (*Bouwstoffen voor de Geschiedenis der Protestansche Kerk in Nederlandsch-Indië*, ed. J. Mooy, vol. i, book 1, p. 330).

forerunner to the detailed and historical description he was to give, at the Abrolhos, of the first Australian marsupials to be examined and reported on in the interest of science.

After retailing further facts about the indigo trade, he writes, "Opinions may differ as to the course to be followed in buying indigo, but my own view, based on several years' experience, is this . . . ."[22] A capable exposition follows, with ways and means of dealing with various buyers neatly summarized with ironic emphasis to drive home his point:

> From repeated personal experience then, my opinion is that at such times it is more profitable for the Honourable Company that buyers should keep quiet, than that they should run about the country from one village to another. Goodness knows, the Armenians do quite enough of that, running and racing about like hungry folk, whose greedy eyes show that they are dissatisfied with the meal provided, who take a taste of every dish, [and] make the other guests hurry to secure their own portions, but directly they have tasted each course, they are satisfied, and can hold no more. In the indigo market they behave just like that, making as if they would buy up the whole stock, raising prices, losing a little themselves, and causing great injury to us and to other buyers who have to purchase large quantities.[23]

Throughout the section devoted to the buying of indigo a keen grip of the subject, enhanced by such apt making of points, clearly reveals the business acumen that was before long to bring gratifying recognition from the Directors at Amsterdam. Quite apart from his report, the Company's operations bear witness to his capabilities. The fact that "He went up to Agra one of a small party of pioneers: when he left it, the Dutch had secured a leading position in the indigo-market"[24] speaks for itself. Good progress in six or seven years; undoubtedly assisted by Pelsaert's mastery of the language of the country.

Yet there remained certain financial difficulties to be overcome if expansion was to reach truly gratifying proportions; and the real value of Pelsaert's report to the Directors lay in his considered opinion that spices should no longer be shipped in such large measures to the east but rather increased on the west (Surat) coast of India. If indigo was the principal purchase made for the European markets, spices were the item most readily sold to the Indians, in particular to the Moslems of Jahangir's Court and cities. Therefore funds for the purchase of indigo could be obtained locally by

[22] *Jahangir's India*, p. 15.
[23] Ibid., p. 16.
[24] Ibid., p. xi (Introduction).

increased sale of spices forwarded from Batavia via Surat, with a correspondingly satisfactory decrease in disbursement of cash imported from Europe. Pelsaert hammers the fact that the Indian merchants who purchased spices from the Dutch on the eastern Coromandel Coast in the end had the advantage at Agra over the Dutch themselves, who did not always get supplies sufficient to their needs from Surat. Thus, since the Company's merchants required cash to purchase indigo, many Hindu merchants were enabled to force down Dutch prices. He suggests that the Governor-General (Coen) did not know that the supplies sent to the Coromandel Coast were not mainly used there, but sent inland. He goes so far as to add a detailed table to demonstrate that by the simple expedient of doubling the Company's shipment of spices to Surat and halving that to the Coromandel Coast, the Company's profits generally would become much larger; and he precedes this statement by remarking: ". . . if this proposal should be doubted or criticised, the certain profit might be proved with uncertain loss to the Company by experiment within two years in the following way."[25] He concludes: ". . . then in the first or second year the books at headquarters will show His Honour whether the profits have increased or not."[26]

Unfortunately, Pelsaert can never have had the satisfaction of knowing that in this matter his recommendation was followed, although he must have gained the impression later in Amsterdam that it had every likelihood of being implemented. Moreland writes:

> In 1627 Pelsart . . . pointed out that the Dutch were injuring their trade in Northern India by excessive imports of spices on the East Coast, and recommended a reduction there coupled with increased supplies to Surat. A few years later general orders were issued from Amsterdam to regulate supplies [of spices] to Persia, Surat and Masulipatam in such a way as to keep prices level throughout the whole region. . . .[27]

From one passage after another of his report, it is evident that Pelsaert was greatly impressed by the trade openings offered in India, and felt it would be wise to "drive the trade" there, with less concentration on monopoly in the Spice Islands. His attitude invites speculation as to what policies he would have advocated had he lived to take his seat on the Council of India, firstly with Coen as Governor-General, and later with his brother-in-law, Hendrick Brouwer, who held the same office from 1632 to 1636.

[25] Ibid., p. 22.
[26] Ibid., p. 23.
[27] *From Akbar to Aurangzeb*, p. 152, footnote.

In his enthusiastic plea for increasing the Indian trade Pelsaert makes lists of particular goods, commenting on articles brought out by the English. He adds acidly:

> Formerly the English maintained an ambassador [Sir Thomas Roe] ... an arrangement which was very expensive to their Company; but it has now been abandoned, because a factor who sells their goods at Court can also look after all their incidental business; and obtain farmans, or rescripts, from the King. Frequently one hears many of the great lords asking (though it may be through the suggestions of our English friends) if precious stones are known in our country, or if there are any skilled craftsmen there, who can make *toffas* [*tuhfa*, rarities], as there are in England, Venice, and other European lands. It is essential therefore, both for the profit of the Honourable Company, and to increase the reputation of our own nation, that we should make it clear that our little country is not only on a level with England, but surpasses the whole world in skill.[28]

He continues with a list of specified items which include such rarities as

> 2 or 3 good battle-pictures, painted by an artist with a pleasing style, for the Moslems want to see everything from close by; also one or two maps of the entire world; also some decorative pictures showing comic incidents, or nude figures.[29]

He lists the type of "rarities" favoured by the English, mentioning that new inventions, or objects that we would call curios, held great attraction for Jahangir, and he also gives precise information concerning Indian trade measurements and currency.

From these particularized details Pelsaert passes to descriptions of the countryside and such towns as he visited, including

> the famous city of Kashmir,[30] which extends over a strongly defended plain, circular, and ringed with terrible mountains.[31]

He notes that the inhabitants of Kashmir are poor but physically sturdy, which surprises him because they eat so little.

> Their children are very handsome and fair, while they are young and small, but when they grow up, they become yellow and ugly, owing to their mode of life, which is that of beasts rather than men. The women are small in build, filthy, lousy and not handsome.[32]

He pays considerable attention to the varying forms of government in the provinces, and states that the land is good, and

---

[28] *Jahangir's India*, p. 25.
[29] Ibid., p. 26.
[30] To which the Court removed in the hot season.
[31] *Jahangir's India*, p. 33.   [32] Ibid., pp. 34-5.

would give "a plentiful, or even extraordinary yield" if the peasants were not so cruelly and pitifully oppressed. Pelsaert is in fact repeatedly shocked and horrified by the callous selfishness of the ruling classes; especially as after the death of a noble his estates revert to the King, and his dependants receive but a bare living.

> I have often ventured to ask great lords what is their true object in being so eager to amass their treasures, when what they have gathered is no use to themselves or to their family. Their answers have been based on the emptiest worldly vanity, for they say that it is a very great and imperishable reputation if it is generally known, or the official records show, that such a man has left an estate worth so much.[33]

He writes that he often urged in reply that surely "a greater reputation for time and eternity" might be expected were they to share their wealth with the poor, and banish oppression and injustice from their doors.

He sums up his attitude towards the administration by remarking that although certain laws do exist they are scarcely observed at all because in fact the government is "absolutely autocratic".

> The Governors are usually bribed . . . [even by such people as murderers and thieves] to remain inactive, for avarice dominates manly honour, and, instead of maintaining troops, they fill and adorn their *mahals* with beautiful women, and seem to have the pleasure-house of the whole world within their walls. . . .[34]

"One must indeed be sorry," he writes, "for the man who has to come to judgment before these godless 'un-judges'; their eyes are bleared with greed".[35]

As for the Emperor, Pelsaert makes a careful study of Jahangir's character, showing him to be a daring and successful hunter of big game, but dismissing him with contempt as a ruler. "The King does not trouble himself with public affairs, but behaves as if they were no concern of his."[36]

Pelsaert's respect for justice as a principle of behaviour is self-evident; and his opinions on government are of particular interest in relation to his personal attitude when later he found himself obliged to deal with the mutineers of the wrecked *Batavia*.

That he was immensely proud of Dutch justice and administration, with a pride based on inner gratitude that he belonged to an advanced and energetic Republic, is clearly shown, not only in open statement but also by constant comparison of the institutions and skills of his own country with the corruption and poverty so

[33] Ibid., p. 55.
[35] Ibid., p. 57.
[34] Ibid., p. 59.
[36] Ibid., p. 50.

rife in India. In religion he discloses himself to be a sturdy Protestant, scornful of "popists" and infidels alike, but innocent of fanaticism.

Up to this point Pelsaert has been mainly occupied by what might be termed legitimate trade interests, with an occasional personal diversion. But from the above passage to the end of the *Remonstrantie* he becomes something of a social historian, at the same time indulging his own obvious interest in human nature. He writes sections or chapters on the manner of life, on religious superstitions, on the Hindu religion; devoting considerable space and much literary endeavour to the erotic aspects of *zenana* life. He pictures the *mahals* as being

> ... adorned internally with lascivious sensuality, wanton and reckless festivity, superfluous pomp, inflated pride, and ornamental daintiness, while the servants of the lords may justly be described as a generation of iniquity, greed and oppression, for, like their masters, they make hay while the sun shines.[37]

He follows with a striking passage retailing the domestic relationships and housekeeping customs of a lord with his three or four wives, and includes details of an evening's entertainment, the manufacture of aphrodisiacs, as well as the enjoyment of much wine because "drinking has become very fashionable in the last few years". He winds up this intimate picture with an equally striking comment:

> The husband sits like a golden cock among the gilded hens until midnight, or until passion, or drink, sends him to bed. Then if one of the pretty slave girls takes his fancy, he calls her to him and enjoys her, his wife not daring to show any signs of displeasure, but dissembling, though she will take it out of the slave-girl later on.[38]

He records with great disapproval the power of the eunuchs and their unpleasant behaviour towards the women under their surveillance. Although he opens this section by remarking that he must turn from the "submissive bondage" of the wretched poor who "may be compared to poor, contemptible earthworms, or to little fishes, which, however closely they may conceal themselves, are swallowed by the great monsters of a wild sea",[39] his ever-ready sympathy for the oppressed in any class is ultimately extended to the fragile inhabitants of the *mahals*. He states that in order to write of the rich and the great

[37] Ibid., p. 64.
[38] Ibid., p. 65.
[39] Ibid., p. 64.

... the pen which has described bitter poverty, clothed with the woeful garments of sighs, the foe of love, friendship and happiness, but the friend of loneliness wet with the daily dew of tears,—that pen must entirely change its style, and tell that in the palaces of these lords dwells . . . wealth which glitters indeed, but is borrowed, wrung from the sweat of the poor.[40]

Nevertheless, his strongly developed sense of humanity is touched, rather than shocked, by the condition of the wealthy women.[41] When later he mentions the annulment of permits for pilgrimages to shrines (on which occasions the "secluded ladies" tried to make contact with the men of their fancy, seen from behind the curtains of their palanquins), he writes:

Assignations were made in the gardens, which are numerous in the neighbourhood, and there passion was given the food for which it hungered, and for which, in the case of many, no opportunity could be found on any other day . . . . Thus nobody more regrets these gardens, or is more grieved, than these pitiable little creatures of Agra. . . .[42]

The *Remonstrantie* has been quoted at length since it is only from his own writings that any true assessment of Pelsaert's character can be made. He stands forth clearly as a keen observer, a shrewd business man, a student of mankind. He was warm-hearted, sometimes even impulsive (as when he allows his pen to run away with him). He was sensitive to beauty, lively, and possessed a reasonable sense of humour. He even makes a little jest in his *Conclusion*, when he commends his report to the Directors:

I have been constrained by zeal to fulfil my duty, to show and make it clear that while in India I have not been like the main-mast, which also travels to India, but rather their servant, who is, and always will be, bound to render them such services as etc., etc. I close by wishing my employers continual expansion and development of their trade, all good fortune and prosperity to themselves.[43]

This confident, jocular ending is in sad contrast to the last letter he was to write to the Directors,[44] from Batavia, two or three years later, after the disaster at the Abrolhos.

At the same time there is also a hint in the *Remonstrantie* that the climate was taking its toll, and that at the moment of writing

---
[40] Ibid., p. 64.
[41] Pelsaert does draw attention to the evil power wielded by the Queen over the self-indulgent Jahangir; but he appears to regard her as an exception.
[42] *Jahangir's India*, p. 72.
[43] Ibid., p. 85.   [44] See Appendix II.

he must already have been thinking of refusing further appointment in India:

> This would be a desirable country if men might indulge their hunger or appetite as they do in our cold lands; but the excessive heat makes a man powerless, takes away his desire for food, and limits him to water-drinking, which weakens or debilitates his body. But as this discussion is irrelevant, I shall close it and turn to—The administration of the country.[45]

The *Remonstrantie* was written in 1626 and probably reached Amsterdam the following year.[46] Pelsaert's appointment terminated in 1627. Despite van den Broecke's expressed wish "readily" to keep him in India,[47] he left Surat (van den Broecke's letter was dispatched by the same ship) aboard the *Dordrecht*,[48] sailing direct via the east coast of Africa for Amsterdam. The chances are that he had contracted malaria. The severe bouts of illness that so handicapped him on the subsequent voyage of the *Batavia* point to some recurring fever rather than dysentery, then called the flux, or the bloody flux, and generally specified. Both diseases took a heavy toll of life amongst the native inhabitants, no less than amongst the Europeans.

An English letter of the period, dated 4th January 1628,[49] notes that the *Dordrecht* sailed "on December 5 or 6, while the English were with the Prince; hence their omission to send letters in her". The same letter also announces the death of the Emperor Jahangir:

> And no sooner were our goods chopt and cleared but a suddaine rumour overspread the land with the Kings death, which filled all men with feare and expectacion, except only rebells and theeves, that make itt their harvest. This newes was first wispered here the 19th November, but within two dayes after publikly divulged.[50]

From orders later placed in Amsterdam by Pelsaert for certain goods he hoped to sell to Jahangir, it appears probable that he either did not hear the public announcement or failed to believe it, despite the fact that the *Dordrecht* seems to have been held up for some time before she cleared from Swally, where she had been at anchor with the English ships. The final date on van den

---

[45] *Jahangir's India*, pp. 49-50.
[46] Ibid., p. xiii (Introduction).
[47] ARAKA, VOC: 1004 (1628^{II}), Letter from van den Broecke to Directors, dated 16th December 1627.
[48] More correctly the *Maagd van Dordrecht*; frequently shortened to *Dort*.
[49] William Foster, *The English Factories in India, 1624-29*, pp. 207-8.
[50] Ibid., p. 202.

Broecke's *Dordrecht* dispatch is 16th December 1627.[51] The *Dordrecht* was not a new vessel. She had been the command of Frederik de Houtman when in 1619 he sighted for the first time the rocks which now bear his name, rocks destined later to bring Pelsaert to ruin.

During the period of inactivity at Swally, Pelsaert and the skipper Ariaen Jacobsz quarrelled violently. No evidence has yet been uncovered to disclose the reason for their dispute, yet its serious nature is attested by evidence given by Jeronimus Cornelisz, undermerchant of the *Batavia*, when on trial for murder and mutiny at the Abrolhos isles.

> He [Jeronimus Cornelisz] being asked why the skipper was so embittered against the Commandeur [Pelsaert], says, that he does not know, for he often wondered that he [the Commandeur] liked him so much and put up with him. But that the skipper had told him that he had started to hate the Commandeur when he was in Souratte, waiting in order to sail to the Fatherland, and when he [the skipper] had gone too far in words one night, whereon the Commandeur Grijph and Wollebrand Gheleijnsen, Uppermerchant,[52] had rebuked him, saying that that was not the manner to sail in peace to the Fatherland, and that he must behave himself differently towards the Commandeur.[53]

There can be no doubt that the hate born of this quarrel played a dominant part in the disaster that was so soon to wreck not only a valuable ship but also the career of Francisco Pelsaert. When two years later Ariaen Jacobsz was arrested at Batavia and brought before a court of inquiry regarding his behaviour both aboard the *Batavia* and during the wrecking of that vessel, it seems more than likely that evidence then furnished supplied also the reason. Unfortunately the records of this inquiry have been lost, although it is definitely stated in a General Letter from the Governor-General, Specx, to the Directors that they were forwarded to Amsterdam.[54]

---

[51] Dr W. Ph. Coolhaas sends the following note from the diary of P. van den Broecke: "Have departed to go aboard and I arrived there on the 16th ditto [Dec. 1627] in the morning; since the ship Dordrecht was just departed, I could still see it sailing from aboard. On the foresaid ship Dordrecht was uppermerchant Francisco Pelsert and the skipper Ariaen Jacopssen." (Translated from the old Dutch by E. D. Drok.) Thus both date of sailing and position of officers are confirmed.

[52] The names of Grijph and Gheleijnsen appear frequently in V.O.C. records. Pelsaert himself mentions the former as being aboard one of the ships he met in the Straits of Sunda when reaching Java in the open boat after the wreck of the *Batavia*.

[53] Pelsaert's Journals: Evidence of Jeronimus Cornelisz, 19th September 1629, on *Batavia's* Graveyard.

[54] ARAKA, VOC: 1009, O.B. (1630¹), Report of Governor-General and Council to Directors, dated 15th December 1629. Signed by A. van Diemen and others.

The evidence given by Jeronimus clearly implies that Pelsaert had himself forgotten the dispute, or had at least not allowed personal antipathy to colour his official attitude towards Jacobsz. There must, however, have been some additional and deep-rooted sense of guilt to feed the hatred of Jacobsz when he found himself once more unexpectedly in close company with a greatly promoted Pelsaert. That such was so is hinted by further evidence given by Jeronimus in self-defence, wherein he stated that he had asked Jacobsz why he did not merely have Pelsaert thrown overboard (if personal hatred was the point at issue) instead of planning a full-scale mutiny, with seizure of the *Batavia*. Jacobsz had then replied: "The Commandeur was not the whole desire." Jeronimus said that Jacobsz went on to "paint to him" the advantages of great riches, adding, "I am still for the Devil; if I go to India, then I have to come to shame in any case."[55]

It is even possible that Pelsaert knew something to the discredit of Jacobsz (such as extensive private trading), implied in another statement attributed to Jacobsz by Jeronimus at the same time as the above: ". . . that it would be to their advantage [to seize the *Batavia*] because there was now so little profit to be got in India." If Pelsaert did possess such information, he must have chosen to ignore the matter when at Surat. At this period the majority of the officials in both Companies, more especially in the English Company which was less organized, regarded private trading as a venial crime; although very soon the V.O.C. Directors were to promulgate strict and harsh prohibitory measures. Moreover in 1627 at Surat, Pelsaert (as well as Jacobsz) believed that he was leaving India for good. When ten months later he changed his mind and was sent out as Fleet President, travelling aboard the new ship *Batavia*, Jacobsz may well have become uneasy. He had indeed been given command of the latest ship to be built for the Chamber of Amsterdam (a fact that suggests nothing was known to his detriment in Holland); but his annoyance must have been considerable to discover that Francisco Pelsaert had not only reconsidered his decision not to return to the Orient, but had also been given added authority and was returning aboard the *Batavia*. Thus was her skipper placed in close proximity to an ancient enemy, with every action open to scrutiny.

---

[55] Pelsaert's Journals: Evidence of Jeronimus Cornelisz, 19th September 1629.

III

DISTINCTION, DISASTER, AND DEATH

WHEN PELSAERT LANDED at Amsterdam from India in June 1628,[1] he must have been amazed. Despite the cessation of the Twelve Years' Truce with Spain and the restless state of Europe, embroiled still in the endless battles of the Thirty Years' war, the great port was secure, serene, and busy—busy beyond the dreams of the first years of the century. A generation had passed since the initial ships returned with their valuable cargoes from the Indies: wealth had poured into the Netherlands, new inventions, new amenities, new ideas, had enriched the lives of all in the ten years of his absence. Wharves, ships, streets, houses, had multiplied. A hundred thousand people lived at Amsterdam.

Across the River Scheldt in Pelsaert's home town of Antwerp, the empty streets still lay desolate, trade drained away by the yet-unmoved barriers the Hollanders had thrown across the river in their struggle for freedom. Yet there the artist Rubens, himself luxurious, was recording for posterity the colour and texture of the magnificent existence of wealthy men and their beautiful wives. In Amsterdam the merchants were no less magnificent, but they walked with zest through a bustling city; whilst the people *en masse* were well clothed, well fed, filled with the same spirit of enterprise as the busy merchants[2]—a striking contrast to the India Pelsaert had recently described, where the princes lolled in their palaces and the wretched peasants often sold their children into slavery in order to subsist.

Despite his assurance to van den Broecke that he would not consider re-engagement or return to India, Pelsaert spent barely five months in the Netherlands. His brother-in-law Hendrick Brouwer was still one of the High and Mighty Seventeen: an elected representative of the Chamber of Amsterdam on the governing body of

---

[1] *Jahangir's India. The Remonstrantie of Francisco Pelsaert*, p. ix (Introduction).

[2] "Amsterdam, the city of refuge from Parma's havoc at Antwerp, became the European emporium of Indian commerce, richer and more powerful by far than Venice, Genoa, or Lisbon in their prime." Sir William Wilson Hunter, *A History of British India*, vol. i, p. 333.

the V.O.C. He was also greatly involved in general politics. It was common talk in Europe that the policies of the Directors of the V.O.C. and those of the States-General were so intermixed as to be inextricable. Brouwer was destined to become Governor-General at Batavia in 1632; it is probable that he already had this possibility in mind, or even under discussion. He must have read and approved Pelsaert's Indian report. The chances are that, quite apart from family considerations, he was not at all inclined to let the Company lose such an able servant. But whatever the persuasion or the reason, October saw Pelsaert once again ready to set sail for the Indies, with greatly increased responsibilities and glowing prospects.[3]

What he did with his time at home, whether he visited his family at Eupen, or travelled to Antwerp, possibly there meeting Rubens in person to discuss the Indian "toy" trade, remains undisclosed.[4] It is certain, however, that in those few months Pelsaert was allowed by the Company to order, and have made to his own design, various *objets d'art* for sale at the Mogul Court at Agra. His personal contact with other merchants also appears from correspondence and jewels found amongst his effects after his death in Java in 1630.[5]

Whilst he had been visiting and ordering in Amsterdam, a new fleet for the Indies had been fitting up and loading,[6] and by the end of August he had accepted another term abroad.

A recommendation to Coen was to follow him to Batavia:

> The person of Francisco Pelsaert who before this has come over with the ship *Dordrecht* from Suratte but has now gone again as President with the ships lately sailed for the Indies, on the ship *Batavia*, this same has asked for our recommendation to Your Hon. and the Councillors of India, and, because we have heard very good reports of his previous services, we therefore recommend him to Your Hon. hereby, asking you to keep in mind his person and to note the future services of the same to advance the said Pelsart according to those services to such positions [*qualiteyten*] as his conduct and contribution shall merit, whereby you will perform an act of

---

[3] It is probable that Brouwer also indicated to Pelsaert that he would press for his rapid appointment to Coen's Council of India.

[4] See Chapter V, Trade Jewels.

[5] ARAKA, VOC: 1011, General Letter to the Directors dated 13th September 1630.

[6] This fleet was originally meant to sail in charge of Councillor Jacques Specx. In the end it was dispatched in two sections: Pelsaert was appointed President in charge of eight vessels which sailed in October 1628; the remaining ten sailed later under Specx.

friendship to us and a service to the General Company. Done in Amsterdam, this 16 December anno 1628. In the name of the High and Mighty [*Bewinthehebberen*] of the East-India Company at Amsterdam, friends of Your Hon.

Six signatures follow.[7]

Some months later a further letter from the Directors to Coen gives notice of Pelsaert's appointment to the Council of India. After mentioning the fact that three Councillors of the Indies have recently arrived back in the Netherlands, and that in consequence Coen would find himself "a little depleted", and although he could expect before long the arrival of the Heeren Specx and Raemburch, and also Gysels, the letter continues:

... still the Seventeen have found good to provide Your Hon. with three extraordinary Councillors, namely: ─────────,[8] going from here, and Philips Lucasz, President at Amboina, also Francisco Pelsaert, the last sailing with *Batavia*, which persons Your Hon. will assume as Councillors of India because some of the places of the eight Councillors will be vacant when you receive this message; namely, successively as they are mentioned here, firstly, ─────────; for second place: Philips Lucasz, and for third: Francisco Pelsaert. ───────── has made his conditions with the Company; the other two persons will enjoy a salary of f. 200[9] per month, for three years from the time of their appointment.[10]

In ten years Pelsaert had risen from a humble assistant at f. 24 per month to wealth and honour. Yet by the time this letter reached Batavia. Coen was dead and Pelsaert the victim of disaster.

According to an official letter of advice from Amsterdam to Batavia, dated 21st March 1629,[11] the fleet sailed on 25th October of the previous year. But in a private letter written by the predikant, or minister, Gijsbert Bastiaensz,[12] who travelled aboard the *Batavia*, he states that they sailed from the Texel (out-going fleets gathered for shelter in the lee of the island) on 27th October. The "outward

[7] H. T. Colenbrander, *J. P. Coen, Bescheiden omtrent zijn Bedrijf in Indië*, vol. v, p. 826. The signatures are Louis Delabeeque, Simon Jacobsz. Schoonhoven, Pieter de Schilder, Andries Rijkaert, Cornelis de Vry, Aernolt Sweers.

[8] The name place of this appointee remains blank. It would appear that he was not able to make his "conditions with the Company" in a manner satisfactory to himself.

[9] Florins (f.), equal in value to guilders.

[10] H. T. Colenbrander, *op. cit.*, vol. v, p. 858. Letter dated 28th August 1629.

[11] Ibid., p. 830. Letter per *Gouden Leeuw*, dated 21st March 1629.

[12] See Appendix IV.

sailing" record of the period gives the date as 29th October;[13] which is probably correct.[14]

In the official letter the *Batavia* is listed as a *retour* ship; in other words a merchantman, although of course she would be armed as all ships then were. Later records show that she also carried a large complement of soldiers en route to Java to fight in the still active war against the Susuhunan, or ruler, of Mataram. A *retour* ship was in fact one intended to trade back and forth from the Indies to the Netherlands, and larger than the yachts and flutes employed on the inter-island trade—though in fact many of the larger vessels voyaged between India and Batavia and often enough the flutes also returned to the Fatherland. The yachts were the fastest sailers; they were frequently used as dispatch carriers.

Big or little, broad-beamed or slender, the ships were all built with high poops and square-rigged; they were gaily painted, generally in green and gold, and all carried the carved red lion of Holland at the prow. The decks and the great square gun-ports were also painted red—in order to lessen the ghastliness of slaughter, on the same principle that later inspired the famous British redcoat. Flags and fifty-foot pendants fluttered and streamed from the mastheads on days of departure and arrival. A fleet about to sail, dressed, gleaming with fresh paint, was indeed a brave sight.

Besides the *Batavia* Pelsaert's fleet comprised six other ships. The *Dordrecht* and the *Galias* (or *Gailliasse*) were also *retour* ships; the others were the flutes *Assendelft* and *Sardam* (later referred to as a yacht), the yacht *Cleenen Davidt* (or *Cleen David*) and a convoying ship of war, *Buren* (or *Bueren*).[15] With the exception of *Galias* and *Cleenen Davidt*, destined for the Coromandel Coast, all

[13] ARAKA. *Uitloop boek van schepen der O.I.C.*
[14] *Uitloop boek van schepen der O.I.C.* also notes her tonnage as being 300 *last*. This is generally taken to equal a modern 600 tons. Moreland notes the *tun* of the period to equal approximately 60 cubic feet of cargo space (*From Akbar to Aurangzeb*, p. 16, footnote); in another place (ibid., p. 80) equating 2,000 *last* to about 3,125 tons weight; in a third (ibid., p. 121, footnote) a *tun* is approximated to half a *last*; and 800 *tuns* measurement shown to equal 600 to 700 tons weight. Thus, assessing the size of these vessels in modern terms is difficult. In a letter to me the Director of the Scheepvaart Museum, Amsterdam, G. A. Cox, wrote: "The ship Batavia . . . had a tonnage of 300 last (600 tons). Though no other information is available we can assume that she was a normal ship of the V.O.C. of that tonnage, with a length of about 150 feet, beam of 36 feet, and depth of 14 feet, and with about 24 guns. I did not find her name mentioned earlier [than 1628]. . . . Nor plans nor pictures of the Batavia are known to me, but any picture of a square-sterned vessel\from the second quarter of the seventeenth century will be almost identical. The ships of the period carried a spritsail below the bowsprit. Flags were carried at the stern and also from the mast-tops."
[15] H. T. Colenbrander, *op. cit.*, vol. v, p. 830.

were Java-bound on Brouwer's route across the southern Indian Ocean, to be sped by the prevailing winds before turning north for Batavia, well clear of the coast of the still unknown Southland. An eighth ship, *'s Gravenhage*, set sail, but the rest of the fleet were not to know her fate for many months.

They ran into a storm. Gijsbert Bastiaensz, the predikant, after noting the date of departure, continued his letter: "On the same day we have run aground with the ship, thinking that we should perish there with the ship: but God the Lord this fore-seeing, we got free, and continued sailing. . . ."[16] A dispatch to Coen dated 22nd December gives added evidence of the fury they encountered:

> Further this letter will serve to bring to the notice of Your Hon. the disaster that happened to our ship *'s Gravenhage* at sea, about 3 or 4 days after it had run out with the other ships under the command of the Hon. Francisco Pelsaert; the same ship has run on to a bank through storm, and also through being too slight in the beam [*ranckheyt*]; but it has come off at last, thanks to God, and has run into the harbour mouth of Veere without a mast and disabled beyond hope to the extent that it has become totally leaky; so that it has been found advisable to unload the mentioned ship completely and to bring it to dock at Middleborch in order to refit it, due to which fact it will not be ready until the Spring, in April.[17]

October-November, April-May were the favoured sailing months for vessels bound for the East Indies. Otherwise, ships could not take advantage of the prevailing winds. From Sierra Leone they crossed the South Atlantic almost to the coast of Brazil (a desired landfall was a small group of islands also then termed the Abrolhos), whence they turned south east for the Cape of Good Hope.

A contemporary skipper of the V.O.C., Willem Ysbrantsz Bontekoe has left a vivid and detailed account of a voyage to the Indies and back.[18] He left the Texel late in December, which was late indeed, and his worry about catching the trade winds is evident. He gives fascinating sidelights on the uncertainties of navigation:

> The wind being now N.W. we bore eastwards to make the Cape of Bonesperance [Good Hope]. After holding this course for some time we saw black-specked gulls of which occasionally we caught some, with sticks covered with a piece of fat and hooks to them, and so pulled them into the ship by way of pastime. The sight of these gulls is a token of the Cape of Bonesperance being near, for they

---

[16] See Appendix IV.
[17] H. T. Colenbrander, *op. cit.*, p. 829. Letter dated 22nd December 1629, per *Hollandia*.
[18] *Memorable Description of the East Indian Voyage 1618-25*, translated from the Dutch by Mrs C. B. Bodde-Hodgkinson and Pieter Geyl, Litt. D. (Leyden).

followed us to the Cape. But there is a trustworthy sign that the Cape be near or that you be at the height thereof, to wit: When you find the compass to hold straight south and North, then look out for land. We did prove this and saw land, namely the Cape of Bonesperance, yet the wind was so strong from the West that we ran with a reefed foresail and durst not attempt to land. Therefore we called the ship's council together and resolved to sail past the Cape, having all our men in good health and no want of water, so we let her go before the wind and continued our way. This was the last of May being five months after we sailed from Holland.[19]

In 1628 Pelsaert's fleet was at least a month earlier at the Cape, and entered Table Bay. His ships were cleaned and he went ashore to buy meat for the convoy[20] from the Hottentots (so called by the Netherlanders because the sound of their speech was said to resemble a duck quacking). Passengers and crew relaxed. But here, as once before at Swally, trouble flared between Pelsaert and the *Batavia's* skipper, Ariaen Jacobsz. What happened, what was said, was destined to be taken down by Pelsaert himself months later, when given in evidence at the Abrolhos trials over which he presided.

A drunken spree of the skipper's ended in a sharp reprimand from the Commandeur. Ariaen's banked-up hate now exploded into a plan for mutiny, given greater violence by a passion he had conceived for Zwaantie[21] Hendrix, the maidservant of one of the passengers named Lucretia Jansz, a "fair" young woman who was travelling to Java to join her husband, Boudewijn van der Mijlen, an undermerchant with the Company. Originally, Ariaen had molested the mistress; repulsed, he became infatuated with the maid. A third party to their desires and schemes was soon found in the undermerchant Jeronimus Cornelisz, thirty years of age and ambitious, an astute schemer who had once practised as an apothecary at Haarlem, where he had been the friend of artists. Ariaen Jacobsz recklessly decided to sail the *Batavia* away from the other ships as soon as they left the Cape.

Fate played into his hands. They were scarcely clear of Agulhas than a storm arose. The *Batavia* ran away from the convoy *apparently* by chance. In addition, Pelsaert became very ill from what-

[19] Ibid., pp. 25-6.
[20] Probably with copper plates. A short time before, Coen, returning to Java in 1627, had found difficulty in trading with the natives for cattle and sheep "because there was only thin copper in our ships, which they did not like much, we only got the worst stock. It is necessary that in order to refresh the crews in Table Bay, ships should be given thick copper plates; [I] request such should be given." H. T. Colenbrander, *op. cit.*, vol. v, p. 6.
[21] Also spelt Zwaantgie, Zwaantje.

ever malady he had contracted in India, and the barber expected him to die. But he did not die. Accordingly the skipper created an "incident" designed to force Pelsaert to take harsh disciplinary measures bound to alienate the sailors. Ariaen planned to pose as a defender of his crew, while the mutiny would be sprung at the same time, the impetus given by several malcontents amongst the soldiers, already enlisted in the plot. Pelsaert clearly endured days of mental torture, racking his mind as to what action he could best take to uncloak and punish the "incident" offenders, painfully aware that the understeersman happened to be the skipper's brother-in-law and that one of the petty officers was his cousin. Doubtless Pelsaert was uncertain whether he would find the ship's council solidly behind him if once again he openly reprimanded the skipper.

The *Batavia* drove steadily eastwards towards the reefs of Houtman's Abrolhos. The skipper himself took over the night watch. All was in order; when he gave the word, his terrible plan could erupt in a sleeping ship and himself alone command action. But "God the Lord did not wish to suffer that extraordinary bad evil, but rather let the ship be wrecked."[22] Grown careless in his calculations, Ariaen Jacobsz piled *Batavia* on a reef—in a wreck that three centuries later remains notorious amongst maritime disasters.[23]

Within twenty-four hours Pelsaert found himself faced by an even more ferocious dilemma. Should he stay with the survivors, landed on two waterless specks he knew not where,[24] or should he depart with the skipper and his chosen crew in search of water and succour? He had small faith in the skipper's will to save any lives other than those of the boat's crew and his own, or in his undertaking to return with water should it be found. Pelsaert played for time. He pointed out that rain might fall, the seas abate, food be salvaged from the wreck, so that he, the Commandeur, might leave with easier mind. Ariaen Jacobsz remained implacable: he would go immediately. The Commandeur could go with him, or remain. Still ignorant of the now delayed mutiny plot, or that Ariaen

[22] Pelsaert's Journals: Summary of evidence at trial of Allert Jansz, 28th September 1629, on *Bavaria's* Graveyard.

[23] From 1616 onwards all ships, once past the Cape of Good Hope, were ordered to sail in S. lat. 36° to 42° on an easterly course for 800 to 1,000 *mylen* (approximately 2,400 to 3,000 miles) in order to benefit from the prevailing westerlies, then to steer north for Java. This was known as Brouwer's Route. The difficulty in calculating correct longitude was responsible for the numerous wrecks on the coast of Western Australia. For order see Pieter van Dam, *Beschrijvinge van de Oostindische Compagnie* (ed. F. W. Stapel), book 1, vol. i (1927), pp. 665-6.

[24] Pelsaert's Journals: First entry. Also Appendix II.

Jacobsz planned to kill him, Pelsaert, practically kidnapped, reluctantly accompanied the skipper.

In a letter to Pieter de Carpentier at Amsterdam, Antonio van Diemen reports from Batavia the arrival of Pelsaert and the skipper Ariaen Jacobsz in the largest of the *Batavia's* open boats. In less than four weeks they had come more than twelve hundred miles from the wreck, skirting the formidable coast of the unknown Southland and crossing to Java. Eventually they were picked up in the Straits of Sunda by the yacht *Sardam* (which, it will be recalled, had sailed from the Netherlands in Pelsaert's fleet). But they passed on (Pelsaert insisting) to another Company ship in the vicinity. This was the *Fredrick Hendrick* [sic], on which the Honourable Crijn Raemburch, a high official of the V.O.C. was sailing to Java. Van Diemen wrote:

By God's truth, the ship *Batavia*, with its full cargo despatched from the Fatherland to India, is on the 4th June 1629 come out of its course, with a clear and full moon, on the Southland 28⅓ degrees, and has been knocked to pieces on the dry [reefs] of Houtman; the Commandeur Francisco Pelsaert, the skipper of ditto ship, Capn. Hans Jacobsz,[25] the uppersteersman and more other officers in total 48 and amongst them two women[26] and a child of 3 months, have arrived here on the 7th July with the boat of the ditto ship, reporting that the rest of the people 250 souls, amongst them 30 women and children, have been left on certain small islands over which the sea breaks at high water, situated about 8-10 miles [i.e. 24-30] from the continent, being in the utmost misery, to perish shortly from thirst and hunger; upon what consideration the Commandeur Pelsaert has separated himself from those desolate people and in the end decided to come to Batavia, and what resulted from all that, Your Hon. will be so good as to hear from his written statement.

The 15th July following on that, the yacht *Sardam* has been sent thither with the Commandeur Pelsaert in the hope of rescuing some people and goods, as apparently in the first place the people, a casket with jewels valued at [f.] 20,409.15., were salvaged on the small island, and 4 chests of Cash have had buoys put on them. What orders[27] have been given to the Commandeur Pelsaert, Your Hon. may see from the letter book of the 15th July 1629. So far the mentioned one has not returned, may God grant he can do something useful.

Considerable disorder and insolence had occurred on the said ship *Batavia*, of which the skipper has been no small cause; the High Boatswain Jan Devertsz of Munnickendam[28] has been hanged on the

[25] Van Diemen not yet certain of the skipper's correct name.
[26] One was Zwaantie Hendrix.
[27] See Appendix I.
[28] Another slight error: the name was Evertsz; the town, Monnikendam.

gallows on account of the mishandling on ditto ship of Lucretia van Mijlen, wife of Boudewijn van der Mijlen.[29]

The skipper himself was on watch when the ship grounded, being, according to his reckoning, so far from land that one would not think to look out, and thinking that the spray from the sea was the glare of the moon. Proper proceedings have been taken against the skipper, but it will be of little comfort to the Company, such a beautiful *retour* ship with 250 thous. guilders in Cash, as well as so much rich merchandise and victuals, so carelessly neglected, and so many poor people brought into the danger of death; may the Almighty make good the damage to the Company and may he have helped the miserable distressed people.[30]

A critical attitude towards Pelsaert can be sensed in this letter of van Diemen's. Whether this was entirely disinterested is matter for conjecture. It is possible that the favourable reception given to the *Remonstrantie*, added to the unexpected return and increased responsibilities of Pelsaert himself, induced in van Diemen a measure of antagonism. The brilliant young councillor had been a known favourite with Coen; in this letter he is addressing himself to Carpentier, a former Governor-General, now back in Holland and a powerful influence in the Company.

Pelsaert's Journals written from the time of the wreck until the return of the *Sardam* with the survivors on 5th December (with the exception of the week he spent in Batavia from 7th to 15th July) give a day by day account of his own experiences. They also include the full record of evidence given at the Abrolhos trials, thus disclosing as far as possible all that happened on the islands during his absence. Earlier writers have sometimes wondered why no similar record remains of the *Batavia's* voyage from Holland, for both skippers and merchants in charge were required to keep such records; and Pelsaert must undoubtedly have noted any incidents that might ultimately have had some bearing on the subsequent mutiny. Full translation of the evidence at the trials has supplied the reason: all documents, including Pelsaert's records, were thrown overboard after the wreck by rioting members of the ship's company.[31]

Together with the Order given by the Governor-General Jan Pieterszoon Coen,[32] mentioned by van Diemen, the record of proceedings provides a picture of Pelsaert making his disastrous report

[29] This was the "incident" created by Ariaen Jacobsz, of which full accounts appear later.
[30] ARAKA, VOC: 1009, O.B. (1630¹), Letter from A. van Diemen to Pieter de Carpentier, dated 30th November to 10th December 1629.
[31] Pelsaert's Journals: Evidence of L. Michielsz. van Os, 23rd September 1629, on *Batavia's* Graveyard.
[32] See Appendix I.

to the Council of India at Batavia, and lists the decisions taken thereon; from which can readily be deduced how urgently he must have been occupied during that week in Java:

> Monday the 9th July 1629. Also informed by the commandeur Francisco Pelsaert (arrived here on 7th inst. with the boat of the ship *Battavia* from the Southland) that on 4 June last on Houtmans Abreolhos situated between 28 and 29 degrees about 9 miles [i.e., 27] west of the land of the Eendracht,[33] the aforesaid ship *Battavia* was wrecked and that it had run off its course at high tide, with 12 feet of water at the bow and 18 feet at the poop, being coral ground, and that 180 souls therefrom, whereof 30 odd were women and children, and a casket with jewels, were landed on a certain coral shallow, that there was not any fresh water at that place and that they had not more than 13 barrels of ships' biscuit with them; that 12 or 13 persons were drowned and that 70 souls were still on the ship when they [Pelsaert and the skipper] had sailed off with the boat (in which 48 persons, whereof 2 were women and one child) in search of water; that the ship had burst and was full of water; that at several places they had been ashore in order to dig for fresh water so that they might have provided those left on the small island, but that they had not been able to find it, whereupon they had resolved amongst themselves to set course to Battavia because they saw that it would not be possible to salvage anything more from the wrecked ship, because of the daily rough weather.
> It was put forward by His Hon. to the Council, since it was apparent that it was possible that some of the people and also some of the goods might be saved and salvaged, whether it was not advisable that they should be sent thither with a suitable yacht to find out what could be done. The Council having taken notice of the proposal of His Hon., it was found good on an unanimity of voices, and it was resolved to despatch the yacht *Sardam*, arrived here from the Fatherland on 7th inst.; to provide the same with provisions, water, extra cables and anchors, and to send back thither Francisco Pelsart, commandeur of the wrecked ship *Battavia*, with a crew of 26, amongst them a few Guseratten,[34] in order to dive for the goods with the express order to return hither as soon as possible after having done everything for the saving of the people and the salvaging of the goods and cash.[35]

The minutes of the Council run straight on:

[33] This was the portion of Australia (seen by J. P. Coen in 1627) named after the ship *Eendracht* (meaning concord, or unity) from which Dirk Hartog landed on the mainland in 1616. It lies in the latitude 25° S.

[34] Men from Gujarat: Indian province of which Surat was the port. These men were native divers.

[35] H. T. Colenbrander, *op. cit.*, vol. v, pp. 756-7; Governor-General in Council, Batavia, 9th July 1629. Signed by J. P. Coen, Pieter Vlack, A. van Diemen.

Besides also, because we are at the moment scarcely provided with suitable *retour* ships for the Fatherland, it has been found good that the ship *Uytrecht* which has arrived here lately on June 19th from Suratte, should be despatched thither also, and if it were suitable, to send the ship *Mauritius* in its place to Suratte.

This recording, "done in the Castle Battavia", was signed by Coen, Pieter Vlack and van Diemen.

A few days later, on 13th July, another entry in the minute book[36] discloses that Pelsaert's former senior officer, Pieter van den Broecke, was at Batavia. In fact, he had arrived aboard the *Uytrecht*,[37] which had been separated from various other vessels coming from Surat; the same ships seen by Pelsaert after the *Batavia's* boat had been picked up by the *Sardam*. It is easy to imagine that Pelsaert drew some comfort from this: it was barely eighteen months since van den Broecke had written to the Directors at Amsterdam praising his knowledge and good services and expressing his own willingness to retain him, had such been Pelsaert's wish. In the terrible moment when the disaster needs must be reported to Jan Pieterszoon Coen, noted not only for his tremendous ability but also for his ruthless and implacable discipline,[38] Pelsaert may well have looked to van den Broecke for support.[39] The critical attitude of van Diemen has already been observed. And Coen was certainly not a man given to making any allowance for extenuating circumstances—his harsh attitude towards any form of sexual misdemeanour was notorious. Not long before, he had executed the sixteen-year-old Cortenhoeff for daring to have a love affair with Sara, the natural daughter, aged twelve, of General Specx. She had been left in Coen's care.[40] The girl herself had been publicly whipped. Batavia was already waiting in anticipation of the explosion likely to occur when Specx returned and learnt what Coen had done to his child.

[36] Ibid., p. 758, Friday 13th July 1629.

[37] Ibid., p. 558, 22nd June 1629: note of arrival "van Zuratte ende Persia", on 19th June, of the ship *Uuttrecht* [*sic*] with van den Broeck [*sic*] aboard.

[38] "Hero worship is not customary among the Dutch, and the stern character of Coen, who never could forget misdeeds even when they resulted from understandable human weakness and whose heart was never softened by the sufferings of his opponents, did not appeal to the imagination of posterity." B. H. M. Vlekke, *Nusantara* (1945), p. 128.

[39] In editing van den Broecke's journals Dr W. Ph. Coolhaas has formed the opinion that he would not be likely to support Pelsaert, despite his earlier recommendation.

[40] H. T. Colenbrander, *J. P. Coen, Levensbeschrijving* (1934), p. 428. Also H. T. Colenbrander, *J. P. Coen, Bescheiden omtrent zijn Bedrijf in Indië*, vol. v, p. 703.

On Friday 13th July 1629 Pelsaert's accusation of the skipper, combined with statements made later by several of the *Batavia's* company who had been in the open boat, brought action:

> Because Adriaen Jacobsz, skipper of the wrecked ship *Batavia* is notorious through allowing himself to be blown away by pure neglect; and also because through his doings a gross evil and public assault has taken place on the same ship, on the widow of the late Boudewijn van der Mijl, in his life undermerchant, it has been decided by His Hon. and the Council to arrest the mentioned skipper and to bring him to trial here in order that he may answer those accusations made to his detriment.[41]

Thus was the skipper arrested before Pelsaert left for the Abrolhos in the *Sardam*, which had been hastily unloaded and refitted as a salvage ship under the command of the uppersteersman Jacob Jacobsz.[42] Claas Gerritsz, uppersteersman of the *Batavia*, and Jacop Jansz, one of his understeersmen, evidently still in sufficiently good health to be likely to prove of use in the search, also returned. It is interesting, incidentally, that the death of Lucretia's husband was obviously known as a fact in Batavia. The loss of this officer is not mentioned anywhere in Pelsaert's Journals; there is no record of his being aboard the *Batavia*. This reference makes it quite clear that he was not amongst those left at the islands, as their fate was still undisclosed.

The *Sardam* sailed two days later. In his Order of Sunday, 15th July,[43] Coen, always the stern upholder of religious observance, had written

> Shalt therefore set sail tomorrow in the name of God, and shalt hasten thy journey with all possible diligence in order to arrive most speedily at the place where thou hast lost the ship and left the people . . . .

Undoubtedly a stab, that sentence, despite the arrest of the skipper; perhaps it served to strengthen Pelsaert's determination to be gone at once. More probably he needed nothing more than the Order safe in his hands and the *Sardam* ready to weigh; at any rate he did not wait for the morrow; Sunday notwithstanding, he cleared from Batavia on the 15th, as his Journal shows.

Little did he guess of the ordeal ahead. They had sailed from the Abrolhos to Batavia in an open boat in thirty days; how could he imagine that it would take them sixty-five days to return in a fast ship? But even though the long weeks must have reduced her

[41] H. T. Colenbrander, *op. cit.*, vol. v, p. 758.
[42] ARAKA, VOC: (1630[II]), Letter written by Pelsaert, 12th December 1629, also throughout his Journals.   [43] See Appendix I.

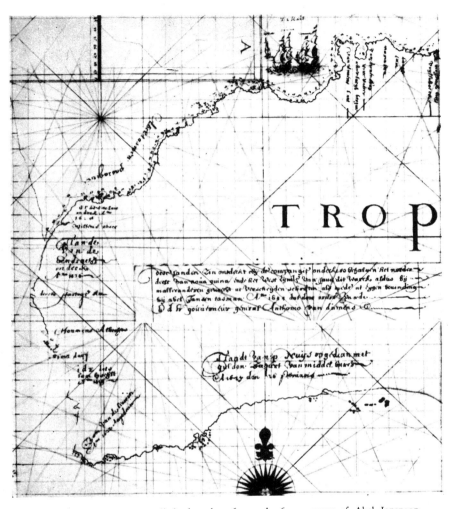

Section of V.O.C. map compiled after the 1642 and 1644 voyages of Abel Janszoon Tasman. The legend at the top right-hand corner of the complete map has here been inset to appear in the centre. The whole map shows all that was known of Australia and New Guinea in 1644.

View of Amsterdam by C. Janszoon Visscher, dated 1614. The clock tower of the Old Church can be seen at the top right. The house named The White Angel is situated amongst the mass of dwellings to the right of the church.

small crew to bitter anxiety, not one of them feared other than natural disaster for the unfortunates for whose sake they were battling against relentless head winds. No rain, no water, no food; sickness and accident—that would be the refrain torturing their thoughts.

At last, on 17th September, they anchored in the lee of one of the "high" islands of the Abrolhos that Pelsaert and Gerritsz had searched more than three months earlier for water. Smoke was rising from another island to the south. Their spirits were high. They dared to expect to find the majority of their erstwhile shipmates alive and perhaps well. Instead, they were soon to listen to one of the most terrible stories of murder and rapine in the annals of the sea.

Thus Pelsaert's able pen was forced, not to "keep a perfect journal", like an explorer taking "notice of lands, shallows, cliffs, inlets, bays and capes which mayest encounter and discover" as directed by Coen, but to set down for the Directors and posterity (as chairman of a disciplinary council) the grim evidence of a series of crimes without parallel in V.O.C. records. Once only, on the morning of 15th November, when at last they "have gone under sail to the continent away from these disastrous Abrolhos", does he find time or heart to turn his attention from the wickedness of men and describe what he had seen at the islands. On this happy occasion he gives a description of the wallabies, or tammars, which had been found on the two largest islands and had served so deliciously as food for wrecked and rescuers alike. He thus became the first person both to report and take note of the characteristics of Australian marsupials. His accurate account of these "creatures of miraculous form, as big as a hare", is as vivid now as then; and compares with his precise descriptions of indigo in the *Remonstrantie*.[44]

When, having previously hanged the principal murderers and recovered the greater part of the treasure of the wrecked *Batavia*, Pelsaert had earlier on that 15th November at last given the order to return to Java, he had also instructed the uppersteersman Gerritsz to cross first to the continent. The acting skipper of the *Sardam*, Jacob Jacobsz, together with three other men, had been lost some weeks earlier in a storm; they had been out in the *Sardam's* boat searching for possible flotsam. It was Pelsaert's intention to see if by any chance they had been blown across to the mainland,

---

[44] Pelsaert was also "the first man to record a land bird in Australia; he wrote that he saw 'a number of grey turtle-doves' on one of the Abrolhos Islands". See A. H. Chisholm, *Strange New World*, p. 54. See also entry in Pelsaert's Journals for date 15th November 1629.

E

and were unable to return. Smoke seen rising to the north-east on earlier clear days had given hope. It was a vain hope; the smoke had doubtless come from native fires or signals.

But on reaching the continent and learning from a landing party that they had discovered fresh water, Pelsaert decided to maroon then and there two of the chief miscreants amongst the remaining prisoners. Accordingly, on 16th November he penned another document, one that gains him a place, not usually remarked, in the social history of Australia; for on this occasion Francisco Pelsaert laid down the first official ruling regarding the proper treatment of the aboriginal tribes of Australia by white men about to inhabit the country.

This document, a copy of which he incorporated in his Journals,[45] contains general instructions to the two men about to be marooned and orders them to "make themselves known" to the inhabitants of the country by gifts of friendship.

> Whereto are being given by the Commandeur some Nuremberg toys, as well as knives, Beads, bells and small mirrors, of which shall give to the Blacks only a few until they have grown familiar with them. Having become known to them, if they will then take you into their Villages to their chief men, have courage to go with them willingly. Man's luck is found in strange places; if God guards you, you will not suffer any damage from them, but on the contrary, because they have never seen any white men, they will honour you with all friendship.

They are also to "observe with all diligence" what materials of value such as gold or silver are to be found, and also what the natives themselves value:

> So that, having come to perfect friendship with them, you may be able to ask by signs and by learning their language, that a look-out should be kept for ships or for people coming from the side of the Sea, in order to obtain from them more of such goods as iron, copper or Nuremberg toys, of which you have with you several samples which without doubt will please them greatly.

The merchant's mind, never willing to miss an opportunity, always a good servant of the Company, can be seen assessing the situation for what it may be worth in terms of trade, as well as pointing out the advantages of encouraging the natives to keep a watch for any ship that might pick up the marooned men. But it is also characteristic of Pelsaert the man, that to the condemned in their terrible straits he offers a very human word of hope about

---

[45] Dated "on the yacht Sardam this 16 November 1629".

so familiar a matter as luck; and at a moment when he himself, as a later letter shows, was feeling near to despair.[46] His sturdy common sense and naturally benevolent attitude to life undoubtedly prompted the instructions both to give and receive friendship: instructions that unfortunately were not to be followed in later centuries. It is to Pelsaert's honour that he should have adopted such an attitude so long ago, in a harsh age. The two marooned men, Wouter Loos and Jan Pelgrom de Bye van Bemel, did in fact find luck, but in a way that no one, that November afternoon, is likely to have dreamed of: their names are remembered in history, not by reason of their crimes, but because they were the first two white men recorded to have lived on the continent of Australia.

Pelsaert and the *Sardam* arrived back at Batavia on 5th December. Coen had died of dysentery on 20th September.[47] It is frequently said that the great Governor-General had mentioned that he wished van Diemen, for long a protégé of his, to be elected in his place; it is certain that he mentioned his brother-in-law, Dr Pieter Vlack. But Councillor Jacques Specx was already lying off Bantam in the *Hollandia*. He reached Batavia a day later.[48] He was then, of course, the senior Company officer present; the Council preferred, waiting on a decision from the Directors, to elect him.[49] This was done on the 24th. "The Heer Jacques Specx has been chosen provisionally as General and has been so acknowledged publicly before all soldiers and burghers."[50] Van Diemen's term as Governor had to wait another five years, because Hendrick Brouwer, Pelsaert's famous brother-in-law, was sent to relieve Specx in 1632 and remained in Java with his wife Agniete and his small daughter Geertruid until 1636.

Van Diemen took up his pen again on 10th December 1629, to continue his long letter to Pieter de Carpentier in Amsterdam:[51]

> The 5th of this month returns here to anchor from the Southland, the yacht *Sardam*, bringing with them 74 souls from the wrecked ship *Batavia* together with 10 chests of Cash, amongst them the chest No. 33 with 9 sacks of ducats. Item, the Cash with Jewels to the value of f. 58,000 and some wrought silverwork, 3 barrels of Cochineal and other baggage, as can be seen in the enclosed memo. Thanks be to the Almighty for this, we would not have expected it to come out

[46] ARAKA, VOC: (1630^II). See Appendix II.
[47] *Dagh Register gehouden int Casteel Batavia, Anno 1624-1629*, ed. J. E. Heeres, pp. 397-8.   [48] Ibid., p. 398, 21st September 1629.
[49] Ibid., p. 399. The clerk's entry of 22nd September reads: "Who will succeed provisionally the Hon. Lord General Coen is not yet known, the same time will show."   [50] Ibid., p. 399, 24th September 1629.
[51] ARAKA, VOC: 1009, O.B. (1630^I).

so well. The big costly jewel of Merchant Caspar Boudaan has also been saved.

How wholly unheard of and beyond all reason is the manner in which shortly after the wrecking of the *Batavia*, when left by the Commandeur and the skipper, those people have behaved towards each other; it is a horror in the ears of all good Christians, and shall not be told here, but will refer you to the enclosed documents and the Journals of the uppermerchant Francoys Pelsaert, only will say that very bad order has been kept on the mentioned *Batavia*, and that some time before the ship came into danger there had been the intention to run off with it, of whom the skipper, as some have confessed, was the principal instigator, about which he will know shortly. This evil intention has been the cause of wicked effect amongst the wrecked folk of *Batavia*. The undermerchant Jeronimus Dircksen [*sic*] of Haerlem (following the beliefs of Torrentius)[52] with some of his accomplices in wicked intent, by rumour having become aware that the previous evil mutiny was known, and should a yacht be sent for them, on arrival at Batavia they would not escape the burden of their misdeeds, have come to more evil things; having the intention to get rid of all except about 40 people, with whom they thought they had a chance to run off with the yacht that would be sent for them, and so seek their fortune. In which evil and horrible intention they proceeded so far that in a short time they murdered and killed in a frightful way 125 souls, namely 96 men, 12 women and 7 innocent children. And they would have continued in this way if 47 persons had not resolved to flee to another island to escape death, where they remained until the arrival of the yacht *Sardam*, thrice being attacked by the aforesaid Jeronimus and his band, numbering 32 men and 5 women. The particulars, as said before, Your Hon. may learn from the enclosed papers; Your Hon. will never have read of more cruel deeds.

268 souls remained on the wrecked *Batavia* and on the islands when the boat left, of whom 74 have arrived here with *Sardam* and the rest have been consumed as follows:

In swimming from the wreck to land:	40
By disease and illness have died:	20
By the undermerchant Jeronimus Cornelis murdered	125
By order of the Commandeur Pelsaert hanged	7
By order of the Commandeur set alive on the Southland ..	2
With *Sardam* brought to Batavia, namely 68 men, 5 women, 1 child } compt.	74

Persons 268

---

[52] Van Diemen wrote *"hebbende een taurensiaens gevoelen"*. The man was Johannes Torrentius van der Beecke.

There are several small errors in this, notably the inaccuracy in naming Jeronimus. It was of course possible that he had also been known in Batavia as Dircksen; but there is no further evidence to support such an idea, and the earlier error made by van Diemen in giving the skipper Ariaen Jacobsz the Christian name of Hans, and also referring to Pelsaert as both Francisco and Francoys, points to minor carelessness on the part of a busy man occupied with many important matters. If the numbers given above are regarded as being accurate, and to them are added the forty-eight people mentioned earlier as arriving in the *Batavia's* boat, then it would appear that the ship was carrying approximately 316 people at the time of the wreck.

One senses again the hint of criticism of Pelsaert in this further statement by van Diemen. In general, one gains the impression that Pelsaert's return to India from the Fatherland was not popular with the current councillors and that his future promotion would scarcely be welcomed. Van Diemen also lists the goods salvaged:

> The Cash and gold destined for India with *Batavia* amounted altogether to [f.] 259,788. 11. 14., of which at the most will miss 40 to 45 thousand guilders and not more, so that the salvaged goods amount to 215 thousand—with the Jewels and the Cochineal.

He then itemizes the amount of money on hand "in India", and continues:

> To this list has to be added the above mentioned salvaged Cash from the ship *Batavia* . . . . . [f.] 215,000
> The Casket with Jewels: 60 thous.
> The three barrels of Cochineal: ——— thous.

He did not apparently know the estimated value of the cochineal. He next assesses the full value of "effects" in "India" as f. 5,688,565. 15. 12., and adds: "Diminished by return with the *Galiasse* going over [to the Netherlands] . . . . [f.] 91,110. 15. 8. Rest at value of goods and effects [f.] 5,597,455. 0. 4.'

Taking the florin at value of ten to the English pound sterling at the time,[53] that would mean that the V.O.C. had slightly over half a million pounds in cash and goods to maintain trade in the Indies and elsewhere in Asia. A considerable sum in those days. The original value of cash and merchandise on the *Batavia* was on this estimate £25,978 odd (indeed a "rich ship"), of which approximately £21,500 was salvaged. But, as van Diemen had remarked earlier in his letter, although proceedings had been taken against

[53] C. W. Kett, *Sir Peter Paul Rubens*, 1882, pp. 65, 85.

the skipper, they would be of "little comfort to the Company" for the loss of such a "beautiful *retour* ship". It may also be noted that although he is subtly critical of Pelsaert, he makes no comment on that officer's valiant and successful efforts in salvage beyond pious thanks to the Almighty that "we would not have expected it to come out so well."

Further substantiation is given to the probability of a generally critical or hostile attitude towards Pelsaert by a note in the minutes of the Council of India early in the following year. The ship carrying the letter of recommendation from the Directors to Coen and the Council, which Pelsaert had requested and been accorded on his appointment as President of the departing fleet, had arrived. But on 28th January 1630, immediately following the sentences passed on the mutineers brought to Batavia in the *Sardam*, comes the following entry:

> Francisco Pelsaert at his request appearing in the Council exhibits a letter from the Hon. Lords High and Mighty of the Chamber of Amsterdam, on behalf of the Council of Seventeen, wherein the person of the mentioned Pelsaert is recommended to be advanced according to merit; whereupon is answered by the Hon. Lord General [Specx] that notice shall be taken of his person and contributions in order to be promoted according to opportunity and merit.[54]

This suggests that Pelsaert wished to be certain that the favourable letter had been received from Amsterdam. It is of course possible that notice of his further appointment as an Extraordinary Member of the Council itself had also arrived by then. Probably Pelsaert had been privately advised of this appointment by either Brouwer or Agniete.

It seems obvious that he wished to consolidate his position. According to Moreland,[55] there does not appear to be any notice or signature to documents to show that Pelsaert actually took his seat on the Council of India; nor has other evidence to that effect been discovered during these researches. It does seem that his appointment to the Council may have been disregarded, although nine months after his death at Batavia, in a delayed report to the Directors, van Diemen writes: "Pelsaertt as before mentioned has died, in whose place the Hon. Jan van der Burch has been appointed, and likewise chosen Councillor of India."[56]

[54] ARAKA, VOC: 1011, O.B. (1631¹), Governor-General in Council, dated 28th January 1630.   [55] *Jahangir's India*, p. x (Introduction).
[56] Letter dated 5th June 1631, "Een Indisch Verslag uit 1631, van der hand van Antonio van Diemen", ed. W. Ph. Coolhaas, *Bijdragen en Mededelingen van het Historisch Genootschap te Utrecht*, vol. lxv (1947), pp. 203-4 (translated by E. D. Drok).

Pelsaert was already ill when he returned to Batavia from the Abrolhos. Study of the Journals shows unmistakable signs of mental and physical stress: as the mounting horrors and long-drawn-out salvaging operations press on his spirit, syntax becomes at times slightly confused; at other times there is a slight deterioration in his firm, level, Gothic script, usually clear and picturesque and far more legible than the handwriting of the majority of his contemporaries. The state he had reached by the time the *Sardam* made Batavia is pitifully attested by the last official document written by him that exists. This is a personal communication to the Lords High and Mighty of the Chamber of Amsterdam, sent as a covering letter to his Journals, and dated 12th December 1629[57]— that is, a week after his return from the islands. At times he becomes incoherent, though his handwriting remains steady.

> Honourable, brave, wise, provident, very discreet Noble Lords—
>
> It is [to] me more than Grief that the Disaster of the woeful Happenings of the ship *Batavia* must be again related, also the remaining of it on the Abrolhos of Frederick Houtman . . . as well as the miserable State experienced by everyone, snare thrown around the neck by the Terrible surf of the reef on to which the ship was de-navigated [*sic*], then no Water could be salvaged from the ship, through which we have come to the extreme of want and been forced to resolve to go in search of Water with every boat. . . .

After detailing the open boat trip to Java and, on arrival, his request for a rescue yacht "which was allowed me by the Lord Gov. Gen., and departed on 15th July, 7 days after our Arrival, although I was wholly ill and reduced to great wretchedness", he relates the terrible "Anguish of the Heart" that followed their first happiness at finding people still alive, when the full iniquity of all that had happened during his absence was disclosed; and how he was "forced to hang the Principal Leaders on the Gallows, punishing them with death earned a hundredfold." He notes that ten money chests, also jewels and other goods "very miraculously and with many Perils had been fished up"; adding that the Directors "will see in full" in his Journal, forwarded by "Lord Gov. Gen. Specx"

> . . . how the loss of the ship, with all the happenings to which by God's Truth it has been subjected right from the beginning out of Texel until at last to my immeasurable Grief it has been denavigated,

---

[57] Appendix II. This letter is in fact the only one written by Pelsaert known to exist. V.O.C. records at the Algemeen Rijksarchief from 1621 to 1628 were checked on my behalf.

is wholly because I so unwisely [trusted] the arrogant presumption of the skipper and steersmen, who still reckoned to be 200 [i.e., 600] miles from land.

He continues:

It is our honour that Zeal towards the service of the Gen. Comp.[58] has been greatly strengthened through continuous Grief and sorrow of the heart, which scarcely can be forgotten or ignored by me; and now for the first time I can clearly see and realise that a human being often finds that his Worldly Welfare has fallen into the hands of two or three perfidious men.

At present the pack of all disasters has moulded together and fallen on my neck, yea, not quite possible to express with the pen, will moderate the same as much as possible, and though I have cried out my eyes, shall be able, by the Grace of God, to resume due service and Duty such as I have always endeavoured in service to the Company, as I did although I was exhausted, due to serious illness and poor health into which I had fallen at the Cabo de Bona Esperansa, until the ship happened to be Wrecked, (so it ended) that I had to come to Batavia 400 [i.e., 1,200] miles with the boat in great Misery, with hunger, thirst and want. . . .

The emotion under which he labours speaks for itself; as does also his evident anxiety, now the ordeal is over, concerning his own future. Especially is the latter made obvious by the remaining part of the letter, devoted to matters of concrete business, and in particular the bills of credit due to the accounts of the *Sardam's* skipper and quartermaster, drowned at the Abrolhos. Pelsaert notes that in the normal way these bills would not be forwarded until the New Year, and adds

. . . therefore I send the bills now, in order that they will not get lost and also that the Hon. Lords will be able to arrange compensation for their Wives; on the back of the bills I have also made a note of what amount they will also be credited with in the new books which, through lack of time [before sailing of ship taking this letter], I have not been able to send along.

Of all Pelsaert's recorded actions and written words, that last passage can be most aptly taken as a key to the inner man, to the fundamental integrity of his character. It is set prosaically enough at the end of what is quite an emotional, even defensive report; yet it stands out like a bright seal to the spirit of true leadership: his final thought and action was taken on behalf of those for whose distress he felt responsible. He could have allowed the bills to take their normal course; instead, in the midst of his own near despair,

---

[58] The word "Comp." was omitted and then written in afterwards.

he remembered the unhappy wives of the lost sailors he had ordered to their doom, and took what ameliorating action lay to his hand. He signed himself: "Your most humble servant to the Hon. Lords".

By April, however, his health had so far recovered that he went, as second-in-command to His Honour Pieter Vlack, on an expedition to Jambi, in Sumatra, where the lucrative pepper trade was then languishing due to Portuguese interference. The minuted resolution of appointment reads:

> And as it is necessary to have a qualified and experienced person of the highest order to be sent in command over those [ships] and other ships already there, it has been found good to commend to that, the Hon. Pieter Vlack, Councillor of India, as Commandeur in addition to His Hon. Francisco Pelsaert, Vice-Commandeur.[59]

Vlack was then the senior Councillor, next in importance to Specx himself; brother-in-law, moreover, to the late Jan Pieterszoon Coen.

The squadron sent was a strong one, as the prince had been beseiged by Portuguese ships. It arrived at Jambi on 11th May, "to help affairs in Jambij against the common enemy".[60] There can therefore be no valid reason to regard Pelsaert's secondary position on this occasion as a sign of de-rating, as some writers have done. It was an important and dangerous mission, for one thing; for another, he had been for so long in India proper, away from the island trade, that it would be advantageous to re-acquaint a possible new Councillor with island conditions.

Pelsaert was present at meeting after meeting that took place on this voyage, the majority held aboard ships lying at anchor in the river off Jambi. Innumerable copies of letters sent from Jambi to Batavia still exist;[61] but all concern themselves with Company activities, mainly trading. There is nothing of personal interest regarding Pelsaert. The mission returned to Batavia in June.

The next reference to Pelsaert is a note in the Council minutes, dated Friday 13th September 1630. This records, obliquely, his death, and raises the suggestion of illicit dealing that for three hundred years has been allowed to smear his reputation to the detriment of his real achievements on behalf of the Company:

> As through the death of Francisco Pelsaert have been found, amongst the goods left by him, certain small jewels sent to him, with the ship

[59] ARAKA, VOC: 1011, Governor-General in Council, 27th April 1630.
[60] ARAKA, Letter Book, Netherlands Factory at Jambi, beginning on 25th September 1629 and ending on 20th September 1630. Letter dated 24th June 1630.
[61] ARAKA. Letters on Jambi Expedition under Pieter Vlack, 1630, Jambi Letter Book.

Gouden Leeuw, by Johannes Dobbelworst [*sic*], Merchant of Amsterdam, valued according to his letters at *f. 1,261*, to be sold here to the profit of the abovementioned Dobbelworst. Item, still a *Mogulian tronie*[62] belonging to Gaspar Boudaen, also Merchant in Amsterdam, taken by Pelsaert from Amsterdam, and as the suchlike sending of jewels is directly opposed to the article briefs, and also opposed to the charter patent [*d' Octroij*] granted to the United East Indian Company, it is therefore felt necessary to proceed towards confiscation. It is not quite certain that the abovementioned jewels have been found here with the consent or knowledge of the High and Mighty; has been found good to send them with the first departing ships to the fatherland, to the Hon. Lords High and Mighty to be disposed of by them as they shall think fit.[63]

By the irony of fate, Dobbelworst sent his jewels on a ship that left Holland in March 1629 and carried also copies of letters announcing Pelsaert's departure to Batavia as Fleet President; Gaspar Boudaen must have given the *second* cameo (a portrait of the Mogul emperor) to Pelsaert in Amsterdam when he handed over his famous "great jewel" with full knowledge and consent of the Seventeen; hence the expressed doubt. Unfortunately for the dead Pelsaert, new stringent orders had recently been issued at Batavia regarding trade in jewels and other goods. On the selfsame day that the resolution to arrest the skipper Ariaen Jacobsz was passed by the Council of India, the following curt memo appears in the minutes:

It has come to our notice that the merchants, skippers and officers of lower ranks are trading privately and are shipping goods and merchandise in a private manner, and that thus they are doing damage to the profit of the Company, therefore it is by this order forbidden that uppermerchants and skippers and all others sailing . . . shall, under threat of confiscation of all their due salaries, trade for themselves in any goods, or in cash moneys, whatever the case may be, without our knowledge and special consent to transport from here to other places, directly, or indirectly, with threat of punishment as before, also with the confiscation of all goods or money.[64]

So far as the jewel trade was concerned, Pelsaert had long been eager that the good market he believed available in Agra should be fully exploited. He had both written from India to this effect and pursued the idea at Amsterdam. When he returned to the Indies he was carrying, with full consent of the High and Mighty, not

---
[62] Visage or face, i.e., cameo. Both price and item underlined.
[63] ARAKA, VOC: 1011, Governor-General in Council, 13th September 1630.
[64] H. T. Colenbrander, *op. cit.*, vol. v, p. 575.

only the precious casket of jewels later saved from the wrecked *Batavia*, but also a fabulous gem belonging to the merchant Gaspar Boudaen and known as the "great cameo".[65] The negotiations regarding this jewel had been both peculiar and secretive, nevertheless the Council at Batavia had been advised of Pelsaert's commission. Specx himself noted its safe return from the Abrolhos:

> Item, a casket of jewels valued at 58 thousand guilders and some wrought silver work . . . the great jewel of the merchant Caspar Boudaen has also been salvaged but has not yet been visited [to see] whether it has suffered any damage; with the death of the great Mogul, through which there is a very big change and a little enough appetite for jewels has been created, doubt whether it will be advisable to send it to Industan; of that Sr. Boudaen will have to take notice and meanwhile following your recommendation we shall execute your order in respect to that as well as possible according to duty.[66]

Apparently Specx, who in Amsterdam had expressed himself as being of the same opinion,[67] was now sceptical about Pelsaert's belief that jewels would prove good merchandise at the Mogul Court. This comment makes it quite clear that by this time Pelsaert was aware of Jahangir's death; it would seem that Specx had already been informed that the emperor's son and successor, Shah Jahan (who later built the Taj Mahal) was displaying more interest in architecture than in "toys". Therefore it appears likely that Pelsaert made no attempt to dispose of the smaller jewels with which he had been personally entrusted, possibly to his own advantage. Originally at least, he had probably seen nothing wrong in accepting a few small pieces on commission: had he not conducted a personal campaign with the High and Mighty in order to bring them to realize the value of a jewel trade? During his years in India he had seen private trading winked at by the English Company; indeed for a time (until it grew out of hand) almost condoned because salaries were low. Doubtless the Hollanders at Surat had also traded a little on the side. It was indeed unfortunate that "certain small jewels" and a second cameo belonging to Boudaen remained unsold amongst his effects at a moment when regulations were being strictly enforced, and when the disastrous loss of the *Batavia* and its dreadful aftermath were clouding his reputation.

The matter did not end there. It was rehearsed again by van Diemen in his report of 5th June 1631, already mentioned:

[65] See Chapter V, Trade Jewels.
[66] ARAKA, VOC: 1009, O.B. (1630¹), Governor-General to Directors.
[67] H. T. Colenbrander, *op. cit.*, vol. v, p. 836.

Francisco Pelsaert who has induced the Compa. and others to the sending of jewels to India, and had instructed regarding the sale of Boedaens jewel, has died at Batta [Batavia] after a long illness; what has been produced from the goods he left behind appears here with the accompanying bills and paybooks from Batta. Among the goods left has been found the tronie of the late Magoll cut in agate, belonging to the aforesaid Boedaen, also several small jewels . . . .[68]

He goes on to express the same doubt as to whether Pelsaert acted with knowledge of the Directors or not, but adds that, although it had first been decided to return the jewels to Holland, in the end they had remained in Batavia "in order, it has been said, to give this affair into the hands of the fiscael [law officer]".

Van Diemen's letter of 5th June 1631 was in fact part of a General Letter to the Directors that should have been finished in time to send to Amsterdam on the ship *Deventer*, but was not. As van Diemen was returning to Holland aboard this vessel, he was ordered to complete the dispatch, and did so. Specx was later rebuked by the Seventeen for not writing the whole letter himself.[69]

Van Diemen states that Ariaen Jacobsz was still imprisoned at Batavia and adds:

> How the case of the same has proceeded with the Council of justice, Your Hon. please see from the accompanying reports and documents of the proceedings; it is certain that a completely Godless and evil life has been conducted on the mentioned ship, of which both the skipper and the President Pelsaertt are greatly guilty, may the Almighty forgive their sin and make good the damage to the Comp.; we think it good that Your Hon. should look again into the proceedings regarding the skipper and give an order in this matter, the accusation is great and the fact that the ship and the people have been so shamefully left, through which such a great disaster has arisen, cannot be excused.[70]

This underlines van Diemen's earlier opinion that Pelsaert was reprehensible in leaving the castaways. It certainly implies that evidence given at the skipper's trial at Batavia pointed to laxity of discipline on Pelsaert's part (as well as the skipper's) before the ship was wrecked. But lacking those important records it is impossible to form a true and just assessment of the case against Pelsaert. There seems to have been an inclination at the time, as with many historians since, to believe that in his Journals and his last letter Pelsaert

[68] W. Ph. Coolhaas, "Een Indisch Verslag uit 1631, van der hand van Antonio van Diemen", *Bijdragen en Mededelingen van het Historisch Genootschap te Utrecht*, vol. lxv (1947), pp. 200-1.
[69] Letter from W. Ph. Coolhaas, Utrecht, dated 14th June 1960.
[70] W. Ph. Coolhaas, *loc. cit.*, p. 202.

endeavoured to excuse himself at the expense of Ariaen Jacobsz. In actual fact, unless the lost evidence was particularly clear (which seems highly unlikely as earlier it had been considered "obscure", and van Diemen writes that the skipper "had been condemned to more acute examination"), the situation dissolves into a matter of one man's word against another's. Pelsaert was probably weak in his initial handling of Ariaen Jacobsz, who was unquestionably a tough customer and considerably older; but Pelsaert was a sick man. One can but set his personality and character as they take life from his *Remonstrantie* and the painful Journals of the wreck, against his own picture of Ariaen and the evidence he recorded on the Abrolhos Islands. It is difficult to feel that the lively, hardworking author of the *Remonstrantie*, so obviously humane and interested in his fellow men, would deliberately choose to abandon the ship's company merely to save his own skin, or seek afterwards to blacken another man without justification. His writings have the ring of sincerity and genuine emotion. It may not be entirely amiss to presume that after his death Pelsaert became, to some extent, a scapegoat.

When in 1632 "his mother and heir" applied to the Company to have her son's will cleared,[71] the question of confiscation of "all due salaries" was curtly raised. Hendrick Brouwer took the matter up on behalf of his mother-in-law when he returned from his period as Governor-General at Batavia; but the attitude of the Directors remained cold.[72] Confiscation and disapprobation seem unnecessarily harsh in the case of a man who had served the V.O.C. so well, and whose sound advice, followed after his death, was yet further to enrich the Indian trade. Possibly, rigid or jealous minds were pleased to discredit the man for the sake of financial benefit to the Honourable Company.

There is a final reference to Pelsaert in the Batavia Day Book of March 1636, which lends colour to the latter idea. The occasion concerned the imprisonment at Batavia of an uppermerchant whose dealings at Agra had been to the prejudice of the Company, and of several other officers who had been living there viciously, or at least riotously. Earlier writers have invariably presumed that the paragraph following accuses Pelsaert of having behaved or lived in the same manner. However, Mr E. D. Drok and Mr C. de Heer, who have studied photostats of the original document, are both convinced that the statement as written is ambiguous. The refer-

[71] ARAKA, VOC: 185, Resolution Lords XVII, Chamber Amsterdam, 17th March 1632.
[72] ARAKA, VOC: 185, Resolution Lords XVII, Chamber Amsterdam, 31st August 1635.

ence could be taken to mean that, in his lifetime, Pelsaert had himself *reported* on loose living at Agra. This would appear the more reasonable view; there could surely be no point in recording such an item of gossip except as evidence *against* the accused men; unless indeed it were for some malicious reason such as a deliberate reminder designed to strengthen the Company's case, still proceeding at Amsterdam, for refusal of compensation to Pelsaert's mother. Such may have been the petty truth.[73]

Whatever the Seventeen or the Council of India may have thought of him, Pelsaert was no mere time-server or money-grasping merchant. His *Remonstrantie* and his Journals remain to arouse admiration and interest for a man whose contemporary reputation was diminished by an early death and posthumous accusations, perhaps unfounded. Today it may well be more just to regard him, as without question he saw himself, as being the victim of evil circumstances; and to accord his memory the esteem he undoubtedly earned by facing, with fortitude, a monstrous union of malice and ill-chance.

---

[73] See Appendix III. To produce a past record as evidence against the accused is common sense. To make an idle statement regarding the life lived by an officer dead for more than five years is pointless unless prompted by jealousy or ambition on the part of some authorizing officer; aided, perhaps, by the fact that Brouwer had left Java the previous January, and gossip about his dead brother-in-law had probably become more free. Moreland states that he was unable to trace further references to this reputed accusation (*Jahangir's India*, p. xii, Introduction), and more recent researches in Batavia and Holland have also failed.

IV

THE SKIPPER OF THE *BATAVIA*, AND OTHERS

In Pelsaert's Journals the extraordinary, ambiguous personality of Jeronimus Cornelisz—the undermerchant who on the Abrolhos islands became a dictator—assumes gigantic proportions, twisting the reader's mind with the same horrified queries that tormented Pelsaert's own; yet that Pelsaert believed the skipper Ariaen Jacobsz to be the primary cause of disaster, as well as his own evil genius, has already been clearly seen. There is little outside information to be gained regarding this arrogant, reckless, and amorous skipper.

That he was a seaman of outstanding ability is evident, not only because he was entrusted with the *Batavia*, a new luxury liner of the day, but because his feat in steering an open boat from the Abrolhos to the Straits of Sunda remains even today an epic amongst such exploits. On de l'Isle's maps of the world (1740, 1750-60, 1775)[1] the "Route de Pelsart" is emphatically marked; thus more than a century later it was evidently regarded as a phenomenon. It is just possible that Ariaen Jacobsz sailed under Willem Bontekoe and so heard at first hand of that undaunted sailor's famous voyage, made after the ship in which he left the Netherlands had been destroyed by fire, some ninety miles south-west of Sumatra. The earliest mention of Ariaen Jacobsz to be found in V.O.C. records kept at Batavia[2] notes his appointment as highboatswain in the *Berger-Boot*, at 20 f. per month, from 19th October of the previous year, 1616; and it is possible that he was still one of her officers when Coen, after Bontekoe's arrival[3] at Batavia in 1619, appointed him skipper of that ship. The *Berger-Boot* traded through the islands, at one time carrying stone for the building of the castle at Batavia.

In 1628 when he took command of the ship *Batavia* at Amsterdam,

[1] Guillaume de l'Isle, Maps of the World. MLS, F 1/79, F 1/41, F 1/48.
[2] H. T. Colenbrander, *J. P. Coen, Bescheiden omtrent zijn Bedrijf in Indië*, vol. iii, p. 392.
[3] Bontekoe's ship *New Hoorn* blew up, having first caught fire when the steward's mate accidentally dropped candle waste into a keg of brandy. Bontekoe and his parched crew, like Pelsaert and his, were finally picked up in the Straits of Sunda; this time the rescuing ship was the *Dordrecht* under the command of Frederik de Houtman, who had discovered, five months earlier in July, the Abrolhos or Houtman Rocks, where later the *Batavia* was to pile up.

Ariaen Jacobsz must have been well on towards middle age. On the voyage he developed a passion for Lucretia Jansz. She refused his advances. He became so inflamed that he went the length of offering money or jewels to buy her favours. Further repulsed, the libidinous skipper apparently transferred his attentions to Lucretia's servant Zwaantie, perhaps from spite, or possibly he was "caught on the rebound". Evidence shows that Zwaantie was "easy" and none too particular; that in addition she became eager not only to comfort the skipper in place of her mistress's contempt but also to enrage him with a desire for revenge. Thenceforward, Ariaen Jacobsz set his mind to mutiny. He became more arrogant than ever, and consequently careless. In this mood he did not trouble, like many another skipper of the times, to exert himself in order to reckon, as best the poor instruments of the period allowed, the distance they had sailed east from the Cape of Good Hope. By his guess they were still 200 [i.e. 600][4] miles from the Southland when the *Batavia* struck the reefs of the Abrolhos, during his own night watch.

Jacobsz was placed under arrest for negligence very soon after his arrival with Pelsaert at Batavia. What actually led him to abandon his original intention of destroying the Commandeur and taking the open boat to Malacca, there presumably to announce his defection from the V.O.C. and beg from the Portuguese[5] a vessel in which to sail back to the rescue, cannot be clearly deduced from the evidence; one imagines that the unforeseen inclusion of ten men he had not himself picked to accompany him— but who arrived by chance in the *Batavia's* yawl at the "high" island before the boat left on its journey to the continent—must have had something to do with the decision. On the other hand, starved and thirst-worn men are not good material for active mutiny. That the plan was still in Ariaen's mind when he decided to leave the Abrolhos is substantiated by the presence of Zwaantie Hendrix in the open boat. A second woman (with infant in arms) was presumably taken as companion to Zwaantie. She remains unnamed in the records.

What ultimately became of the skipper Ariaen Jacobsz has not so far been discovered. An enlargement of Antonio van Diemen's letter is found in another document:

> Very great insolences, yea, monstrous actions, have been committed on the mentioned ship [*Batavia*] before her wrecking, wherefore

---
[4] See Pelsaert's letter, Appendix II.
[5] Or possibly to purchase with bills of credit against the treasure he hoped to plunder.

amongst other things the Highboatswain of the ship [Jan Evertsz] has been punished here with death, having confessed to being the principal culprit when a certain woman named Lucretia Jans was dragged by the legs along the ship and maltreated very indecently on her body, as cannot be imagined by Christian people, as Your Hon. will be able to see from the enclosed declarations and statements of the [legal] processes, the skipper scp. *Batta* [*sic*] was very much suspected that the previous had happened with his knowledge, yea, even with his aid and at his instigation; about this he, and a certain other female who had been the servant of the previously mentioned Lucretia have been examined by the Fiscal [legal official] and brought before the Council of Justice, but through the obscurity of the case no verdict has yet been given; we do not think that he is wholly free, being certain that if he had publicly maintained authority and justice as well as he secretly undermined both, many of the committed insolences would not have happened aboard the ship nor would previous actions have remained unpunished.[6]

Unfortunately the declarations and statements recorded as being sent to Amsterdam cannot be traced in V.O.C. records. What Ariaen Jacobsz and Zwaantie had to say on their own behalf remains unknown. The above document was written before Pelsaert's return from the islands with the damning evidence of the Abrolhos trials. It is regrettable that the Day Books of Batavia also happen to be missing between 7th October 1629 and 9th January 1631, the period in which one might expect to find further comment on the *Batavia* wreck and its aftermath. Van Diemen's already quoted letter of 5th June 1631 announces that

> Adriaen Jacobsz, skipper of the wrecked ship *Batta*. is still imprisoned, although has several times requested a relaxation and a return to the fatherland; on the strong indictment of having had the intention to run off with the ship *Batta*. [he] has been condemned to more acute examination and has been put to the torture. . . .

Van Diemen also states that "reports and documents of the proceedings" accompany this letter, and requests that the Directors should issue an order "in this matter". That is the last known reference to Ariaen Jacobsz. The fate of the arrogant skipper and his light-of-love Zwaantie remains obscure.

So too, for centuries, remained the fate of Lucretia Jansz. A variety of ends, a diversity of characters, have been devised for her by many writers. And for several years after these researches began it appeared that no further trace could be found of the fair Lucretia whose destiny it had been to arouse the evil passions of

---

[6] ARAKA, VOC: 1009, O.B. (1630[1]), Governor-General and Council to Directors, dated 15th December 1629.

men; that fiction and speculation must continue to suffice in the place of truth. Inquiry after inquiry in Java and Holland brought no advancement. Historical research has much in common with the detection of crime. In this case, it was in fact necessary to unravel the threads of a terrible multiplex crime several centuries old but as yet never fully comprehended or made public. As in crime detection, so in historical research: the investigator, steeped in the whole known situation, occasionally conceives an idea begotten of trying to think collaterally with the writers of old manuscripts. In short, it seems to him that certain things "are so", despite lack of documented evidence.

From an early interest in the wreck of the *Batavia* and my initial reading, years ago, of Siebenhaar's translation of *Ongeluckige Voyagie*, I had felt convinced that far more significance should be attached to Lucretia Jansz; that, in fact, the true story of the crime would prove it to be a classic example of *cherchez la femme*, and that a full translation of Pelsaert's own Journals would provide more subtle motives for such wholesale murder than sheer brutality or love of monetary gain. Now the summary of the episode with which Pelsaert concludes his record makes it clear that Ariaen's illicit passion for Lucretia and his subsequent infatuation with Zwaantie, backed by his hatred of Pelsaert, did indeed begin a horrible sequence of events that ended in the undermerchant Jeronimus Cornelisz assuming dictatorial power and *himself* possessing Lucretia Jansz, against her will.

After those fruitless inquiries regarding Lucretia Jansz in Holland and Batavia (now Djakarta), a final rather hopeless plea to Djakarta brought the unexpected and illuminating reply that a notice of the remarriage of Lucretia Jansz of Amsterdam, widow of Boudewijn van der Mijlen, had been traced.[7] This supplied the much needed clue. Lucretia had been a native of Amsterdam: in the records of that town there might remain some mention of this undermerchant's wife who was yet sufficiently important, or wealthy, to travel abroad with a personal servant.

[7] "Notitie van d' afcondinghe der namen
der genen die Haer in houlyck willen begeren.
A dom 1630   Octob/r 12
                    voor de III reise
Jacob Cornelisz Cuick van Leyden, weduwen/r van
Catharina Bernardi van Groeningen, Sergeant Capn
Hans Jurjaen
           met
Lucretia Jans van Amsterd/m, weduwe
van Boudewyn van der Mijlen."

THE LIFE AND TIMES OF FRANCISCO PELSAERT 65

Until now, it has been generally assumed[8] that her husband was either murdered or drowned at the Abrolhos Islands. That never at any time appeared likely to me. One very good reason for Lucretia's retaining a maid was the possibility that she was travelling without him. In addition, the attack on Lucretia could scarcely have been recorded without some mention of her husband (other than his name to distinguish her as a married woman) had he been aboard the ship. Furthermore, van der Mijlen is never mentioned as being amongst those killed or drowned, as one would expect an officer to be; nor was it likely that there would be two undermerchants below Pelsaert on the one ship. But such reasoning was far from conclusive. Study of the available van der Mijlen family records of the period, in Holland, disclosed no scion named Boudewijn.[9] But in a letter from the V.O.C. factory at Masulipatam to the Governor-General at Batavia, dated 10th October 1627, mention is made of the undermerchant Boudewijn van der Mijlen's being dispatched[10] with a cargo to Arakan, a river port in Burma, where he was to remain till further orders. It would have been practically impossible for him to return later to Masulipatam, thence to Batavia and finally to the Netherlands, in time to sail out again with Pelsaert aboard the ship *Batavia*, less than a year later. Positive proof, however, comes from the notice, already quoted, of the arrest of Ariaen Jacobsz at Batavia on 13th July. In that Lucretia is referred to as "the *widow* of the *late* Boudewijn van der Mijl" so that his death was known in Batavia *before*[11] the return of the *Sardam* from the islands. It is thus clear that he did not perish at the Abrolhos, for had he done so, Pelsaert and the crew in the open boat must have been those who imparted the news; and it is unbelievable that Pelsaert would not have noted an undermerchant's death in the record of the wreck or on the voyage to Java.

Records at Amsterdam have now disclosed that Lucretia married

[8] I am told that an exception is to be found in *The Dutch Flag on the Seven Seas*, by J. C. Mollema (Amsterdam, 1942), a popular account.

[9] Letter from Mrs Meilink-Roelofsz of the Algemeen Rijksarchief, The Hague, dated 26th November 1953, states that no Boudewijn is mentioned in the van der Mijlen genealogy by J. H. van Balen in *Geschiedenis van Dordrecht*.

[10] ". . . the ship Brouwershaven . . . has been despatched hence to Aracan on 21 ditto [September 1627] with a cargo amounting to f. 7,891. 19. 5. Cornelis van Houtten and Boudewijn van der Mijlen, undermerchants, have been ordered to use the profit from this in buying good slaves, which we hope will be here with the mentioned ship towards the middle of December." A later statement gives the same information but adds, "Van Houtten will return but van der Mijlen is to be left there." W. Ph. Coolhaas, *J. P. Coen, Bescheiden omtrent zijn Bedrijf in Indië*, vol. vii, pp. 1174, 1186.

[11] The italics are mine.

van der Mijlen at the Old Church on 18th October 1620. He was then twenty-one, living in the Liesdel (though he hailed from Woerden) and working as a diamond polisher.[12] His father only is named as giving consent to the sexton for the marriage, which suggests that his mother was dead or unable to attend. He was "supported" on the occasion of the calling of the banns by a brother-in-law. Lucretia herself was eighteen (which makes her not more than twenty-seven at the time of the wreck), and an orphan. Her guardian, Jacob Jacobs, present when the banns were called, gave his consent. At this time the bride was living in the Herenstraat; which, as the name denotes, was then one of the most fashionable streets of the wealthy city.

Lucretia had money of her own. Her affairs are recorded in the archives of the Orphan Chamber of the City of Amsterdam[13] because she and her elder sister Sara eventually became the heirs of their mother's uncle, Nicolaes van der Leur. Her mother, Steffanie Joosten, had first married Hans Meynertsz, a cloth merchant, and by him had Sara and Lucretia. They lived in a house called The White Angel, on the Nieuwendijk.[14] Meynertsz died in 1602 (a

[12] GAA: D.T.B. 425, fol. 40 verso: 1st October 1620. Proclamation banns of Boudewijn Adamss van der Mijlen (from Woerden, 21 years old, living in the Liesdel, diamond polisher; assisted by Niclas de Ploeis, his brother-in-law; the father gave his consent to the sexton (J. Jacobs) and Lucretia Jans (18 years old, living in the Herenstraat); assisted by the aforesaid Jacob Jacobs, her guardian).
D.T.B. 969, p. 433: celebration of the marriage in the Old Church, Amsterdam, 18th October 1620.

[13] Archives of the Orphan Chamber, Amsterdam, papers dated 1624 to 1685, re the heirs to Nicolaes van der Leur:
(a) 16th August 1602, burial of Jan, or Hans, Meynertsz, clothier (father of Lucretia Jans): burial register of Orphan Chamber, No. 16.
(b) 31st July 1604, proclamation banns of Dirk Krijnen (captain on a warship), widower of Lijsbet Claes Plempend/r, living beside the Gasthuispoort on the Singel, and Steffanie Joostend/r, widow of Hans Meynertsz., declaring that she had been a widow during two years, living on the Nieuwendijk. D.T.B., No. 411, fol. 137 verso.
(c) 15th August 1604, celebration of the marriage in the Old Church, Amsterdam. D.T.B., No. 969, p. 259.
(d) 2nd December 1604, instrument executed before the Notary J. Ghijsberts. Testament of Dirck Crijnen and his wife Stephania Joosten; heirs are Weijntgen Dircx [daughter of Dirck Crijnen] and the children of Stephania Joosten, named Saertgen and Luijtgen [Lucretia] Jans. Not.Arch., No. 26, fol. 363.
(e) 3rd November 1612, instrument executed before Notary J. Ghysberts. New Testament of D. Crijnen and S. Joosten. Heirs as above. (Not.Arch., No. 29, fol. 366-8.) They then lived on the Leliestraat, having sold the house named "The White Angel" on the Nieuwendijk on 23rd June, 1608; but Crijnen still retained a mortgage on it.
(f) 19th May 1613, burial of Stephanie Joosten, buried in Nieuwe Zijds chapel in own tomb; burial register of the Orphan Chamber, No. 16.

[14] This house still exists. See Appendix VII.

year before Elizabeth I of England), which was also the year of Lucretia's birth. He was buried in the Nieuwe Zijds chapel. Two years later the mother married again, this time a widower named Dirk Krijnen, captain of a ship of war. Krijnen already had one child, a girl named Weijntgen. At the time of the marriage, Lucretia's mother was noted as being still the owner of the house called The White Angel. A few months later, she and her new husband made wills in favour of the three little girls. Eight years later, in 1612, another will was drawn up. They had evidently prospered; in 1608 they sold the house on the Nieuwendijk, retaining a mortgage on it, and went to live in a new home of their own on the Leliestraat, a more fashionable and wealthier quarter. They had also made provision for a tomb for themselves in the Nieuwe Zijds chapel. The three girls were again named as heirs. But Steffanie was ill; and she died the following year. By 1620, the date of Lucretia's marriage, the affairs of the family had been taken over by the public Chamber, and Lucretia possessed also a guardian to give consent to her marriage. It is thus reasonable to assume that her stepfather died in the intervening period.[15]

Lucretia's sister Sara married twice, first Jacob van Kuyk, and secondly Gerrit de Leur; she had five children. Lucretia had none. Apparently Boudewijn van der Mijlen decided to join the V.O.C., and must have gone overseas some time before 1628, when Lucretia, following him, embarked with her maid on the *Batavia*—there to meet with unpleasant attentions from the skipper that culminated in the disgusting and humiliating ordeal to which his malice subjected her; and afterwards, on threat of death, to become the unwilling concubine of Jeronimus Cornelisz during his reign of terror at the Abrolhos.

At this point can be mentioned a strange discrepancy between the 1647 edition of *Ongeluckige Voyagie* and Pelsaert's Journals. The former work was compiled directly from the evidence given at the Abrolhos trials as set down by Pelsaert in his Journals. Nevertheless, there is one item that does not appear in the latter. The fact that Lucretia Jansz was the unwilling victim of Jeronimus Cornelisz is stressed by Pelsaert many times, but the passage quoted below appears only in *Ongeluckige Voyagie*. There it follows immediately on a statement dated 28th September 1629, which is itself a third-person précis of Pelsaert's own account of the final arraignment of Jeronimus on that date.

The marginal note (these are a feature of *Ongeluckige Voyagie*)

[15] Dates are not easily available, for the ordinary burial records of 1553-1731 of Amsterdam are not alphabetically indexed.

reads: "There follows another confession in aggravation of the charges against Jerome Cornelisz aforesaid." The date given is 2nd October. This was not the date originally set for execution of the condemned, when sentences were pronounced, but the day on which they actually took place. Prevailing winds had made it impossible to transport the condemned to the isle on which gallows had been erected. This factual date lends substance to the statement:

> We, the undersigned, Webbye Hayes, of Winschoten, sergeant; Claes Jansz Hooft of Ditmarssen, trumpeter; Allert Jansz, corporal; and Jan Kastensen of Tonninge, musketeer, attest and testify on our manly truthfulness, that we have seen with our eyes and heard with our sober ears, today, the 2nd October, 1629, that Lucretia Jans, the widow of Boudewijn van der Mylen, one hour before Jerome Cornelisz was to be executed for his great misdeeds, bitterly lamented to the said Jerome over the sins he had committed with her against her will, and forcing her thereto. To which Jerome replied: "It is true, you are not to blame for it for you were in my tent for twelve days before I could succeed." He continued further relating how in the end he had complained to David van Seevanck that he could not accomplish his ends either with kindness or anger. Seevanck had answered, "And don't you know how to manage that? I'll soon make her do it." He had then gone into the tent and said to Lucretia: "I hear complaints about you." "On what account?" she asked. "Because you do not comply with the Captain's wishes in kindness; now however, you will have to make up your mind, either you will go the same way as Wybrecht Claes, or else you must do that for which we have kept the women." Through this threat Lucretia had to consent that day and thus he had her as his concubine for the time of two months. In sign of the truth we have heard every one of the above words from the lips of Jerome Cornelisz and in the presence of several witnesses, we have put our ordinary signatures to this. And we shall be at all times prepared, if it should be required, to confirm it with our solemn oath. Actum on the island, "Batavia's Graveyard," near the wreck of the foundered vessel Batavia. *Datum ut supra.*[16]

This passage is composed more or less in the style of Pelsaert's own Journals,[17] but differs from other evidence recorded by Pelsaert in that it is signed by those offering it (and not by the ship's disciplinary council, as in Pelsaert's documents); it also appears to be in the form of a voluntary statement. All other confessions and statements were offered as evidence before the council. There are

---

[16] BLWA. W. Siebenhaar, *Western Mail*, Christmas Number, 1897, p. 10.
[17] One of the major differences is the change from the first person to indirect narrative in *Ongeluckige Voyagie*.

three possibilities: either that a page has been lost or at some stage removed from the original Journals now in the Rijksarchief at The Hague, despite the fact that neither the microfilm nor the photostats used in these researches shows any place where this might have occurred; or else that it is indeed a true statement made by those men (who existed in fact, and who would actually have been the soldiers of the guard) made at some later date and inserted by the compiler of the story; or, thirdly, that it was invented by the compiler, who wished to make quite sure that Lucretia Jansz was not accused of complicity, and, since he ends his story far short of all the evidence given, chose that way to establish her innocence.

Apart from the soundness of the supposition of authenticity from the evidence of the date given, there is also a certain ring of truth about the statement as a whole that discounts the third possibility. Zevanck (or Seevanck) did cut the throat of Wybrecht Claasz, the predikant's maid, and had "stood over" various other reluctant accomplices. The date of the postponed execution is not found anywhere else in *Ongeluckige Voyagie*, but is fully documented in the Journals; therefore the most likely supposition is that the statement was made at some date later than the writing of the Journals and inserted by the compiler of *Ongeluckige Voyagie*. In the Hartgers edition of 1648,[18] a letter by the predikant, Gijsbert Bastiaensz, has been included, the authenticity of which is difficult to doubt. This letter was apparently sent from Batavia to his relatives, and is so convincing from internal evidence and the self-revealing style of the writer, that there seems no reason to believe that the publisher had not acquired a genuine document to enhance further that particular edition of the popular story. This inclusion lends colour to a belief that the same might apply to the passage under discussion. People who had been present on the islands, and survived, or relatives of the victims, would be sought out and questioned by publicists in 1629-47 no less than today. It is also possible that the quoted statement was actually written by those who signed it on the given date, but not included by Pelsaert in the documents sent forward by him, remaining instead in the hands of the men concerned and so later finding its way to the publishers of the story in Amsterdam. Whatever the fact, the item in no way conflicts with evidence given before the examining council and recorded by Pelsaert. It can be assumed, fairly reasonably, to be true in substance.

None of the women concerned was called to appear as a witness at the Abrolhos trials. (No reason is given for this omission, but

[18] Also in the Lucas de Vries edition of 1649 and also in Saeghman's.

several present themselves.) Judith Bastiaens, the daughter of the predikant, however, asked, or was incited by her father, to give a report on one of the mutineers, Wouter Loos.[19] The opinion of Lucretia Jansz remains undocumented. Her own character can only be guessed from the effect she had on others.[20] Her acknowledged attraction for men, the jealousy of other women, the fact that she repulsed the skipper and was an unwilling victim of Jeronimus Cornelisz, yet remained able to maintain her own integrity after Jeronimus was captured and his place and tent occupied by Wouter Loos, is proof of strong character. On what depths of resolution or inward convictions she drew in order thus to live through the ordeal must remain matter for surmise. That she was regarded contemporarily as more sinned against than sinning could be deduced from her remarriage at Batavia, in October 1630, to Jacob Cornelisz Cuick of Leyden, a sergeant in the company of Captain Hans Jurjaen; and the further fact that both in 1633 and 1635 she was named godmother at two christenings in Batavia.[21]

Soon after the last date, June 1635, Lucretia and her new husband must have returned to the Netherlands. Church records at Leyden reveal that two years later they were together named as godparents to the twin sons of Pieter Willemsz Cuyck and Willempje Dircx. Making allowance for the extraordinary deviations in all spellings of names (for instance, in the records, the name of Lucretia's

---

[19] Pelsaert's Journals: Evidence at further trial of Wouter Loos, 27th October 1629, on *Batavia's* Graveyard.

[20] Pelsaert's attitude seems clear in his Summary, wherein he assesses the whole story and also notes that the first attack on her person "was taken [i.e. objected to] very violently and to the highest degree, by the Commandeur".

[21] AND: Gedoopt Batavia Holl. Kerk. 29 Sept. 1633.

Jan

ouders [parents]	Lucas Barentsz, van Roodemaer
	Grietje Jans, van Ams/dm
getuigen [witnesses, godparents]	Adriaan Sonnius, Middelburg
	Hoopman Simon Bollentijn (Antwerp)
	Jacob Gouijn van Hoorn, vrijburger
	Anna van den Heuvel, van Macao
	Lucretia Jans, van A'dam

Gedoopt Batavia, Holl. Kerk. 30 Juni, 1635
Jeannetie

ouders	Robbert Dircksz. Kistemaker, van A'dam
	Geertruyt Gillis
getuigen	Harmen Jacobsz
	Bartholomeus van Warmond
	Grietie Cornelis
	Lucretia Jans
	Neeltje Gerrits

mother is spelt Steffenye, Steffanie, Stephenia; and Lucretia varied to Luijtgen) it seems probable that Lucretia's second husband Jacob Cuick was in fact brother-in-law to her own stepsister, Weijntgen Dircx. At Batavia it was Lucretia only who became a godparent, but in Leyden she and her husband together made the promises. They repeated them in 1641, when once again the same parents had another pair of twins, a boy and a girl.[22] Thus was Lucretia, childless herself, godmother to six children in an epoch when such offices were not lightly undertaken. It would also appear that she and her husband settled in Leyden, although no record of the death of either can be found there, or in Amsterdam.[23] There is, however, one anomaly, in that the records of the Amsterdam Orphan Chamber name Johannes Hilkes as being husband to Lucretia Jansz after her earlier marriage to Boudewijn van der Mijlen. But this alliance has not been traced in the marriage records. Nor could it be traced at Leyden, where it is possible that she might have contracted a third marriage had Cuick died before her. One can but assume that the naming of Hilkes was an error, or more likely, that it was indeed a third marriage, because the record of the marriage of Lucretia Jansz, widow of Boudewijn van der Mijlen, to Jacob Cuick, at Batavia, is undisputed.

A search of both Coen's records[24] and the Day Books of Batavia failed to reveal any further information regarding Jacob Cuick, although his Captain, Hans Juriaen, is mentioned more than once in orders, and presumably Cuick fought in the same engagements against the troops of the Susuhunan of Mataram. On 17th September 1629, the very day that Pelsaert arrived back at the Abrolhos with the rescue yacht *Sardam*, a sortie was made from Batavia on the beleaguring Javanese—probably Lucretia's future husband went with the musketeers. The Day Book entry gives a rousing picture:

> First a party of sailors and crew with grenades and fire-workers, who attacked so courageously that it was miraculous; whereon immediately the soldiers, the musketeers and the Chinese began to attack in 2 parties. Over one party was Hr. Antonie van Diemen, Councillor of India. . . . Due to continuous firing and courageous entering of our troops, the enemy is beginning to flee, being a thous-

---

[22] Gemeente-Archief van Leiden: 4 Sept. 1637, Jacob Cornelisz and Lucretia Jans became godparents to twins Willem and Dirck, sons of Pieter Willemsz. Cuyck and Willempje Dircx. On 3 Dec. 1641, the same stood as godparents to twins Willem and Neeltje, of the same parents.

[23] It is possible that Lucretia may have been buried in the Nieuwe Zijds chapel family tomb, but the original building has been destroyed, and another built on the same site.

[24] H. T. Colenbrander, *op. cit.*, vols. iii-v.

and men strong as we have advised. . . . It is said that about 300 of
the enemy are dead and with our nation, not more than 2 and some
blacks and Chinese dead and wounded; captured a brass gun, pikes
and muskets.[25]

The next entry states that news has been received that Jacques
Specx, Councillor of India, had arrived in the Straits of Sunda in
the *Hollandia*. On the 20th it is recorded that Jan Pieterszoon Coen
"has gone to rest in the Lord after he had suffered for considerable
time from the flux, but only slightly ill, suddenly dying of a heart
failure, some would say of a spasm . . . . On that date his wife was
in child-bed of a young daughter, 4 days old; how great an afflic-
tion that has been your Honours can imagine."[26]

The great Governor-General was accorded an impressive funeral.
The Day Book continues:

> Firstly, marched in front the free-burghers, mostly in mourning,
> very solemnly in 27 rows of 4; followed a company of soldiers being
> 100 men strong, then a company out of the castle of 27 rows of 5
> men, thereafter followed the horse of the Hr. Gen. very solemnly
> robed in black velvet, and he was led by the master of the stables
> and his valet; then the Commissary vander Lee, carrying his weap-
> ons; thereafter followed Job Christiaense Grij [*sic*] carrying his
> helmet and black plume. Thereupon followed the upper merchant
> Nachtegael carrying his staff [baton]. Then the upper merchant van
> der Burcht carrying his iron [*iseren*] gloves, then also the Com-
> mandeur van den Broecke carrying his spurs; thereafter the Heer
> Treasurer, carrying his pedarm.[27] Thereafter followed the corpse of
> the Hr Gen. being carried by [*van*] four Uppermerchants, the cap-
> tain of the burghers, 3 lieutenants and the skippers of the ships.

Two days later, on 24th September, Jacques Specx was provisionally elected Governor-General at Batavia. On 3rd October the
Day Book states that the Javanese had abandoned the siege over-
night. After that date the entries tail off. The last one for the year
1629 is made on "7th and 8th" October. It merely notes that the
enemy had been "forced to leave the town with dishonour and in
an ignominious manner after they had made a siege for six months
minus one day". Nor are the Day Books of Batavia for the following year still in existence. There is a gap until January 1631. Thus

[25] *Dagh Register gehouden int Casteel Batavia, Anno 1624-1629*, ed. J. E.
Heeres, p. 396 *et seq.*, translated from the Old Dutch by E. D. Drok.
[26] Ibid., pp. 397-8.
[27] More often *pede*, name of a weapon in the form of a stick or club, metal-
coated or provided with a metal point. On the use of *van* meaning "by" in the
following sentence see Appendix III.

no records other than the official letters and dispatches already quoted remain to report the return of the *Sardam* from the Abrolhos Islands, and the repercussions that followed. While Batavia mourned for the great Governor-General, at the islands Pelsaert had been listening in horror to evidence given at the disciplinary council he had immediately set up. On the day of Coen's funeral this council was engaged in examining Jeronimus Cornelisz. And on 2nd October, the last day of the siege of Batavia, those condemned to die (with the exception of Jan Pelgrom de Bye) were hanged on Seals Island. Pelsaert wrote in his Journal that the condemned men "requested that Jeronimus should be hanged first, so that their eyes could see that the seducer of men died".

What sort of man was this Jeronimus Cornelisz, who seized dictatorial rights on the windswept isles, having risen to power by subtle and bloody means? His nature remains ambiguous, even after close study of Pelsaert's detailed reports. At his trial he is stated to be aged about thirty, once an apothecary, a native of Haarlem.[28] Inquiries at Haarlem uncovered no trace of him, either in baptismal records (so that he appears to have spoken the truth when he declared that he had not been baptized) or in any other available or apposite records. No lists of apothecaries were kept at Haarlem before 1661. Therefore one is obliged to seek some clue to his behaviour in the teachings of Johannes Torrentius van der Beecke, of whom he confessed himself a follower.

Born at Amsterdam in 1589, Torrentius van der Beecke (as he is known) became a painter of pictures of still life, small and exquisite, remarkable for their delicacy of tone and colour. He made a name and a fortune and lived in considerable luxury, but very shortly abandoned his charming interiors and "conversations" for subjects grossly obscene. His conduct and manners also deteriorated. Originally a Catholic, he began to mock religion, to preach "the commonaulty of women", and next to preside over gatherings of Adamites. He left Amsterdam for Haarlem, where in 1627 this

[28] Jeronimus Cornelisz has been mentioned more than once in the *Medical Journal of Australia*: "The Discovery of Western Australia, with Some Early Medical History", by B. C. Cohen, 13th June 1953, p. 840; "A Tragedy for Tradition", by B. Gandevia, 5th October 1957, p. 505. However, Jeronimus was merely an apothecary; claims for the privilege of being first medical practitioner in Australia can more justly be advanced for Mr Frans Jansz, the Upperbarber and surgeon of the *Batavia*, later murdered at the instigation of Jeronimus. Pelsaert's use of "Mr" (Maistre) before his name indicates that Jansz was so addressed in deference to his position; a customary practice.

sect and its peculiar religious morality drew the attention of the magistrates of that city. Torrentius tried to save himself by denying all religions. He was arrested on 30th August 1627 and accused of leading a very scandalous life, with loathsome blasphemy and shameful heresy. Persisting in denials, he was condemned to be "put to the question", but he resisted all torture and no reply could be drawn from him. It was thus found impossible to convict him as chief of the Adamites; but his pictures of orgies were sufficient to merit punishment: a sentence of twenty years' imprisonment. At this point the English Ambassador (Sir Dudley Carlton) and many other distinguished people, including the Stadtholder himself, intervened on his behalf. He was allowed to escape to England. Charles I had been a great admirer of his earlier works; at the English Court the painter for a time re-established himself. But his new successes did nothing to improve his outlook and morals. Possibly he fell from favour for that reason, for in private life Charles was an upright and God-fearing man. At any rate, Torrentius returned eventually to Amsterdam, where he lived in hiding until his death in 1644. Shortly after, the government ordered that all his paintings be collected and burnt by the public hangman.[29]

The original Adamites flourished in the second century. They were a Christian sect whose members stripped naked in places of worship they called Paradise, in hope that by imitating the nudity of Adam they might also recapture the primeval innocence. Part of their doctrines was adopted by the Brethren of the Free Spirit, a pantheistic group flourishing in Western Europe in the early thirteenth century. Almaric, who died in 1209, maintained that salvation did not depend on the sacraments of the Church, but in serving God in freedom of spirit, that those who became united with God in love might yield without sin or remorse to the demands of the flesh and that the sole faith needed to be saved was to believe firmly that one was a Member of the Body of Jesus Christ; thus, only "la charité" or "la grâce" was essential. Expelled from the University of Paris in 1204 for his teachings, Almaric appealed to the Pope. He lost the appeal, retired, and died soon after. But his disciples went to extremes; they considered that all crimes were justified, all passions satisfied, all scruples dissipated, by their doctrines. Three hundred years later the Anabaptists, the most extreme of the Reformation groups in the northern Netherlands and Westphalia, coupled some of these doctrines with other revolutionary ideas. They believed in adult baptism (hence the

[29] *Biographie Universelle, Ancienne et Moderne*, ed. L.-G. Michaud, vol. xlvi (1826), p. 284.

name) and also in the community of goods and women. They later abandoned their more extreme practices, nevertheless remained strong enough to engage attention in the years of bitter religious-political strife that followed. Torrentius van der Beecke was also accused of trying to establish in Holland the creed of the Meritorious Order of the Rosy Cross, or the Rosicrucians, whose first manifesto had been published in Germany in 1614.

Such then, were the beliefs that Jeronimus Cornelisz preached to his own followers on the forlorn isles west of the unknown Southland, a convenient dogma that enabled him to murder and steal without scruple. There his nimble mind and glib tongue, doubtless aided by his much better education, enabled him to gain a fantastic hold on the less vivid imaginations of those he chose to influence. The evidence of the trials shows that he not only followed the philosophies of Torrentius but also, when accused, his practice of denial. It is true that Jeronimus was unable to withstand torture as his teacher had; yet again and again he retracted all that he said under duress, unquestionably filling Pelsaert's mind with doubt to a degree that led to much re-questioning and considerable heart-searching on the part of the Commandeur and his council. When Jeronimus saw that his situation had become hopeless, he resorted to pleas of postponement of sentence in order that he might have time to repent and so save his soul; finally he attempted suicide. But he had not the will even to endure the pain caused by whatever it was he ate, and begged for an antidote. Only beneath the gallows did he find strength to denounce both followers and judges alike, and declare himself unjustly condemned. In Pelsaert's words:

> ... Jeronimus could not reconcile himself to dying or to penitence, neither to pray to God nor to show any face of repentance over his sins. But they all shouted at each other, "Revenge", some evil-doers shouted at Jeronimus, and Jeronimus shouted at them. At last he challenged them, as well as the council, before God's Judgement Seat, [saying] that he wanted to seek justice there with them, because he had not been able to get it here on earth. And so he died stubborn.[30]

As Pelsaert's Journals unfold, the strange beliefs and horrible acts of Jeronimus create an elusive picture of a personality that was subtle, even paranoic, capable of fascinating and deceiving many, of attracting devotion, of demanding and receiving deference. Physically, Jeronimus was a coward: he clung to the wreck until forced to leave, fearful because he could not swim. He led to

[30] See Journals, 2nd October 1629.

attack, but he did not appear to fight; he incited to murder, but he did not stain his own hands with blood. To Pelsaert, he changed from a trusted officer of the Company to a "tiger animal devoid of all humanity". Nor was the peacock absent; he adorned himself with magnificence on the bleak limestone rock of *Batavia's* Graveyard, in scarlet cloth and gold braid vaingloriously ruling his pitiful territory, not half a mile long and far less in width.

Religious belief was of major importance in those times. Motley describes how an entire people, from rulers to beggars, from peasants to crews of the East Indiamen, exercised their wits and their tongues in endless argument on the conflicting doctrines of free-will or absolute fore-knowledge.[31] Although it can be seen that a logical extension of several of the Seven Points of the Calvinistic Contra-Remonstrance could be argued in favour of the no less extreme and scarcely more fantastic dogma of the Adamites, the heresies of Jeronimus Cornelisz were in fact almost as shocking to his fellow officers as were his murderous deeds.

A few years earlier, during the period when the principal actors in the *Batavia* tragedy were growing up, the fiercest controversies had raged round the respective interpretations of the Calvinist faith as propounded by Gomarus and Arminius:

"By an eternal decree of God," said Gomarus in accordance with Calvin, "it has been fixed who are to be saved and who damned. By His decree some are drawn to faith and godliness, and, being drawn, can never fall away. God leaves all the rest in the general corruption of human nature and their own misdeeds." "God has from eternity made this distinction in the fallen human race," said Arminius, "that He pardons those who desist from their sins and put their faith in Christ, and will give them eternal life, but will punish those who remain impenitent. Moreover, it is pleasanter to God that all men should repent, and, coming to knowledge of truth, remain therein, but He compels none."[32]

Bloodshed and violence marked the controversies, and the aftermath was bitter.

An addendum to the report from Specx and his Council on the return of the *Sardam* is significant:

Your Hons: Considering what evil can arise through a godless man, we request that Your Hons. please instruct in particular regarding the main officers that they are of good repute and are reared in the true Christian religion, and of that give public witness; now and

[31] J. L. Motley, *Life and Death of John of Barneveld*, vol. i, p. 387.
[32] Ibid., pp. 393-4. See also pp. 384 and 395 for points of both creeds.

then different persons of strange opinion come here [to Batavia]; Your Hons. please prevent this as far as possible and look to it that all such as almoners, students of divinity, and all other clericals come with due commission and having proper knowledge of the church.[33]

By 1629 the proper knowledge required was that of the Calvinistic creed. The Arminians had been routed. Motley writes: "Even the illustrious Grotius was . . . repudiating the notion that there could be two religions in one State. 'Difference in public worship,' he said, 'was in kingdoms pernicious, but in free commonwealths in the highest degree destructive.' "[34]

The very strictest conformity was demanded if not always obtained, despite savage punishments, by the V.O.C. Very probably Pelsaert's reluctant humanity, his desire to temper justice with mercy, in other words an evident inclination towards the softer beliefs of Arminius, told in his disfavour with the High and Mighty Seventeen, and led less sensitive but more ambitious men to consider him weak.

Gijsbert Bastiaensz, the official predikant, or minister, on the *Batavia* became an important actor in the shocking drama staged at Abrolhos during the absence of Pelsaert. One is tempted to wonder if there might not have been a different outcome had Bastiaensz been a man of character. That he suffered greatly cannot be denied, but the ignominous part he played is more clearly manifest in a document written by himself than in all the recorded evidence of the trials.[35]

A native of Dordrecht, Bastiaensz was an elder in that city until called to become a predikant in the East Indies in September 1628. For this he did a preparatory examination, was re-examined and appointed.[36] He embarked with his family on the *Batavia*. His wife, Maria Schepens, had borne him seven children; the eldest son, Gijsbert, must also have been appointed by the V.O.C. as a junior assistant, or clerk, because he is mentioned in that capacity in the evidence. Three of the seven appear to have been girls; Judick (or Judigh or Judith) is constantly referred to in the evidence as being the eldest daughter, and later Willemyntgie a "middle daughter" is also mentioned. Three other children remain nameless, but the baby was a son called Roelant. Bastiaensz also

[33] ARAKA, VOC: 1009, O.B. (1630¹).
[34] J. L. Motley, *op. cit.*, vol. i, p. 393.
[35] See Appendix IV. It is useful to read this letter before the Journals.
[36] C. A. L. van Troostenburg de Bruijn, *Biographisch Woordenboek van Oost-Indische Predikanten*, pp. 25-6.

took abroad a servant for his wife, a maid named Wybrecht Claas.

The account the predikant has given of the wreck and its aftermath is apparently the one private, non-official report extant. His statement was made in a letter to relatives and friends in Holland which he wrote after the survivors reached Batavia. Presumably this was dispatched on the same ship as Pelsaert's letter to the Chamber of Amsterdam. They both mention the need for haste.

The predikant's letter appeared first in 1648, in the Hartgers edition of *Ongeluckige Voyagie*. Lucas de Vries also printed it in his 1649 edition, and subsequent publishers followed suit.

Jan Jansz, as original publisher of *Ongeluckige Voyagie* in 1647, became incensed with Hartgers. In 1648 he published his own second edition, which carries the title *Nieuw en vermeerdede [New and enlarged] Ongeluckige Voyagie* and is prefaced by a note of "Advice to the Reader". In this, Jansz states that the story had come into his hands through "a Dillettante" (or amateur, in distinction to an acknowledged author). He continues:

> ... the compiler, later discovering that Joost Hartgers (to my harm and perhaps with little profit to himself) has copied the same out of envy and jealousy, has therefore taken it in hand again, and has improved and enlarged it out of various writings and particularly out of the notes of Gijsbert Sebastiaensz., Predikant on the same ship (since come to his hand), thereby adding what was lacking in the first impression, especially what horrors happened on the islands amongst the survivors whilst their Commandeur, Fr Pelsaert, had gone to Batavia for help. ...

Jansz appears to have no doubt that Hartgers used an authentic letter. Since the predikant had been dead for more than ten years, it is not likely that Jansz's Dillettante, or compiler, found other "notes" to improve his tale; probably, tit for tat, he drew on the Hartgers material.

The letter itself has the ring of truth. The unnamed author of the rest of the text in the original and re-published editions of *Ongeluckige Voyagie* does not show himself able, or even eager, to make any creative effort (unless the pre-cited passage regarding Lucretia is to be reckoned as such); nor does he attempt character delineation; he merely transposes Pelsaert's text carelessly, with slight variations and some altered names, into third person narrative; very occasionally condensing, but frequently altering sequence. The predikant's letter, on the other hand, is intensely personal and self-revealing—notably a touch regarding the writer's distaste for eating grass as salad, without oil and vinegar—a touch unlikely to have occurred to a seventeenth-century author dealing with a hor-

Francisco Pelsaert, a reputed portrait from a copy of an etching or engraving supposedly made in India about 1625. It was presented by E. Das Gupta in Lahore in 1945 to K. Wallace-Crabbe Esq. of Melbourne, who gave it to the author.

The Emperor Jahangir (Selim Ghe-hangier Shah), from a contemporary drawing reproduced in *Purchas His Pilgrimes*.

ror story, unless it had in fact happened to him. In addition, the revelation of self is scarcely flattering, although the vanity of the author is plain. There are also several points that clarify and complement the picture as presented by evidence given at the trials, and, to one who has visited the islands, greatly assist in identifying the Wallabi Group as the site of the wreck.

It is thus a very important letter—quite apart from the fact that it appears to have been the first private letter ever to have been written by any person who spent some time ashore, close by the great southern continent![37]

Several fresh points of significance appear in it: first, the existence of a beach on the island named *Batavia's* Graveyard; second, the fact that the skipper Ariaen Jacobsz was still in prison when the *Sardam* reached Batavia on 5th December; third, that Jeronimus had his right hand struck off before his execution, although no mention is made of that in Pelsaert's Journal other than in the sentence which condemned him to the loss of both hands (and the rest of the condemned to the loss of one only, although Bastiaensz, who was present at the executions, makes no mention of that also happening); fourth, a note to the effect that some of the sentences were finally carried out aboard the *Sardam* on the return trip.

Despite the initial apology for lack of clarity, the letter is well written in an individual style that distinguishes it from all the other documents. It enlarges and gives precise personal details of life on the islands in such a way as to seem the true statements of an eyewitness; for instance, sea-fowls' "eggs by the basketsfull", and the delicious taste of wallabies. It is difficult to dispute its claim to being regarded as genuine.

Notwithstanding his terrible bereavement, Bastiaensz was sufficiently recovered to marry at Batavia, in July 1631, Maria Cnijf, the widow of IJsbrand van Swaenswijk, Bailiff of Batavia.[38] Very probably van Swaenswijk had been the uppermerchant of the same name who sailed out in the *Dordrecht* with Pelsaert's fleet,[39] although on that occasion he was called Isaac. After his marriage Bastiaensz must have been posted to the island of Banda; he died there of dysentery in March 1633.[40]

---

[37] See Appendix IV for translation of this letter from Lucas de Vries edition. The note of "Advice to the Reader" is printed at the beginning of the Jan Jansz 1648 edition, following the title page. See also Chapter I, footnote I, for list of various editions of *Ongeluckige Voyagie*.
[38] C. A. L. van Troostenburg de Bruijn, *op. cit.*, p. 25.
[39] *Ongeluckige Voyagie*, Jan Jansz. ed. 1647, p. 1.
[40] C. A. L. van Troostenburg de Bruijn, *op. cit.*, p. 25.

Mention of him[41] is made in the letters of Jean-Sigismond Wurffbain,[42] originally published by the author's father at Nuremburg in 1646. Wurffbain was indignant at his private letters being published without his permission and declared the book to be full of inaccuracies not due to himself. He bought up practically the entire edition to destroy. His own son later republished the substance, but the interest of the first-person observation was lessened by being transposed into the third person and edited. Wurffbain travelled extensively in India and the islands of Indonesia; his letters home must have been of exceptional interest.

From the dates available, it appears that Wurffbain met Bastiaensz very soon after his arrival in the East Indies. One can imagine his satisfaction on meeting a survivor from the *Batavia* wreck, and his curiosity regarding a story that must still have been the subject of considerable talk. Had the original letters remained in existence, further light might have been thrown on the character of Bastiaensz and the part he played.

Judith (or Judick) the predikant's eldest daughter, forced by the mutineers to live with Coenraat van Huyssen, that "otherwise handsome young nobleman" mentioned in her father's letter, was apparently very quickly married off on return to Batavia: by February 1631, at her marriage in the same city to the predikant Helmichius Helmichii, of Utrecht, she is recorded as being already a widow and the name of her first husband is given as Pieter van

[41] *Tijdschrift voor Indische*, ed. W. Stortenbeker and L. J. J. Michielsen, vol. xviii, 6th series, vol. i, p. 353. The predikant Bastiaensz is also mentioned by Seyger van Rechteren, who sailed on one of the ships in Specx's fleet, which left the Netherlands little more than a month after Pelsaert's and very nearly piled up on the Western Australian coast. The reference is found in *The Discovery of Australia*, by George Collingridge, p. 273, and is in turn drawn from *Voiages de la Compagnie*, vol. ix, p. 131. Rechteren is not very accurate: he remarks that he had himself talked "au Pasteur qui y étoit, de qui la femme et les enfants furent égorgez par nos propres gens, à la réserve d'une fille que ces scélérats violérent"; and he goes on to say that the "Commis" (i.e., Jeronimus Cornelisz) and his adherents "se rendirent à Batavia" where they were arrested on the complaints and testimony of the rest, whom they had outraged, and who had also gone to Batavia.

[42] Born at Nuremburg, Wurffbain went in his youth to Holland. "The war having destroyed all industry and commerce in Germany and no one having the courage to start new enterprises," he decided, with the consent of his parents, to go to the East Indies. He enlisted as a common soldier in 1632 in V.O.C. troops; but since by 1635 he had become a senior assistant, he must early have displayed the talent that eventually led to his becoming the first German to reach the status of uppermerchant. The original 1646 edition was later included in toto in *L'Epistolische Schatzkammer de Martin Zeiller*, Ulm, 1700. From *Biographie Universelle, Ancienne et Moderne*, vol. li (1828), pp. 264-5.

der Hoeven.⁴³ If, therefore, she observed the usual year's mourning, she must have been both married and widowed between 5th December 1629, the date of arrival at Batavia, and February of the following year. Such was life in the Indies in the seventeenth century; only the hardiest survived. Judith's second husband, like her father, was dead of dysentery by 1634; at Amboina. Thus destitute, her plight was brought to the notice of the High and Mighty Seventeen. They made a generous gesture. Because of her widowed state she was granted the sum of 300 guilders, with the addition of a similar amount in recognition of her trials and privations "on the wrecked ship *Batavia* close to the Southland". This compensation appears also to have been mentioned by Wurffbain. Possibly he met Judith; unfortunately not even his son's edition of his letters has been available for study during these researches, or rather more might have been disclosed about the predikant's daughter.

Of the rest of the survivors from the wreck, some were rewarded, some savagely punished after arrival at Batavia. The tale is told in a document dated 28th January 1630,⁴⁴ as well as in later references to the trials at Abrolhos.

The V.O.C. did not forget either the money chest left submerged at the wreck site, or the two men marooned on the mainland by Pelsaert. Ships sailing in the vicinity had general orders to watch for the men, and in 1636 the commanders of two yachts, sailing from Batavia to see what could be discovered regarding the Southland, were ordered to give a passage home to the miscreants if they desired to leave.⁴⁵ In 1644 Abel Janszoon Tasman received more specific instructions.⁴⁶

Van Diemen was by now Governor-General. He had become extremely interested in the discovery "of the supposed rich Southern and Eastern lands". It was he who dispatched Tasman in 1642 on the famous voyage that led to the discovery of Van Diemen's Land (now Tasmania) and of New Zealand. Tasman in fact sailed right round Australia without touching it. However, the instructions he received from van Diemen and the Council on 29th January 1644 revived the story of *Batavia's* wreck.

There is quite a preamble dealing with previous voyages under-

---

⁴³ C. A. L. van Troostenburg de Bruijn, *op. cit.*, p. 177.
⁴⁴ See Appendix V.
⁴⁵ J. E. Heeres, *The Part Borne by the Dutch in the Discovery of Australia 1606-1765*, p. 66.
⁴⁶ *Dagh Register gehouden int Casteel Batavia, Anno 1643-1644*, ed. H. T. Colenbrander, p. 20.

taken to discover New Guinea and the unknown Southland, but none of these discoveries found out the situation and condition of this vast land . . .

> [only] that it has barren and dangerous coasts, green fertile fields, and exceedingly savage, black, barbarian inhabitants, as has been sufficiently proved by the well-known wrecking of the ship Batavia and the horror and miseries consequent thereon, and by the experiences gone through by the crew of the yacht Sardam in sailing along its coasts.[47]

Therefore, the time being considered apt, Tasman, provided with three ships, is directed to discover if New Guinea is separate from the Southland, and if there is a passage through to the South Seas. Having, it is hoped, made this discovery, he is to

> further continue your course along the land of d'Eendracht as far as Houtmans Abrolhos, and come to anchor there at the most convenient place, in order to make efforts to bring up from the bottom the chest with eight thousand rixdollars,[48] sunk with the lost ship Batavia in 1629, owing to a brass half cannon [*een metael half cartouw*][49] having fallen upon it, and which the men of the Yacht Sardam dived for without success, and so save the same together with the said gun, which would be good service done to the Company, on which account you will not fail diligently to attend to this business. You will likewise make search on the mainland to ascertain whether the two Netherlanders who, having forfeited their lives, were put ashore here by the Commander Francisco Pelsert at the same period, are still alive, in which case you will from them ask information touching the country, and, if they should wish it, allow them to take passage hither with you.[50]

The possibility of trade was not overlooked:

> If . . . you should happen to come to any country peopled by a civilized race of men, you will give them greater attention than to savage barbarians . . . showing them the goods and samples of the commodities you have taken on board for that purpose . . . as duly specified in the invoice amounting to a sum total of f. 2809. 12. 6.[51]

---

[47] *Abel Janszoon Tasman's Journal of His Discovery of Van Diemens Land and New Zealand in 1642 with documents relating to his Exploration of Australia in 1644 . . . to which are added Life and Labours of Abel Janszoon Tasman by J. E. Heeres*, ed. Frederik Muller, Amsterdam, 1898, Appendix M, p. 148.

[48] Funk and Wagnalls Dictionary (1956), p. 522 gives this as a silver coin varying in value, but in the Netherlands approximating 4/0½d. to 4/2½d.

[49] In a footnote, p. 50, *Early Voyages to Terra Australis*. R. H. Major gives this as being a 24-pounder.

[50] Abel Janszoon Tasman's *Journal*, Appendix M, p. 150.

[51] Ibid., p. 151.

This invoice is attached.⁵² The list of articles includes many yards of materials, including four parcels of tinsel, as well 200 pieces "of various assortments of china porcelain", "143 lbs. of elephants' teeth at 25 stivers per lb.", mirrors, "indifferent knives", eight small pearls, three pounds of ebony, pepper and needles.

One guesses that most of these goods went back to Batavia unbroached. Tasman did not sail east through Torres Strait nor did he sail sufficiently far south to reach the Houtman Rocks. The money chest remained submerged somewhere on the reefs of Abrolhos. As for the two young men, they were either dead by 1644 or else successfully established amongst the aborigines; either way, they had passed for ever from European ken.

---

⁵² Ibid., p. 155

V

TRADE JEWELS

THE HISTORY of the famous jewel that, with others, was sent ashore by Pelsaert immediately after the wreck and survives to this day adds further extravagance to the already fantastic record. Listed as "the great jewel of Gaspar[1] Boudaen", it was on its way to be sold to the Mogul Emperor at Agra, who, unfortunately for Pelsaert, was no longer the King Jahangir of his acquaintance.

A British writer of the period gives a picture of Jahangir that displays him as a jolly toper, virile, brutal and obstinate. Listed amongst his "toys" were an elephant harnessed in gold, a new set of clothes, jewels; a cornet was a great success—Jahangir himself blew it for hours. Amongst the gifts presented by the British Ambassador, Sir Thomas Roe, are mentioned, in the correspondence of 1616, cases of Burgundy wine and mastiffs to bait tigers.[2]

This extensive trade in "toys" paid dividends when subtly promoted amongst the fabulously wealthy Indian princes, and did for merchants what advertising does today. It will be remembered that Pelsaert, arriving at Agra five years later than Roe, was not long in deciding that it would be more effective and in the end cheaper if the V.O.C. also entered the "toy" trade. He advised the use of presents: on the one hand, by way of ingratiation with the higher officials; on the other, as a means of advertising the wares of the Netherlands so that a desire to possess European objects of art or amusement was aroused amongst the wealthy. His list of popular jewels is interesting: "large pearls; large and fine emeralds (old and new); sapphires, rubies and balas-rubies[3] of rich colour". He also specified "various rarities" that had been recommended to him by different Indian nobles, such as:

- 10 small gold chains, of the most ingenious work.
- 20 sabres, costing 10 to 15 guilders each, embellished with some gold-work, slightly curved, of which I can show a sample.
- 20 handsome musket barrels, wrought with gold and set with agates of various colours, in which heads are carved, of the kind brought here overland by the Venetians.

[1] Also spelt Caspar.
[2] C. E. Carrington, *The British Overseas*, p. 153.
[3] Red spinel resembling a ruby.

Some sea-horse [walrus] teeth, marbled on the inside with black stripes, much esteemed. . . .

Many of the great men [Pelsaert continues] express surprise that we do not have the gold and silver (coined and uncoined), which we import in large quantities, manufactured by us into articles that are here in common use. . . . It would be well therefore, for the first trial, to manufacture such goods as the following to the value of 8000 to 10,000 reals-of-eight,[4] and to the same amount in gold:

Feet for *katels*, or bedsteads, hollow, and as light as possible, but artistically wrought.

Aftabas, or ewers used by Moslems for washing the hands.
Betel boxes.
Fan handles.
Handles for fly-switches.
Dishes and cups with covers.

If necessary, the style or fashion of these could be shown or explained.

Most of these goods could be sold in the Palace or the Camp, to the good profit, honour, and reputation of the Company, by an agent familiar with the language and customs of the country.[5]

In a letter to Coen dated 21st March 1629 that followed on Pelsaert's return to the Indies aboard the *Batavia*, notice is given of the dispatch of gold jewels sent for trading in India with the Great Mogul and other great lords "on the advice of Sr.[6] Francisco Pelsaert and the Heer Specx" because "we are of the belief and they also are of the same opinion, that they can be sold there with a good profit of 60 to 70 percento." Immediately there follows yet another reminder that "many persons transport many jewels and other costly goods to the great detriment of the Company. Also, that many complaints and calumnies are made about it." Coen is therefore requested to "look keenly into shipping by such persons" and to see that the practice is prevented.[7]

The next month Coen is "recommended" to

. . . take very good care of the great jewel that Sr. Gasper Boudaen has handed over on 29 October 1628[8] at Texel, on commission to Francisco Pelsaert, in order that the mentioned Pelsaert and others who are in charge of the administration and the care of the jewels

---

[4] Moreland estimates the *real* as worth about 2 rupees at this time in India; a rupee was equivalent to 24 Dutch stivers, and a Dutch guilder equal to 20 stivers.
[5] *Jahangir's India*, pp. 26-7. Pelsaert spoke the language.
[6] *Singeur, sinjeur*, now *señor*: as then used in Spanish Netherlands to denote a man of some standing, but who was not addressed as "de Heer".
[7] H. T. Colenbrander, *J. P. Coen, Bescheiden omtrent zijn Bedrijf in Indië*, vol. v, pp. 835, 836, 840.
[8] Here again is the "out sailing" book date. The jewel was obviously handed to Pelsaert at the last possible moment.

and the costly goods of the Company, will keep that jewel as a jewel belonging to the Company, and that the jewel will be handed over according to the instructions given by the mentioned Boudaen when he handed the mentioned jewel to the mentioned Pelsaert.[9]

A week later several of Pelsaert's desired items follow:

> Herewith [i.e., with the same ship as the letter] goes a case numbered as No 4., in which are four posts for a bed, a chamber-pot, a ewer, and a big dish, all made from pure gold, which were made to order and on the advice of the merchant Francisco Pelsaert, to be sent to Suratte and from there to the land of the Great Magor [sic] to be sold to that person or to the mighty men of the same Realm.[10]

Thus, backed by Jacques Specx and probably also his brother-in-law Brouwer, Pelsaert at this stage appears to have been given practically a free hand in putting into practice his own ideas for the Indian "toy" trade. When he left on the *Batavia* he took with him not only the "mentioned" jewel, but also gold and silver services for domestic use likewise made to his own specifications and valued at 62,811 guilders;[11] the items shown above as following on a later ship were evidently not ready in time for dispatch aboard *Batavia*.

Today Boudaen's great jewel, handed over with secrecy (so much so that even the High and Mighty Seventeen were allowed to see no more than a picture of it) can be admired by anyone able to visit the Royal Coin Cabinet at The Hague. Measuring 8.3 by 11.7 inches, the gem is one of the world's largest and most distinguished cameos.

> It is a large agate of two layers of grey and brown and shows an Emperor and his family on a chariot drawn by two centaurs trampling on fallen enemies while a flying Victory holds a wreath. Both the style and the scene depicted point to the fourth century: Constantine the Great is pictured with his spouse Fausta, his son Crispus and his mother Helena. Comparison with Constantinian coins and a close scrutiny of the scene portrayed lead to the conclusion that this work of art was produced in the years 312-315 and served as a present on the occasion of the tenth anniversary of the Emperor's accession, in 315.[12]

The gem was presented to the Royal Coin Cabinet in 1823 by William I of the Netherlands, who bought it for the sum of 55,000

---

[9] H. T. Colenbrander, *op. cit.*, vol. v, p. 840, 20th April 1629.
[10] Ibid., p. 842, 28th April 1629.
[11] A. N. Zadoks-Josephus Jitta, "De Lotgevallen van den Grooten Camee in het Koninklijk Penningkabinet", *Oud-Holland*, 1951, pp. 191-211.
[12] Ibid., pp. 210-11.

guilders (£5,500) from the family of van Pabst van Bingerden. Previously, Napoleon had been negotiating for its purchase, but he set out on the disastrous Russian campaign before agreement was reached, and eventually his defeat and banishment put an end to such private transactions. To this period belongs an engraving that shows the cameo mounted in a most beautiful jewelled and enamelled frame of silver gilt. Today, nothing remains of this frame[13] but the inner setting surrounding the agate, which can be easily removed but which shows clearly the small holes in which the four points of the larger frame were attached (Plate facing p. 158). There is evidence to support the theory that the whole frame was made by the famous goldsmith Theodore Rogiers of Antwerp, a friend and associate of Rubens and van Dyke, and that in 1628, the year that the *Batavia* sailed for the Indies, Rubens was himself the owner of the gem.

The artist was known to possess one of the finest gem collections in Europe and to take an immense and informed interest in antiquities. The year before he had indeed sold his collection of pictures and statues, advantageously, to the Duke of Buckingham; but it is known that he did not part with all his jewels. In 1622 he was discussing with his friend Fabri de Peiresc, the noted French antiquarian, the possibility of including prints of his own gems in an edition of engravings of famous cameos, including Parisian and Viennese gems, which they planned to publish. In one letter Peiresc asks Rubens for depictions of his own beautiful cameos, and promises secrecy. Having been sent what he requested, the Frenchman replied with so much discretion that although he indeed expresses great admiration for Rubens's "most stupendous cameo", exact identification is impossible.[14]

Such is not the case, however, with the splendid engraving by Paulus Pontius, after a drawing by Rubens, which was indeed published at this time for the projected series or "Corpus of Cameos": a truly magnificent "depiction", wherein the stark classical lines of the artist who originally cut the jewel have gained "a dynamic movement, breadth and depth";[15] in short, all the opulent grandeur of which Rubens remains the undisputed master. The artist had vanquished the antiquarian. Nor is there difficulty in establishing that "the great jewel of Gaspar Boudaen" was the same cameo as that drawn by Rubens. Its description, and that of the magnificent frame, appear in the V.O.C. records of 1632 when, two years after Pelsaert's death, it eventually went forward to Agra:

[13] I have been informed privately that members of the van Pabst family retained the frame and only recently disposed of the jewels.
[14] A. N. Zadoks-Josephus Jitta, *loc. cit.*, p. 194.   [15] Ibid., p. 193.

A great antique agate stone, on which is cut according to life, a triumphal chariot with some imperial persons standing, in a silver gilt frame studded with several jewels, large and small, the face of the agate belonging to a certain jeweller of Amsterdam, Gaspar Boudaen.[16]

Boudaen, like Pelsaert, came from Antwerp; and Rubens lived there. It is known that about 1626, through his future father-inlaw, Daniel Fourment (who as a dealer in silks and tapestries was associated with the V.O.C.), Rubens did send various agates to be traded in India. These of course went "under the lap" in the care of friendly or obliging merchants—the very trade the Directors were bent on breaking. What then more likely than his arranging for Boudaen to enter into all negotiations on his behalf, even when this particular cameo was being sent with the Directors' knowledge and permission? It is indeed more than probable that the painter-diplomat would not wish his name to be used in connection with any company trading in cut stones, however legitimate.

Despite his wish to interest the Indian lords and display to them the skills of his country's craftsmen, Pelsaert cannot have been very pleased with this commission. The contract with Boudaen relieved the Company from any responsibility for disposing of the jewel, that being left to Pelsaert and putting him more or less in the position of a private agent; at the same time it provided for a commission to the Company of 28 per cent.[17]

But the cameo was never sold in India. Along with the other jewels it fell into the hands of Jeronimus Cornelisz and his gang. One of Pelsaert's first acts after he had captured the leaders was to have a search made for all jewels; the majority were quickly restored to the casket, only a ring and a chain being missing. A marginal note in his Journal states that the ring was found "later".

[16] Ibid., p. 195.
[17] "Enclosed there goes a copy of a certain contract made at the last meeting of the Seventeen with one Gasper Boudaen, jeweller, in regard to, as Boudaen declares, a costly jewel, of which neither the Seventeen nor anyone else of the Company, has seen any more than the picture, which the aforesaid Boudaen has given to Sr. Francisco Pelsaert to go to the East Indies, who has sailed to the Indies with the previous fleet, as President, last October, in order to sell the aforesaid jewel of the mentioned Boudaen in India with the greatest profit, of which proceeds the Company shall receive 28 in the hundred. The cash that comes therefrom shall be paid into the comptoir [account] of India, which shall again be paid here to the aforesaid Gasper Boudaen on the first advice from India, with profit of 8 in the hundred of the exchange; referring further to the written contract, to give with that an order as is implied in this content." Dated 18th December 1628 "in the name of the High and Mighty of the East India Company at Amsterdam", this document was signed by ten of the Directors, including Hendric [sic] Brouwer and Pieter de Carpentier. H. T. Colenbrander, op. cit., vol. v, pp. 828-9.

Other personal jewels, such as a medallion of his own, were also seized by the cut-throats, the medallion being wantonly thrown overboard. Also, a discrepancy in figures[18] suggests that still more valuables may have been stripped from those who were murdered, and points to the likelihood of other undisclosed items (such as "the Rubens Vase", to be discussed later) being also recovered. However that may be, Pelsaert must have been grimly relieved to find that at least he would not be called on to explain the loss of such a magnificent gem as the Great Cameo. Lacking knowledge of the historic and aesthetic value of this particular jewel entrusted to his personal care (and possibly also the priceless vase), some earlier writers have found Pelsaert's anxiety over the jewels slightly repellant: to any artist or antiquary it would appear amply justified, and not purely a matter of self-interest.

Despite the deaths of the two principals, Jahangir and Pelsaert, efforts were eventually made to dispose of the Cameo in India; it was sent there, along with the gold and silver services, in 1632. After six months haggling the plate was sold for "a vile price" instead of bringing the expected 50 per cent profit;[19] but the jewel was returned unsold to Batavia the following year. It travelled twice more to Surat; it was sent fruitlessly to Sumatra, Persia and Siam. By then it should have been obvious that however much the baroque beauty of the frame may have appealed to Oriental taste, the cold classic lines and alien mythology of Rome left potential buyers unmoved. Nevertheless in 1647, the same year that Jan Jansz published the first edition of *Ongeluckige Voyagie*, Gaspar Boudaen's son travelled out to Java and himself took the jewel again to Surat. He had no better success than the merchants of the V.O.C. By 1656 the cameo was back in Holland.

The Rubens drawing, from which the Paulus Pontius engraving still in existence was made, marks the first recorded appearance of this cameo. Its earlier history remains unknown, but antiquarians generally assume that it came to Western Europe in the hands of some Crusader returning from Byzantium. It is the opinion of Mrs Zadoks-Josephus Jitta, of the Royal Coin Cabinet, that Rubens not only made a drawing of the cameo but also owned it; she believes, moreover, that Pelsaert either directly or indirectly influenced the great painter to send the gem for sale in India on commission, through the V.O.C. She also presumes that the famous Rubens vase, of the Walters Art Gallery, Baltimore, U.S.A., was

---

[18] Of approximately f. 40,000. Van Diemen's first estimate of the value of the casket with jewels, and his statement after the *Sardam* returned, can be seen on pp. 42 and 51 of this book.

[19] A. N. Zadoks-Josephus Jitta, *loc. cit.*, p. 200.

sent to Pelsaert at the same time, for the same purpose, but *without* reference to the High and Mighty Seventeen.

This vase is an even more beautiful example of antique gem-carving than the cameo, and did without question once belong to Rubens. For beauty and rarity it ranks as one of the most important gem carvings in the world. A note written by his correspondent Peiresc tells how the artist picked it up in Paris at the Foire St Germain in 1619.[20]

Over seven inches high, the vase has been cut from a single mass of agate that shades from honey colour to milk white. It is carved in high relief in a design of vine leaves and bunches of grapes solid enough to give strength to the walls, which have been worked down to the thinness and translucence of porcelain. At the shoulders, two handle-like knobs have been carved into heads of Pan. This vase has been known to collectors and scholars for about sixty years, but when in 1941 the Trustees of the Walters Art Gallery purchased it, the question of its period was reopened.

In his exhaustive article in the Walters Art Gallery journal Marvin C. Ross traces the possible owners of the vase back through medieval days,[21] and eventually, from the nature and the carving of the vase itself, arrives at the conclusion that it belonged originally to the late fourth or early fifth centuries A.D.

To detail the many surmises and clues that led to the vase being finally established as once belonging to Rubens is here impossible. Sufficient to state that an engraving (probably by Paulus Pontius) after a drawing by Rubens was eventually discovered in the Berlin Print Cabinet. There can be no mistaking this for the picture of any other vase than the one in question, the beautiful agate that Rubens mentioned lovingly more than once in his correspondence with Fabri de Peiresc.

An obscure sentence in one of Rubens's letters to Peiresc, considered in conjunction with several other letters later written to the V.O.C. regarding the same vase, gives colour to the belief that this exquisite gem was very probably aboard the *Batavia* at the time of the wreck. The letter to Peiresc, dated Antwerp, 18th

---

[20] Marvin C. Ross, "The Rubens Vase. Its History and Date." *Journal of the Walters Art Gallery*, vol. vi, 1943, p. 18; also Appendix V, p. 39 of that journal. Rubens paid *"duo mille scudi d'oro"* (2,000 gold *scudi*) for the vase. The Coins and Medals Department of the British Museum estimate the corresponding French *écu d'or* of the period as worth 7s. English at the time. Thus Rubens paid £700 for the vase if he paid for it in French money. On the other hand, if he used *duo mille scudi* to represent the actual cost, then he paid £400, for a *scudi* was worth approximately 4s.

[21] Marvin C. Ross, *loc. cit.*

December 1634, is written in Italian,[22] as was most of the great painter's correspondence. In his *Recollections of Rubens*, Jacob Burckhardt has translated the relevant passage as follows:

> Signor Rockox is alive and well, and kisses your hands with sincere devotion. I still have the drawing and the model of the agate vase you saw (which I bought for two thousand gold scudi), but not the mould. It was, however, no bigger than an ordinary carafe of somewhat thick glass. I remember measuring it and it held exactly one "pot", which is the stupid name of this measure in our language. The jewel itself was sent to the East Indies in a carrack and fell into the hands of the Dutch, *sed periit inter manus rapientium ni fallor*, and though many inquiries were made of the Eastern Company in Amsterdam, it has never been heard of again. *Iterum vale*.[23]

In Burckhardt's footnote the "*sed periit*" sentence is translated to read: "But unless I am mistaken, it perished in the hands of the pirates." It must also be noted here that in the original Italian version of this letter, as published by Marvin C. Ross, "*repientium*", not "*rapientium*", is the word used. A more literal rendering of Rubens's letter as given in Mr Ross's article[24] has been made for me by Mr C. de Heer, and reads thus:

> Signor Rockox is alive and well, and kisses with a true heart the hands of Your Hon. I still have the drawing and the model of the Agate vase that Your Hon. saw (which I bought for two thousand gold scudi), but not the mould. It did not have a greater size than that of an ordinary carafe of somewhat thick glass. I remember having measured it and it had exactly a measure that we call in our language by the inept word Pot! That jewel was being sent to the East Indies in a ship[25] and came into the hands of the Hollanders, *sed periit inter manus repientium ni fallor*, because, having made every attempt possible with the Eastern Company at Amsterdam, I have not been able to obtain any further news.

Mr de Heer translates the Latin as: "But it perished in the hands of those who took it, if I am not wrong."

The divergence of meaning, especially of the Latin tag, allows quite a different assessment of fact to be made, especially by those conversant with the Pelsaert story. "Those who took it" has an altogether different connotation from "the pirates". The Burckhardt rendering suggests that the ship concerned was captured by pirates, then must later have been *recaptured* by the Company,

22 See Appendix VI for the original Italian as printed by Marvin C. Ross.
23 Jacob Burckhardt, *Recollections of Rubens*, p. 237.
24 Marvin C. Ross, *loc. cit.*, p. 37.
25 *Carrack*, the word used, is an ordinary Italian term for "ship", so there is no need to presume that the gem was sent overseas with either Spanish or Portuguese merchants.

since the vase "fell into the hands of the Dutch"—and because later on Rubens appeared to think that the V.O.C. knew something about his missing treasure.

If, however, one assumes that the painter gave, or sent, the vase to Pelsaert, he must eventually (but not until the end of 1630 at earliest, and probably later) have heard about the wreck of the *Batavia* and the resulting mutiny. The Company was outraged by the disgraceful episode; one does not imagine the news was broadcast, especially as considerable tension still existed with England over the Amboina executions; was indeed coming close to breaking point. More time must necessarily elapse before Rubens could hear of Pelsaert's own death, which would be the logical moment to begin making inquiries. Even so, Rubens might have refrained for a period from asking direct questions. There appears to be no record of this vase being sent to the Indies "on commission", as was the great cameo. Whether Pelsaert or another took the vase, it seems fairly certain that it was sent secretly. It is known that in 1626-8 Rubens "disposed of certain gems to Daniel Fourment for nine hundred florins",[26] and that Fourment sent jewels secretly to India. What would seem more likely than that Rubens, aware that Pelsaert believed a good price could be got for the cameo at the Mogul Court, should decide to send his even greater "rarity" to be offered in the same market? One can be certain that he would not have applied to the V.O.C. for news of his vase unless he had very good reason to know the Company was the most likely source of information. "Came into the hands of the Hollanders" has therefore special significance, for Rubens would not think of Pelsaert as being a Hollander: he came from Antwerp, and was Flemish. It is therefore possible to assume that when the artist in his letter to Peiresc alludes to the vase's having perished in "the hands of those who took it" he means either those who took it *after the wreck*, i.e. the mutineers, or those who took it after the death of Pelsaert when it came into the hands of the Company. In either case, the reference seems to fit very aptly with the conditions required for both sending, and losing, the gem, through Pelsaert.

If that were so, what in fact became of the vase? It is possible that Pelsaert forwarded it to India, still privately; and died before he heard what became of it or before he could carry out his part of the transaction. As this appears to have been a secret venture, written references would have been unlikely, especially between two such men as Rubens and Pelsaert. The vase may even have been found amongst the other effects left by Pelsaert, confiscated,

---

[26] Marvin C. Ross, *loc. cit.*, p. 18.

and ultimately sold in India by the Company. If there was no note attached, the Council of India would have felt entirely justified. Or, again, it is possible that some reference to it may have been made in the missing Day Books of Batavia that covered the period immediately following the return of the *Sardam*. Whatever the true facts, the vase must have lingered in India or the Far East for a long time: Rubens heard no more of his treasure. Its existence remained unrecorded in the East or in Europe until 1823 when it reappeared in Fonthill Abbey, in England, as part of the famous collection of William Beckford. One clue only suggests that it had been for a time in Italy: the gold band around the lip bears the French gold-standard stamp for the years 1809-19 and the guarantee stamp of the Department of Ain for the same decade; in the opinion of Marvin C. Ross it is very probable that the vase had been brought from Italy by some tourist or merchant returning to France or England; but how it arrived in Italy from India remains a mystery.

It is indeed fantastic that three hundred years ago two such gems of the ancient world for a time rested (one for certain and the other more than probably) on a coral rock close by the shores of Australia, as yet the unknown Land of the South. It is even more remarkable that, after who knows how many more hazardous adventures, these fabulous and fragile jewels should come at last to secure and permanent homes, one in Europe, the other in the United States of America.

VI

THE JOURNALS, AND SOME LEGAL ASPECTS

THE ORIGINAL MANUSCRIPTS of Pelsaert's journal of the *Batavia* wreck and the boat journey to Java, and of his *Sardam* journal are in the Algemeen Rijksarchief at The Hague. They were inspected in 1954 by the late Professor Neville Burkitt, who wrote:

> Pelsart's journal or day book consisted of about 84 pages of handmade paper in sheets of about 15 in. long, 10 wide, without any covering; being simply bound together with other records of a similar nature in a huge folio . . . . It was signed by various members of the crew as well as by Pelsartt. . . . The writing was clear-cut old fashioned script [Gothic] in old Dutch, with a clear left hand margin of about 2 in. There were occasional notes in the margin, also large flourishes and excursions into it . . . . The writing was still perfectly clear, distinct, and copy-book, and impressed me as being written by someone of strong character. The sheets were written on both sides and the dates sometimes in the margins. It was mostly signed from time to time by six or seven people . . . the signatures were not always in the bold clear script of the journal itself, but seemed to be the true signatures of the people concerned.[1]

The form of the Journals as revealed by the microfilm of the full text is also of interest.

Headings are written in the top right-hand corner, and the pages then filled with uniform symmetry in a manner to delight the eye. Italian script is used instead of Gothic for place-names and ships' names and generally for signatures when these are not actually written by the men signing. The sole exception is that of Salomon Deschamps, who had been senior assistant on the *Batavia*. His signature is always in Italian script, which nevertheless appears to be written personally: it ends with flourishes not common to other Italian writing penned by Pelsaert.

The Journal of the wreck and the open boat journey to Java is one continuous document, broken only by paragraphs. The first pages exhibit what appear to be signs of dampness, the writing on the back often showing through. This is hardly surprising; what is surprising is that Pelsaert managed to write so evenly and clearly under the existing circumstances.

---

[1] Personal letter from the late Dr Neville Burkitt (formerly Professor of Anatomy in the University of Sydney) sent from The Hague, dated 16th May 1954.

Hendrick Brouwer (brother-in-law to Pelsaert), Governor-General for the V.O.C. at Batavia 1632-6.

Antonio van Diemen, Governor-General for the V.O.C. at Batavia 1636-45.

Both from Vies des Gouverneurs-Généraux, Du Bois, 1763.

Jan Pieterszoon Coen, from a seventeenth-century portrait.

The Old Church, Amsterdam, towards the end of the sixteenth century. Lucretia Jansz was here married to Boudewijn van der Mijlen on 18th October 1620.

A view of Batavia about 1625 (from *Vies des Gouverneurs-Généraux*, Du Bois, 1763). The larger ships are two of the *Batavia* class, and there are several yachts or flutes, as well as large ships' boats similar to that in which Pelsaert made his journey from the Abrolhos to Batavia. Some small *schuits*, or yawls, can also be seen, with native craft on the right.

The *Sardam* Journal, on the contrary, is broken into various parts. The first long section resembles a ship's log, giving daily entries of position, winds, etc. The writing varies in size occasionally, a variation doubtless due to weather conditions and the movement of the ship. However, when Pelsaert found himself faced by the necessity of setting up a council to examine a pack of mutineers and murderers, and at the same time direct salvage operations, he had to arrange his daily notes as best he might to achieve some coherence.

The first interrogation of prisoners by the ship's council took place on the afternoon of arrival, 17th September, aboard the *Sardam*, following the capture of some of the castaways who had planned to over-run the yacht. That same evening Jeronimus Cornelisz was also brought aboard by Wiebbe Hayes as a prisoner to be questioned by the council. These facts are recorded as usual in the daily entry under the relevant date, as also Pelsaert's own landing on *Batavia's* Graveyard the next day and the various activities which followed; including sending the remaining mutineers, who were there overcome, to be guarded on Seals Island. On the 19th Pelsaert orders the prisoners still incarcerated on the yacht to be brought to *Batavia's* Graveyard; it has become obvious that he has dangerous criminals to cope with, and that some decision must be taken regarding their confinement and possible punishment. Whether the majority of the prisoners were kept all the time under guard on Seals Island never becomes clear; but the principals were not, since their trials continued on *Batavia's* Graveyard whenever the weather became unpropitious for salvage work.

Hitherto it has been customary to presume that the major trials took place on the yacht. An error largely due, one imagines, to one of the *Ongeluckige Voyagie* engravings which shows prisoners being "put to the question" in what is presumably a ship's hold, despite the fact that the text makes it clear that they were brought ashore for trial. Possibly the publisher had that particular illustration to hand and found it convenient to use. Under this date (19th September) Pelsaert also includes copies of various of the mutineers' documents discovered on *Batavia's* Graveyard, probably in the tent of Jeronimus Cornelisz.

But from 19th September until the 28th the daily entry is confined to reports of what one might call normal activities, although sittings of the disciplinary council are noted as occurring. On the 28th, under a new heading, comes a long report of the decisions taken by the council, followed by the sentences passed on the principal evildoers, as well as decisions taken regarding the rest; it ends with a list of rewards granted to several of the castaways who remained loyal, notably the soldier Wiebbe Hayes.

This section is signed by the full council of the *Sardam*: Pelsaert; Jacob Jacobsz, skipper; Claas Gerritsz, uppersteersman (late of the *Batavia*); Jacob Jansz, understeersman (also late of the *Batavia*); Symon Yopson, high boatswain; and a sixth member, Jan Willemsz Visch, who cannot write so puts only his mark. The exact status of this extra member, Visch, never becomes clear. But he sat on every trial. Later there are variations in the number signing, notably after the skipper was lost or when the understeersman Jansz was absent on other duties; sometimes there are only the statutory five.

The most extraordinary feature is the frequent inclusion of Salomon Deschamps, the senior assistant of the *Batavia*, who signed even his own sentence. This would suggest that Pelsaert was hard put to it to find some officer of sufficient intelligence to sit on the council, and that Deschamps was himself prepared to make an act of contrition. Moreland suggests that he may have been the clerk who made copies of the *Remonstrantie*.[2] If so, he was probably well known to Pelsaert, who may have been prepared to believe him truly led astray and as truly penitent. If that were so, his presence at the trials would have been an asset; one of the major difficulties must have been the lack of reliable witnesses amongst those who remained on *Batavia's* Graveyard throughout the entire period.

Pelsaert then inserts the whole of the evidence given at the trial of Jeronimus Cornelisz, from the opening examination on 17th September aboard the *Sardam* to the delivery of sentence on the 28th on *Batavia's* Graveyard. This includes all the evidence given against Jeronimus by numerous witnesses, as well as his own confessions, made sometimes under torture, but finally of his own free-will after twenty-four hours free from torture, as was necessary under Dutch law. Pelsaert wrote all evidence incorporated in the Journals, himself; references by witnesses to him as "the Commandeur" have sometimes led to incorrect assumptions that the Journal records were in fact made by a clerk; but the handwriting refutes this idea.[3] The record of Jeronimus's evil doings, of his many shifts and twists, is signed by the original six already mentioned, and by Salomon Deschamps as well; his name follows immediately below that of the skipper of the *Sardam*, thus placing him as the next in rank after Pelsaert on the commercial register

[2] See *Jahangir's India*, p. xiii (Introduction).
[3] It is possible that during proceedings notes were taken by a clerk, later written up by Pelsaert. But I incline to the idea that he handled the whole matter personally.

of the Company. It is possible that Pelsaert called on Deschamps to sign the evidence merely as a reasonably reliable spectator of all that had occurred; but more probably Pelsaert was not at this stage aware of the assistant's own culpability; Deschamps' complicity was not disclosed until later. The evidence ends with a declaration of belief in its truth made by the signatories on their "manly truth in place of the duly attested oath". Pelsaert next makes a summary of the evidence, which is followed by the sentence, signed by the full *Sardam* council, but not by Deschamps.

The same pattern is followed in each subsequent examination; thus the strictly official form of the Abrolhos trials becomes remarkably clear. It differs little from the pattern of our criminal procedure today, apart from the legal use of torture and the lack of jury and counsel. Whenever the accused wished a particular witness called, he was called. Moreover Jeronimus, who protested his innocence again and again, was heard again and again.

Obviously the council, and Pelsaert in particular, were considerably exercised in mind over this extraordinary man, unwilling to condemn until thoroughly convinced of his guilt. As to whether, on the nature of the circumstantial evidence offered, an able defence might have persuaded a modern jury to acquit him, is a not uninteresting speculation. Pelsaert's own attitude is also interesting. At first he sets down the evidence with careful impartiality; but as the dreadful tale of murder deliberately planned, of licence and rapine unfolds its full horror, he cannot always restrain a reaction of shock or disgust. Emotive words begin to creep in. In his final summary —the "Declaration in Short" with which the Journal concludes, a fine piece of condensation, a report and assessment worthy of the author of the *Remonstrantie*—his handwriting is not so steady. It appears to show signs of nervous strain and the deterioration of health that was to come. Again according to Dutch law this summary, as well as the individual ones preceding, was required of a Public Prosecutor;[4] an office filled in this case by Pelsaert.

After the large sheaf of papers covering the trials of the principal criminals, Pelsaert continues with his daily notes, beginning with a further addition on 28th September regarding a new request made by Jeronimus, and including, on 2nd October, details of the executions on Seals Island. From then until 13th November he continues with daily notes of salvaging operations. He next makes a long entry recording the decision of the *Sardam's* council that nothing further is to be gained by remaining at the Abrolhos, wherefore they have decided to sail. He also notes here the

[4] Sir William Wilson Hunter, *A History of British India*, vol. i, p. 399.

decision to maroon Wouter Loos and Jan Pelgrom de Bye, and records sentences passed on some of the "less guilty" (including Salomon Deschamps); all these are signed by the council, now aboard the *Sardam* ready to sail. But at this point Pelsaert inserts the evidence given at the trial of Wouter Loos on the island on 24th September as well as the sentence itself, (which was passed on the yacht), together with a copy of the letter of Instructions to be given to Loos and de Bye before they were marooned on the Southland. The record of de Bye's trial, however, is listed before this, along with those of the major criminals: he had been reprieved from hanging on account of his youth. More evidence given at the lesser trials follows the letter of Instructions. At last, on 15th November, the *Sardam* sails. Under this date the weary Commandeur takes time to write a long report on the Abrolhos Islands, and to set down what has now become his well-known historical description of the "cats" or wallabies—the "miraculous" pouched animals of the Southland.

From then on until 2nd December the daily record continues. Immediately after that date Pelsaert inserts the record of yet more trials, held at the special request of the men concerned, as well as that of the ship's company. The sentences imposed are also listed. Whether these were ever carried out during the voyage, is not mentioned by Pelsaert, although the letter of Gijsbert Bastiaensz states that some were. On 3rd December they sighted the Princen Islands and Java Head. The last three entries describe their joy. The record ceases as they enter the Straits of Sunda. The "Declaration in Short", presumably written during the homeward voyage, completes the *Sardam* Journal.

The decision Pelsaert was forced to take as to whether the worst criminals should be tried and possibly punished cannot have been easy for him. It is clear that he and the *Sardam* council "searched their hearts" considerably. It is unlikely that he had ever been obliged to take severe disciplinary measures at Agra, but at the Abrolhos he found himself chairman of a council faced with an unprecedented and horrifying record of crimes, not only against the Company but, as he himself writes, "against humanity". It will be recalled that the crew of the *Sardam* numbered only twenty-six, a skeleton crew because of the many people they hoped to bring back to Java. Also, half of those Pelsaert found alive at the islands had become mutineers and murderers. A considerable portion of the treasure of the wrecked *Batavia* would be carried aboard the *Sardam*, and could thus remain a temptation once the entire company was crowded together on the yacht. It was obviously impossible to keep under close guard all the followers of Jeronimus. At best only the most desperate could be confined; and even those amounted to a score. Also, it was the stated policy of the Company that known evil-doers should not be taken to Batavia.

The decision to examine, and if necessary to punish with death, was reluctantly taken. That Pelsaert's reluctance was real cannot be doubted. His attitude towards the corrupt Indian government that allowed peasants to starve; his scrupulously objective account of the burning of the Rajput widow that nonetheless sickened as much as it amazed him; the fact that he reprieved Jan Pelgrom de Bye from death at the last moment because he was but eighteen years of age and begged and wailed for his life; most of all the petitions of the remaining prisoners en route to Java, that they also should be tried by the *Sardam* council, all underline Pelsaert's humane attitude. The fact that some degree of torture was used during the trials was not only in accordance with Dutch law of the time, but in some cases a necessity under the law. One of the chief interests of the trial documents is that they show how earnestly Pelsaert endeavoured to conduct proceedings with the utmost formality and legal punctiliousness.

Apart from Coen's Order and his own methodical inclination as shown in the *Remonstrantie*, a third factor may well have entered his mind. It is impossible that, while he was in Amsterdam, he should not have heard about (and probably discussed) the English claims made against the judges (V.O.C. officials like himself) at the Amboina Trials in 1623. In 1627-8 envoys and dispatches were being hotly exchanged, the English demanding recompense for what they called "the massacre of Amboina". Moreland writes that the term is misleading:

> The English merchants, who were resident in the Dutch fort under the agreement of 1619, were charged with conspiracy to seize it; they were convicted on confessions obtained by torture, and most of them were executed. The Dutch admitted that the proceedings were in some respects irregular, and the "massacre" may be regarded either as a judicial murder or a tragic failure of justice according to the view formed of the intentions of the judges.[5]

Coen was absent in the Netherlands when this unfortunate episode occurred but there is reason to believe that the officials concerned were over-zealously interpreting his wishes, expressed before leaving Java, to gain absolute monopoly of the Spice Islands. The uproar and opprobrium that followed cannot have pleased Coen. Ruthless as he was, even he expressed horror at the action of the

[5] W. H. Moreland, *From Akbar to Aurangzeb*, p. 23, footnote.

Susuhunan of Mataram when that prince slew 800 of his own troops because they failed to dam the river in order to cut the water-supply to Batavia during the seige, and so force the city to surrender. In fact, stupidity was more displeasing to Coen than cruelty. In both the instances cited, lack of vision would, to him, constitute the greater offence. With this knowledge in mind, faced at the Abrolhos with the aftermath of a true massacre, "without any real hunger or need of thirst but solely out of bloodthirstiness",[6] and with none but seamen on his council to assist in the difficult decision, Pelsaert must have felt grievously concerned as to which was the better procedure: to carry the murderers back to Batavia, or to try them then and there.

Under its Charter of 1602 the V.O.C. was empowered to appoint public prosecutors in its fortresses beyond the Cape of Good Hope. Later in 1617 the ordinances for the Governor-General at Batavia authorized him not only to effect all civilian and criminal sentences, but also to delegate this function to the subordinate councils and proper officers of settlements at which the Governor-General and Council could not be present.[7] This power of on-the-spot decision was formally delegated by Coen to Pelsaert in the concluding sentences of his Order[8] for the rescue voyage of the *Sardam*, thus reinforcing by personal emphasis an authority already held *ex officio*. Pelsaert's decision to try and, if necessary, to torture and execute the criminals was entirely legal.

At the Abrolhos Islands he found himself called on to try men not only for murder, but also for conspiracy and what amounted to treason: the association of the V.O.C. and the States General was not only fully documented, it had become all but mystical.[9] The general law of Europe prescribed torture as a proper and almost necessary means for arriving at the truth. Dutch jurisprudence went farther: in cases of conspiracy and treason, a public prosecutor could *demand sentence of death only on the confession of the accused*.

> The judges therefore, after satisfying themselves by independent proof of the guilt of the accused, had to obtain his confession: without torture if possible, by torture if not.[10]

[6] Pelsaert's Journals, 17th September 1629.
[7] Sir William Wilson Hunter, *op. cit.*, vol. i, pp. 416-17.
[8] See Appendix I.
[9] ". . . 'the Government of the Low Countries is so intermixed with Bewinthebbers that in a trial they will be both parties and judges'. *Court Minutes*, July 20, 1627." W. H. Moreland, *From Akbar to Aurangzeb*, p. 311, footnote.
[10] Sir William Wilson Hunter, *op. cit.*, vol. i, p. 418.

This explains repeated attempts to get the "straight truth" from the lips of Jeronimus Cornelisz, as well as various other repetitions in the course of the trials that to modern minds appear hardly necessary. There were, however, Dutch ordinances providing safeguards against abuse of this method. There had to be a reasonable presumption of guilt before torture was resorted to; the Dutch law also recognized that there could be a miscarriage of justice arising out of confessions thus wrung forth, so that the use of torture had to be noted in the minutes of proceedings and the various witnesses confronted with each other after torture, and themselves brought also to free (i.e., unbound) confessions of guilt not less than twenty-four hours after the cessation of torture.[11] These requirements were all carried out at the Abrolhos trials, and it is Pelsaert's fulfilment of them that gives the Journals much of their significance. Unlike the fiscal or legal officials at Amboina, who kept an irregular and incomplete record of their notorious action, Francisco Pelsaert made every effort to set down all that went forward.

Regarding the type of torture applied, the *Ongeluckige Voyagie* illustration already mentioned shows the rack and other methods then in use. It is quite certain that no rack would be carried on the *Sardam*. Authorized ships' punishments of the time were keelhauling, dropping from the yard-arm, lashing, and confining with heavy irons. These were frequently employed. Swearing and blasphemy were savagely punished, under Calvinistic code, by lashing. Actual instruments of torture were not part of the V.O.C. ships' equipment; but very efficient means could be readily devised when need arose. The water torture, similar to that used at Amboina, was employed at the Abrolhos.

All that this method required was rope, canvas, and a can or two of fresh water. The accused was tied up, sometimes hoisted spreadeagled in a doorway or between posts, then the guards "bound a cloth about his neck and face so close that little or no water could go by. That done, they poured the water softly upon his head until the cloth [canvas] was full up to the mouth and nostrils."[12] Carried to extremes (which does not appear to have been necessary at the Abrolhos as the majority of the men "begged surcease" very soon) the result was horrible. The pouring continued until the body of the victim "was swollen twice or thrice as big as before, his cheeks like great bladders, and his eyes staring and strutting out beyond his forehead", as recounted by an eye-witness

[11] Ibid., pp. 416-20.
[12] Ibid., pp. 396-7.

of the period.[13] The historian notes that "it was the slow agony of bursting joined to the acute but long drawn out agony of suffocation".

To discover the reason for the chopping off of hands prior to execution has not been possible. It may have been a common practice; more probably it was associated with the crime of "picking and stealing" and was passed on Jeronimus and his followers in token of their seizure of the Company's goods. Pelsaert's entry covering the executions on 2nd October makes no mention of its being carried out. But the lopping of the right hand of Jeronimus (he was sentenced to lose both, the others the right only) is noted by Gijsbert Bastiaensz; and a pile of hands lies gruesomely in the foreground of the execution picture in the 1647 edition of *Ongeluckige Voyagie*.

There is likewise only the statement of Bastiaensz to show that the lesser sentences were carried out. The *Sardam* was a small ship; to be keel-hauled three times and given a hundred lashes before the mast possibly would not kill a man. But her masts would be tall; the unfortunate dropped from the yard-arm by a rope attached to arms pinioned behind his back, would stand as bad a chance of being maimed as when that punishment was inflicted on larger ships. If, as Bastiaensz writes, these sentences were carried out on the *Sardam*, it seems scarcely credible that the accused should be re-tried in Batavia, and the majority condemned to death. But whatever may have happened on that ship, they were certainly punished—or re-punished—in Batavia. Details of the executions were officially recorded.[14] Such ruthlessness makes it only too apparent why the prisoners returning to Java aboard the *Sardam* begged to be tried by the Commandeur and the ship's council: for one thing, they knew that Pelsaert had reprieved a youth at the gallows, even if he later marooned him. It would seem that the remaining prisoners thought, rightly, that a larger measure of "mixing grace with justice" could be expected from their Commandeur than from the Governor-General and his Council at Batavia.

Research has shown that the true character and stature of Francisco Pelsaert can only be assessed from his own record of the events in India and at the Abrolhos in which he played a part. For more than three centuries he has remained a dubious figure hovering in the shadowy fringes of Dutch and early Australian history, the existence of his writings scarcely known. There can

[13] Ibid., p. 397.
[14] See Appendix V.

surely be no other man of legendary repute for whom it is more apt to quote the words of the medieval poet Maurus,[15] offered to a friend on the completion of his book:

> The written word alone flouts destiny,
> Revives the past and gives the lie to Death.

---

[15] The Latin lyric is by Hrabanus Maurus (A.D. 776-856): "To Eigilus, on the book that he had written", from *Mediaeval Latin Lyrics*. A Translation by Helen Waddell (Penguin Classics), 1952, p. 119.

THE JOURNALS OF FRANCISCO PELSAERT

Officers, Crew and Others Aboard the *Batavia* who are Mentioned in the Journals
Diary of Events Following the Wreck of the *Batavia*, 1629
Text of the Journals

OFFICERS, CREW AND OTHERS ABOARD THE *BATAVIA* WHO ARE MENTIONED IN PELSAERT'S JOURNALS

Spellings of many of these names and place-names are varied in the Journals.

V.O.C. OFFICERS

Uppermerchant (and Commandeur)	Francisco Pelsaert
Undermerchant	Jeronimus Cornelisz
Senior Assistant	Salomon Deschamps
Assistants and Book Keepers	Gijsbert Bastiaensz, Predikant's son
	Daniel Cornelisz
	Hendrick Denys
	Isbrant Isbrantsz
	Cornelis Jansz
	Andries de Vries
	Davidt Zevanck
Predikant	Gijsbert Bastiaensz
Provost (Officer of Law)	Pieter Jansz

SHIP'S OFFICERS, N.C.O.s AND CREW

Skipper	Ariaen Jacobsz
Uppersteersman	Claas Gerritsz
Understeersmen	Gillis Fransz, Halffwaack
	Jacop Jansz, Hollert
High Boatswain	Jan Evertsz
Constable or Chief Gunnery Officer	Unnamed
Upper Barber	Mr Frans Jansz
Under Barber	Aris Jansz
Chief Steward (Butler)	Reyndert Hendricxsz
Butler's Mate	Lucas Gerritsz
Cook	Unnamed
Cabin Servants	Rogier Decker
	Jan Pelgrom de Bye
Quartermaster	Harman Nannings
Boatswain	Pauls Barentsz

Bos'n's Mate	Relative of Skipper, unnamed
Blacksmith	Gillis Phillipsz
Locksmith	Rutger Fredricxsz
Upper Cooper	Jan Willems Selyns
Coopers	Jacob Jacopsz
	Cornelis Aldersz, a youth
Gardener	Jan Gerritsz
Tailor	Jacop de Vos
Sailors	Pieter Arentsz
	Jan Cornelis
	Gerrit Haas
	Bessel Jansz
	Cornelis Jansz (*Boontje* or "Little Bean")
	Jeurian Jansz
	Obbe Jansz
	Pieter Lambertsz
	Wagenaars I
	Wagenaars II
	Thomas Wensel
	Gerrit Willemsz
	Nicklaas Winckelhaack
Carpenters	Hendrick Claasz
	Warner Dircxsz
	Jan Egbertsz
	Hendricks Jacop ⎫ Same man?
	Jacop Hendricks ⎭
	Hans Jacobs, joiner
	Hendrick Jansz
	Teunis Jansz
	Egbert Roelofsz
	Stoffel Stoffelsz
Ship's Boys	Cornelis Arentsz
	Andries de Bruyn
	Fran Fransz
	Abraham Gerritsz
	Claas Harmansz of Campen
	Smoert
	Unspecified number (15 or more) killed on Seals Island
	Several killed on *Batavia's* Graveyard
Gunners	Jan Carstensz
	Cornelis Dircxsz
	Jan Dircxsz
	Arian Ariaanz

Gunners	Passchier van den Ende
	Hans (?) (on deck at time of wreck)
	Abraham Hendricks
	Jan Hendricx of The Hague
	Abraham Jansz
	Allert Jansz of Assendelft
	Jan Jansz Purmer
	Ariaen Theuwissen
	Ryckert Woutersz
Schotsman	Wouter Joel
Chief Trumpeter	Claas Jansz of Dortrecht
Upper Trumpeter	Jacop Groenewaldt
Under Trumpeter	Cornelis Pietersz ("Fat")

CADETS

(*Adelborsten*: naval cadets, Military Ensigns or Company appointees)	Daniel Cornelisz
	Lucas Gellisz
	Johan (Hans) Jacobsz Heylwech
	Allert Jansz of Elsen
	Coenraat van Huyssen
	Andries Liebent
	Lenart Michielsz van Os
	Hans Radder
	Otto Smit
	Gysbert van Welderen
	Olivier van Welderen

SOLDIERS

Corporal	Gabriel Jacopsz
Lance-Corporal	Jacop Pietersz (*Cosijn*, or "Window-frame")
Soldiers	Mattys Beer
	Teunis Claasz
	Hendrick Jaspersz (*Cloet*, or "Clumsy Fellow")
	Hans Fredericxsz
	Dirck Gerritsz
	Hans Hardens
	Wiebbe Hayes
	Claas Harmansz of Maagdenborgh
	Cornelis Helmigs
	Jan Hendricxsz of Bremen
	Hendrick ("Squinting"). May be Abraham (gunner).

110 VOYAGE TO DISASTER

French Soldiers
Hendrick Jansz (*Maftken* or "Zany")
Andries Jonas van Luyck
Wouter Loos
Jan Michielsz ("Deaf")
Cornelis Pietersz of Utrecht
Jan Pinten (English)
Cristoffel Quist
Marcus Symonsz
Jacques Pilman
Jean Boniver
Eduward Coo
Jean Coos de Sally
Jean Reynouw
Jean Thiriou
Thomas de Villiers
Jean Hongaar

WOMEN AND CHILDREN

Maria Schepens	Wife to Gijsbert Bastiaensz, Predikant
Judith Bastiaens	His eldest daughter
Willemyntgie	His middle daughter
Unnamed girl	His youngest daughter
Roelant	His infant son
Two unnamed boys	Sons to Predikant
Wybrecht Claasz	Maid to Predikant's family
Lucretia Jansz	Wife (later widow) to Boudewijn van der Mijlen, Undermerchant
Zwaantie Hendrix	Maid to Lucretia Jansz
Vrouw Pieter Jansz	Wife to Pieter Jansz, Provost
Unnamed child	Child of above
Claudine Patoys and her child (unnamed)	
Vrouw Harmansz	Wife to Claas Harmansz, soldier
Anneken Hardens	Wife to Hans Hardens, soldier
Hilletje Hardens, aged six	Child of Anneken and Hans Hardens
Laurentia Thomasz	Wife to Gabriel Jacopsz, corporal
Gertje Willemsz	Widow
Anneken Jansz, known as "Gunner's" (*Bosschieters*)	Wife to Jan Carstensz, gunner

Janneken Gist	Wife to Jan Hendricx, gunner
Mayken Soers	
Tryntgien Fredricxs	Wife to Claas Jansz, Chief Trumpeter
Sussie Fredricxs	Sister to Tryntigien
Marretgie Louys	
Mayken Cardoes and her infant (unnamed)	
Three children mentioned at Seals Island*	

* These three children bring the number up to 30, as mentioned by Antonio van Diemen in his letter regarding the wreck, dated 30th November 1629. See page 42.

DIARY OF EVENTS FOLLOWING THE WRECK OF THE SHIP *BATAVIA*, 1629

THE detailed sequence of events is not clearly set out in the Journals; especially is this so in regard to the crimes committed at the Abrolhos Islands during Pelsaert's absence. What happened, and when, is only slowly revealed in evidence given at the trials by many witnesses. This Diary has been compiled to give a picture of the affair as a whole, with the dates of all the main events shown in relation to each other as well as in order of sequence, in the hope that it will be a useful guide to the Journals. Two significant events before the wreck were that on 13th May, Pelsaert, who had been ill, reappeared on deck; and that on 14th May an assault, to spring a mutiny, was made on Lucretia Jansz.

1629

4 June Monday morning, second day of Whitsuntide (Gregorian Calendar). Ship struck at 2 hrs before daybreak, in watch of skipper. Mainmast cut. Ship burst at 10 hrs. Before that, skipper returned from inspecting two islands. Boat did 3 trips to land 180 people on one island. Skipper reports disobedience over drinking water. Pelsaert goes ashore; weather prevents return to ship. Remains on smaller island. On board, rioting starts. Pelsaert's chest looted, all papers thrown over.

5 June Some people with Pelsaert on smaller isle, landed on larger. Pelsaert and skipper try to reach wreck but fail; 70 men still aboard. In evening skipper Ariaen Jacobsz informs Pelsaert he means to leave in search of water. Pelsaert protests. On board, drinking and rioting continue.

6 June Jacobsz leaves, with Pelsaert. He takes also Zwaantie, and another woman, with baby. They sail past two separate larger islands, but find only brackish water in rock pools.

7 June Remain on largest island to heighten gunwhale of boat. At nightfall joined by Gillis Fransz, understeersman, and 10 more men, arriving in yawl, also in search of water. Wells dug in sand. No water.

8 June Sail in morning for mainland, taking yawl and men from it. At noon, lat. 28° 13′, and shortly after see mainland. Wind high. Ran seawards after 3 hrs, but set course back at midnight.

9 June	In morning still some distance from coast. Approach small inlet and decide to land, but surf too high. Wind, some rain. At Abrolhos, much rain at night; drinking water collected, but relief too late for many.
10 June	Sunday. Sailed north with hard winds. Obliged to cut yawl adrift. Much rain; also at Abrolhos.
11 June	Calmer weather for boat.
12 June	Pelsaert considers the continent "a dry cursed earth". Still not possible to land. At Abrolhos, Jeronimus Cornelisz comes ashore on a mast. (Pelsaert states "after 8 days" in his summary; Jeronimus says 10 in his evidence.) He discovers the mutiny plot has been disclosed by Woutersz, but does not disclose his own hand, continuing to act "subtly and gradually" for 20 days.
13 June	Boat at latitude 25° 40′ at noon.
14 June	Those in boat see blacks, after 6 men swim ashore in vain search for water.
15 June	At 23° reef opening found by boat, and small supply of water discovered ashore in rock-holes. Resolve to sail for Java, having given up hope of finding sufficient water. At Abrolhos, during following days, Jeronimus orders some to seek water on neighbouring isles, using rafts. These return without success, but are ordered to remain silent, and others are sent (presumably in expectation that they will perish); yet others go voluntarily, in order to see if there really is no water on the larger isles. (See letter of Predikant, Appendix IV.) About 45 men, women and children are also transported from *Batavia's* Graveyard to Seals Island
25 June	Pelsaert and crew sight floating seaweed in lat. 11° 30′.
27 June	They sight Java towards evening; anchor all night.
28 June	They land, find a waterfall, and praise God.
29 June	2nd quarter of moon. By evening they are about 3 miles from Java Head.
30 June	Sail between Princen Islands; but becalmed in Sunda Straits.
1 July	Sunday. Becalmed. In afternoon manage to pass Thwartway Island.
2 July	Lie becalmed by Topper's Hat Island. At sunset see a sail astern.

3 July   Daybreak discloses 3 ships. Pelsaert boards nearest, which turns out to be yacht *Sardam*. Learns Heer Raemburch, Councillor of India, is on largest vessel, and immediately seeks him.
At Abrolhos mutiny gathers to a head. First murders ordered. Some evidence gives this as date of first murders, but in his Summary Pelsaert places them on 4th July; in fact, mutiny appears to have begun on night of 3rd. Andries Liebent is spared.

4 July   Pelsaert sails on to Batavia in large vessel with Raemburch.
At Abrolhos, a soldier taps keg of wine and gets drunk. Jeronimus says he and his companion must be drowned at once in punishment. Island "Council" objects to second condemnation. Jeronimus bursts out in rage. Two carpenters killed.

5 July   At Abrolhos, Jeronimus dismisses elected "Council" and appoints his own: Coenraat van Huyssen, Davidt Zevanck and Jacop Pietersz Cosijn. Huyssen and Zevanck, with 5 others, during the night, secretly, have taken 4 men on a raft to Traitors Island and drowned them. Andries de Vries is spared.

7 July   Pelsaert arrives at Batavia at dusk. "God be thanked and praised."

8 July   Sunday. At Batavia, Pelsaert interviews Governor-General, Jan Pieterszoon Coen.
At Abrolhos, Jeronimus invites Hans Hardens, soldier, and his wife Anneken to supper in his tent, while their little girl is murdered by Jan Hendricxsz.

9 July   At Batavia, Governor in Council decides to send Pelsaert to rescue the castaways, with yacht *Sardam*.
At Abrolhos, Jeronimus sends his 3 "Councillors" with others to kill Provost, his wife and child, other women and 9 men who have been put on Traitors Island. Murderers now have a small boat; they overtake victims, who, having grown suspicious, are escaping to the "High Island" on raft. All are killed. Smoke signals have now been seen on the High Island, showing that water has been found; but are disregarded.

10 July   At Batavia, High Boatswain of *Batavia* is hanged for his part in assault on Lucretia Jansz.
At Abrolhos, Jeronimus and his council force de Vries to cut throats of sick, at night. Other secret murders.

12 July	At Abrolhos, murder of Passchier van den Ende and others, called at night from their tents. (Also given as on 10th.) First pact between mutineers is drawn up and signed.
13 July	At Batavia, skipper, Jacobsz, arrested for negligence in wrecking the ship *Batavia*. At Abrolhos, de Vries forced to murder remaining sick.
14 July	At Abrolhos, de Vries seen talking to Lucretia, which was forbidden him. Reported to Jeronimus, who orders him to be killed. He is chased into sea and killed by Lenert Michielsz, at noon, in public. First open murder. More at night.
15 July	Sunday. At Batavia, Governor-General hands his order to Pelsaert to sail on morrow. But Pelsaert sails with *Sardam* before noon. They sight and speak to several V.O.C. ships. At Abrolhos, Jeronimus sends his councillors with others to kill some people already sent by him to Seals Island. 18 men and ship's boys are killed. Some escape; women are spared.
16 July	*Sardam* nears Princen Islands. At Abrolhos, a second pact is drawn up and signed by 26 men, including Jeronimus.
17 July	*Sardam* leaves islands in her wake and steers S. by W. At Abrolhos, murder of cabin boy Andries de Bruyn.
18 July	At Abrolhos, women and boys remaining alive on Seals Island are killed—15 or more. Three boys escape in the bushes.
19 July	At Abrolhos, English soldier, Jan Pinten, murdered.
20 July	At Abrolhos, Deschamps is forced to strangle an infant, already half-poisoned by Jeronimus.
21 July	At Abrolhos, Predikant and daughter Judith invited to sup with Jeronimus and van Huyssen in latter's tent; meanwhile rest of their family is murdered. Aris Jansz, underbarber, escapes in skiff to the High Island.
22 July	Sunday. At Abrolhos, Jan Hendricxsz kills assistant Denys at night.
23 July	At Abrolhos, Daniel Cornelissen sent by Jeronimus to High Island with a letter to some French soldiers there, hoping to win them over. Daniel is, however, kept prisoner there.

24 July At Abrolhos, murder of 2 of boys remaining on Seals Island; third is obliged to help on pain of death.
25 July At Abrolhos, boy Rogier Decker stabs carpenter Hendrick Jansz, after being given wine and a dagger by Jeronimus. Two others drowned.
27 July At Abrolhos, probably the day on which Zevanck and others made first attack on men gathered at the High Island under leadership of soldier Wiebbe Hayes; without success.
28 July At Abrolhos, Anneken Hardens strangled. (Given as 30th also.)
5 Aug. Sunday. *Sardam* still battling with head winds; at noon, latitude 24° 45′, long. 130° 8′ (Ile de Ferro).
At Abrolhos, Jeronimus visits those on island of Wiebbe Hayes, leaving Zevanck and others to kill Mr Frans Jansz, upperbarber, on the other High Island.
6 Aug. At Abrolhos, Jan Hendricxsz publicly stabs Stoffelsz to death on order of Jeronimus, who openly watches. About this time, plans for seizing the first-coming rescue yacht begin to be discussed.
10 Aug. At Abrolhos, Hendrick Jansz, walking with Deschamps, is stabbed by Rogier Decker. (This is also given as happening on earlier date.)
16 Aug. At Abrolhos, Cornelis Aldersz, boy, decapitated at noon by Mattys Beer, the boy being first blindfolded by Jeronimus on pretext of a joke.
20 Aug. At Abrolhos, Jeronimus declares himself Captain General, and requires all to take an oath of allegiance to him. This document is signed by 36 men, including the Predikant, but not by Jeronimus.
22 Aug. *Sardam* reaches lat. 29° 19′ and, running on a N.E. course, is estimated by the steersmen to be 15 (45) miles from the wreck.
25 Aug. *Sardam* crew think they see surf and islands, but discover it is only reflection of sun.
28 Aug. *Sardam* at noon, lat. 28° 45′. Expecting shortly to see land.
At Amsterdam, Pelsaert is appointed to Council of India.
1 Sept. *Sardam* on lat. 29° 16′ at noon.
At Abrolhos, Jeronimus and followers visit island of Wiebbe Hayes and try to win them over. He agrees to

bring them wine and clothes if they will hand over the small boat. The Predikant remains behind as go-between.

2 Sept. *Sunday.* At Abrolhos, Jeronimus returns with wine, etc., and leaving most of his followers on a small islet crosses to other with van Huyssen, Zevanck, and three others. They are attacked and captured, except Pietersz who escapes in their skiff. Jeronimus is kept prisoner, but the the other four are immediately killed, as it appears the others mean to attack. Instead, they postpone attack, but elect Wouter Loos, a soldier, as their leader in place of Jeronimus.

3 Sept. *Sardam's* company at last see main Southland.

8 Sept. *Sardam* still beating about trying to sail in to islands on lat. 28° 20', where they believe wreck to lie. At noon, lat. 29° 7', course N.E. See surf in evening and obliged to bear seawards.
On *Batavia's* Graveyard, Wouter Loos demands oath of allegiance, which is duly signed by all mutineers.

13 Sept. On *Sardam*, Pelsaert resolves to risk sailing through passage below "extreme" shallow, or most northerly point of Abrolhos Islands, in order to approach from east. This manoeuvre is successfully accomplished, but stiff winds keep *Sardam* held up, to north.

16 Sept. *Sunday. Sardam* sails S.W., and towards evening Pelsaert sees land that he is convinced is the High Island.

17 Sept. Wouter Loos leads his men to attack Hayes, rescue Jeronimus and recover skiff. During the attack Hayes spies incoming *Sardam*. Leaps into small boat and rows round north point of High Island to warn whoever may be aboard. Pelsaert meanwhile lands on nearest High Island, and is surprised to find no one. Hayes arrives. Pelsaert returns hastily to *Sardam*. A boatload of mutineers rows up; they are eventually persuaded to come aboard *Sardam*, where they are captured and bound. Examination of mutineers begins at once. In evening Hayes brings Jeronimus and Predikant aboard, the latter well bound.

18 Sept. Before daylight Pelsaert, *Sardam's* skipper, and some crew go with boat and yawl to Wiebbe Hayes's island, and take him aboard with 10 armed soldiers. They sail to *Batavia's* Graveyard and quickly overpower rest of mutineers. Jewels found. In afternoon Pelsaert goes to wreck. Later orders all mutineers to be taken to Seals

	Island for security, whence they can be fetched for examination when needed.
19 Sept.	Prisoners on *Sardam* brought to *Batavia's* Graveyard for examination, which continues all day.
20 Sept.	Examinations continued; Pelsaert sends yawl to Wiebbe Hayes's island to fetch water. Two women go on this trip, and are later reported to have indulged in loose behaviour. At Batavia, Governor-General Jan Pieterszoon Coen dies.
21 Sept.	Examinations continue at Abrolhos. Cannot go to wreck, nor can yawl return, because of bad weather.
22 Sept.	At Abrolhos, reach wreck, but surf too heavy for swimmers; yawl returns. At Batavia, funeral of J. P. Coen.
23 Sept.	Sunday. Prisoners brought from Seals Island for examination. Steersman sent with divers to wreck, but work impossible.
24 Sept.	Skipper sent with boat to wreck, no work possible. Examinations continue. At Batavia, Jacques Specx elected provisional Governor-General.
25 Sept.	At Abrolhos, skipper with yawl crew raise 2 chests. Pelsaert goes in skiff to wreck. In all, 4 chests salvaged. In afternoon, examinations.
26 Sept.	Too rough in morning for salvage. Boat sent to search islands for wreckage. Yawl for water, with orders to bring back Aris Jansz as witness. Calm afternoon, 3 more chests raised. One left because of cannon and anchor on top.
27 Sept.	Wind fresh. Examinations. Yawl returns with witnesses.
28 Sept.	Wind still fresh. *Sardam* council, on *Batavia's* Graveyard, considers all evidence. Condemns Jeronimus Cornelisz and 7 others to death. Public reading of examinations and sentences in afternoon. Execution fixed for 1st Oct. Jeronimus begs postponement in order that he may repent and be baptised.
29 Sept.	On *Batavia's* Graveyard Jeronimus passes two letters to one of the understeersmen, in which he asserts his innocence to friends in Holland, and declares himself wrongly condemned. He is again threatened with torture. Confesses he was only trying to prolong his life, and that he was in truth guilty. At night he tries to commit suicide.

30 Sept.	Sunday. Pelsaert orders prisoners to be fetched to hear sermon. Jeronimus refuses to come.
1 Oct.	High wind and showers. Impossible to take condemned to be hanged on Seals Island.
2 Oct.	Eight condemned taken to Seals Island. Men request that Jeronimus be hanged first, so that they may see him die. At last moment Pelsaert reprieves Jan Pelgrom de Bye on account of his youth. Same day Wouter Loos is re-tried because of statement made by Predikant's daughter, but he is sentenced to be marooned along with Jan Pelgrom.
3 Oct.	High Wind. No work possible on wreck. At Batavia, the Susuhunan of Mataram lifts his siege.
10 Oct.	At Abrolhos, bad weather has prevented work at wreck for a week. Pelsaert sends men to burn off on the High Island under which *Sardam* lies anchored, to get more wallabies and to see if more water can be found, as caverns on Wiebbe Hayes's island have grown brackish. Water found.
11 Oct.	Water kegs filled and taken aboard *Sardam*. Men fishing in skiff find barrel of vinegar.
12 Oct.	Pelsaert sends skipper with boat to fetch vinegar and anything else to be found, warning him to take care and stay out all night if necessary. At wreck, divers raise loose coin, but not chest.
13 Oct.	Pelsaert awaits skipper with boat to try again for chest.
14 Oct.	Sunday. Hard storm.
15 Oct.	Still blowing.
16 Oct.	Beautiful weather. Pelsaert visits wreck, but surf too high for divers. At noon, sends skiff to *Sardam* ordering high boatswain to man yawl, provision it, and set out to search for skipper and crew lost in boat.
17 Oct.	Pelsaert sees yawl leave *Sardam*.
18 Oct.	Uppersteersman arrives in yawl at *Batavia's* Graveyard, having returned to *Sardam* previous night without finding any trace of skipper, but had seen large island N.N.W. of ship; says he had also seen boat being blown away in storm on evening of 13th Oct. Pelsaert orders yawl to be strengthened, and to continue search for skipper.
18 Oct.	Pelsaert sees yawl leave *Sardam* about noon.
20 Oct.	Stiff wind. Skiff unable to bring ordered food and water from *Sardam* to *Batavia's* Graveyard.

21 Oct. Sunday. As before. No food on island.
22 Oct. As before.
23 Oct. Calm weather; but skiff does not come until sunset.
24 Oct. Pelsaert sees yawl return to *Sardam* at noon. In afternoon reaches *Batavia's* Graveyard with general news, but no word of skipper.
27 Oct. Yawl comes with uppersteersman and high boatswain from *Sardam* before noon to continue examinations of more prisoners on *Batavia's* Graveyard. Yawl sent back to *Sardam*. About noon water extremely low round wreck so signal yawl with smokes to return. Meantime try to raise another chest with skiff and fail. Yawl returns too late.
28 Oct. Sunday. Bad weather.
4 Nov. Sunday. Wind S.S.E., very clear weather; see smoke columns N.N.E. of Abrolhos. Pelsaert hopes may be skipper on main Southland.
5 Nov. Divers raise another chest, etc.
9 Nov. Work at wreck impossible, but 4 money chests sent aboard *Sardam*.
10 Nov. Pelsaert himself boards *Sardam*, taking 3 more money chests.
11 Nov. Sunday. Day spent getting water for *Sardam*.
12 Nov. Divers sent once more to wreck; return with silver dishes and a carpenter's chest, but say any further endeavours useless. Examinations of more prisoners continued on *Sardam*.
13 Nov. Beautiful weather. Council decides to sail for Batavia on 15th.
15 Nov. *Sardam* sets sail, heading first for Southland in search of skipper. Pelsaert writes his historic account of island wallabies, or tammars. At noon sight mainland but see no sign of skipper.
16 Nov. See a small inlet, also smoke signals. Landing party find fresh water and signs of blacks but no white men. Pelsaert maroons the two condemned. In afternoon it is decided to sail for Batavia, as there appears to be no hope of finding skipper. Set course W.N.W.
22 Nov. Change course to N. and N.E. in order to "get in view" the Cocos Islands.

26 Nov. At noon lat. 12° 3'; have passed Cocos Islands without seeing them.
30 Nov. Fine weather. Examinations and sentences of remaining prisoners, who have begged to be tried aboard by ship's council.
3 Dec. Princen Islands sighted.
5 Dec. *Sardam* arrives in Batavia Roads.
10. Dec. Antonie van Diemen writes to Pieter Carpentier re mutiny.
12 Dec. Pelsaert writes to V.O.C. Directors at Amsterdam.

1630
28 Jan. Governor-General Specx and Council of India condemn remaining mutineers at Batavia. Executions set for 31st.
Sept. 1630. Pelsaert dies, having first gone on an expedition to Jambi. Lucretia Jansz remarries.

THE JOURNALS

[Pelsaert's original MS., hand-written in Gothic script in Old Dutch, obviously cannot be reproduced in facsimile here. But in order to preserve the flavour of the times and his own method of presentation, the original form has been retained as far as possible, as well as Pelsaert's inconsistencies and occasional omissions; where the Journals leave a blank space for omissions, a blank is left here.]

SAD daily notes of the loss of our Ship *Batavia*, being sailed off on to the Abrolhos or Rocks [*Clippen*] of Frederick Houtman, situated on the Latitude of $28\frac{1}{3}$ degrees, 9 Miles[1] from Southland on the —

FOURTH OF JUNE, being Monday morning, on the 2 day of Whitsuntide, with a clear full moon[2] about 2 hours before daybreak during the watch of the skipper [Ariaen Jacobsz], I was lying in my bunk feeling ill and felt suddenly, with a rough terrible movement, the bumping of the ship's rudder, and immediately after that I felt the ship held up in her course against the rocks, so that I fell out of my bunk. Whereon I ran up and discovered that all the sails were in Top, the wind South west, that during the night the course had been north east by North, and that lay right in the middle of a thick spray. Round the ship there was only a little surf, but shortly after that heard the Sea breaking hard round

[1] In his *Remonstrantie* Pelsaert uses *mijlen* or *mylen* in all land measurements. No reason to believe that here, three years later, he uses it to specify any other distance than the one he meant there, for which Moreland gives the note: "The Holland mile was nearly three English miles." (*Jahangir's India*, p. 2, note 2.) Cf. distance meant by mile in Coen's Order (Appendix I, footnote 1). Also cf. Pelsaert's own use of *mijle* and minute in the instructions to the two men sentenced to be marooned (p. 230, note 135). If Moreland's assessment is accepted, the positions given by Pelsaert generally prove to be more correct than if reckoned by the Snellius mile, which equals approximately 3·85 British nautical miles.

[2] Continental countries were using the Gregorian Calendar. In early June, sunrise at Geraldton, Western Australia, is at 7.10 a.m. approximately. Allowing 55 minutes for nautical twilight, one can assume that the *Batavia* struck about 4 a.m. The precise moment of Full Moon (Greenwich Mean Time) on 6th June 1629 has been estimated as 11 p.m., which, allowing for the eight-hour delay between Amsterdam and Geraldton, is approximately two days after the actual time of wrecking. Thus Pelsaert was referring to a condition of bright moonlight, not to a full moon.

about. I said, "Skipper, what have you done that through your reckless carelessness you have run this noose round our necks?" He answered, "How could I do better? I did not sleep, but watched out very well, for when I saw the spray in the Distance I asked Hans the gunner,[3] What can that be? Whereupon he said, Skipper, it is the shine of the Moon; upon which I trusted." I asked him, "What counsel now? Whereabout do you think we are?" He said, "God knows; this is a shallow that must be lying quite a distance from the unknown Land, and I think we are just on the tail of it. We must see now to putting out an anchor astern; perhaps it is low tide, so that it will be possible to wind it from it." I asked him how deep it was there. He answered that he did not know. I ordered the lead to be fetched, which was in the cabin of the steersman, and I found that astern there was only 17 to 18 feet of water, but at the forepart of the ship still less. At the moment, I did not know any better than that it was an unknown shallow in the Sea as the skipper said. ——— So we started to throw all our cannons overboard in order to make it lighter, and the yawl[4] with the boat was put out, and I ordered them to sound round about, and found at an arrow's shot[5] at the back of the Ship, 7 fathoms of Water. But forwards very dry; we made a kedge [*worp*] anchor ready, to put out at the stern. Meanwhile it began to blow harder with showers, and the boat was smitten overboard by a gush, so that it floated quickly away and we had to send the yawl to help it row up. But before it could be put aboard again, it had become daylight and we found ourselves then amongst rocks and shallows on every side, and very suddenly through the fall of the waters (for we had sailed there by high tide) it began to surf and foam around the ship, so that through the bumping of the ship, could not stand or walk. Therefore we decided to put overboard the main mast, in order that it would not immediately push into the ground.[6] But when it was cut down we found that it caused much damage, for we could not get it

[3] *Bosschieter*: a ship's gunner, sometimes carrying a musket. A term still used in the Dutch navy.

[4] *Schuijt* (*schuit*): boat; but as Pelsaert uses this term for the smaller of the two boats carried by the *Batavia* (they would normally lie athwartship, the larger one over the smaller, in the waist) and refers to the other as the *boot* (i.e., boat), yawl, a type of jolly-boat capable of carrying eight to ten persons, appears to be the best translation. The larger boat was capable of carrying forty or more.

[5] This can be taken to approximate 100 yards, as that was regarded as the distance at which great accuracy of aim could be expected, although targets could be hit at more than twice that distance.

[6] Either grind through the ship's bottom, or else the weight of it wedge the ship farther into the reef.

from aboard, so that we could not get the boat aboard through the big surf. —— I saw no Land that I thought would remain above at high water except an island that by guessing lay at least 3 miles from the ship; therefore I sent the skipper to 2 small islands or rocks not so far from the ship in order to see if the people and some of the goods could be saved there. —— About the 9th hour the skipper returned because it was nigh impossible to get there through the stones and rocks, for at one spot one could not get over with the yawl, whilst at another it would be several fathoms deep. He reported that the Islands would not be flooded so far as he could see. —— Because of the great Yammer [*sic*] that there was in the ship, of Women, Children, Sick, and poor-hearted men, we decided to put most of the people on land first and meanwhile to get ready on deck the money and the most precious goods, for which I did my utmost. But God the Lord chastised us with many rods for in spite of all the duty [*devoir*] we made to cant the ship to leeward or to land, it turned out exactly the opposite because of the uneven rocks upon which it was set, which so caused it that *the people*[7] could only come out of the ship very slowly. Secondly, the Ship had already burst at the 10 hour, and all speed and skill had to be used to get some bread [*broot*][8] out of the bread cabin. Of water we hoped to get enough but our goodwill and diligence were impeded by the godless unruly troops of soldiers, as well as crew, and their women [*consorten*] whom I could not keep in the hold on account of the liquor or wine, so that one could not get there [to the bread cabin] and in the meantime the entire hold started to float, so that hardly 1½ *leggers*[9] were filled with tankards [*kitten*] and buckets and lay ready on the deck of the ship. So that day went by and the boat had only done three trips with folks, with which we had put on land 180 Souls, 20 Casks of bread and some small barrels of water. —— About Sunset the skipper came aboard with the sloop [*sloep*],[10] which had taken to land a Casket of Jewels and some people, and said to me, "It won't help at all that we save water and bread, for everyone on land drinks as much as he can, and to forbid this has no result unless you order it otherwise." Whereupon on account of our water the which, as far as I could see, would be very little available, moreover there was such a great number of people that it had to be better used,

[7] This was underlined by Pelsaert, doubtless to stress the urgency of saving life, which was difficult enough without trying to save the cash.
[8] Hard bread like ship's biscuit, kept in casks.
[9] Measure containing about 120 Old English wine gallons, which would approximate to 100 Imperial gallons.
[10] Presumably the *schuijt* or yawl; there seems no evidence of a third boat, and a few lines farther on Pelsaert reverts to *schuijt*.

I jumped into the yawl, with the intention of returning immediately in order to get the money from the ship with the next boat, according to our resolution.[11] But by God's Truth, I was scarcely from aboard than it began to blow so hard that it was outside human power to reach the ship with the boat. Yea, we could hardly prevent it from drifting away. In the morning before daylight, the 5th, we put some folks, with some bread and water, on the largest of the islets,[12] for we had been separated in the night into 2 parties, and I sailed from there in the sloop and the skipper in the boat, to go aboard; where I arrived at last about noon after much rowing, and the boat could not sail up against the wind because it had no sweep oars, and I went back to the island. Also, on account of the big surf, for the waves broke over the poop, I could not come by the ship with the sloop. I remained a long time in the vicinity of the ship to wait for an opportunity for me to get aboard, but in vain. At last there was a carpenter Jan Egbertsz of Amsterdam, who was bold enough to come to the sloop through the surf, whom the under Merchant Jeronimus Cornelisz, with at least another 70 Men who were on the ship, sent with the request to help them, for there was for them no longer any safe place on the ship. How great a grief it was to me all reasonable people can imagine; I asked if there were no means of getting 5 or 6 planks or pieces to make sweeps for the boat. Secondly, that they should make one or two rafts to save themselves, and with the first boat that could come aboard [alongside] I would get the money. Whereupon the before mentioned Jan Egbertsz swam again aboard and they immediately threw six planks overboard, which we got. Whereupon with great regret I returned to the island, where I found the carpenter very busy making a sweep out of a piece of topmast which had floated to land. In the afternoon it started to blow very hard out of the North-west and the ship was pounded very much that day by the waves, so that one could hardly see it and it was a miracle that it remained together. In the evening we calculated our water which we had in the small barrels and we found ourselves, on the smallest islet where we were with the folks of the boat and the yawl, with about 80 *kannen*[13] of water, where we were about 40 people, and on the largest island, where there were 180 Souls, was still less.

[11] A reference to the decisions made by the ship's council; the word used is *resolutie*.
[12] As the Dutch language has no comparative, this means the larger of the two small islets previously mentioned.
[13] *Kan* (pl. *kannen*) is a measurement equivalent to 1 litre = $1\frac{3}{4}$ pints, approximately.

Thereupon the people murmured, asking why we did not go to the islands round about in search of water, for otherwise we could not help them, or they us, and we should perish in that way, all of us together; which was what the skipper told me, or otherwise it was apparent the folk would take the boat, towards which resolution I would not give my consent. I proposed that we should see the outcome of the weather and the ship. For to leave such a large group of fine people and the goods of the Company, I would be responsible before God and my High Authorities at Batavia. They protested very much against, and promised that on whatever land we should find water, be it on the islands or on the main Southland, they were willing to turn back in order to assist the other people with as many water trips as were found to be necessary. At last, after having discussed it very well and weighed up that there was no hope of getting water out of the ship unless the ship should fall to pieces and it [water in barrels] should so float to land, or that there should be a good daily rain with which we could quench our thirst (but as these were all very uncertain means), resolved after long debating, as appears out of the resolution,[14] that we should go in search of water on the islands most nearby or on the continent [*vaste landt*] to keep them and us alive, and if we could find no water, that we should then sail with the boat without delay to Batavia, with God's grace there to relate our sad, unheard of, disastrous happening. But first I requested the skipper that he should order some men to sail with me with the yawl to the other islet, to tell them first of all our intention. But he advised me not to go to the island, saying, "They will keep you there; and you will regret it; secondly, there is no one who will sail with you." I persisted that without going to the island I had no intention of sailing in search of water, but that it was better and more honest to die with them if we did not find it than to stay alive with deep grief of heart. At last I consented that the High Boatswain[15] with six men in the yawl, should put me off on the island on condition that if they saw I was kept there against my will, they were permitted to make off with the yawl. I took a barrel of Water with me to give to the people, but when they came near the shore they did not dare touch land, saying, "They will keep you and us, we will not come any nearer." And as they were thinking that I would jump overboard, the High

---

[14] This suggests some document drawn up and signed, later lost, as the one included was signed on 8th June. On the other hand, Pelsaert probably did not write this account until a few days later, and that may be the only resolution.

[15] Jan Evertsz of Monnikendam, later hanged at Batavia for his share in the assault on Lucretia Jansz.

Boatswain pulled me backwards, and they rowed away before the eyes of all the people; who had seen the foresaid, so that by God's Truth, I was prevented from my intention and returned back [to the smaller islet] at night.

On 6 ditto with the day, I wrote on a leaf of a table-book[16] that we were going with the boat to the islands round about or to the main Southland and would return as soon as possible, and put this under one of the bread barrels which we left there behind, and went off with the boat under sail.[17] Moreover, that day to two particular islands[18] on the largest of which we found some brackish water that was left by the rain in the holes of the rocks on the beach, but the sea water had already washed into most.

On 7 do. we remained here in order to build up our boat with planks, for we saw that otherwise it would not be possible to reach the continent. Against nightfall we saw the sloop, which I had left in the neighbourhood of the ship, come rowing; in it was Gillis Fransz Halffwaack,[19] with yet another 10 Men, also come in search of Water, but when, by the many wells we had dug, they saw there was none, they requested to be allowed to go with us to the continent, which I permitted. We took also the yawl [*schuijt*][20] with us in order that it would be better or easier for us to get through the surf in search for water. Also, another reason, there was no one who wanted to sail back with the yawl to the other island or to the Wreck.

On 8 do. in the morning we sailed from this island to the continent, after I had read to all people the resolution taken by us, and commanded them to take the oath, which they did, and as follows—

Since on all the Islands or Rocks here in the neighbourhood of our wrecked ship *Batavia*, do not find water to keep the saved people alive, for that reason the Commandeur has earnestly besought us and pro-

[16] A book consisting of some tables, or leaves, joined together for the purpose of taking notes.
[17] From the "smallest islet".
[18] East and West Wallabi; the latter is the larger, and later became "the island of Wiebbe Hayes". With the exception of North Island these are the only isles of any size or height in the whole archipelago. Fresh water, as described by Pelsaert later, is to be found on both; as also the wallabies which he also described later and to which the castaways gave the name of "cats".
[19] Understeersman on the *Batavia*. There were two of these officers; the other was Jacob Jansz. One of them was also brother-in-law to the skipper Ariaen Jacobsz, but which remains undisclosed. *Halffwaack* could be a nickname meaning "half awake", or possibly refer to his having "the wake" or the first half of the night watch.
[20] This establishes beyond doubt Pelsaert's use of this word or of *sloep* to denote the same small boat.

posed that we should sail to the continent in order to see if God will grant that we find water there, to assist the people with as many trips from there until we can estimate that [they] will be able to remain alive for some considerable time; and meanwhile command someone to bring our sad happenings to the Hon. Lord Gov. Gen., to which we the undersigned have consented now that the need has been placed before us of how greatly important it is to be responsible before God and Higher Authority—

Have decided and resolved to do our utmost duty [*devoir*] in order to help our poor companions in dire distress. In token of the truth have signed with our own hand and have sworn in the presence of all people this 8th June 1629.

Was signed

    Claas Jansz Dor [trecht]   *FranCo. pelsars*
    Claas Willemsz graaf   Ariaen Jacopsz
    Michiel Claasz   Claas Gerritsz
        Hans Jacobs joiner [*binder*]
        Jacob Jansz Hollert
        Jan Evertsz[21]

At noon had the latitude 28° 13 minutes; saw shortly thereafter the continent, and guessed to be 6 miles N. by W. of our ship;[22] the Wind West; had ground at 25 and 30 fathoms in the evening about 3 hours. In the night we again went away from the land, and after midnight we ran again towards it.

On 9 do. in the morning we were still about 3 miles from the coast, the wind mostly N.W. with some rain; this 24 hours, by guessing, covered 4 to 5 miles; held N. by W.; the coast here stretches mostly N. by W. and S. by E. It is a bad [*slecht*][23] Rocky land without trees, about as high as Dover in England. Here we saw a small Inlet as well as low dune land, where we intended to

[21] This is a *copy* of the original, as the signatures are all in Pelsaert's ordinary hand and his own name is written in Italian script as well as being spelt in an unusual form; the other names are written clearly and carefully: *graaf* is a Dutch word for the title *count*; but since there is no record of such a personage it is more probably a contraction of *graafijzer*, a pickaxe, or *graafwerk*, the act of digging, and denotes the man's trade, as Hans Jacobs is shown to be a joiner. The division of names shows those on the left were not members of the ship's council, as those on the right are. In order of signing, their ranks are: Commandeur, skipper, uppersteersman, joiner (or carpenter) (replacing another merchant officer), understeersman, high boatswain. Of these men the uppersteersman Gerritsz and the understeersman J. Jansz later returned with Pelsaert in the *Sardam*. The three on the left appear to be extra witnesses to general willingness.

[22] The wrecked *Batavia*, in my opinion; but Pelsaert is ambiguous; see page 294.

[23] Pelsaert uses *slecht* later to mean level, as well as bad, and could mean level here. The adjective means bad, mean, ill, plain, silly, etc. The verb *slechten* means to level, raze, demolish, decide, etc.

land, but approaching, noticed that there was a big surf and many breakers near the shore; very suddenly the swell out of the West became so heavy and ran so high against the coast that we could not readily keep off it, and the wind increased more and more.

On 10 do. we kept hovering off and on the whole 24 hours because of the hard wind and had to set adrift the sloop which we had taken with us, on account of the storm that blew out of the N.W.; and we also threw overboaord portion of our bread, and everything in our way, because we could not get rid of the water. In the night we were also in great peril of Sinking through the hard wind and the hollow seas. Also could not get away from the coast because we could not carry a sail as we could only fight the sea; it rained the whole night so I hope that our people at the island have also had these rains.

On 11 do. in the morning, the weather began to calm down and the wind ran to W.S.W., and then we steered round to the North, but the waves ran high as ever.

On 12 do. in the afternoon, had latitude 27 degrees. Ran close along the coast, the wind S.E., but could not find an opportunity to get to land with the boat because of the heavy surf. The Coast very steeply hewn without any foreshore or inlets as have other countries, but it seemed to be a dry cursed earth without foliage or grass.

On 13 do. at noon had latitude of 25 degrees 40 minutes. We found that we drifted speedily towards the North and were round the corner [*hoeck*] where the coast stretches out mostly from N.N.E. to S.South West; have held during these 24 hours mostly N., the land still entirely red stone hewn off without a foreshore, and generally everywhere at the same level; also it has not been possible to get ashore because of the surf.

On 14 do. in the morning we had a Slight breeze, but during the day it became very quiet. At noon we had latitude 24 degrees, held N. and the wind S.E.; the current took us daily against our wish [to] the North, for we ran close along the coast with little sail. In the afternoon seeing some smoke inland, rowed thither hoping to find an opportunity of landing. Were quite rejoiced for I imagined that where there were people there would also be fresh water. I noticed that the ground on shore rose very steeply, full of stones and rocks, and there was also a very big surf, yet 6 men swam ashore, and we remained with the boat at 25 fathoms outside the breakers. Our folk were searching for water everywhere until nightfall but found none. Saw also four men creeping towards them on hands and feet. When our folk, coming out of a hollow upon a height, approached them suddenly, they leapt to their feet and fled full speed, which was clearly seen by us in the boat; they were black savages, entirely naked, without any cover. At night time our folk swam aboard, all very much injured by the Rocks upon which they were thrown by the surf. Then, getting ready and lifting the kedge, started in search of a better opportunity, sailing close to the coast all night with small sail and keeping outside the breakers, until

On 15 do. in the morning we found ourselves at the point where a large reef stretched about one mile to Sea [*den punt bevonden daar een groot reciff afstreckten, ontrent wel een mijl t'zee*]: then we ran between the land reef and the sea reef, which we guessed to be at 23 degrees, and sailed thus along the Coast, alongside which stretches a reef where between the land [and the reef] appears to be very smooth and still water, we did our best to get into it, but found no opening till nearly noon, when we found an opening where there was no surf; ran into that, but it was very rocky and sometimes not more than 2 feet of water. ———— This coast had a dune foreland of about one mile width before one comes to the High Land, therefore began to dig in this place; there was salt water, a party of folk therefore went to the High land where they found by chance some small holes in a rock that were full of fresh water that the rain had left there. It seemed that the blacks had been there a little time before, for there lay bones of Crabs and ashes of fires. We quenched our great thirst a little, for we hardly were able to do more, for since the wrecking of the ship we had been without Wine or other drink except for one or two small mugs [*mutskens*][24] of water. Also collected a fair provision, about 80 *kannen* of water, and remained there the whole night until

The 16 do. in the morning we continued to see whether there were more such holes in the range. But our search was vain, it appeared it had not rained there for a long time, nor was there any sign of running water, for beyond the heights the country was flat again, without trees, foliage or grass, except for high anthills thrown up of earth, which in the distance were not unlike the huts of people. Was also such a host of flies, which came to sit in the mouth and the eyes, that they could not be beaten off. ————
We next saw eight black men, each carrying a stick in his hand, and these approached to the distance of a musket shot, but when we went towards them they ran away and we could not get them to stop where they were so that we might come up to them. ————
Towards noon, seeing that there was no more water to be come by, set sail, and ran through another opening of the reef which lay

[24] *Mutsken=mutsje*: one-eighth of a bottle. Taking a bottle as holding 1¼ pints, this suggests they were not receiving more than ¼ pint per man per day.

a little more to the North. Where we were in the latitude of 22 degrees 17 minutes. I had the intention to run to the river of Jacop Remmessens[25] but the wind ran to the N.E. so that we could not keep to the coast. Therefore we were forced to take a resolution, because we were more than 100 miles[26] away from the People left by us and had up to now not found water to assist them, as for ourselves only [enough] that we might have the benefit of 2 *mutskens* daily; to do our utmost in the name of God to further our journey to Batavia as quickly as possible in order that through the Hon. Lord Gov. Gen. some order or means might be set to work towards succour.

On 17 do. at noon, had no latitude, but by guessing sailed 15 miles, held N.W. by North, Wind N.E., a topgallant breeze and dry weather.

On 18 do. at noon had no latitude, but by guessing sailed 10 miles this 24 hours [*etmaal*], held W.N.W. in rough weather, with rain; wind N.E. and about noon the wind veered to the North; then we lay round to the east.

On 19 do. at noon had no latitude; by guessing sailed 7 miles, held N.N.E., the wind N.W. by West, rough weather with rain.

On 20 do. at noon had the latitude of 19 degrees 29 minutes, this 24 hours sailed 22 miles, held North, the wind W.S.W., a shaky topgallant and sometimes rain.

On 21 do. at noon, had no latitude, by guessing sailed 23 miles, held North, the wind ran from the S.W. to the S.E.; gradually more breezy, then again somewhat quieter.

On 22 do. at noon, had the latitude of 16 degrees 10 minutes, sailed this 24 hours 24 miles, held North, the wind ran from the S.W. to the S.E., shaky topgallant, with dry weather. It appeared that the storm ran round North, otherwise we could not have made so many degrees.

On 23 do. at noon, had no latitude, by guessing sailed 16 miles, held N. by W., the wind ran to and fro from the East to the West, then some breeze, some calmness with rain. In the afternoon a breeze blew from the S.S.East.

On 24 do. at noon, had the latitude of 13 degrees 30 minutes, this 24 hours sailed 25 miles, held North by West, the wind mostly S.E. by S., topgallant, with dry weather.

On 25 do. at Noon, had the latitude of 11 degrees 30 minutes, this 24 hours sailed 31 miles, held N. by W., the wind more to

[25] Present-day Yardie Creek. See Appendix X, The Landings in Australia.
[26] From 28° 20' (their estimated wreck site) to 22° 17' is 363 miles taking Pelsaert's mile as equal to 3 English miles (or 121: i.e., "more than 100 miles"). It is almost exactly 370 miles from Noon Reef to Yardie Creek.

S.E., topgallant, with dry weather, nevertheless we saw much seaweed [*steenkroos*][27] floating.

On 26 do. at noon had the latitude of 9 degrees 56 minutes, this 24 hours sailed 24 miles, held N. by W., the wind mostly S.East with dry weather.

On 27 do. at noon, had no latitude. By guessing this 24 hours sailed 24 miles, held N. by W., the wind S.E., topgallant, with some rain. Towards afternoon sighted the land of Java, by guessing, on the latitude of 8 degrees, and were 4 to 5 miles off. We set our Course W.N.W. along the coast, until in the evening we saw a cape in front of us, off which lay an Island [Nusa Kambangan] covered with trees. In the evening Sailed past this cape, off which stretched a reef and found behind this a big Inlet, so sailing N.N.West, we dropped the kedge in 8 fathoms, hard ground, for the whole night till

On 28 do. in the morning with daylight, when we lifted the kedge, we rowed ashore to seek fresh water, where to our luck we found a waterfall. Thanks and praise to God, we could quench our great thirst at last; here we filled our casks and before Noon were again under sail.

On 29 do. in the morning, in the second quarter [of the moon] we saw a little island ahead which we passed on the starboard side; with the daylight we were near the western Inlet, hence the course lies W.N.West, though one leaves the coast on account of the curve. But before one reaches the Trouwes Islands [Trouvens Islands], land is seen again. At noon had the latitude of 6 degrees 48 Minutes, this 24 hours sailed 30 miles, held mostly N.W.West. About the middle of the afternoon, we sailed between two Trouwes islands; where, on the more Westerly stand many Coconut palms; In the afternoon we were still a mile away from the South cape of Java [Java Head], and at the third hourglass of the second watch we began to enter the straits that separate Java from the Princen Islands.

On 30 do. in the morning we were sailing through the Princen Islands, in the afternoon drifted about 2 miles due to calmness, until evening when a slight breeze came from the land.

ON 1st JULY, in the Morning weather was again calm; at noon we were still 3 miles from Dwars in de Weegh [Thwartway Island], the wind variable, towards night held West then North West, it became very calm and the whole night through we had to row.

On 2 do. in the morning we came by Toppers Hoetgien [Top-

[27] Seaweed torn from rocks, generally a sign of land.

per's Hat], there we lay until 11 hours and waited for a Sea wind, then getting only a slight breeze; so that the whole day we had again to row, making only 2 miles by evening. In the setting sun we saw a sail astern behind Dwers in den Wegh [*sic*]; whereupon we dropped the kedge under the shore in order to wait for it.

On 3 do. in the morning, I let the kedge be lifted before daybreak and ran towards the ship in order to get some weapons as we did not know how those of Java stood towards us, but as we approached we saw that there were three ships, of which the nearest was the yacht *Sardam*, aboard which I went. I understood from the Merchant, van Dommelen, that the largest ship was *Frederick Hendrick*, on which was the Heer Raemborch, Councillor of India. Therefore I sailed immediately to him, where I told his Hon. with heart's grief of our sad disaster. He showed me much friendship and permitted that I should stay on the ship with him until we reached Batavia. The other ships were *Brouwers Haven* and *Weesp*, with which was the Commandeur Grijph[28] coming in company of the Heer Commandeur Pieter van den Broeck from Suratte,[29] but had been parted from each other.

On 4 do. the ship *Bommel*, sailing from Souratte, also came by us, saying that still some ships had been seen outside the Straits [of Sunda], but not knowing whether they were English or our own ships.

On 7 do. we arrived towards evening in the roads of Batavia. God be praised and thanked.

---

[28] Present when earlier Pelsaert and Ariaen Jacobsz, skipper of the *Batavia*, quarrelled at Surat, aboard the *Dordrecht*.
[29] On the ship *Utrecht*, arrived Batavia 19th June.

DAILY notes on my return journey to the Southland, sent by the Hon. Lord Gov. Gen. Jan Pieters Coen, with the Yacht *Sardam*, to search for the people of our wrecked Ship *Batavia*, and to bring [them] back with all the cash, and goods, that can possibly be fished up, and we, in God's name

ON 15TH JULY, in the Morning, have sailed with a land wind —— in the afternoon near Man Eaters Island, met the ship *Leijden*, which had sailed from the Fatherland on 8 May, Anno 1628, in the company of the ship *Wapen van Enchuijsen*, which had been blown up on 12 October passing near the Sierra Lionas, and only 57 persons from that have been saved by the ship *Leijden*, up to that time more than 170 have died, but the rest of the people were in fair health as they had been refreshed at Celebar in Sumatra[30] —— Towards evening also saw the ship *Beets* or *Wigge van Hoorn*, which had sailed in the fleet of the Hon. Lord Jaques Specx.

On 16 do. was mostly calm, so that we advanced with sail but were carried by the current quickly out of the Strait, in the evening we saw the Prince Islands.

On 17 do. in the Morning, we had the Princen Islands E.N.E. from us, it had been calm the whole night, then before sunrise it began to blow from the S.E., our course S.S.W., towards noon we ran one degree more east, so that we could sail only S. by West, guessed have sailed   miles, and held S.W. by South.

On 18 do. at noon had latitude of 8 degrees 25 minutes, Southern

---

[30] "With the arrival of the ship Leyden, which through a long delay in Sierra Liona, as well as through many contrary winds between the Cabo and Java has had a very long journey and has lost 175 souls, received here the sad tidings of the wrecking of the ship Wapen van Enckhuysen which in company of ship Leyden the 8th October sailed from Sierra Liona, getting on fire the 12 ditto in latitude 10 degrees about 35 miles from land, and has burst open, whereon 184 people were lost and 5 [space was left here] were picked up by the ship Leyden; the uppermerchant and the skipper of the Leyden, who had sailed there to help quench the fire, have also died there." From report of Governor-General J. Specx and Council to Directors dated 15th December 1629 (VOC 1009, O.B. 1630[1])). The same report details the wreck of the *Batavia*. One imagines that Pelsaert, at this stage, drew comfort from this apparently even greater disaster. Pelsaert gives the number saved by *Leyden* as 57 but, as indicated, the digit after 5 is left blank in the report. The town of Celebar (also Celeber, Selebar, Silbe) lies on the west coast near Benkulen, but is not shown on maps published after 1900.

hemisphere, the wind S.E., course S.S.W., guessed to have sailed 25 miles, held S.W. by West.

On 19 do. at noon had latitude of 9 degrees 56 minutes, the wind S.E., course S.S.West, guessed have sailed 24 miles, held S.W. by S.

On 20 do. at Noon, had latitude of 11 Degrees, the Wind S.E. by East, Course S. by West, guessed to have sailed 20 miles. Held S.S.W.

On 21 do. the Wind variable, and sometimes calm. In the morning had some rain, so that we gathered about 30 to 40 *kannen*; at noon the latitude of 11 degrees 38 minutes, held S.W. by South. Guessed to have sailed 11 miles.

On 22 do. had a topgallant gale, the wind S.E. Course S.S.West, at noon had the latitude of 12 degrees 41 minutes, guessed to have sailed 19 miles, and held S.W. by South.

On 23 do. a topgallant gale, although the weather was altogether variable, with gentle showers; at noon had the latitude of 14 degrees, guessed to have sailed 22 miles, and held S.W. by South.

On 24 do. the Wind S.E., course S.S.W. and held S.S.W. by South, at noon had the latitude 15 degrees 14 minutes, and sailed 22 miles.

On 25 do. the Wind E.S.E., course held S.S.W., the latitude of 16 degrees 16 minutes, and sailed 17 miles.

On 26 do. the Wind East. Course S.S.East, and held South, at noon had the latitude of 17 degrees 52 minutes. ——— Guessed to have sailed 23 miles.

On 27 do. at noon, had the latitude of 18 degrees 55 minutes, the wind E. by South, with lulls, guessed held South and sailed 15½ miles.

On 28 do. in the morning the Wind ran S.S.E., therefore turned easterly, with misty rain and beautiful calm; at noon, the latitude of 19 degrees 45 minutes, guessed held South.

On 29 do. the Wind S.S.E. with dark misty rain, at noon had no latitude, guessed to have sailed 20 miles, and held E.N.E.[31]

On 30 do. the Wind again S.East with dark Weather, at noon had no latitude, guessed to have sailed   miles, and held S.West.

On 31 do. at noon the latitude of 20 degrees 7 [or 9] minutes, and the longitude 132 degrees 8 minutes,[32] as now the wind turned Southerly, so that we have sailed towards the East, and at night sailed S.East by East, because the Wind ran West S.West.

THE 1ST AUGUST, at Noon had latitude of 21 degrees 13 minutes, the Longitude 133 degrees 35 minutes, held S.West by South, the wind S.East.

[31] Probably a slip, and should be E.S.E.?
[32] Ile de Ferro reckoning (see p. 295, note 4).

On 2 do. at noon the latitude of 24 degrees 55 minutes, the wind S.East, held S.W. by S.

On 3 do. at noon, the latitude of 23 degrees, longitude 132 degrees 3 minutes, the wind variable, but most S.S.East, and held S.W.

On 4 do. at noon had Southern Latitude 23 degrees 59 minutes, longitude 131 degrees, 1 minute, beautiful weather, the wind southerly but most variable, have turned for a certain time eastwards.

On 5 do. at noon had Southern Latitude 24 degrees 45 minutes, longitude 130 degrees 8 minutes, the Wind S.S.East, and sailed S.West until night, the wind very variable, run round and round, and turned altogether.

On 6 do. at noon Southern Latitude of 24 degrees 32 minutes, had a strong swell from the S.West, and the wind variable so that we turned altogether to the East and again to the South.

On 7 do. at noon had the Southern Latitude of 24 degrees 49 minutes, sailing towards S.W., the-wind most S.S.East with strong gusts until night when the Wind ran E.S.East, and could sail South again.

On 8 do. at noon had Southern Latitude of 25 Degrees 20 minutes, longitude 129 degrees 47 minutes, again had the wind E. to Southerly and could sail South to East.

On 9 do. at noon had Southern Latitude of 26 Degrees 23 minutes, the wind E.N.E. Ran towards S.E., also altogether E.S.E. after the wind increased, with very bad [*slecht*] water.

On 10 do. at noon, we had the Southern Latitude of 27 degrees 54 minutes, the Wind North East, ran most to East according to the Wind, in and out, with bad weather at night, the Wind running to the North east.

On 11 do. at noon the latitude of 27 degrees 57 minutes, the wind before noon ran west, went Wt. by North at night coming from out the S. and S.S.West with a stiff gale.

On 12 do. at noon had the Southern Latitude of 27 degrees 2 minutes, the wind S. to West. Course eastwards, in the afternoon variable weather, and the wind ran S.E. and turned in the morning S.S.West, with great hollow waves.

On 13 do. at noon, the latitude of 25 degrees 50 minutes, rather calm, the wind S.E., sailed S.S.West, and S.W. by South, variable weather, turned altogether again after the wind came up.

On 14 do. at noon had no latitude, then guessed to be on the above mentioned latitude, the wind S.S.Wt. to South, sailed East S.East, with high seas from the South.

On 15 do. at noon had Southern Latitude of 26 degrees 30 minutes, the Wind South, were able to sail E.S.E., with a stiff gale with showery and rainy weather.

On 16 do. at noon the Southern Latitude of 26 degrees 16 minutes, the wind South, at night the wind ran S.E. by South, turning mostly S.West by South, again seawards.

On 17 do. at noon had no latitude but guessed to have gained 2 miles South, with a stiff gale and high seas from the S.S.Wt. In the morning bad weather came up and the wind veered to the East.

On 18 do. at noon had no Latitude, but guessed Southern Latitude 27 degrees 15 minutes, the Wind E.S.E., with beautiful weather, sailed Southwards the whole 24 hours.

On 19 do. at noon Southern Latitude of 28 degrees 29 minutes, the wind E.S.E. with mild weather, in the morning the wind came from the Wt. then S.S.West, and it became very calm.

On 20 do. at noon, the Southern Latitude of 29 degrees 10 minutes, the wind South, held East by South, at night mild weather with a variable wind.

On 21 do. at noon, no Latitude, guessed latitude as before, had held East, the wind S., the swell of the sea from the S.S.Wt., continued to hold east to South.

On 22 do. at noon the Southern Latitude of 29 degrees 19 minutes, the wind South, Course North east. The steersmen guessed to be now 15 miles from the wreck.

On 23 do. had the Southern Latitude of 28 degrees 14 minutes, the wind S.West, Course east, guessed now in the longitude of the Land. Therefore drifted at night, 2 quarters [watches] with the foresail on the mast.

On 24 do. at noon the Southern Latitude of 28 degrees 25 minutes, the wind S.West, Course east.

On 25 do. at noon, the Southern Latitude of 27 degrees 56 minutes, we found that a current had carried us this 24 hours round to the North in a very unusual fashion, and we also saw many strong cross-currents [*ravelingen*]. We thought about this time that we saw surf and some islands, but it was the reflection of the Sun; the wind South; held over to the East; at night in the first quarter the wind ran S.S.E. Therefore ran westwards, it became calm, and the sea ran very hollow from the S.S.W.

On 26 do. at noon had the latitude of 28 degrees 5 minutes, the wind South by West, with very high seas; towards noon the wind shot S.S.E., then turned westwards and ran so about 9-10 glasses[33] but on account of the hollow swell turned again to the east.

[33] Hour-glasses were still used at sea, although clocks were gaining in popularity on land.

On 27 do. at noon, the Southern Latitude of 28 degrees 13 minutes, this day it became calm so that we drifted aimlessly westwards, towards evening the sea rose strongly from the South; began to sail somewhat towards the S.West, held S.E., but at night was most calm.

On 28 do. at noon, the Southern Latitude of 28 degrees 35 minutes,[34] the wind S.S.W., ran Easterly, and I then saw floating around, the first seaweed [kroos], from which we guessed that we should shortly see land, and ran for two quarters with swift advancement, but during the day watch drifted with the foresail on the mast; in the morning the wind ran again S.E. by East.

On 29 do. at noon the Southern Latitude of 28 degrees 10 minutes, the wind S.E. by South, with hard weather, the topsail at half [halvenstenge], so that have again lost Southern Latitude; at evening turned again seawards, and sailed S.W. to West, during the whole night.

On 30 do. at noon the Southern Latitude of 28 degrees 55 minutes, the wind S.E. by South, the sea came up hard from the S.S.West.

On 31 do. at noon, the Southern Latitude of 29 degrees[35] 49 minutes, before noon very calm, no wind, but after noon began to blow westerly and became fresh. Set our Course N.East by East, for we did not know how far we were from the land; in the morning the wind ran again S.E., after that E.N.East.

ON 1ST SEPTEMBER, at noon the Southern Latitude of 29 degrees 16 minutes, the wind variable, so that it was not possible to come round to the East.

On 2 do. in the morning the wind ran North, with a topgallant gale; at noon the Southern Latitude of 30 degrees 16 minutes, found ourselves now quickly drifted to the south, at night the wind turned north west: our Course N.E. to North.

On 3 do. in the morning the Wind west; saw floating round much seaweed [kroos] with some cuttlefish bones [sasbeen]. Therefore set our Course Eastwards; at noon saw the main Southland, stretching out N.N.W. and S.S.E., were about 3 miles away, and saw the land still stretching out Southwards, by guessing about 4 miles, where the horizon ended;[36] had here clean sand ground at 25 fathoms. —— It is Bare level [slecht] Land with some sand dunes as round the North; had the Southern Latitude of 29 degrees

[34] Pelsaert wrote 45 first, then substituted a 3 over the 4.
[35] Another erasure: this time Pelsaert has begun to write the minutes figure first and altered it to 29 degrees. There is another slight correction in this entry: signs of mental agitation as the goal comes near?
[36] Probably Green Head.

16 minutes, took our Course N.Westwards, the wind W.S.West, then the hollow swell sent us very much towards the coast, so that at night we had to anchor one mile from land; and, 2 hourglasses in the first watch, our anchor broke into 2 pieces; let another drop speedily.

On 4 do. in the morning, the wind S.W. to S. with still hollow swell, during the day [it] ran S.S.W., then we lifted our anchor, and before noon got under sail, took our Course W.N.W. to Sea, in order to get off the lee shore; at noon the Southern Latitude of 28 degrees 50 minutes, where the land began to fall off one point, to wit, N. by West and S. by East.[37] After noon, the wind ran S. and went towards the Wt. and towards night we noticed a shallow straight in front, or west, of us and were only a musket shot away from it.[38] —— But had 25 fathoms clean Sand ground. We turned and ran half a mile E.S.East away from it, there we anchored at 27 fathoms clean ground; had held W.N.W. from noon till evening, and were 5 miles from the continent. At night it became very calm and beautiful weather, the wind S. by East.

On 5 do. in the morning the wind S.S.East, and lovely weather; lifted our anchor and sailed one hour S.S.Wt., then we noticed in front and alongside our Course more breakers, a shallow and some small islands, the wind veered meanwhile and ran more towards the East, so that we could sail Southerly and S.S.E. This reef or shallow stretched out S.S.Wt. and N.N.East;[39] found along here 27-28 to 29 fathoms sand ground; at 11 hours before noon the continent had disappeared from our sight; at noon had the Southern Latitude of 28 degrees 59 minutes, and the corner of the reef was W.S.West from us, with dirty steep ground with depths from 50 to 60 fathoms. —— After noon it began to become calm, but the current took us towards the West, and the rocks here stretched out wholly Westerly;[40] guessed to be about 8 miles[41] away from the continent; the whole night it was dead calm, and drifted alongside the rocks so that we heard the surf the whole night, until

---

37 At that latitude they would observe Point Moore.
38 This could be either Little North Island (so named by the fishermen) off the Easter Group, or Hummock Island, or King Reef, off the Pelsart Group. The first appears the most likely.
39 Pelsaert Island. Exact position of Wreck Point is given. Sentence "at 11 hours . . ." should have opened the paragraph.
40 Could be southern reefs of Easter Group.
41 In *The Part Borne by the Dutch in the Discovery of Australia 1606-1765*, p. 54, Heeres writes *87 miles*, but he has mistaken an overlong flourish from the W of *Westerly* for the figure 7. Pelsaert set his 8 within the tail of the flourish. Eighty-seven miles is here untenable.

On 6 do. in the morning, when we had lost sight of the rocks, about 10 hours, a light wind came from the W.N.Wt.; ran then slowly towards the rocks. At noon had the southern latitude of 28 degrees 44 minutes, began to blow hard from the N.Wt.; tacked off and on in the afternoon and found that the current ran us towards the North West. At night turned to Sea again away from the rocks; cast 40 fathoms ground, but dirty rocks [klippen]; this shallow stretches further out S.E. and N.West.[42] ——— At night it began to blow very hard and ran with shortened sails [huckende schover zeylen], the wind variable.

On 7 do. in the morning the weather took up, and set sail; at noon found Southern Latitude of 29 degrees 30 minutes and ran northwards in order to get the continent in view again; then the wind freshened very much towards W.N.Wt., so that we again had to veer.

On 8 do. at noon, the Southern Latitude of 29 degrees 7 minutes, Course N.East, at evening have seen the breakers. Therefore ran the whole night W.S.Wt., the Wind N.West; it began to blow so hard that the topsail had to be taken in again.

On 9 do. in the morning, have turned again towards land. At noon the Southern Latitude of 29 degrees; the rest of the day have turned on and off; towards evening such a storm blew that were obliged to lessen sail; the wind N.West.

On 10 do. in the morning set Sail again, had at noon Southern Latitude of 29 degrees 30 minutes, the wind west, with a topgallant gale.

On 11 do. in the morning was calm, but very hollow seas, the wind out of the W.S.Wt. so that we could not make way Northwards, either we were on to, or near, the rocks; at noon the Southern Latitude of 28 degrees 48 minutes, furthermore the wind variable, ran at night with the foresail, and drifted round until it was daybreak.

On 12 do. with the day, again set Sail eastwards until Noon, when took latitude 28 degrees 13 minutes. ——— Therefore ran somewhat Southerly, to reach the land straight on 28 degrees 20 minutes[43] the Wind S.West, with big breakers. ——— In the afternoon 2 hrs. before Sunset have seen again the rocks, which guessed to be 2 Miles away from us. Cast the lead at 100 fathoms clean Sand ground, but going half a mile nearer had 30 fathoms dirty stony ground. We turned this night 2 watches to seawards, and in the day watch again to the coast.

[42] Western Reef of the Easter Group lies thus in the same latitude; but could refer to the whole archipelago.
[43] The position at which they reckoned to find the wreck.

On 13 do. in the morning, 3 hours after Sunrise, we again noticed in front of us, a churning [*barningh*] and [this place] being known to us, we noted had lost one mile North, as the wind had been S.S.East; this was the most Northerly point of the Abrholos [*sic*]. Therefore I resolved because we came always too high or too low, and because it was very perilous to approach it from outside on account of the high seas and dirty ground, to keep bearing beneath the extreme shallow [*dragende te houden beneden d' uytterste droogte*][44] and tacked slowly towards that again, the wind S.S.E., Course East, coming in a little immediately had clean Sand ground at 30 to 35 fathoms; at noon, the latitude of 28 degrees Southern Latitude; shortly after saw again the main Southland. At night, because it began to blow very hard, we anchored about 2 miles from the coast in 30 fathoms clean ground.

On 14 do. the Wind S.S.E., but blew hard, so that we could not wind our anchor, and remained lying here the whole day.

On 15 do. still blew hard, but towards noon calmed down a little so that we could wind up our anchor; at noon Southern Latitude of 27 degrees 54 minutes, the wind S.S.E., tacked the whole day to gain South, and towards evening found to have made two miles; being dark, anchored in 30 fathoms clean ground.

On 16 do. in the morning with daylight, again lifted our anchor, the wind was W.S.W., went near enough South, at noon the Southern Latitude of   degrees   Minutes, the wind ran towards the West, and after that Northerly, so that we could sail South West; towards evening saw the rocks of our wrecked ship *Batavia*, and I recognised [*wierdt jch verkendt*] the High Island, although the Steersmen sustained that it was the other land; 2 hours in the night anchored in 27 fathoms clean Sand ground until

On 17 do. in the morning, with daybreak, lifted our anchor again, the wind North; were then about 2 miles from the High island, ran towards that for   .[45] ——— Before noon, approaching the island, we saw smoke on a long island 2 miles West of the Wreck, also on another small island close by the Wreck, about which we were all very glad, hoping to find great numbers, or rather all people, alive. ——— Therefore, as soon as the anchor was dropped, I sailed with the boat to the highest island, which was nearest, taking with me a barrel of water, ditto bread, and a

---

[44] Heeres translates *uytterste* as "outermost", but "uttermost" has a more precise meaning, i.e., "the most extreme" or "northerly" in this case. His translation puts a different aspect on what actually happened. Instead of translating *dragende* as "bearing" he writes: ". . . to keep tacking off the outermost shoal. After this we went over again nearly to weatherward with a S.S.E. wind, keeping an eastern course." (Heeres, *op. cit.*, p. 60.)   [45] Time omitted.

keg of wine; coming there, I saw no one, at which we wondered. I sprang ashore, and at the same time we saw a very small yawl with four Men rowing round the Northerly point; one of them, named Wiebbe Hayes, sprang ashore and ran towards me, calling from afar, "Welcome, but go back aboard immediately, for there is a party of scoundrels on the islands near the wreck, with two sloops, who have the intention to seize the Yacht." —— Furthermore, told that he was Captain [*Capiteyn*] over 47 Souls, who had kept themselves so long on one island in order to save their lives, as they [the scoundrels] had Murdered more than 125 persons, Men, Women and Children as well, and that 14 days ago he had captured Jeronimus Cornelisz, undermerchant, who had been the chief of the scoundrels, also at the same time they had killed 4 of his [Cornelisz's] principal councillors and Accomplices, namely, Davidt van Sevanck, assistant, Coenraat van Huyssen, and Gysbrecht [*sic*] van Welderen, cadets [*adelborsten*],[46] and Cornelis Pietersz of Wtrecht, soldier, had been killed; because they had been attacked twice by them in a felonious way. But they had bravely repulsed them. —— And they next tried treacherous means to overpower and murder them. For they had then come to [try to] establish Peace with each other under Oath, and not to remember any more what had passed. Nevertheless, whilst Jeronimus was engaged in pretending to make an agreement through the agency of the Predikant, whom they compelled to go backwards and forwards, at the same time Davidt van Sevanck, and Coenraat van Huyssen, were engaged in bribing some of the soldiers to treason by offering them six thousand guilders each if they, the next day when they [the scoundrels] came back, would come to their side under cover, as friends, in order to help murder the others. So when the People perceived that their lives were at stake, they have killed the above mentioned, as has been told above. —— Moreover, that some one named Wouter Loos, who had been made their Captain after the capture of Jeronimus, had attacked them this same Morning with 2 sloops of men; whom they had also repulsed, and there were in the party of the ditto Wibbe [*sic*] Hayes, four very seriously wounded Men.

With all these sad tidings which I had briefly learnt, I returned immediately aboard, whilst I ordered Wiebbe Hayes that he should go back again in the little yawl and bring Jeronimus Cornelisz,

[46] *Adelborst*: now naval rank of midshipman, but then applied to a young man of better class, appointed by the Company in capacity of very junior officer of naval or military rank; ensign; appointee.

No. 113 The Nieuwendijk, Amsterdam, in 1960, known in the seventeenth century as The White Angel. Here Lucretia Jansz was born in 1602.

Van 't Schip BATAVIA.

COPYE,

Uyt den Originelen Brief / van

GIISBERT BASTIAENSZ.

Geschreven uyt BATAVIA, al-hier
aen sijne Broeders van sijn periculeuse ende
distructieuse reyse, gaende in den
Jare 1628. naer *Indien.*

Godt met ons, Amen.

NAer hertelijcke groeteniße ende wenschinge alles goets aen mijn Broeder Jan Bastiaensz, Hugo mijn Swager / Suster Anneta, Sara Suster / den Rent-meester Pandelaer / mijn Couzijn Schepens / ende alle den sijnen / alle de Predicanten aldaer / Willem Reyersz Swanen-burgh, Janneken Maertens: met een woort alle den ghenen die ghy-lieden weet dat van my behooren ghegroet te werden: dit weynigh dient daer toe / hoe-wel nochtans met groote droefheyt / als verschrickt zijnde om de penne op het Papier te setten / om u van mijn wedervaren op de reyse te verwittigen. Eben-wel de saeck nu een goeden tijdt gepaßeert zijnde / ende mijn selven onderwerpende de voorsienigheydt des Heeren / die den sijnen beproeft tot haren besten: ende wederom door des Heeren ghenade waer kracht ende sterckheydt ontfanghen hebbende; want ick naeuwelijcks en hebbe konnen staen van swackheydt / ende dat met goede reden. Dit is dan de somma ende in-houdt kortelijck / van mijn weder-varen in dese groote ende sware reyse: Wy zijn / gelijck als u kennelijck bekent is / den 27. October / 1628. uyt Terel t'zeyl ghegaen / ende des selven daeghs aen de grondt met het Schip ghekomen / meenende dat wy aldaer met het Schip souden ghebleven hebben: Maer Godt de Heer sulcks versiende / zijn los gheraeckt / ende den 28. dito voorsz voort-ghezeylt / eerst tot onder Engelandt / ende voorts daer naer aen Siara-leonis, ende ten derden aen de Caep. Wat hem heeft toeghedragen in die tijdt op de reyse/ zijnde saken van kleynen gewichte/ sal P. L. t' Amsterdam konnen verstaen/ uyt het Journael/ by de E. Heeren Bewinthebbers zijnde. Van de Caep afgevaren / heeft hem de saeck aldus toegedragen: daer is soo wat moeyten gheresen tusschen den Schipper ende den Commandeur / ende het onstont meest uyt twee Vrouw-luyden/ waer van de eene op het Schip was mishandelt/ daerom veel moeyten op het Schip is gevallen: Ende wy van de andere Schepen

The first page of the Predikant's letter about the wreck and mutiny, from the Lucas de Vries 1649 edition of *Ongeluckige Voyagie*.

bound, to the ship; which he did. ------ But before we got aboard, I saw a sloop with people rowing come round the Southerly point of the High island. ------ Therefore we made all preparations to capture the above mentioned scoundrels. ------ When they came near the ship, it could be seen that they were dressed mostly in red *laken*,[47] embroidered with *passementerie*.[48] ------ I called to them, "Wherefore do you come aboard armed?" They answered me that they would reply to that when they were on the ship. I ordered them to throw their weapons into the sea before they came over, which at last they did. ------ When they came over, we immediately took them prisoner, and we forthwith began to examine them, especially a certain *Jan Hendricxsz from Bremen*,[49] soldier, who immediately confessed that he had murdered and helped to murder 17 to 20 people, under the order of Jeronimus. I asked him the origin and circumstances of this, why had they practised such cruelties. Said that he also wished to explain how it had been with him in the beginning, ------ saying, that the skipper [Ariaen Jacobsz] Jeronimus Cornelisz, the Highboatswain [Jan Evertsz] and still more others, had it in mind to seize the ship *Batavia* before it was wrecked; to kill the Commandeur [Pelsaert] and all people except 120 towards whom they were more favourably inclined, and to throw the dead overboard into the sea and then to go pirating with the ship. Wherefore Jeronimus and all the people who had been on the island had been certain that the skipper would have murdered the Commandeur on the way [to Java] or have thrown him overboard into the sea. So that Jeronimus, having been for a month on the island after the wrecking of the ship, thought that one should either murder all the people to 40 or less, or else help them to some land, so that when the Yacht came, one could seize it, which has been put into action to that purpose. But they could not fulfil their plan because Wiebbe Hayes had been sent with a party of people to a long island, to seek water, which they found after a search of 20 days, and therefore they made, according to arrangements, 3 fires as signals. But because they were in those days busy with the murdering, Jeronimus did not care about the water; whereupon several parties from 4 to 5 strong, saved themselves on pieces of wood or rafts, and escaped to Wiebbe Hayes's island, at last 45 strong. ------ As they understood what had been decided and that daily so many were being murdered, made themselves ready to counter-attack if they should come to fight them, and made weapons from hoop-iron

---

[47] A fine woollen material in which the Company traded in India.
[48] French trimming of gold or silver lace, braid, beads, etc.
[49] Name underlined by Pelsaert, but not written in Italian hand.

and nails, which they bound to sticks. —— After they had murdered most people, except 30 men and 4 Boys, they decided to go to the high island with 2 flat-bottomed sloops to overpower Wiebbe Hayes with his men, for they said, "If the Yacht comes by the inside passage [*binnendeur*], he will warn them, and our plan will not succeed; therefore they must go." And they had already done three trips against them, but they were unable to do any harm to them except on this day [17th] when they shot some.

Towards evening Wiebbe Hayes brought Jeronimus aboard, bound; I looked at him with great sorrow, such a scoundrel, cause of so many disasters and of the shedding of human blood, and he had still had the intention to go on; however, it was not according to the plan of God. I examined him in the presence of the council, and asked him why he allowed the devil to lead him so far astray from all human feeling (to do that which had never been so cruelly perpetrated amongst Christians), without any real hunger or need of thirst, but solely out of boodthirstiness to attain his wicked ends. —— He answered, that one should not blame him for what had happened, laying it on Davidt van Sevanck, Coenraat van Huyssen, and others who had been killed, that they had forced and willed him to it; that also one often had to do a great deal to save oneself; denied that he ever had the intention to help in the plan to seize the ship *Batavia*, and as to the idea of seizing any Yacht that might come, he said that Sevanck had proposed this, to which he had only consented on account of his own safety without meaning it, for, firstly, he believed that they would never be delivered; [secondly] he had also heard here on land from Ryckert Wouterssen that skipper Arians [*sic*] intended to seize the ship and to throw the Commandeur overboard, which made him presume that he would never take the boat to Batavia but that they would veer off to Malacca, or if the other had occurred, and he or the Commandeur had arrived at Batavia, and some Yacht were sent to rescue them, he [Jeronimus] would have given warning. In this manner he tried to talk himself clean, with his glib tongue telling the most palpable lies, making out that nowhere had he had a hand in it, often appealing to the people, who would say the same thing. —— At that the matter was left this day, and he was again imprisoned.

On 18 do. before daylight, I and the skipper of the *Sardam* [Jacob Jacobsz] went with the yawl and the boat to the island of Wiebbe Hayes and got 10 soldiers to whom I gave weapons and muskets, and thus we sailed to the island named *Batavia's* Graveyard, which was near to the Wreck, where the rest of the scoundrels were, in order to capture and secure them. When they saw us coming they lost their courage, and said to each other, "Now our necks are in the noose," thinking that they would be killed immediately; and when I came ashore I had them bound hand and foot and so secured. Afterwards, the first thing I did was to seek for the scattered jewels. These were all found, except a ring and a gold chain.[50]

Towards evening we went to the Wreck, and found that the ship was lying in many pieces, that a piece of the keel, with the flat of the hold, all above water had been washed away except a small piece of the bulwark which was above water, it was almost exactly in the same place where the ship had first struck, — a piece of the front of the ship was broken off and thrown half on the shallow, there also were lying 2 Pieces of Cannon, one of brass and one of iron, fallen from the mounts [*rampaarden*]. ——— By the foreship was lying also one side of the poop, broken off at the starboard port of the gunners' room. Then there were several pieces of a lesser or greater size that had drifted apart to various places, so that there did not look to be much hope of salvaging much of the money or the goods. ——— But I understood from the steward[51] Reyndert Hendricxsz, which comforted me a little, that on a day one month ago when it was very calm, a thing which hardly ever, or rather rarely happened, he went to the wreck fishing (at which they kept him), and that with a pike he hit some money chests, and hoped that they had not drifted away in this time. ——— I also took the opportunity to ask him how matters had fared regarding the Ship or wreck, and how long it had remained whole after having been wrecked. He said that for 8 days it had held together, then the poop and the higher parts had been washed away first of all, in which days it had mostly blown very hard and there was a terrible surf, and at last the larboard [port] side had been burst, and the wrecking went on so quickly and easily that it was like a miracle. Then at different times floated ashore five[52] *leggers* water, one *legger* French wine, 4½ ditto Spanish, one ditto vinegar. ——— But before that God sent on the nights of 9 and 10 June, a hard steady rain, the same rain by which we who were in the boat near the continent, were in danger of drowning, from which they gathered much water; and after fished up the above mentioned, so that they could certainly have given all people three *mutskens* of water and 2 *mutskens* of wine for a long time, had the Devil not tempted them.

50 Here in the margin of the MS. Pelsaert has written: *Note: That the ring has been recovered hereafter.*
51 *Bottelier*: butler; or, aboard ship, steward.
52 Pelsaert wrote *five* above *three* scratched out.

In the evening I ordered the principal scoundrels and other accomplices whom I had bound here on the island, to be taken to Seals Island, from whence one could get them at an appropriate time if one wanted to examine them, so that in the meantime we would have more security.

On 19 do. in the morning, I sent the skipper to bring ashore those who have been kept imprisoned in the ship in order to inquire how they had conducted their lives; namely, Jeronimus Cornelisz, under Merchant; Jacop Pietersz from Amsterdam, Lanspesaat,[53] here Lieutenant Gen., and had been one of their councillors; Jan Hendricxsz of Bremen, soldier, one of the principal murderers; Rutger Fredricxsz of Groeningen, locksmith; Hans Jacobsz Heylwech of Basel, cadet; Lucas Gellissz from the Hague, cadet; Hans Fredericx of Bremen, soldier; Jan Willemsz Selyns[54] of Amsterdam, upper cooper; Hendrick Jaspersz Cloet[55] of Montfoort, soldier; Hans Hardens from Ditmarssen, soldier; Jaques Pilman of Pres du Verdun, soldier; Gerrit Haas of Zanten, sailor. ——— I have that day in part begun to comprehend from questioning and free confessions, what a godless life is that which has been lived here. The goods of the Company which they have fished up, as *laken*, stuffs, *passementerie*, and other wear, were very shamefully misused by making them into clothes embroidered with as much *passementerie* as possible. Jeronimus set the example, as appeared from his clothes found here. Moreover, all my clothes or goods he made his own, yea, none was exempt, and he used it [all] as if it had been left to him by will [*testament*], whereby he gave free rein to the utmost to his pride and devilish arrogance, on these poor miserable islands. More, by changing daily into different Clothes, silk stockings, garters with gold lace, and by putting on suchlike adornments belonging to other persons. Moreover, to all his Followers whom he could best trust, and who were most willing to murder, he gave clothes made from red *laken* sewn with 2 or more [bands] of *passementerie*. And created a new mode of Cassock[56] believing that such evil vain pleasure as this, could last for ever. ——— Furthermore, when the most murders had been committed, they shared the women who remained, or rather whom they had meant to keep as booty. Namely, Jeronimus took Lucretia Jansz, wife of Boudewyn van der Mylen; Coenraat van Huyssen; Judith Gysbrechtsz, eldest daughter of the predikant. Furthermore,

[53] Soldier with rank approximating to lance-corporal.
[54] Selyns may be a nickname; it is possibly derived from old Dutch word *zelling*, denoting the mark left by the keel of a ship, or an anchor, in sand.
[55] *Kloot*; ball; or clumsy fellow, a nickname.
[56] *Cassiacke*: It. *casacca*, a long coat.

the sisters Trynt and Zussie Fredricx, and Anneken Gunner [*Bosschieters*] should be available for common service. Jeronimus made several Articles to which the Women had to be put on oath if they wanted to remain alive — that they had to be obedient to the men in all that they should desire of them. ——— Of such [Articles] Jeronimus has made several, and he has also taken the oaths of the Men he wanted to save, that they should be obedient to him in every way in whatever he should order them, and that they should be faithful to him; he pledged himself on his Soul and salvation that those who signed the same, and whom he included, need not have any fear or mistrust that they would be murdered; though it has, nevertheless, happened that some of those who signed, or took the oath, had to be killed by hatred or distrust; therefore he tore the Oath of agreement publicly, by which action he dismissed the same, and so those who had to die were murdered at night, and then a new agreement was made. ——— Of these, I have found some, and [they] read as follows,

WE UNDERSIGNED persons, in order to remove all distrust that may be amongst us, or that may arise between us, and nevermore to have any recollection of such, will promise with this written unbreakable agreement, making to each other the greatest oath that anyone can take, to be faithful in everything, *so truly as God shall help us*, and will take the same on the salvation of our souls, to be faithful in everything, also that we shall do no harm to any of us undersigned, nor make any plan before the one has warned the other, nor shall anyone, without the other knowing it, undertake anything, be it by favour or by hatred, but assist one another in brotherly affection in all matters that may happen. ——— And towards further security we have signed this separately this 12 July Anno 1629, thus done on the island named *Batavia's* Graveyard.

Furthermore, dated as below, another similar, reading,

WE UNDERSIGNED persons, in order to remove all distrust that may be amongst us or that may arise between us, and nevermore to have any recollection of such, will promise with this written unbreakable agreement, making to each other the greatest oath that anyone can take, to be faithful in everything, *so truly as God shall help us*, and on our souls' salvation, also that God shall punish us here and Hereafter in Eternity, in as much [as] we undersigned persons may undertake any plan without revealing it to each, and that none shall undertake any plan separately be it by favour or by hatred, but in all matters that may happen assist each other in brotherly affection for the common welfare. And to maintain the given laws with the following women, Lucretia Jansz, Anneken Hardens, Judith Gysbertsz, Tryntien and Zussie Fredricx, Anneken Gunner [*Bosschieters*], and Marretgie Louys. In the same manner we have written our names with our own hands here below. Thus decided on the Island *Batavia's* Graveyard, the 16 July Anno 1629.[57]

Also,

WE UNDERSIGNED persons being present on this island, councillors as well as soldiers, sailors, as well as our Dominij,[58] no one excepted Whoever it may be accept as our chief, as Captain General, *Jeronimo Cornelij*, whom we with one accord, and each separately swear *so truly as God shall help us* to be faithful and obedient in all that he shall order us, and in so far as the Contrary happens, we shall be the Devil's own.

To which we have bound ourselves with a common hand herewith destroying [*te niet doende*] and casting away all previous promises, public and particular, and Oaths which have been taken before this, under which are included the secret comradeships, tent-ships, and others. ——— Also that the ship's folk amongst us will not be called sailors any more, but will be reckoned on the same footing as Soldiers, under one company. ——— Thus done on the island *Batavia's* Graveyard, 20 August Anno 1629.[59]

This following letter is by Jeronimus Cornelisz, on 23 July, translated into French, with Daniel Cornelisz sent secretly to the isle of Wiebbe Hayes in order to bring some French soldiers there to treason and to murder their own people—this was as follows,

Beloved Brothers and Friends, Jean Hongaar, Jean Reynouw de Miombry, Thomas de Villier, Jean Boniver, and Eduward Coo. ——— The more we consider amongst ourselves your previous faithfulness and brotherly friendship, the more we wonder that you who left willingly at the request of the Merchant to survey the High island, do not return to bring us word; for we have always considered you our greatest and truest brothers and friends, and have desired still more bonds and mateships (which we consider as valuable as our own lives), and still endeavour to strive therefor. ——— More, we think it strange that you seemed to give hearing to the tale-bearing of some evil-doers who here had deserved death on account of mutiny, and therefore were sent by us to another island, but came to you without our knowledge.

That on the island we have bound Jean Coos de Sally, only happened on account of Jean Thiriou, whom we also sent (because he had

---

[57] Pelsaert gives the names of those who signed later on in his Journals (see p. 165).

[58] *Dominie*: the predikant Gijsbert Bastiaensz.

[59] The names of those who signed this oath are given later in the Journals (see p. 166).

swilled drink from the *legger* [barrel]), and because we feared that Jean Coos helped him, which was otherwise, as we learnt later on, for Jean has offered to stab him, if he [Jean Coos] were allowed to live and die with us, with which [killing] he would have done a particular friendship for us, and still shall do so. ———

Now then, beloved Brothers and Friends, Jean Hongaar, Jean Renouw, Thomas de Villier, Jean Boniver, Eduward Coo, and Jean Coos, come to us, help us (to maintain justice and to punish the evildoers) in particular to give into our hands alive those who so treacherously the day before yesterday robbed us and Your Hons. (because we and you are one) of our greatest help, the little yawl, and also give to our hands Lucas the steward's mate, Cornelis the fat trumpeter, Cornelis the assistant, deaf Jan Michielsz, Ariaen the gunner, squinting Hendrick, Theunis Claasz, Cornelis Helmigs, and other sailors who are with Your Hons., for they have in their possession (unknown to you) a Compass, in order thus to go secretly with the little skiff to the High land. ——— The Merchant, who has a particular liking for, and trust in Wiebbe Hayes, wishes and requests that you should inform him secretly of this. ——— Furthermore, we refer everything to a report Your Hon. Confrère, Daniel Cornelisz will make verbally, if Your Hons. will give him free hearing. Herewith, beloved Brothers and friends, we commit Your Hons. altogether to the protection and safekeeping of the Highest. This 23 July Anno 1629 on the Island *Batavia's* Graveyard.

Was signed
Jeronimus Cornelisz

Those were the means, because they saw that they could not overcome the people on the High Island with force, to overcome them in such a manner, by treason; and with that purpose they wrote more suchlike letters, of which not all Copies have been found, in order to deceive them. ——— But it seemed that when the cruel things they had started, although they still had the intention to do more, were at the culminating point, God Almighty had stopped their evil intention by destroying some of the principal leaders by the sword and by causing Jeronimus, the Author of all, to be captured, as before mentioned, in order to make more known to all men the wonder of His justice.

On 20 do. before Noon, I have sent the boat aboard,[60] also the yawl to the island where the people of Wiebbe Hayes were, to fetch water, because they had found, very miraculously after they had been on the island 20 days, 2 pits with fresh water, which with ebb and high tide flow up and down, therefore they thought it was salt water, as I shall relate later on in more detail.

[60] Back to the *Sardam*.

On 21 do. the Wind E.S.E. with a hard gale though noticed that the water here remained very low, and because of the hard wind the yawl could not return; we spent this day with examinations.

On 22 do. the Wind as before. But no yawl to be seen; before noon, I went with the skipper and 3 men in a skiff to the Wreck in order to see if one could inspect the whole situation, but the breakers were running so high that the Swimmers could not get through; towards evening the yawl came back.

On 23 do. the Wind as before. In the morning I had the scoundrels who had been held secure on Seals Island, fetched from there for examination. I have been busy with this the whole day. ——— Meanwhile I sent the steersman [Claas Gerritsz] to the wreck, in order to see if any work could be done, but he has come back with the information that it was impossible to get near it because of the heavy breakers.

On 24 do. the Skipper went aboard with the boat for some necessities, because it was impossible to work at the wreck.

On 25 do. in the Morning when the weather was Calm, I sent the Skipper with the steersman to the Wreck in order to see if it were possible to begin work. When they came near it, I noticed that they were busy hauling something up. ——— Therefore I sent them another boat, with a crew, in order to help them, and I also went in the smallest skiff with 2 cabin boys and a Man, to the same spot, and saw that they had fished up a chest with Tinsel [*Clater gout*][61] as well as a money chest, which they brought to a shallow a little way from the wreck. I stepped into another boat, which was also engaged in fishing up, and we got yet another money chest above water. ——— The Gouseratse[62] divers said they saw yet another six that could be got. Meanwhile, I brought the money chest which we had buoyed, to the shallow also, and the divers prepared yet another for when the skipper should come, so that we had now 4 chests. Again it started to blow very hard, and the surf came up so that we had to leave the wreck. Therefore we fetched the money chests that had been put in the shallows and brought them to the Island *Batavia's* Graveyard. The rest of the day was spent in examining.

On 26 do. a hard Wind out of the S.W. so that we could not work at the wreck, therefore a boat has been sent to an island on the opposite side [*een over eijlandt*] in order to fetch several empty oil barrels, amongst other things, and a capstan that was lying there; before noon also a yawl has been sent for water, and I have ordered Cornelis Jansz of Amsterdam, assistant, and Aris Janssz

---

[61] Modern Dutch: *klatergoud*.   [62] Divers from Gujarat, in India.

of Hoorn, barber, to be fetched, in order to examine them regarding what had happened to them when they were escaping, at the time when they were to have been killed. But after noon it started to become very calm and the sea was smooth, therefore I sent the skipper immediately to the Wreck in order to haul up the chests with money (which we had seen yesterday); in the afternoon he has returned with 3 chests with money, and there was yet one chest which was impossible to get for the time being because on it was a cannon with an anchor across it, which would have to be pushed away with force.

On 27 do. the wind out of the South, hard gale; not able to do anything about the Wreck. Before noon the yawl has come from the high island with the 2 above mentioned persons, Cornelis and Aris, so that we went on with the examining of the scoundrels.

On 28 do. the wind Southerly, with hard gale, so that we have not been able to do anything at the wreck. ——— Therefore, after completing a thorough examination of the principal Murderers and Villains, from their own confessions as well as from numerous witnesses, and by God's Truth have got enough information, as seen by the following written testimonies ——— I have called together the council, and after ripe deliberation have put to them the question whether those against whom innocent blood is calling for revenge, should be taken to Batavia before the Hon. Lord Gov. Gen., or whether they should be punished here with death as an Example to others, in order to prevent all disasters that might arise on the ship through suchlike Men as Jeronimus and his Accomplices. Because some, more hardened, are already impregnated with the bad life, whilst others have sipped a little of the poison, and they could easily become wholly corrupted by the richness of the salvaged wealth which belongs to our Lord Masters, which we have now fished up. ——— Therefore it would not be without danger for the ship and the goods to set off to sea with so many corrupt and half-corrupted men, have decided, as appears from the following resolution ———

> TODAY the 28 Sept. 1629 on the island named *Batavia's* Graveyard situated near by the Wreck of the lost Ship *Batavia*, on the latitude of 28½ degrees Southern latitude, about 9 miles from the main Southland, the Commandeur *Franco pelsart*, and the ship's council of the Yacht *Sardam*, resolved as follows—

We have, thanks to God, at last arrived with the Yacht *Sardam*, on the 17th of this month, after suffering many dangers, at the High Island 2 miles from the wreck, where a small boat with four Men came to the Commandeur, who had gone ashore with bread, water and wine in order to assist, because of the smoke that we saw rising up there, to warn that he had to go back immediately on board, because there was on the islands near the Wreck, a party of scoundrels who had the intention to seize the Yacht; also that they had been able to capture Jeronimus Cornelissz (who was chief of the scoundrels), whom the Commandeur immediately ordered to be brought on board, and had himself returned with the yawl to the ship and had imparted the said tidings of what he had briefly understood, upon which we prepared ourselves for defence, and shortly afterwards 11 men from a flat-bottomed yawl have come on board, who were all taken prisoner and examined, as well as Jeronimus Cornelisz, who was brought aboard that day, bound. Out of which, as well as from the other scoundrels, we have realized with great grief the gruesome and abominable murders which the said Jeronimus, with Davidt van Sevanck, assistant, Coenraat van Huyssen, cadet, and Jacop Pietersz, lanspesaet, who 14 days ago had been killed on the High island, except Jacop Pietersz, having the intention to reduce the number of people to 40, and who to that purpose did attempt to master a certain party of 47 souls who had escaped out of the murdering on the High island and so saved their lives (and to master them with force and murder them) in order thus, according to their confessions, to seize the first Yacht that should come to rescue them, and then sail to Spain, Barbary, or suchlike places.

Furthermore, we learned from their own confessions and the testimony of all the living persons, that they have drowned, murdered and brought to death with all manner of cruelties, more than 120 persons, men, women and children as well, of whom the principal murderers amongst those still alive have been: Leenert Michielsz van Os, soldier; Mattys Beer of Munsterbergh, cadet;[63] Jan Hendricxsz of Bremen, soldier; Allert Janssz of Assendelft, gunner; Rutger Fredricx of Groeningen, locksmith; Jan Pelgrom de Bye of Bemmel, cabin servant, and Andries Jonas of Luyck, soldier, with their Consorts. ——— Therefore we have been busy from 17th onwards daily, with examinations in order to come to the straight truth, and from the examinations and freewill confes-

---

[63] Pelsaert has here confused the status of these two men. Later evidence shows that Michielsz was the cadet, Beer the soldier.

sions of Jeronimus Cornelisz we found that, on the Ship *Batavia*, after sailing from *Cabo de bone esperansa*, he, with the skipper Ariaen Jacobsz, conspired to seize the Ship; they would have murdered all but 120 persons, with which they would have started first on robbery, and after that they would have sailed to Spain and suchlike countries—but because the ship was wrecked they have not been able to carry this out. ——— Further confesses that all people had been murdered on his order and with common agreement of his council, in order, as has been said, to reduce them to a small number. ——— Also confesses that he, with Sevanck, Coenraat van Huyssen, and Jacop Pietersz, had decided to seize the first-coming Yacht; namely, after they had mastered the folk on the great [*sic*] island, or won them over, that then, when a ship should come, they would allow the boat to come ashore, and they would make the crew of it drunk, in order to kill them easily; and then with the same boat to surprise the Yacht at night, which as far as they thought, could not possibly fail, because they reckoned that on it would come only 20 to 30 Men.[64]

THEREFORE after long examination of all people who have been on the island, in order to come to the straight truth, which, praise be to God, we have found, the question has been put by the Commandeur, whether one should take such a gruesome villain (who is besmirched with all thinkable misdeeds and the horror thereof) in captivity on our Ship to Batavia to bring him before the Hon. Lord Gov. Gen., who could give him the justly deserved punishment, or whether, because according to the strict order of our Lord Masters, villains and Criminal evil-doers must not be brought to Batavia, in order not to put ships and men in such like danger (should be punished here)—

THEREFORE WE HAVE exchanged our thoughts thoroughly and maturely and have considered; because we found one gruesome sin in the above mentioned Jeronimus, besmirched in every way not only with abominable misdeeds but also with damnable heresy, declaring that there is neither devil nor Hell, and has tried to imprint that into the people here on the island—moreover that it is still his daily work to bring with his tongue well-intentioned people to a wrong opinion and lead them from the straight path. ——— Have therefore unanimously resolved and found good, in the best service of the Company and our Hon. Lord Masters, in order that their ship and the valuable goods that have been fished up here, praise be to God, may be safe against further disaster, to sentence the said Jeronimus Cornelisz, with the worst and most

---

[64] Sound reckoning: the *Sardam* carried a crew of 26.

willing Murderers, who have made a profession of it [heresy].
────── Accordingly we sentence and condemn with this, that firstly
JERONIMUS CORNELISZ, of Haarlem, Apothecary, and late under
Merchant of the ship *Batavia*, on Monday, being the first of
October, as he has requested to be baptised, [shall be taken] to
Seals Island, to a place made ready for it in order to exercise Justice,
and there firstly to cut off both his hands, and after shall be punished on the Gallows with the Cord till Death shall follow, with
confiscation of all his money, gold, Silver, monthly wages, and all
claims which here in India he may have against the profits of the
Gen. East India Company, our Lord Masters.

JAN HENDRICXZ of Bremen, soldier, aged about 24 years, who according to his confession and examination in full [*int largo*]
appears to have murdered 17 to 18 people and helped murder
them, as well as having the intention to seize the Yacht that came
to rescue them, shall also be taken to the above mentioned Seals
Island, at which place Justice shall be exercised, in order that there
firstly his right hand shall be cut off, and after that he shall be
punished on the gallows with the Cord till death shall follow, with
confiscation of all his kit [*plunjen*], monthly wages and all that
he may have to claim against the Hon. Lord Masters. ────── Also,

LENART MICHIELSZ van Os, cadet, aged about 21 years, who according to his freewill confession has murdered 12 people or has helped
to murder them, and who has slept with married Women and has
used as his concubine Anneken Gunner [*Bosschieters*] wife of
Jan Carstensz of Tonningen. ────── Therefore he shall be taken to
Seals Island in order that there, firstly, his right hand shall be cut
off, and after that he shall be punished on the gallows with the
Cord till death follows, with confiscation of all his kit, monthly
moneys, and all that he may have to claim against the Hon. Lord
Masters. ────── Also,

MATTYS BEIJR of Munsterbergh, soldier, aged about 21 years old,
who according to his freewill confession in full, has murdered 9
people or has helped to murder them, also has kept as his concubine Zussie Fredricx, married Woman. ────── Therefore he shall
also be taken to Seals Island in order, firstly, to cut off his right
hand, and after that to punish him on the gallows with the Cord
till death follows, with confiscation of all his kit, monthly moneys,
and all that he may have to claim against the Hon. Lord Masters.
────── Also,

ALLERT JANSSEN of Assendelft, gunner, aged about 24 years, who
according to his freewill confession in full, has confessed to being

persuaded by Jeronimus Cornelisz to help to seize the ship *Batavia*, to which he had consented. As well, he has cut the throat of Andries de Bruyn of Haarlem, Boy, also has helped to murder Jan Pinten, Englishman, and that, one night with the others, he had the intention to kill Aris Jansz of Hoorn, barber, but through the bluntness of his sword, though he gave him a blow on the shoulder, it did not go through it, and the above mentioned Aris escaped in the darkness in the water; as well, has committed many wilful deeds during the wrecking of the ship. —––— Therefore he shall also be taken to Seals Island in order that there first his right hand shall be cut off, and after that he shall be punished on the Gallows with the Cord till Death follows, with confiscation of all his kit, monthly wages, and all that he may have to claim against the Lords. —––— Also,

JAN PELGROM DE BYE of Bemel, aged about 18 years, late cabin servant [*kayuitwachter*] on the ship *Batavia*, who according to his own freewill confession has behaved in a godless manner in words and deeds, more fitting to a beast than a man, has also murdered on Seals Island the cabin boy Smoert and Janneken Gist, wife of Jan Hendricxsz from the Hague, gunner, and has also helped Andries Jonas to kill. —––— And on 16 August required very urgently that he should be allowed to behead Cornelis Aldersz of Ylpendam, cooper, but this was allowed to Mattys Beyr, about which he [de Bye] has wept. —––— He also has had carnal knowledge of Zussien and Tryntgie Fredricxsz, both sisters, and Anneken Gunner [*Bosschieters*] all married women. —––— Therefore he also shall be taken to Seals Island in order there to punish him on the Gallows with the Cord till death shall follow, with confiscation of all his kit, monthy wages and all that he may have to claim against Lord Masters. —––— Also,

ANDRIES JONAS of Luyck, soldier, aged about 40 years, who according to his freewill confession has also put a spear through the throat of Pauwels van Harderwych when he was stabbed to death in the water, and has cut the throat, on Seals Island, of Mayken Soers, who was pregnant, and also has helped, together with Jan van Bemmel, to kill Janneken Gist. —––— And he has allowed himself to be used of his own freewill at all enterprises. —––— Therefore he also shall be taken to Seals Island in order to be punished there on the Gallows with the Cord till Death shall follow, with confiscation of all his kit, monthly wages, and all that he may have to claim against Lord Masters. —––— Also,

RUTGER FREDRICX of Groeningen, locksmith, aged about 23 years, who according to his freewill confession bound the hands and feet of Jacop Groenewaldt, upper trumpeter, when he was to be drowned, and was carried into the Sea by Sevanck and de Vriese. —— Also, when Pieter Jansz, provost, was thrown into the Sea with 14 others, and Pauls Barentsz with Bessel Jansz, both from Harderwyck, Niclaas Winckelhaack, Claas Harmansz of Maagdenborgh, escaped by swimming and fled here on this island [*Batavia's* Graveyard], it was then ordered by Jeronimus that they should be slain; and he, Rutger, has given Pauwels Barentsz 2 strokes with his sword, and from that he has gone towards Claas Harmansz, whom he had killed single handed. —— Also, when Andries de Vries, assistant, was ordered to be killed, the above mentioned Rutger, Jan Hendricx and Lenert Michielsz were called by Jeronimus into his tent, and each was given a sword in order to smite de Vries to death—whereto he allowed himself to be used willingly, without protest. When de Vries saw that his life was forfeit, he fled into the water, and Lenert Michielsz followed him into the water and killed him with 2 strokes, so that he [Rutger] had not been able to have a hand in that. —— Secondly, Jeronimus affirms that the mentioned Rutger has of his own freewill allowed himself to be used in all things, together with Mattys Beer or suchlike, and therefore cannot talk himself clean. —— Therefore he also shall be taken to Seals Island to be punished there on the Gallows till death follows, with confiscation of all his kit, monthly wages, and all that he may have to claim against Lord Masters.

HAVING resolved, as there are still some evil-doers here in captivity, because we are not as yet fully informed or certain of all their misdeeds, and secondly, insofar as we are in doubt concerning some, whether they should be considered guilty of death or whether their lives may be spared without [our] falling into disgrace with the Hon. Lord Gov. Gen. —— Therefore the under mentioned persons shall be kept in captivity, thus to bring them to Batavia to the Hon. Lord Gov. Gen., or to punish them on the way, according to time and occasion —— Namely—

> Wouter Loos of Maastricht, soldier, but who has been made Captain of the rebel troop after the capture of Jeronimus Cornelis
> Jacop Pietersz of Amsterdam, lanspesat, councillor of Jeronimus as well as
> Sevanck and Coenraat van Huyssen
> Hans Jacop of Basel, cadet
> Daniel Cornelisz of Dort., cadet

Andries Liebent of Oldens, cadet
Hans Fredrick of Bremen, soldier
Cornelis Jansz of Haarlem, sailor
Rogier Decker of Haarlem, late Boy to
    Jeronimus
Jan Willemsz Selyns of Amsterdam, cooper.

AND the rest of the prisoners shall be let free until later decision, unless something detrimental arises.

ALSO, because we notice from manifold testimonies that Wiebbe Hayes of Winschooten, soldier, all the time that he has been with 47 people on the high island, has faithfully protected and defended them when they were three times attacked by the party of murderers who had intended to kill them all ——— Have decided, God willing, as there are no officers over the soldiers, to appoint the above mentioned Wiebbe Hayes Sergeant of the same; we do so forthwith, with the salary of 18[65] guilders per month, beginning from today. ——— Also,

Otto Smit of Halverstadt } cadets
Allert Jansz of Elsen

On account of their good conduct, to be promoted as well as Wiebbe Hayes, to Corporals with a salary of 15 guilders per month, beginning from today. ——— Thus done and laid down on the Island *Batavia's* Graveyard, date as above.

FranCo. Pelsartt
Jacob Jacobsz *houten man*
Claas Gerritsz
Jacop Jansz
Sijmon IJopzoon
This is the mark of
Jan ⚓ Willemsz
    Visch[66]

[65] The figure 2 has been erased, and 1 written above it; it would appear that Pelsaert had second thoughts about such a high salary as 28 guilders, and thought the authorities might not approve. The usual pay of a soldier was about 10 guilders per month. Soon after arrival at Batavia, Hayes's salary was lifted to 40 guilders per month on appointment to the rank of cornet. See Appendix V.

[66] These signatures are the originals and the handwriting differs greatly. In order of rank they are: Commandeur; skipper of the *Sardam*; uppersteersman, late of the *Batavia*; understeersman, also late of the *Batavia*; high boatswain of the *Sardam*; and probably a sailor convened for the council, Visch, who was unable to write. Pelsaert has written his name for him and made him attach his mark. *Houten man* literally means "wooden man". On 29th September Pelsaert writes *Holloch* after the name of Jacob Jacobsz, but reasons remain obscure.

[Pelsaert next details the examinations of the various prisoners as they took place from 17th September onwards.]

FIRST there will follow the examinations of Jeronimus Cornelisz, from the day when he was brought to us as a prisoner until today; have been busy with him daily; as well as his freewill confession concerning the great evil misdeeds done and intended by him. ——— Whereupon his sentence has been passed on him, as well as on his Accomplices ——— follows—

> TODAY 17 Sept. 1629, after noon has been resolved by the Commandeur *Franco. pelsart* and the Ship's council to bring forward the captured Jeronimus Cornelisz of Haarlem, Apothecary, and later under Merchant on the Ship *Batavia*, in order to examine the gruesome deeds which had done, and still had in mind to do, and if necessary to put to torture; on the Yacht *Sardam*—date as above.

JERONIMUS CORNELISZ, brought in, has been asked by the Commandeur why through the devil he has denuded himself of all humanity, and why he was more evil than if he had been changed into a tiger animal, so that he had to let flow so much innocent blood; and also has had the intention also to do that with us. Whereon he says, "Everything that has been done is not my fault, but Davidt Sevanck, Gysbert van Welderen and Coenraat van Huyssen have thought of it and forced me to it, otherwise I had to die." And furthermore has desired to be heard in order to plead himself free, and has been ordered to tell from the beginning ———
SAYS, that after the wrecking of the Ship, he had been 10 days on the Wreck and that the same had been smitten to pieces during that time, so that he sat for 2 days in the bowsprit top-mast [*marsse*] and at last has come ashore with the pole of the same bowsprit. He found that a cask [*legger*] of water, ditto wine, ditto vinegar, washed at the same time to the island. Having been on the island for about a month, Davidt Sevanck and Coenraat van Huyssen, cadet, with another 12, have come to his tent about 10 or 11 hours, armed, the above mentioned persons saying that there were too many people and the food was too little; that they had the intention to surprise all the people in the tents and to kill them

The Great Cameo of Gaspar Boudaen. Antiquarians consider that it was carved in A.D. 312-315. It was once in the hands of the mutineers on the Abrolhos Islands, and can now be seen at the Royal Coin Cabinet, The Hague.

An engraving of the Great Cameo by Paulus Pontius, after a drawing by Peter Paul Rubens. The stark classical lines of the carving have been transformed by Rubens into opulent curves, and the whole given movement and vitality.

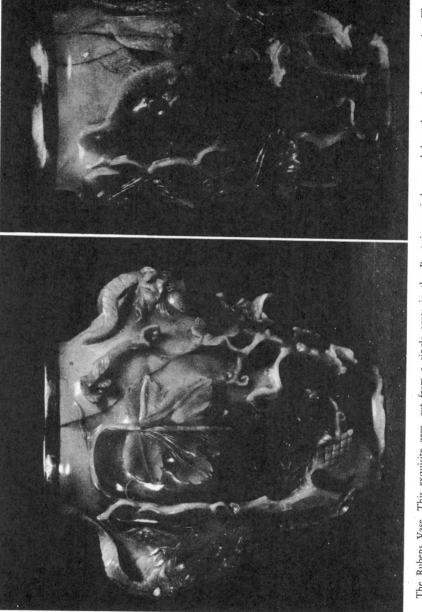

The Rubens Vase. This exquisite gem, cut from a single agate in the Byzantine period, once belonged to the great artist. There is evidence to suggest that it was amongst the jewels landed on the Abrolhos Islands from the wrecked *Batavia*. It can be seen today in the Walters Art Gallery, Baltimore, U.S.A.

all except 40. ———— Whereon he, Jeronimus, has requested them that they should not do this, but that it was better to send the folk to the high island in order to go there in search of water as 22 other men who had been sent previously; which they would scarcely permit; but because he implored it, a party had been sent away.[67]

———— 17 days after that happened, Sevanck went with a sloop of people to the island where the above mentioned party of people were, and he with his associates have murdered them all, except 7 Boys and some Women.—Coming back, the said Sevanck told Jeronimus that he had done that, and that he also wished that had also happened to the rest who were on the high island, then they would not have to expect any damage from them. ———— 7 to 8 days after that, they have come again to Jeronimus and said that they would sail to the opposite side to fight against the other folk, the more because Pieter Lambertsz, sailor, with a little self-made boat had saved his life and gone over; and in order to get it back if possible. ———— Whereto they chose 22 Men, which the forementioned Jeronimus said was not to his liking; but he would have requested them to get ready a boat or sloop in order to go to the continent and afterwards to India, which to them seemed impossible;[68] but they have gone out, according to the before mentioned resolution, with the 22 Men. When they returned Jeronimus would again have requested them to make a vessel in readiness, but on the contrary they have gone out again with three little yawls with 37 men, amongst whom was Jeronimus, in order to prevent as much as possible the fighting, if it came to that. ———— They went straight at them, but the others guarded the beach and stood up to their knees in water, so Jeronimus requested to talk with them and to come to accord. Meanwhile, through the mediation of the *dominij*, who went to and fro, to keep from fighting that day and promised to bring them the next day some *laken* to dress themselves; in exchange, the others would hand over the small boat. Whereon the people became very angry and wanted to fight. Coenraat van Huyssen said, he would fight them the following day, against the wish of everybody. ———— The next day Jeronimus has returned with *laken*, with six persons; namely, himself, Davidt Sevanck, Coenraat van Huyssen, Gysbrecht van Welderen, Wouter Loos, and Cornelis Pietersz of Wtrecht, of whom 4 persons have been killed through a fight that arose. Wouter Loos escaped, and Jeronimus was taken prisoner.

[67] To Seals Island.
[68] In 1727 when the *Zeewyck* was wrecked in the Pelsart Group, that is exactly what her crew did.

M

> The Commandeur proposes to bring to torture the above mentioned Jeronimus in order to learn from him the straight truth, as he tries to exonerate himself with flowery talk, shoving his dirt on to persons who are dead and cannot answer for themselves; the which we councillors thought very necessary.

JERONIMUS CORNELISZ, being bound, and having started to torture him a little, requests a postponement, for he wished to tell that which one had asked him, and what he knew. Has been permitted to be heard; and the Commandeur has desired to know from him why, and in what manner he desired to seize the Yacht. He declares, that at the time when the 22 Men had gone to the island for the fight, and he called them back, Sevanck has told, when he was in the sloop, of a dream of Lucas Gelisz, cadet, when there would come a Yacht and that it was necessary to seize it to sail to Spain or other places near there, and such at last has been decided.

FURTHERMORE asked in what manner they would have done it, said, that if a Yacht came, they would have let the boat come ashore and then they would have made the crew drunk in order to kill them easily, and so, without any doubt, they would have seized it; whereupon they had desired to see the jewels of the Company and have them shared, how much the portion would be for each; Jeronimus has opened and has shown them.

YESTERDAY the 18 Sept. in the afternoon, Jeronimus Cornelisz, sitting locked up in the foredeck of the ship *Sardam,* with Jan Hendricxz, soldier, close to him, while Jan Willemsz of Dort., sailor, was lying on the foredeck above their heads, and has heard that Jeronimus Cornelisz asked the ditto Jan Hendricxsz why on the Morning of the 17th they had not got the little skiff when they were fighting with them [the party on the High Island]; and why the musket had not gone off, whether the gunpowder had been wet, Jan Hendricxsz answered, "Had we shot immediately with the musket then we should certainly have got them, but the gunpowder burned away 3 to 4 times from the pan."[69] Whereon Jeronimus said, "If you had used some cunning, you would have got it all ready on the water and then we should have been ready." This we have verified with Jeronimus, and the said Jan Hendricxsz confesses that the same has happened thus.

[69] Part of lock that held the priming in obsolete types of guns.

TODAY the 19 Sept. on the island named *Batavia's* Graveyard,

JERONIMUS CORNELISZ, bound, and made ready for torture, requested pause; that he would say truthfully what he knew. And he has been asked by the Commandeur why he advised the skipper Arian Jacopsz to seize the ship *Batavia*. Denied the same, yea, that he knew anything about it; but wished to tell in full the origin of his shameful living, to wit. —— When we have gone under sail from Sierra Lionas, he noticed that the skipper made great familiarity with Lucretia. For which he chided him, and asked what he intended with that woman. —— The skipper answered that because she was fair, he desired to tempt her to his will, and to make her willing with Gold or other means. Sometime later the above mentioned Jeronimus has asked him why he was no longer so familiar towards Lucretia, but had become crazed anew by Zwaantgie. Said, that he understood from the cook's wife that she was a whore, and that, moreover, he had more pleasure to talk with Zwaantgie and to spend time with her. When they had come to the *Cabo* and the Commandeur had gone ashore, Jeronimus Cornelisz, coming unexpectedly into the Cabin, and opening the privy in the gallery,[70] found the skipper and Zwaantie in the act of carnal knowledge with each other; therefore he closed the door and went away. Two days after that, the Commandeur has again gone ashore in order to seek beasts [cattle] inland. Shortly after he left, the skipper, taking with him Jeronimus and Zwaantie, has gone ashore, and they went on a pleasure trip thus until evening, when they then sailed to the Yacht *Assendelft*[71] where the foresaid Ariaen behaved himself very pugnaciously [*moetwillingh*] and at night time they went to the Ship *Bueren*,[72] where he behaved himself worse, and at midnight they came again aboard. —— The next day in the Morning, the Commandeur called him [Ariaen] into the gallery and chided him over his arrogance and deeds committed by him, and also because he had taken with him, without permission, Jeronimus and Zwaantie, saying that if he did not refrain from his unheard of behaviour, he [the Commandeur] would take a hand; with more other good admonishments. Skipper Ariaen, coming above again, said to Jeronimus, "By God, if the ships were not lying there, I should get at him so that he

---

[70] A gallery overhanging the sea on each side, astern, at the level of the Great Cabin, was a new feature of shipbuilding at this date, and was considered a great advance in comfort and convenience; officers' privies, baggage, etc., were so situated.
[71] One of the ships in Pelsaert's fleet.
[72] Warship with fleet.

would not be able to come out of his bunk within 8 to 14 days, but I swear that as soon as I go under sail from here, that I soon will be away from the other ships, and then I shall be able to be my own master." Whereupon Jeronimus said, "How would you manage that, for the steersmen also have the watch?" Answered, "That is nothing. I will manage it in my own watch. But I do not like the uppersteersman [Claas Gerritsz] and still less my brother-in-law [Gillis Fransz or Jacob Jansz], nor that they should fall in with my plan." ———

The Commandeur asking him [Jeronimus] further, because he wished to know when the decision to seize the ship had been made, denied knowing anything about it.

Therefore again made ready to torture.

And after a little water[73] has been poured out, says that he will say all that he knows; That he has heard for the first time on the day that the Ship *Batavia* was wrecked, from the mouth of Ryckert Woutersz, in public, at the time when the Commandeur and the skipper sailed with the sloop to the nearest island, that if the ship had not stranded, they would have seized the same within a short time, and they would have thrown the Commandeur overboard, with all people except 120, and that they were only awaiting a good opportunity, one they considered to be best, when the Commandeur should put in irons those who had laid hands on Lucretia. ——— They would have run with the Ship firstly to Madagascar or St Helena. Declares, to have heard the same also out of the mouth of Coenraat van Huyssen, that when the foresaid persons were punished, or put in irons, he [Coenraat] would have been amongst the first who would have jumped with a sword into the Cabin, in order to throw the Commandeur overboard. ——— Again asked if he did not know anything about this before the ship was wrecked, denies, No.

> Have ordered to go on with the torture; has again desired to hear some of his accusers, which has been granted him.

JAN HENDRICXSZ, soldier, being called, asked whether he has been one of the conspirators in the seizing of the Ship. Says that he was not one of them, and that he had not known anything of it on board, but that he had heard from several people after the wrecking of the ship, who were dead now, that the skipper, Jeronimus,

[73] The water torture was the one used: see Chapter VI, p. 101.

the High boatswain [Jan Evertsz], Ryckert Woutersz, Allert Jansz of Assendelft, Cornelis Jansz of Haarlem, alias *Boontie*,[74] Gysbert van Welderen, Coenraat van Huyssen, with 10 to 12 others would have started the same, and that they would have nailed the soldiers' hatch until they had their will with the ship. But that Allert Jansz of Assendelft was certainly one of the Accomplices.

ALLERT JANSZ of Assendelft being called, has been examined, free and unbound, in what manner would they have mastered the ship *Batavia*, and who had put them up to that? Has answered, that he did not know about it, but he had heard it said on land, by Jeronimus, that they wanted to do that, and that parties had swords lying in their hammocks; but would not confess any more.

> Put to torture about this, persisted that he knew nothing of it.

After beginning of the torture, he prays to be let free, as he will speak the truth. Says, that Jeronimus has come to him on the ship and has made a proposal to him, whether he would take a hand in the seizing of the ship. But had said neither yea nor nay. ——— When more water has been poured out for the torture, confesses that the High boatswain [Jan Evertsz], Jacop Pietersz Steenhouwer,[75] and he, with still others, had swords lying in their hammocks [*koyen*] ——— Threatened him further ——— confesses, that the skipper was the ringleader, and that as far as he knew they were only 10 to 12 Men strong, and that it would have happened at night and they would have nailed the Hatch in order to master the Ship more easily.

JERONIMUS CORNELISZ, again brought into the tent, and being bound for torture, as one could not get from him the straight truth, and asked whether he had not sounded Assendelft for that, confesses, Yea. But that the skipper Ariaen has ordered him such, and that he was seduced by him. He, being asked why the skipper was so embittered against the Commandeur, says, that he does not know, for he often wondered that he [the Commandeur] liked him so much and put up with him. But that the skipper had told him that he had started to hate the Commandeur when he was in Souratte waiting to sail to the Fatherland,[76] and when he had gone too far

---

[74] *Boontje*: little bean, a nickname.

[75] *Steenhouwer*: stone-cutter. Pietersz held the rank of *lanspassaet*, but perhaps *steenhouwer* was a nickname. Farther on this man also has the added name of *Cosijn*, which means a window-frame. Both names are added to his sentence. See Appendix V.

[76] Pelsaert left Surat aboard the *Dordrecht* in December 1627. See Chapter II.

in words one night, whereon the Commandeur Grijph and Wollebrand Gheleijnsen, Upper Merchant, rebuked him, saying that that was not the manner to sail in peace to the Fatherland, and that he must behave himself differently towards the Commandeur, or that he should dissemble a little on their behalf. ——— Furthermore asked why the Commandeur should not have been thrown overboard secretly if it was only [a matter of] hate, because then they would not have brought so much damage to Lord Masters and would not have had to murder so many innocent people. He says, the Commandeur was not the whole desire, but the skipper said to him [Jeronimus] that it would be to their advantage and because there was now so little profit to be got in India, he would do wonders with that Ship. Jeronimus asked him would it not be dangerous, and whether they would be able to bring it off; the skipper said, "Let me go my way, I will manage it. For I can trust my cousin [*neef*], the bos'n's mate [*schieman*], but I put little trust in the understeersman my brother-in-law [Gillis Fransz or Jacop Jansz] or in the uppersteersman [Claas Gerritsz]." ——— Furthermore asked when they would have done it, said, when the Commandeur would have put in irons the folk concerned in the deed with Lucretia. Him further asked whether the Company and the Commandeur had deserved that from him, says, No. But that he has enjoyed more favour and consideration than he deserved, but the skipper had brought him to it, and painted to him great riches. The skipper said, "I am still for the Devil; if I go to India, then I have to come to shame in any case."

Further examined why he had put about the story among the people that the Commandeur when he left the Ship, had ordered him that he should reduce the number of people to 40, he denies that, and that the Commandeur had not said it to him, but that Davidt Sevanck thought it necessary to put that to the people— Confesses also that Davidt Sevanck and Lucas Jelisz had resolved between themselves to seize the first Yacht that came, in order to sail with that to Spain or some place nearby, for they all thought that the skipper [would have] certainly smitten the Commandeur overboard from the boat, and that he had run with the boat to Mallacca in order to get a yacht there, to get in that way the folks and the money; or, if he had the hardihood to go to Batavia, he would certainly have got a Yacht from the Hon. Lord Gov. Gen. in order to reach again the Ship and the people, and if that had happened, they would be ready.

Being asked why he had ordered Mr Frans Jansz of Hoorn,

upperbarber,[77] to be killed without more ado, he said that he was in the way of Sevanck, and secondly, that he would not dance exactly to their pipes, so they had little confidence in him.

Being asked who the most innocent were, he says, Jacques Pilman; Jeurian Jansz of Bremen, sailor; Reynder Hendricxsz of Barklooster, steward; Abraham Jansz of Yperen, gunner; Teunis Jansz of Amsterdam, carpenter; Jan Egbertsz of Amsterdam, carpenter; Jan Willemsz Selynsz of Amsterdam, cooper.

Says also, that the Council consisted of 4 persons, namely, Jeronimus Cornelisz, Coenraat van Huyssen, Davidt Sevanck, and Jacop Pietersz Steenhouwer, and what has been decided by them, whom one should kill, was immediately carried out.

And because of the want of trust that was among the leaders and other principals, they have made an Oath of trust amongst themselves, and whoever had been included in it and had signed it, would be spared; and this went as follows—

[Here Pelsaert again inserts a copy of the oath taken on 16th July by the mutineers,[78] but here he also writes out a list of the names of those who signed.]

    Hieronimus Cornelisz, Merchant
    Coenraat van Huyssen, councillor
    Jacop Pietersz Cosijn, councillor
    Davidt van Sevanck, councillor
    Isbrant Ysbrantsz, assistant
    Olivier van Welderen, cadet
    Gysbert van Welderen, cadet
    Jan Pelgrom de Bye of Bemel
    Jan Hendricx of Bremen, soldier
    Lenert Michielsz van Os, cadet
    Mattys Beer of Munsterbergh, soldier
    Allert Jansz of Assendelft, gunner
    Hans Hardens from Ditmarsen, soldier
    Rutger Fredricx of Groen., locksmith
    Gerrit Willemsz of Enchuysen, sailor
    Cornelis Pietersz of Wtrecht, soldier
    Johan Jacop Heylwech of Basel, cadet
    Lucas Jelisz from the Hague, cadet

---

[77] The upperbarber was also the ship's surgeon; the prefix of Mr, short for the Fr. *Maistre*, or master, was given in courtesy.

[78] See pp. 147-8. Note that Jeronimus himself signs this oath, using the Latin form of his Christian name, and taking the title of Merchant; Jan Pelgrom de Bye omits his status of cabin servant, or boy, as later evidence shows that it was no longer necessary for him to consider himself a servant.

Reynder Hendricx of Barklooster, steward
Daniel Cornelisz of Dort., cadet
Wouter Loos of Maastricht, soldier
Gerrit Haas of Santen, sailor
Jan Willemsz Selijns of Amsterdam, cooper
Jeurian Jansz of Bremen, sailor
Hendrick Jaspersz of Montfort, soldier
Salomon Deschamps, undermerchant

ALSO confesses that at last he did not any longer like the name of Merchant, because there was no trade whatsoever. —— Therefore has given himself the title of Captain General, and that this was sworn to, and undersigned by all persons, 36 altogether, that they had to call him thus, and recognize him as such; the people as follows—

[Here Pelsaert again also inserts a copy of the oath of allegiance made to Jeronimus Cornelisz, and taken on 20th August,[79] and once more enters a list of the names or (as he notes this time) "the marks" of those who signed, if they were unable to write; but he gives names only.]

Coenraat van Huyssen
Davidt van Sevanck
Jan Pietersz Cosijn
Wouter Loos of Maastricht
Gysbert van Welderen
Gysbert Bastiansz, predikant
Reynder Hendricx, steward
Jan Hendricx of Bremen, soldier
Andries Jonas of Luyck, soldier
Rutger Fredericxsz of Bremen, locksmith
Mattys Beer of Munsterburgh, soldier
Hans Frederick of Bremen, soldier
Jacques Pilman of Pres, soldier
Lucas Gillisse from the Hague, cadet
Andries Liebent of Oldenberg, cadet
Abraham Jansz of Yperen, gunner
Hans Hardens from Ditmarsen, soldier
Olivier van Welderen, cadet
Jeurian Jansz of Bremen, sailor
Isbrant Isbrantsz of Purmerent, assistant

[79] See page 148. Jeronimus does not sign this document. There are here eleven more signatures, including those of the predikant and the runaway ship's boy Abraham Gerritsz of the *Leyden*, picked up at Sierra Leone.

Jan Willemsz Selijns, cooper
Jan Egbertsz, carpenter
Cornelis Pietersz of Wtrecht, soldier
Hendrick Jaspersz of Montfort, soldier
Jellis Phillipsen of Malmediers, soldier
Tewis Jansz of Amsterdam, carpenter
Johan Jacop Heylwech of Basel, cadet
Gerrit Haas of Zanten, sailor
Claas Harmansz of Campen, *hooploper* [youngster]
Allert Jansz of Assendelft, gunner
Rogier Decker of Haarlem, Boy
Gerrit Willemsz of Enchysen, sailor
Abraham Gerritsz of Sierra Liones
Jan Pelgrom de By of Bemmel
Lenert Michielsz van Os, cadet
Salomon Deschamps, undermerchant

> TODAY the 22 Sept. 1629 on the Island *Batavia's* Graveyard,

JERONIMUS CORNELISZ has again been asked whether he has consented to the seizing of the ship *Batavia* or whether he has been brought to it by the skipper; says, that he had not given counsel for it, but that the skipper persuaded him to it. Asked if he would have seized the Yacht when it should come, confesses, that when he had been able to overpower the other people on the island, for which they daily did their best, for otherwise they knew that they would have warned the ship—he would have done it.

Confesses also, in the presence of Jan Hendricxsz, that when Niclaas Winckelhaack, Paulus Barentsz and Bessel Jansz, of Harderwyck, and Claas Harmansz of Maagdenburgh fled out of the water in which they had the intention to kill them, and came fleeing to the tent of Jeronimus, that he ordered the foresaid Jan Hendricxsz to kill them; which he did. ——— Also, when the family of the predikant was murdered, that he said, "The *domini* will not be here much longer." ——— Also, when the sick were murdered, that Jeronimus, Gysbert van Welderen, Coenraat van Huyssen, have taken Andries de Vries and brought him to all the sick huts and ordered him to cut their throats, which he did; eleven people altogether. ——— Also, when Cornelis Pietersz of Wtrecht had cut the throat of Hendrick Claasz, under carpenter, that it had been done in the presence of Jeronimus. ——— Was further accused by Allert Jansz of Assendelft, in his presence, that when he ordered him to cut the throat of Andries de Bruyn, Boy, he pretended to him that they would catch birds, and Assendelft has followed him, and so the order has been carried out.

Jeronimus Cornelisz has read to him the above mentioned complete examination and confession, and is asked whether it is altogether true; confesses free and unbound, without torture, that everything has happened that way.

On the 23 ditto, Jeronimus Cornelisz, present at the examination of Lenert Michielsz, cadet, confesses freely without torture, that he has sent him, together with Sevanck and Mattijs Beer, with a raft to Traitors Island, in order there to drown Andries Liebent, Hendrick Jansz of Oldenburgh, alias Zany [*maftken*],[80] Thomas Wensel of Coppenhagen, sailor, and Jan Cornelisz of Amersvoort, that Andries Liebent was brought to other thought by Lenert Michielsz. ——— Confesses that this is true.

Secondly, that he has sent Lenert Michielsz, Coenraat van Huyssen, Jan Hendricxsz, Sevanck, Daniel Cornelis and Mattijs Beer with the biggest raft, also sending with them Hans Radder of Danisch, cadet, and Jacop Groenwaldt, upper trumpeter; tie their hands and feet and throw them into the Sea.

Thirdly, confesses that the said Lenert, also Cornelis Pietersz of Wtrecht, Hans Jacopsz, Jan Hendricxsz and Mr Frans the barber, have been ordered by him to get out of the tents and sail with the little yawl, along with Sevanck and van Huyssen to Seals Island, in order to murder all the people there; which they did, except 17 persons.

Fourthly, Jeronimus has called the said Lenert, also Jan Hendricxsz and Rutger Fredericxsz into his tent and has given them swords in order to kill Andries de Vries, assistant; which they did.

Fifthly, he confesses that when they had the intention to murder the family of the Predikant, he has given some food to Coenraat van Huyssen, saying that with that he must invite the Predikant and his daughter, as well as himself. ——— In the afternoon he has called the said Lenert Michielsz, also Jacop Pietersz, Jan Hendricxsz, Wouter Loos, Andries Jonas and Andries Liebent, and said that when in the evening he was a guest in van Huyssen's tent, they must kill the whole family of the predikant; which they have done also.

Sixthly, confesses that the said Lenert Michielsz and Lucas Gillisz, with Jan Hendricxsz, on the night of 12 July, had been hauled by him out of the tents to cut the throat of Passchier van

---

[80] *Maftken = mafje*: as in *iemand voor het mafje houden*, which means "to make a laughing stock" of one.

den Ende, gunner, also Jacob Hendricxsz, carpenter; which they have done also.

Seventhly, confesses that on the 6 August in the morning, he stood in the tent of Davidt van Sevanck and called Jan Hendricxsz and gave him his own dagger, which he carried in his pocket, saying, "Stick Stoffel Stoffelsz, the lazy fellow, who stands there working as if his back is broken, through the heart;" which Jan Hendricxsz did.

Eighthly, confesses that also on 16 August he handed over his sword to Jan van Bemel to cut off the head of Cornelis Aldersz of Ylpendam, youngster, in order to prove whether his sword was sharp; (the foresaid Jan van Bemel being too light) Mattijs Beer has cut off his Head in his presence.

Ninthly, confesses that although he is a married man, has taken Lucretia Jansz, the wife of Boudewyn van der Mylen, into his tent and used her as his concubine for two months against her will, and has known her carnally.

On 24 September, JERONIMUS CORNELISZ, present at the examination of Rogier Decker of Haarlem, late cabin servant on the ship *Batavia*, confesses that on 25 July he called the said Rogier into his tent and has given him a beaker of wine to drink, also a dagger, saying, "Stab this into the heart of Hendrick Jansz of Purmerent, carpenter;" which Rogier has done; confesses the above written to be true.

On the 28 ditto, BECAUSE Lucas Gellisz from the Hague, cadet, following the above mentioned confession of Jeronimus, should also have been present at the murder of Passchier, confesses in the presence of Jeronimus that he [and] Sevanck, together with Lenert Michielsz and Jan Hendricxsz have been ordered by Jeronimus to go and kill Passchier van Ende, gunner, and Jacop Hendricx, carpenter; and, coming near the tent, Jan Hendricxsz has sprung into it and cut the throat of Passchier, and Jacop Hendricx was ordered to remain in the tent and Sevanck, going to Jeronimus, said, "Jacop is a good carpenter [*timmerman*]; order him to live." But Jeronimus said, "He is only a turner [*drayer*] and half lame, tomorrow he might chatter; he must go too."

Towards broader confirmation if such is true, have called Lenert Michielsz and Jan Hendricxsz; confess on the Salvation of their Souls and willing to die on it, that it has so happened as is written here above.

But Jeronimus denies it, saying they are lying, also that all he has confessed he has confessed because he has been threatened with torture; also that he knew nothing of the seizing of the ship *Batavia*.

THEREFORE, on account of his unsteady and variable confessions, practising crooked means though by all people accused in his own presence, in order to prove same to be lies. ——— Have again and for the last time, threatened him with torture and asked why he mocked us, because he has confessed and told everything freely several times before this without torture, [both] the origin and the Circumstances concerning the seizing of the ship *Batavia* as well as the gruesomeness that came about afterwards. ——— Confesses, that all that he has said before this, is so.

But that what he asks for is delay, in order that he may be brought to Batavia in order to speak again to his wife, and that he well knows that all he has done is evil enough, and he desires no grace.

JAN HENDRICXZ and ALLERT JANSEN OF ASSENDELFT have freely informed without being examined, that one night Jeronimus has invited them, and among other proposals, informed them that if the Ship had not been wrecked, then it would have been seized, and that the principals were the skipper [Ariaen Jacobsz]; he, Jeronimus; High boatswain [Jan Evertsz]; Coenraat van Huyssen and others, and that they would have nailed up the soldiers' hatch; which has been confronted with, and confirmed as true.

On the same date in the afternoon, THE COMMANDEUR has read these examinations and confessions publicly before all the people on the Island, in the presence of Jeronimus Cornelisz, and asked him was it not thus. Said, something was in it of which Assendelft, Jan Hendricxsz and others accused him wrongly. ——— Therefore the Commandeur has again said to the prisoners who had been witnesses sworn before God, that if they lied to him in the least respect they would have to be responsible before the divine judgment chair. ——— Have said and called out as one Man that they would die on it, on the salvation of their souls, not to have lied in the least in the things heretofore confessed. ——— Thus has the Commandeur again asked Jeronimus why he has mocked the council through his intolerable desperation, saying one time that they spoke the truth, another time that they all lied; confesses at last that he did it to lengthen his life. But that he had done enough evil, as said.

On 29th ditto, JERONIMUS CORNELISZ wrote 2 letters to his friends in Holland and has given them to the understeersman Jacop Jacopsz Holloch[81] to deliver secretly, which the latter has handed over to the Commandeur, which have been opened in the council and read. Found what was mentioned therein was contrary to the truth, in order to cover up his gruesome misdeeds. Thus, he by all Men has been accused with false lies, and therefore he has had to die, innocent.
—— Therefore has the Commandeur read those letters to the whole Community and has asked them again, on the salvation of their souls, if they in anything have wronged or unjustly accused him. They answered all together and each in particular, that all they have done has been at his order and that he had been the instigator of all murders, and that all that had happened or was going to happen, giving the salvation of their souls as pledge, that the same was true. —— Also, Allert Jansz of Assendelft confesses that so far as the seizing of the ship *Batavia* was concerned, he also was implicated in it. But that Jeronimus Cornelisz had firstly brought him to it on the ship. —— In order to make an end to these variable evasions, have ordered Jeronimus to speak the straight truth or he should be tortured; confesses that all the evasions he tries are to prolong his life, or to be taken to Batavia.
—— Is asked why he mocked the council and why he wished to accuse them of wanting to kill him unjustly. Says, as before, to prolong his life. —— And confesses on his soul's salvation that all this of which he is being accused, is true.

WE UNDERSIGNED persons of the council, declare upon our Manly Truth in place of the duly attested Oath, that all the above mentioned examinations have taken place in our presence, and that Jeronimus has confessed, mostly free and unbound, without torture; whereupon the Commandeur for further confirmation of his Criminal Offences [*Delicten*], which were unpardonable before God or our High Authorities, has read this examination today before all the people being on the Island, in the presence of Jeronimus Cornelisz; and has asked him if this was not indeed the truth; confesses at last, (Yea), and because we have heard this same with sober ears and seen with own eyes, are ready, coming to Batavia, to attest this at all times before all high and subaltern judges of the Hon. Lord Gov. Gen. Jan Pietersen Coen, and if requested

---

[81] This is the acting skipper of the *Sardam*, unless Pelsaert makes an error and means Jacop Jansz, the understeersman of the *Batavia* who went with him to Batavia and returned, and signed *Hollert* after his name: see document of 8th June.

there, to testify and to confirm on Oath. —— In token of this being true, have undersigned this with our own hands on the island named *Batavia's* Graveyard, this 28 Sept. Anno 1629 ——

> FranCo. Pelsartt
> Jacob Jacobsz *houten man*
> Salomon Deschamps[82]
> Claas Gerritsz
> Jacop Jansz
> Sijmon Yopzoon
> This is the mark of
> Jan ⚓ Willemsz
>   Visch

[Pelsaert's summary of the crimes of Jeronimus Cornelisz, and the sentence passed on Cornelisz, follows.]

BECAUSE JERONIMUS CORNELISZ of HAARLEM, aged about 30 years, apothecary, and late under Merchant of the ship *Batavia*, has misbehaved himself so gruesomely and has gone beyond himself, yea, has even been denuded of all humanity and has been changed as to a tiger; namely, that before the ship *Batavia* was wrecked, he has allowed himself to be persuaded by the skipper Ariaen Jacopsz of Dulierdam, that with the accomplices they already had and still others whom they would persuade, they would seize the same ship and murder all, the Commandeur as well as the others, except 120 persons who would have been of use to them, whereto Jeronimus has invited Allert Jansen of Assendelft, gunner, to the same fact, and has consented to it at last, according to his own confession.

Furthermore, after the wrecking of the Ship, when the Commandeur *pelsart* and the skipper were gone in search of water to the Islands lying around and the main Southland, and it had not been possible, according to the testimony of all Men who had been present, to find water, though they searched up to 22 degrees [of latitude] and then were forced through their own thirst to sail to India—so has Jeronimus, who was here the chief and Master of the people on the island, thought of evil, yea, even devilish means, and has carried them out, taking as his council persons of his own nature such as Davidt van Sevanck and Coenraat van Huyssen, who have decided to have murdered or destroyed all people until

---

[82] Deschamps signs here for the first time; he also signs the other declarations of truth of evidence, but not all the sentences. His signature is placed in accordance with his status as next after Pelsaert in commercial rank. Italic script is used —probably he affected this; other signatures are the same as usual. Why Deschamps was called as councillor and witness to truth of evidence is a matter for interesting speculation.

the amount of 45 or less; of whom the first ones have been Jan Cornelis of Amersvoort, Hendrick Jansz of Oldenburgh, soldier, and Thomas Wensel of Coppenhagen, sailor, whom Sevanck and Huyssen have been sent secretly with a raft to drown; which was done.

Item, on 4 July he and the council have decided to kill Egbert Roeloffsz and Warner Dircxsz, carpenters, under the pretence that they had intended to get away with the little yawl; which thus has happened.

Item, on the 5 July, he and the council have decided that Hans Radder of Danisch, cadet, and Jacop Groenewald, upper trumpeter, should be taken to an island and that there their hands and feet should be bound, and they should thus be carried into the Sea; which has happened, although neither have done any misdeeds whatsoever.

Item, that the party of cabin Boys, Men and Women, about 45 in number who had been put on Seals Island—Jeronimus, with his council, has decided should be killed, and they were slain on 15 July, about 18 Boys with whom were several Men; and on the 18th he has ordered that the rest, with whom were 4 women, should all be killed; which thus has happened. ——— But Cornelis Jansz of Amsterdam, assistant and Marcus Symonsz of Holsteyn, soldier, and two sailors named Wagenaars, have escaped.

Item, that Pieter Jansz of Amsterdam, provost, with his wife and child; Claudine Patoys with her child; Claas Harmansz of Maagdenburg, with his wife; Cristoffel Quist, soldier; Wouter Joel, soldier; Nicklaas Winckelhaack, soldier; Pauls Barentsz and Bessel Jansz, both of Harderwyck, sailors, and yet others, to the amount of 15 strong, who through Jeronimus had been put on Traitors Island, should there make a raft to sail with that to the High island, but when they have made two rafts and gone on the way with them, then have Jeronimus and his council decided that the same should be killed or drowned in the Sea, and so Sevanck, Coenraat van Huyssen, Gysbrecht van Welderen, Cornelis Pietersz of Wtrecht, Lenert Michielsz, Jan Hendricxsz and Lucas Gellisz, have been ordered to go with the little yawl thereunto, and some of them were thrown into the Sea, and some of them sprang of their own accord into the water and were drowned. But Nicklaas Winckelhaack, Pauls Barentsz, Bessel Jansz and Claas Harmansz escaped by swimming, and thought to save themselves here on land. ——— But Jeronimus being here on the Island, verbally ordered Jan Hendricxsz and Rutger Fredericx to kill them; which was done.

Item, Jeronimus, together with Sevanck, Coenraat van Huyssen and Gysbert van Welderen, having called Andries de Vries, assistant, have gone out on the night of 10 July and forced him to cut the throats of a party of sick people; which he had to do.

Item, about three days after the above mentioned events, Jeronimus, Sevanck and Coenraat van Huyssen, have called again the mentioned de Vries in order that he should cut the throats of some remaining sick, and they have forced him to it.

Item, on 12 July at night Jeronimus has called to his tent Jan Hendricxsz, Lenert Michielsz and Lucas Jellisz, being present Davidt van Sevanck and Coenraat van Huyssen, and ordered them to cut the throats of Passchier van den Ende, gunner, Jacop Hendricx, carpenter, also a sick Boy, which Jan Hendricxsz and Lenert Michielsz have done.

Item, on 14 July, Davidt van Sevanck has seen that Andries de Vries stood from afar and talked to Lucretia Jansz (during the day) and furthermore, because de Vries had been made to promise that if ever in his life he talked to her, he would have to die, therefore have decided to have the above mentioned de Vries killed; and Jeronimus has called Jan Hendricxsz, Lenert Michielsz, and Rutger Fredricx to his tent and ordered them to kill de Vries, and given them a sword with which to kill him, and so they have slain him.

Item, on 21 July, Jeronimus and the council have decided that the family of the predikant, except the Predikant and his eldest daugther, should be murdered at night. ——— To that purpose Jeronimus has allowed some food to be brought to the tent of Coenraat can Huyssen, saying that they must invite him together with the predikant and his daughter, at night; and thus Jan Hendricxsz, Lenert Michielsz and Mattys Beer were verbally ordered by Jeronimus, with Sevanck and others whom he should take with him, to kill the predikant's family at night, and Jan Hendricxsz has stabbed Wybrecht Claas,[83] and Lenert Michielsz has beaten in the skull of the predikant's wife[84] with an adze [*dissel*] as well as that of one of the children, and Mattys Beer has killed Willemyntgie, the middle daughter, beating in her skull with an adze; the rest, because it was night and people could see nothing,[85] have been slain by Zevanck and Cornelis Pietersz from Wtrecht and others.

Item, on the 25 July, Jeronimus and the council have decided to drown Jan Gerritsz of Leyden and Obbe Jansz of Franiker, sailor;

---

[83] Young maid to the predikant's wife.

[84] Maria Schepens. See *Biographisch Woordenboek van Oost-Indische Predikanten*, C.A.L. van Troostenburgh de Bruijn, p. 26.

[85] Presumably these killers could not be distinguished.

and Sevanck, Coenraat van Huyssen and Gysbrecht van Welderen have gone to the mast[86] and drowned them there.

Item, on the 5 August, Jeronimus Cornelisz, Sevanck, Coenraat van Huyssen and Jacop Pietersz have decided, when they were at the High island, to kill Mr Frans Jansz of Hoorn, upperbarber, because they were afraid that he would go over to the other party; which Sevanck, since Jeronimus had gone to the island where Wiebbe Hayes was with his people,[87] has undertaken [to order], and so the forementioned Mr Frans has been killed by Lenert Michielsz, Mattys Beer and Hans Jacops. —— Furthermore, when Jeronimus, with Sevanck, Coenraat van Huyssen and 23 Men in 2 yawls, were coming from the above mentioned High Island to this island,[88] Sevanck, sitting in the yawl, said to Jeronimus, "I have thought of a good new plan;" whereon Jeronimus asked, "What is that?" So he said, "If a yacht comes to rescue us we should seize it and go pirating and sail to Spain." Whereon Jeronimus answered, "Ho, ho, that I have long thought of and had in mind." —— And so it has been decided at last, and have resolved to do this. But that firstly they should endeavour to overpower the other party, in order so to make it, that, if a Yacht came, they should not warn it; and, if they carried out the plan, then they should let the boat first come to shore, and then make the crew drunk, the easier to kill them, and so then they would have been able easily to overpower the yacht.

Item, on 6 August in the morning, Jeronimus has verbally ordered Jan Hendricxsz that he should cut the throat of Stoffel Stoffelsz, carpenter, who stood there working; whereto he pulled his own dagger out of his pocket and handed it to him; and so Jan Hendricxsz has done the same.

Item, on the 10 August Jeronimus Cornelisz has personally called Rogier Decker of Haarlem, late cabin servant, out of his tent where he was frying fish, and has said to him, after giving him a beaker of wine, that he must stab to the heart Hendrick Jansz of Purmerent, carpenter, who went walking (but bound) with Salomon Deschamps, undermerchant; whereto he, Jeronimus, put the dagger in the hand of Rogier, and the forementioned Rogier has done it.

Item, on 16 August, Jeronimus has said to Jan of Bemmel (late cabin servant), "Here is my sword, go kill Cornelis Aldersen of

[86] Probably the same on which Jeronimus floated ashore, left stranded on beach or shallows.
[87] Clear indication that the "High Island" was *not* the island on which Wiebbe Hayes was camped.
[88] *Batavia's* Graveyard, where Pelsaert was when writing.

Ylpendam, youngster [*hooploper*]; cut off his head in order to see if it is sharp enough." —— But Sevanck, who heard, said that the forementioned Jan van Bemel was too weak for that, and then Mattys Beer was named thereto, who in the presence of Jeronimus, in broad daylight, has cut off the boy's head almost with one blow; whereat Jeronimus stood laughing.

Moreover, although he is a married Man, he has nevertheless taken Lucretia Janssen [*sic*] into his tent and has kept her for 2 months against her will as his concubine.

All these and still more gruesome deeds which through the death of Sevanck and Coenraat van Huyssen remain hidden, by the free-will confessions of the evil-doers and perpetrators of the murders, whom he verbally and personally has ordered and forced to do so, who have all confessed to it in his presence, thereto pledging the salvation of their souls, to die on it if they had ever in anything unjustly accused him; which they have done [sworn]. —— As well as from the full examinations and freewill confessions of Jeronimus Cornelissen [*sic*] who, after it has been read to him, has confessed publicly before all people, that everything is true. —— As because, even under Moors or Turks, such unheard of, abominable misdeeds would not have happened or been left without being punished, still less amongst Christians, that they should murder each other without extreme hunger or thirst, as they have not had, and have thought to do still further. —— But because it is clear that it has been an inspiration of the devil that they should come to such a decision in order to reduce the amount of people to 40 and thereby be able to come to their intended misdeeds, and in order to give it more pretence of authority, he deceived the people, [saying] that the Commandeur *pelsart* had ordered him thus. —— Also, he now publicly before all people confesses and is still confessing, that he and Davidt van Sevanck should say so in order to keep the people in greater obedience; Jeronimus said that to this purpose he had been so ordered.[89]

THE COMMANDEUR and WE THE UNDERSIGNED persons of the council of the ship *Sardam*, having given the matter our utmost consideration after long examinations and much searching, and after much discussion and weighing, in order to turn from us the wrath of God and to cleanse the name of Christianity from such an unheard of villain—have sentenced the foresaid Jeronimus Cornelisz of

[89] In several places in the foregoing paragraphs Pelsaert's construction is vague, though his meaning clear. In addition, the repetition of Jeronimus's statement that the Commandeur had himself ordered the killings, suggests that Pelsaert was emotionally disturbed.

Haarlem. —— Thus we sentence him hereby, that on Monday being the first of October, Anno 1629, as he requests to be baptised, he shall be taken to Seals Island, to the place prepared for that, to execute Justice; and there first to cut off both his hands and after that punish him on a gallows with the Cord till death follows—with confiscation of all his goods, Moneys, Gold, Silver, monthly wages and all that he may have to claim here in India against the General East India Company, our Lord Masters. —— Thus done and attested on the Island named *Batavia's* Graveyard, this 28 Sept. 1629.

                FranCo. Pelsartt
                Jacob Jacobs *houten man*
                Claas Gerritsz
                Jacop Jansz
                Sijmon Yopzoon
                This is the mark of
                Jan A Willemsz
                        Visch

                TODAY 17 Sept. in the afternoon, on the ship *Sardam*, has been resolved by the Commandeur *Franco. pelsart* and the ship's council, to examine Jan Hendricx of Bremen on the great murders so understood to have done, and, if necessary, to bring him to torture —— date as before.

JAN HENDRICXEN of BREMEN, soldier, aged about 24 years, brought in, is asked by the Commandeur why they had wanted to seize the ship; answered, free and unbound, without torture, that over 6 weeks [ago] Jeronimus Cornelisz, undermerchant, and his council had taken that plan and sworn to make themselves masters of the first Yacht that should come; but that he is innocent of that and in no way consented to it, though several times was requested about it.
                And in order to come to the straight truth of it, is put to torture.
Has promised of his own freewill to say what he knows. Says, that he was persuaded thereto, as well as [were] all persons who were on the island; the Commandeur asked him again why he wanted to do that; answered, that he did not know. Furthermore examined how they would have brought it about, says, that already before Jeronimus had been captured by the other party, they had

had the plan, if a Yacht should come, to let the boat come to land first and then make the crew drunk in order the easier to kill them, and they should then have mastered the yacht easily at night time, with the boat, because they guessed that there would only be 20 to 30 Men. But no decisioin was yet taken as to how they would begin it, because while they were fighting with the other party, they suddenly saw the ship.

He, further examined as to where they would have sailed had they seized it, and how many people would have been left alive, answered, that the plan was to run off to Spain, Barbary or suchlike places in order to sell the ship and share the booty; that they would have spared the lives of the skipper, the steersman, with 5 or 6 of the sailors who would serve them, but would have murdered the rest.

Further examined as to how many people he has murdered; whereto confesses of freewill that he has killed 18 to 20 by the order of Jeronimus, but that he did not know their names, therefore requested respite till the following day, in order to bethink himself how and when he has done all this; which is allowed.

> On 19 do. on the Island *Batavia's* Graveyard, before the ship's council,

Jan Hendricxsz, before mentioned, called again and being asked by the Commandeur if he would have been one of the conspirators in the seizing of the ship *Batavia*, says, that he was not one of them, and has not been one on the Ship, but that he had heard from several persons (now all dead) that the skipper [Ariaen Jacobsz], Jeronimus, High boatswain [Jan Evertsz], Ryckert Woutersz gunner, Allert Jansz of Assendelft, gunner, Coenraat van Huyssen and Gysbert van Welderen, soldiers,[90] with about 10 to 12 others, had undertaken this first and had made the plan to nail the soldiers' Hatch at night, until they had become masters of the ship; then they would have chosen those of the soldiers who were on their side, but the rest they would have murdered, all except about 120. Said also that he knew Allert Jansz of Assendelft was one of the accomplices.

Towards evening he has been called again and asked if he has now remembered how many people he has murdered. Confesses as follows—

---

[90] That Hendicxsz classes these two as soldiers definitely ends the supposition that *adelborst* can be assumed to mean midshipman, and establishes its use in these Journals as referring to a Company cadet, or appointee. See p. 142, note 46.

That he one day (being 5 July last), together with Davidt van Sevanck, Coenraat van Huyssen, Cornelis, Mattys Beer, Lenert Michielsz and Wouter Loos, were ordered by Jeronimus to go with the biggest Raft, and that they should take with them and drown Hans Radder, cadet, and Jacop Groenewald, upper trumpeter; whom he has helped to bind hand and foot, and in that way have been drowned.

Confesses further that on the day (being the 9 July last) he was ordered by Jeronimus, together with Sevanck, Coenraat van Huyssen, Gysbrecht van Welderen, Jacob Pietersz *lanspesaat*, Lenert Michielsz and Lucas Jelisz, to go with the little yawl and do what Zevanck ordered them to do. They had then gone to where on another island [Traitors Island], Pieter Jansz, provost, with his wife and child, Claas Harmansz of Maagdenburgh with his wife, Claudine Patoys with her child, Jacop Jacopsz, cooper; Pauwels Barentsz, Bessel Jansz, sailors; Cristoffel Quist of Rokema, soldier; Nicklaas Winckelhaack, soldier; Pieters Arentsz of Monickendam, sailor; and Wouter Joel, *schotsman*,[91] had made 2 small rafts with which they thought, according to a promise under oath which Jeronimus at that time had made, to sail to the High island; coming to them, they forced the men to jump from the rafts and help to push them further towards *Batavia's* island; when they came to the shallows Davidt Zevanck ran on the land to Jeronimus and asked him something, whereon Zevanck came back and called out: "Kill" at which Jan Hendricxsz did his utmost; but many escaped and thought to save themselves on the island by Jeronimus, but he ordered that they should be killed, and Zevanck, with Coenraat van Huyssen and Gysbert van Welderen went in the same little yawl and took the three above mentioned women, who were still sitting on the Raft, and took them to the deep, where they were thrown overboard and drowned.

Item, confesses that one day the 8 July, he was ordered by Jeronimus, when Zevanck was by, to strangle the child of Hans Hardens, named Hilletgie, which he did while Jeronimus invited the mother.

Item, confesses that one day, being the 10 July last, together with Allert Jansz of Assendelft, gunner, he has cut the throat of Jan Pinten, English soldier.

Item, confesses that one day (being 12 July last) he was called by Jeronimus into his tent, together with Lenert Michielsz and Lucas Gellisz, and that they were ordered to cut the throats of Passchier van den Ende, gunner, Jacop Hendricxsz, carpenter

[91] Either a soldier who used a gun, or one who was in charge of ammunition, or else a sailor concerned with part of the rigging.

[*timmerman*], and a sick cabin boy; whereupon he, together with Davidt Zevanck and others who were so ordered, took a lamp and went into their tent and asked Passchier if he had any goods hidden there, to say so. He answered weepingly, "No," and begged that he might be allowed to say his prayers, because he thought that it would cost him his life. —— But Sevanck said, "Get on with it." Thus Jan Hendricxsz threw him to the ground and cut his throat. The other one Jacop Hendrix Drayer[92] begged bitterly for his life, whereupon Zevanck and they also went to Jeronimus and said that Jacop was a good carpenter and should he not be spared. But Jeronimus answered, "Not at all, he is only a turner, furthermore, he is half lame. He also must go. He might become a babbler now or later." Whereon they have gone back to the small tent and Jan Hendricxsz threw the foresaid Jacop to the ground and Lenert Michielsz sat on his body and Jan Hendricxsz stabbed 2 knives to pieces on his breast, also 2 knives on his throat, whereupon Lucas Gellisz handed him one of his knives, but he could not bring him to death, so that at last he cut his throat with a piece of knife; after that did likewise to the boy.

Item, confesses that one day (being 14 July last), he has been called by Jeronimus into his tent, together with Lenert Michielsz and Rutger Fredericx, and that they were ordered to kill Andries de Vries, assistant—he gave them each a sword therefor, and poured each a beaker of wine; which [order] they have done publicly.

Item, confesses that he one day (being 15 July last) has been fetched out of his tent by Jeronimus and ordered, together with Sevanck, Coenraat van Huyssen, Cornelis Pietersz of Wtrecht, Hans Jacopsz of Basel and Mr Frans Jansz of Hoorn, barber, that they should go with the little yawl to Seals Island to kill all people there, about 40 altogether, of whom he, Jan Hendricxsz, as soon as they arrived, has killed 5 Boys, and after that 2 Men, but he did not know their names. —— But Cornelis Jansz the assistant, with 3 to 4 others who were chased by Hans Jacopsz, escaped on rafts; and also at that time they spared the lives of 4 women, namely, Mayken Soers, Jannetgie Gist, Gertien Willemsz, widow, and Laurentia Thomasz; also some children were spared.

Item, confesses that he one day (being 21 July) has been called by Jeronimus into his tent, and that he gave him to know that at night time he must help with the murder of the Predikant's family, and that he must do that which Zevanck ordered him to do. At

---

[92] *Drayer* = *draaier*: turner. The man was nicknamed for his trade of carpenter or turner.

night, when Jeronimus, with the Predikant and his eldest daughter had been invited into the tent of Coenraat van Huyssen, then he, Jan Hendricxsz, with Zevanck, Wouter Loos, Cornelis Pietersz, Andries Liebent, Jacop Pietersz and Andries Jonas, have gone to the predikant's tent; Zevanck has called outside Wybrecht Claasen, a young girl, whom Jan Hendricxsz stabbed with a dagger, and inside, all people, the mother with 6 children, had their heads battered in with adzes, and so they were dragged into a hole that had been made therefor.

Confesses also that on that night, after the foresaid woeful tragedy had been committed, he has battered in the head of Hendrick Denys of Amsterdam, assistant, with an adze, in front of his tent, so that he died immediately.

Item, furthermore confesses also that one day, being 28 July, he has been called by Jeronimus into his tent and ordered to take with him Andries Liebent and Jan van Bemel in order to strangle Anneken Hardens wife of Hans Hardens. Whereon he went into the tent; meanwhile Gysbrecht van Welderen came to help him, who made a halter out of her snood and with that strangled her.

On 28 do. before the ship's council, Because Lucas Gellisz has been accused that he also has stabbed a knife to pieces on Jacop Henricks, has been confronted with Jan Hendricxsz, whether he has seen that, and says that he himself [i.e., Jan Hendricxsz] has stabbed to pieces 4 knives on the mentioned man, but that Lucas has handed him his knife for that purpose.

Further, asked again if when a Yacht should have come and they should have come to the execution of their plan, he would have helped in the seizing of it, confesses, "Yea," for there were very few who would not have had a hand in it.

Item, confesses of freewill that he had been called one day (being 6 August last) by Jeronimus, who in the morning stood in the tent of Zevanck, and that he said to him, "Go and stab to the heart Stoffel Stoffelsz of Amsterdam, carpenter, that lazy dog who stands there working, for he is not worth his keep." And thereupon gave him his own dagger which he carried in his pocket. ⸺ Whereon Jan Hendricxsz killed him with 2 blows.

Furthermore he declares, unasked, that he has brought to mind that one evening Jeronimus has invited him, together with Allert Janssen of Assendelft, and amongst other things he has told them that if the ship *Batavia* had not wrecked, they would shortly have seized it and so made themselves rich men; and also in what manner they thought to have brought it about, and that they would have nailed the soldiers' quarters because they thought that that could not miscarry. —— Therefore confronted with Allert Jansz of Assendelft, found his declaration to be in accord with that of Jan Hendricxsz.

WE UNDERSIGNED PERSONS of the council of the ship *Sardam*, declare upon our Manly Truth, in place of the duly attested Oath, that all the above mentioned examinations have taken place in our presence, and have been confessed by Jan Hendricxsz, mostly free and unbound, without torture. Out of abundant goodness of heart, this examination and confession has been read to him again, and he has been asked whether it was not all true; confesses, free, unbound and at liberty, that it so indeed happened; and because we have heard this same with sober Ears and have seen with own eyes, are ready, coming to Batavia, to attest this at all times before all high and subaltern judges, also to the Hon. Lord Gov. Gen. Jan Pietersen Coen and the councillors of India, and to testify, and if being requested, to confirm on Oath. In token of this being true, have undersigned with our own hands this 28 Sept. Anno 1629 on the Island *Batavia's* Graveyard.

[Signed by the Council: Pelsaert, Jacobsz, Deschamps, Gerritsz, Jansz, Yopzoon, and marked by Visch.]

[Pelsaert's summary of the crimes of Jan Hendricxsz, and the sentence passed on Hendricxsz, follows.]

BECAUSE Jan Hendricxsz of Bremen, soldier, aged about 24 years, has behaved with such gruesomeness, yea, with very great cruelty, according to his confessions, made of his own freewill and without torture, here on the island near the wrecked ship *Batavia*, behaving inhumanly and going outside himself, namely, because he has allowed himself to be freely persuaded by Jeronimus Cornelisz, under Merchant, together with other evil-minded wicked persons, to several murders wherein he has killed or helped to kill every tyranically without any compassion or mercy, though it were their own companions sharing the same fate, up to the number of people, according to his own numbering; furthermore he has decided to seize the first Yacht that would come to rescue them and to murder all those who would not be obedient in that respect; and it has happened as follows—

On 5 July, Jan Hendricxsz has been ordered by Jeronimus to go with the biggest raft, together with 6 persons, and to take with

The wreck and the two small islands, from an illustration in the Jan Jansz 1647 edition of *Ongeluckige Voyagie*.

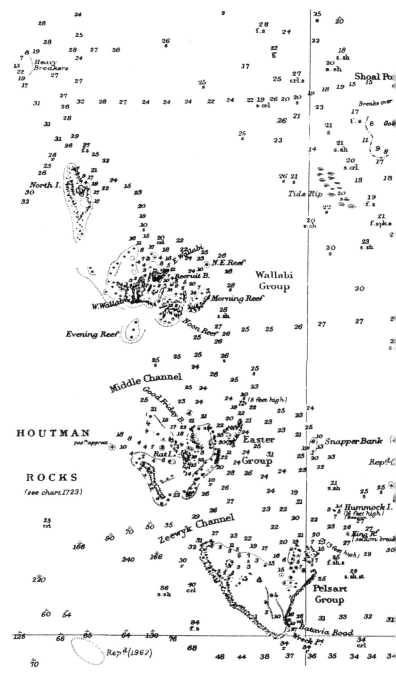

Detail of the Houtman Rocks and the coast, reproduced from British
Office and of t

art No. 1056 with the permission of the Controller of H.M. Stationery
er of the Navy.

them Hans Radder and Jacop Groenewalt, upper trumpeter, and to drown them on the way; Jan Hendricxsz has also helped to bind their hands and feet, and so they have been drowned.

Item, on the 9 July, has been ordered by Jeronimus to go in the little yawl together with Zevanck and still 5 others, and to do what Zevanck ordered them to do. They have sailed to two small rafts upon which were Pieter Jansz, provost, with wife and child, and still other 12 persons having the intention to get to the High island, and they have forced the men to jump from the raft and to push it forward in order to bring it to their island [*Batavia's Graveyard*]. But when they reached the shallows, there came an order from Jeronimus that they should be killed, of whom Jan Hendricxsz has killed the sailors Pauwels Barentsz and Bessel Jansz.

Item, on the 8 July, he had been ordered to strangle the child of Hans Hardens, named Hilletgien Hardens, aged 6, which he has done while Jeronimus invited the father and mother.

Item, on 10 July[93] he has been ordered by Jeronimus with 2 others to cut the throats of Passchier van Ende, gunner, Jacop Hendricxsz, carpenter, also a sick cabin boy. Therefore he, together with Zevanck, Lenert Michielsz and Lucas Gellisz, have gone to the tent of Passchier and have thrown him on the ground and have cut [the throat] in haste, though he begged to be allowed to say his prayers; and they would have spared the life of Jacop Hendricxsz with pleasure, but Jeronimus said that he was half lame and that he must go, he would only sooner or later become a babbler; therefore they went back to Jacop Hendricxsz and threw him on the ground and Jan Hendricxsz struck 2 knives to pieces on his breast as well as 2 on his throat, so that at last they had to cut his throat with a piece of the last knife. After this was done, he also stabbed to death the mentioned cabin boy.

Item, on the 14 July, Jan Hendricxsz, together with Lenert Michielsz and Rutger Fredricx, were called by Jan van Bemmel about noon, and were ordered to go to Jeronimus, who ordered them to kill Adries de Vries, assistant, and he gave each one a sword for that purpose; which they have done publicly.

Item, on the 15 July, he has been ordered by Jeronimus to go with the little yawl, together with Sevanck and four others to Seals Island in order to kill most of the people, children as well as some men, and to leave alive for the time being only the women who

[93] In the evidence given before, the English soldier Jan Pinten is killed on this date, and the murder of Passchier, Jacop Hendricxsz and the boy given as occurring on the 12th.

were there; and as soon as they have come there, Jan Hendricxsz has stabbed to death 5 cabin boys and 2 Men.

Item, on the 21 July, Jan Hendricks has been called by Jeronimus who made known to him that he must murder the family of the predikant that night, except the Predikant and his eldest daughter who he [Jeronimus] would invite into the tent of Coenraat van Huyssen. —— Night having come, he has been called by Zevanck and they went together to the tent of the predicant, also Jacop Pietersz, Wouter Loos, Cornelis Pietersz, Lenert Michielsz, Andries Liebent and Andries Jonas, and Zevanck called outside Wybrecht Claasz, a young girl, who was at once stabbed by Jan Hendricxsz, and also the predikant's wife with her 6 children, inside the tent, have immediately had their heads battered in with adzes, and they were dragged into a hole which had been made ready, for that purpose. Item, after this woeful tragedy has come about, Jan Hendricxsz has called out of his tent the assistant Hendrick Denys of Amsterdam, and because he would not come out for fear, they dragged and tore him outside and Jan Hendricxsz battered his head in with an adze.

Item, on the 28 July, Jan Hendricxsz has been called by Jan van Bemmel to the tent of Jeronimus and there told, with Andries Liebent and Jan van Bemmel, that they must strangle Anneken Hardens, wife of Hans Hardens. When they came near her tent Gysbrecht van Welderen came to help them, and they made a halter of her hair ribbon and Jan Hendricxsz has strangled her.

Item, on 6 August, Jan Hendricxsz was called by Jeronimus in the morning when he was standing in the tent of Zevanck, and he gave him a dagger which he carried in his own pocket, with the words, "Go and stab Stoffel Stoffelsz, that lazy dog who is not worth his keep, to the heart;" which Jan Hendricxsz did with 2 stabs so that he was killed immediately.

Item, he has kept Sussien Fredricx, married woman, as his concubine and had carnal knowledge of her for two months.

Which host of gruesome murders he has very willingly lent himself to do, as well as what they still had intention to do, if Almighty God had not foreseen it; moreover still daily mocking God, while he was one of the first who forbade to pray or to preach the word of God; has very shamefully prevented this, though he says that Jeronimus had ordered it to him; also he has outraged the Women, as well as many misdeeds which it would seem have to remain hidden, Criminal offences which weight very heavily and which cannot be allowed to be suffered by God or mankind, as nature teaches us sufficiently that such evil-doers cannot as an example to others be allowed to remain unpunished. —— Therefore the

Commandeur *Franco. pelsart* and we undersigned persons of the council of the ship *Sardam*, having given the greatest attention to this matter, after long examinations and interrogations, having exchanged our thoughts with each other and weighed and pondered, in order to save ourselves from the wrath of God and to cleanse Christianity from such a villain—have sentenced the foresaid Jan Hendricxsz as we sentence him herewith, that he shall be taken on Monday the first of October 1629 to Seals Island, to a place made ready for that, to execute Justice, and there firstly to cut off his right hand and after that to punish him on a Gallows with the Cord till death shall follow, with confiscation of all his goods, kit, monthly wages and all that he may have to claim here in India against the General East India Company, our Lord Masters. Thus done and attested on the Island *Batavia's* Graveyard, this 28 September, Anno 1629.

[Signed by the council: Pelsaert, Jacobsz, Gerritsz, Jansz, Yopzoon and marked by Visch.]

> TODAY the 23 Sept. 1629 on the Island *Batavia's* Graveyard, has been resolved by the Commandeur *Franco. pelsart* and the ship's council, to examine Lenert Michielsz van Os, cadet, on his great murders thus so understood to have done, and if necessary to bring him to torture —— date as before.

LEENERT MICHIELSZ VAN Os, cadet, aged about 21 years, asked why he, with his accomplices, as soon as the Commandeur and the Skipper have gone from aboard with the sloop to the Island in order to maintain order over the little water that had been saved, and who has been promised by him that he should be fetched as soon as possible, broke open all the chests and goods, without any exception, and plundered. Says, that he has broken open the chest of Passchier van den Ende and that they have shared the contents amongst each other.

Put to torture, because we are enough convinced of his wanton deeds, he begs not to be tortured, and that he will say all that he knows. Says, that he was in the Commandeur's cabin when his chest was broken open by Ryckert Woutersz, and has helped the same to share round and to give parts to others. Further, that the next day in the morning Jeronimus Cornelisz has taken out of the desk of the Commandeur all his papers as well as the notes regarding the fact concerning Lucretia, and has read the same publicly before all people [still aboard] and after that they have been torn up by the above mentioned Ryckert and thrown overboard. ——— But each one has done his best in the plundering and opening up because they said and assured each other they no longer had anything to do with the officers.

Further interrogated in the presence of Jeronimus Cornelisz about the number of men he has murdered or helped to murder, confesses, that one day, being 3 July[94] last, Jeronimus has called him in the presence of Zevanck and has ordered him, with Zevanck and others who he should take with him, to sail with the biggest Raft in order to drown Thomas Wensel, Jan Cornelisz of Amersvoort, Hendrick Jansz of Oldenburgh, and Andries Liebent; that they have gone with the above mentioned 4 persons and that he has helped the next day in the morning to bind their hands and feet, and that Daniel Cornelisz, cadet, has pushed Hendrick Jansz into the Sea; and Coenraat van Huyssen, Thomas Wensel; and Gysbert van Welderen, Jan Cornelisz; but Andries Liebent had been spared on his supplication.

Confesses also, that one day, being 5 July last, he was ordered by Jeronimus to go in the same way on the biggest raft with Davidt Sevanck, Coenraat van Huyssen, Jan Hendricxsz, Cornelisz Pietersz, Mattys Beer and Wouter Loos and drown Hans Radder and Jacop Groenewald, trumpeter. Having come to Traitors Island, Rutger Fredricxsz and Lenert Michielsz bound the hands and feet of Jacop Groenewald, and the others those of Hans Radder, and carried them after that into the deep, where they suffocated or were drowned.

Item, confesses that on one day, being 10 July, Jeronimus Cornelisz has ordered him to get out of his tent at night, together with Jan Hendricxsz and Lucas Gillisz, to cut the throats of Passchier van den Ende, gunner, Jacop Hendricxs, carpenter, and a cabin boy who was ill. Therefore the same 3 have gone with Zevanck, and Jan Hendricxsz has cut the throat of the above mentioned Passchier. After that, when they had thrown Jacop Hendricxs to the ground, Lenert sat on his body and Jan Hendricxsz has struck 2 knives to pieces on his breast and two on his throat, of which one was the knife of Lucas Gillissens, and so they dragged him into a Hole, which they had made ready.

Item, confesses that one day about noon (being 14 July last), has been called by Jan van Bemel into the tent of Jeronimus, together with Jan Hendricxsz and Rutger Fredricxsz, and that he has ordered them to kill Andries de Vries, assistant, and that he has

[94] The figure 3 has been written in over an erasure.

given each a sword and a beaker of wine. Therefore they went to him, whereupon de Vries, because he knew that his life was in jeopardy, started to run ——— but Lenert Michielsz, following him the quickest, chiefly hacked him to death.

Item, confesses, that one day (being 15 July last), he has been fetched out of his tent by Jeronimus, and that he has ordered him, together with Zevanck, Coenraat van Huyssen, Jan Hendricxsz, Cornelis Pietersz, Hans Jacopsz, Mr Frans Jansz of Hoorn, to sail with the little yawl to Seals Island and there kill most of the people, who numbered about 40, except the women. So Lenert, immediately after he arrived, has stabbed one boy right through his body and another boy through his buttock, and also Jacop de Vos, tailor, right through his side. ——— After that he has helped to drag many wounded, who were not yet dead, into the water.

Item, confesses also that on 21 July, he has been ordered by Jeronimus to go at night and help to murder the family of the Predikant when it was dark, except the Predikant and his eldest daughter, whom he would invite as guests at night into the tent of Coenraat van Huyssen. Then Lenert Michielsz, together with Davidt Zevanck, Jan Hendricxsz, Wouter Loos, Jacop Pietersz, Andries Jonas and Andries Liebent, have gone to the predikant's tent where Zevanck has called Wybrecht Claasz outside, whom Jan Hendricxsz has stabbed immediately; meanwhile Zevanck with others has gone inside and said that some of the goods belonging to the Company were hidden there, which they had come to search for; during his talking the lamp has been blown out, and Lenert Michielsz has battered in the head of the predikant's wife with an adze, and one of the children who had also had a blow, he killed later; and they had been ordered to take adzes and axes as weapons as they could use them better to strike amongst a crowd in the tent.

Item, confesses also that when they were on the High island on 5 August, Zevanck has ordered him, together with Mattys Beer, Hans Jacopsz and Lucas Gillisz to go and take with them Mr Frans Jansz of Hoorn, upper barber, under pretext of going in search of seals, but to kill the said Mr Frans on the way. When they had gone part of the way, Lenert Michielsz has stabbed him right through with a pike, whereupon Hans Jacopsen struck him a blow on the head with a morning-star,[95] Mattys Beer has split his head with a sword and Lucas has stabbed him in the body with a sword.

[95] A morning-star was a spiked club. On the islands they were made with wood and nails.

TODAY the 28 do. before the ship's Council,

HE has been called back and asked again whether he also would have helped to seize the first Yacht coming to rescue them, after overpowering the people on the High island; confesses, that he would have helped just like any other.

Further asked how many women he has known carnally on this island, says that Tryntgien Fredricxsz has come to him one night and so he has done his will with her, but that he has kept Anneken Gunner [*Bosschieters*] as his concubine.

WE UNDERSIGNED persons of the council of the ship *Sardam* declare upon our Manly Truth . . . .

[The declaration to truth of evidence is signed by the ship's council and Deschamps; it follows the form of declarations previously made at trials of Jeronimus and Hendricxsz. Pelsaert's summary of the crimes of Michielsz follows.]

BECAUSE LENERT MICHIELSZ VAN OS, cadet, aged about 21 years, has behaved himself very gruesomely, yea, terribly, according to his own freewill confessions got by examinations mostly without torture, that he, on the ship *Batavia* in the night following the day it was wrecked, has committed himself by getting drunk, by breaking open chests, plundering, and other insolent deeds, as well as behaving himself very inhumanly on the Islands near the Wreck, and has gone outside himself, namely, that he has willingly allowed himself to be persuaded by Jeronimus Cornelisz, under Merchant, with other evil-doers, to several murders which he has carried out very tyrannically without any compassion or mercy (though they were all brethren and friends); has killed and has helped to kill up to the number of   people by his hand, according to his confession, as is apparent here below in full; furthermore, he has resolved with others to seize the first Yacht to come to their rescue, and to the murder of all who would not have been of service to them; and his murders have happened as follows ——

[Pelsaert next gives an itemized summary of the crimes as already listed in evidence, without any additional information beyond (in the following paragraph) the name of the husband of the woman they called Anneken Gunner.]

Has also here on the island slept with Tryntgien Fredricx, wife of Claas Jansz,[96] chief trumpeter, and has known her carnally. As

---

[96] One of this name, of Dordrecht, signed the resolution taken to leave the islands to look for water, so that Tryntgien's husband was apparently absent.

well, has kept Anneken Jansz, wife of Jan Carstensz, gunner,[97] as his concubine for a long time.

In all such hosts of gruesome murders he has let himself be used there willingly, as well as others he had in mind to do, had not the Almighty God prevented it. Moreover, he was one of the principals in daily mocking at God, and who has prevented praying and the preaching of God's word, and has behaved himself very scoffingly, although he says he was ordered by Jeronimus; as well has brought the women here into dishonour, with still other misdeeds that appear to remain hidden, being Criminal Offences which cannot, or may not be, tolerated by God or man . . . .

[The sentence on Michielsz follows here, taking the same form as that passed on Jan Hendricxsz, and signed by the ship's council, but not Deschamps.]

TODAY 23 Sept. 1629 on the Island *Batavia's* Graveyard, has been resolved by the Commandeur *Franco. pelsart* and the ship's council, to examine Mattys Beer of Munsterburgh, soldier, on his great murders which understood to have done, and if necessary to bring him to torture —— date as before.

MATTIJS BEER of MUNSTERBURGH, soldier, aged about 21 years, asked why, on the day that the ship was wrecked, as soon as the Commandeur and the skipper went with the sloop to the nearest island to maintain order over the little water that had been saved, and was told by them that they would be fetched as soon as possible, he with his accomplices had broken open and plundered all chests, making no exception. Confesses, that he broke open the chest of Passchier van den Ende, gunner, also that of the skipper and has plundered them. But Lenert Michielsz had given him a medallion (which he had looted in the Commandeur's cabin) which he has sold later to Coenraat van Huyssen for a hundred guilders.

Further asked, in the presence of Jeronimus Cornelisz, how many people he has murdered or helped to murder, confesses that he had an evil intent towards Hans Radder and Jacop Groenewaldt,

[97] Here it can be seen why Anneken Jansz is distinguished as Anneken Gunner (*Bosschieters*) or, more literally, Gunner's Anneken. Her husband, the gunner Jan Carstensz, as appears later, was absent on the island of Wiebbe Hayes. Carstensz is one of those who signed the evidence re Lucretia Jansz in *Ongeluckige Voyagie* (see Chapter IV, page 68). The second Anneken was the wife of Hans Hardens, soldier. Again, the distinction between the naval "gunner" and "soldier" becomes clear.

trumpeter, and therefore had requested Jeronimus to consent that he should murder them because they were loose tongued, thereupon on the same day Jeronimus has ordered Mattys Beer, Davidt Zevanck, Coenraat van Huyssen, Jan Hendricxsz, Wouter Loos and Cornelis Pietersz, with Rutger Fredricx, to take Hans Radder and Jacop Groenewald with them on the biggest raft, and then drown them on the way. They have then taken them to Traitors Island, bound them hand and foot, and so dragged them into the deep where they left them to be suffocated.

Furthermore asked how many people he has helped to kill on Seals Island, says, that Zevanck has ordered him to kill the women, but he has refused (so he says) and that the same had then been ordered to Andries Jonas, who killed Mayken Soers and Janneken Gist. But that he, Mattijs Beer, had wounded some and had subsequently killed some, and after that had helped to drag them into the water.

BECAUSE we were sufficiently convinced of the murders and cruel deeds committed by him, we have put him to torture in order to draw the straight truth from him, and, asked whom he had killed in the predikant's tent (because he also had entered there with an adze) confesses, after having endured pain, that he also was one of those and that the youngest child Roelant ran between his legs and behind him, so that he could not hit him, but that somebody who was behind him had killed him, without [his] knowing who, because it was dark and they could not see each other, but further he had killed or touched no one.

Item, confesses that when they were on the High Island, being 5 August, he was ordered by Zevanck, because he had the order from Jeronimus Cornelisz who was absent that day, to take, together with Lenert Michielsz, Hans Jacobsz and Lucas Gillissen, on the pretence of looking for seals, Mr Frans Jansz of Hoorn, and to kill him on the way. —— Therefore being gone a little way, Mattijs cleft him after Michielsz had pierced him with a pike and Hans Jacobsz beat his head with a morning-star, and furthermore struck his head with a sword so that he died.

Item, confesses, that one day, being the 16 August last he had heard that Jan van Bemel was to cut off the head of a Boy named Cornelis Aldersz of Ylpendam, and that Jeronimus had handed him a sword for that purpose; whereon Zevanck gave as his opinion that the foresaid Jan van Bemmel was too light; therefore Mattijs has offered his services and has requested to be allowed to do it, which was accorded him; therefore he took the sword from the foresaid Jan who would not willingly give it because he wanted to do it himself, but he tore it out of his hands and took it immediately to Gillisz Phillipsz of Malmediers in order to sharpen it, and took it so under his cloak again. Meanwhile Jan van Bemel was busy to blindfold the boy and Jeronimus, who stood next to him, said, "Now, boy, sit still, we are only having some fun with you," and Mattijs Beer with one blow near enough struck off his head.

The 24 ditto, before the ship's Council,

HE has been again brought to torture in order to get from him the straight truth, namely, when and how many people he has helped to kill in the predikant's tent; he maintains as before that he was present there, but that he has not killed anyone. ——— After water has again been poured out to torture him, and after suffering pain, confesses that with an adze he has battered in the head of the predikant's wife, who was not then quite dead, and also that he had thrown one of the children to the ground. Furthermore asked at what other murders he had been present, confesses that when Jan Cornelisz of Amsvoort, Thomas Wensel and Hendrick Jansz alias Zany, were to be drowned, he helped to bind their hands and feet.

The 28 ditto, before the ship's Council,

MATTIJS BEER brought again and being asked whether, if they had been able to execute their intention, he would have helped to seize the first Yacht coming to rescue them, confesses, that he would have been in the same, just as another. ——— Further asked as to how many women he has known carnally on the island, says, that he has slept with Zussie Fredricx and further with none.

WE UNDERSIGNED persons of the council of the ship *Sardam* declare upon our Manly Truth . . . .

[The declaration to truth of evidence is the same as that following the evidence given at the trial of Jan Hendricxsz and is signed by Pelsaert, Jacobsz, Deschamps, Gerritsz, Jansz, Yopzoon, and marked by Visch. On the remainder of the page, originally left blank, a note has been added in smaller handwriting.]

MATTIJS BEYR [*sic*] of Munsterberg, soldier, today 2 October on Seals Island, standing with the noose on his neck ready for death, has confessed to the predikant Gysbert Bastiansz, to clear his conscience, that on the night of   July, in the presence of Jeronimus Cornelisz, he has cut the throats of still another 4 men and a Boy, names unknown to him, about which he has thus far kept silent;

which the above mentioned Predikant has immediately reported to us, and which we ourselves also have heard. As a sign of truth have undersigned this with our own hands, this 2 October 1629.

GysBert Bastiaensz[98]   FranCo. Pelsartt
Claas Gerritsz
Symon Yopzoon
This is the mark of
Jan ⚕ Willemsz
Visch

[The summary of crimes which follows contains one or two extra points and is printed here in full.]

BECAUSE MATTIJS BEER of MUNSTERBERGH, soldier, aged about 21 years, has behaved himself very gruesomely and horribly according to his own confession under torture as well as of freewill, that he, at night on the ship *Batavia* the day after it was wrecked, got drunk, broke open chests and plundered them and committed other wanton deeds. —— Also, that he has behaved himself very inhumanly here on the island near the Wreck, and has gone outside himself, namely, allowing himself to be used willingly by Jeronimus Cornelisz, under Merchant, together with other evil and cruel people, to several murders, in which he has murdered or helped to murder, very tyrannically without any compassion and mercy though they were their brethren and friends, up to the number of people by his hand, according to his confessions as appears underneath in full; moreover, he had in mind, together with the others, to seize the first Yacht that should come to rescue them, and to murder all who would not have been of service to them; and the murders have happened as follows—

ON the 3 July, Mattijs Beer has been ordered by Jeronimus together with Davidt Zevanck, Coenraat van Huyssen, Gijsbrecht van Welderen, Daniel Cornelisz and Leenert Michielsz, to drown with the biggest raft, Jan Cornelisz of Amersvoort, Thomas Wensel, Hendrick Jansz of Oldenburgh, and Andries Liebent; at which Mattys has helped to bind their hands and feet; and so they have been pushed from the rafts into the Sea, except Andries Liebent, whom they spared.

Item, on the 5 July, the aforesaid Mattijs, being a great enemy of Hans Radder and Jacob Groenewaldt, trumpeter, has requested

---

[98] The predikant's signature is large and obviously written with a shaky hand. It would appear that the skipper of the *Sardam* was not at hand to sign this. That he was present is substantiated by his signature to another gallows confession, made by Andries Jonas.

Jeronimus to allow him to kill them because they were cacklers; Jeronimus has promised him this, and on the same day he, together with Zevanck, Coenraat van Huyssen, Jan Hendricxsz, Lenert Michielsz, Cornelis Pietersz from Wtrecht, Wouter Loos and Rutger Fredricxsz, have sailed with the biggest raft and they have taken with them Hans Radder, Jacop Groenewaldt and Andries de Vries, assistant, in order to drown them; they have brought them to Traitors Island and there have bound their hands and feet and taken them into the deep and drowned them, except Andries de Vries who had been bound was set free and his life spared for the time being.

Item, on the 18 July, the foresaid Mattys was ordered by Jeronimus, together with Davidt Zevanck, Andries Jonas, Jan Willems Selijns, Jan van Bemmel, Coenraat van Huyssen and Gysbert van Welderen, to go with the little yawl to Seals Island, to kill there the 4 women and the remaining Boys, and he, Mattys, has killed some boys who were wounded and has helped to drag them into the water.

Item, on the 21 July, Mattys was ordered by Jeronimus to go at night to Zevanck, to help to murder the family of the predikant, except the predikant who with his eldest daughter he would invite as a guest to the tent of Coenraat van Huyssen. ——— Being night, Mattys, together with Zevanck, Jan Hendricxsz, Jacob Pietersz, Andries Jonas, Lenert Michielsz, Cornelis Pietersz, Wouter Loos, Andries Liebent, have gone to the predikant's tent, and Wybrecht Claasz has been called outside, whom Jan Hendricxsz immediately struck dead, and Mattys Beer, together with Lenert Michielsz, with an adze battered in the head of the old woman, and also one of the children who was lying on the ground.

Item, on 5 August on the High Island, Mattys, together with Leenert Michielsz, Hans Jacobsz and Lucas Gellisz, by order of Zevanck, have cleft with a sword, the head of the barber, Mr Frans Jansz of Hoorn after Lenert Michielsz had pierced him with a pike and Hans Jacobsz had battered him on the head with a morning-star.

Item, on the 16 August, Mattys has offered his services and requested (because Jan van Bemmel was to cut off the head of a Boy named Cornelis Aldersz) that he should do the same because Zevanck maintained that Jan van Bemmel was too light for that— whose head, after he had sharpened his sword, he cut off with one blow in the presence of Jeronimus about noon, just to pass the time; at which Jeronimus, Zevanck and the others were laughing.

Has also had carnal knowledge of Zussie Fredricx, a married woman.

To all which mentioned gruesome murders he has let himself be very willingly used, as well as those he had still in mind to do, if the Almighty God had not prevented him. —— Moreover, daily still mocking at God, as he was one of the principals who has prevented the praying and the preaching of His holy word, and who has scoffingly forbidden the same, though he says Jeronimus has so ordered him; also that he has dishonoured the women; with still more misdeeds which apparently remained hidden, Criminal Offences of very evil consequences which may not be suffered by God or Man, because nature teaches us sufficiently that such evil-doers may not be left unpunished as a [bad] example to others.
—— Therefore the Commandeur *Franco. pelsart* and we undersigned persons of the council of the ship *Sardam* . . . .

[The sentence on Mattys Beer which follows the summary of his crimes has here been omitted: it is similar to that passed on Jan Hendricx and is signed by the ship's council, but not Deschamps. Pelsaert begins his examination of Allert Jansz on a new page.]

TODAY 19 Sept. Anno 1629 on the Island *Batavia's* Graveyard has been resolved by the Commandeur *Franco. pelsart* and the ship's council, to examine Allert Jansz of Assendelft, gunner, on his great murders so understood to have done, and if necessary to bring him to torture —— date as before.

ALLERT JANZEN of ASSENDELFT, gunner, aged about 24 years, asked why he got drunk in the night following the day on which the ship *Batavia* was wrecked, why he had committed so many wanton deeds, why he had caused so much misery to all people (having gone too far), with a knife chasing out of the bottle room the steward's mate, Lucas Gerritsz, calling, "Out, cats and dogs, you have been masters here long enough, now I for a while,"—and has cut him with a knife across his back; confesses that he, with others, has committed some evil deeds and that he got very much drunk, so that he does not know whether he has committed the above-mentioned things.

He being further asked in what manner he, together with the other accomplices, had thought to seize the ship *Batavia* before it was wrecked, and who had put him up to it, confesses, that he had heard nothing about it when they were still on the ship but that he had heard from Jeronimus here on land that if the ship had not wrecked, they had meant to seize it, and that they had also already persuaded a party of people, who slept with their swords in their hammocks. ——— Therefore, in order to get the straight truth out of him, we have brought him to torture, and after he has suffered a little pain, he begs to be released and then will say the truth, if released. ——— Assures that Jeronimus Cornelisz, under Merchant, has come to him on the ship, south of the *Cabo de bone esperansa* and has made a proposal and asked him if he would help to seize the ship, then they would be rich men for their whole lives; whereupon has said neither yea nor nay, and he had spoken about it no more. ——— Because the above said does not seem to be the straight Truth, have brought him again to torture. ——— Confesses, after having suffered pain, that he had been willing, and that the principal instigators were Ariaen Jacopsz; Jeronimus Cornelisz, under Merchant; Jan Evertsz, High boatswain. As far as he knew they were only 10 to 13 strong, because one did not dare reveal it to another. ——— Further asked when and how they would have done it. ——— Says, that the best opportunity seemed to be when the Commandeur would have put in chains those men who had laid hands on Lucretia Jansz, which, according to the skipper, would take place when they had seen the Southland, because they thought that then they would find the best opportunity to rouse the people, and so run into the Cabin in a violent way, and to throw the Commandeur overboard from the gallery and to nail the soldiers' hatch until they had seized the ship, which as far as they thought, could not fail, for everyone would very much have wanted to keep his life, though they would have left alive only 120 Men. If they had seized the ship, they would have run to Mauritius to victual, and from there to rob the ships of the Company until they should have become altogether very rich.

Furthermore asked whether he also had part on the ship *Batavia* in the shameful deed done to Lucretia Jansz ——— confesses, that he sat forward in the ship one afternoon, together with Ryckert Woutersz, Cornelis Jansz *boon*,[99] Dirck Gerritsz of Harderwyck, Jan Purmer of Amsterdam, Abraham Hendricxsz, Harman Nannings, quartermaster, and Cornelis Dircxsz of Alcmaer, where the High boatswain Jan Evertsz came to them, saying, "Men, there is an assault on our hands, will you help to give the prince a pleasant outing?"[100] Upon which Allert asked, "What will that be?" So he said, "Tonight we have to blacken Lucretia and have to play a trick on her." Whereupon Cornelis Dircxsz of Alcmaer, gunner, said, "I will not have anything to do with it, for surely something

[99] *Boon*: bean; a nickname.
[100] Idiomatic speech: "to have a right royal time".

else will follow on that." Then the High boatswain answered, "Not at all. I shall take the consequences, whatever comes from it." Then at last Allert Jansz consented, together with all the others except Cornelis Dircxsen of Alcmaer; and they have laid hands on the above mentioned woman at night, between light and dark, and have plastered her with dung and other filth on the face, and next over the whole body.

He being further asked how many men he has killed here on the island ——— confesses that he on one day, being 17 July last, has been called by Jan van Bemmel to come to Jeronimus, and that the last one ordered him to kill Andries de Bruyn, Boy; whereon Allert has called the Boy and said to him, "Andries, we have to go and catch some birds,"[101] but when they came to the beach, he has cut the boy's throat.

Item, confesses also that one night, being 19 July last, together with Jan Hendricxsz, he has helped to cut the throat of a sick English soldier named Jan Pinten.

Item, confesses that one night, being the 14 July last, Jeronimus himself came and called him out of his tent and has said, "Go get Hendrick Claasz of Apcou, carpenter, out of his tent and say he has to come to me, and when he comes outside, you, with the help of de Vries, must cut his throat;" which they have done.

Item, he declares, unasked, that when the ship *Batavia* was south of the *Cabo de bone esperansa*, the Commandeur being ill, the skipper had come one night to the Constable's[102] cabin and had ordered wine, with which they were for a time quite happy; at last the Skipper had gone away and had left Zwaantie with Allert, who has done his will with her, because the skipper thought that she was pregnant and that she should wed Allert.

This same, Allert Jansz confesses in presence of Jeronimus Cornelisz, who also knows this to be true because the skipper had told him.

THE 27 do. before the ship's council,

Aris Jansz of Hoorn, underbarber, come from the High Island, has declared that in the night when the predikant's family was murdered, he, being in his tent was called by Allert Jansz of Assendelft with the words, saying, "Aris, come, we have to go and search for birds for the Merchant." The foresaid Aris has gone

---

[101] Probably mutton birds, which come ashore on these islands at night-time and burrow in the sand, and are good eating.
[102] Officer in charge of guns.

with him although he was very much afraid, but when they came near the beach, Allert cut him across the shoulder, and he received still more blows from others who were there, but through the bluntness of their swords he was only very slightly wounded, so that Aris escaped in the water in the dark. ——— Whereupon we have called Allert Jansz and have confronted him with him. ——— Says, and confesses, that he had been called by Zevanck after the predikant's family had been murdered, and that he had ordered him, together with Cornelis Pietersz of Utrecht, to call the foresaid Aris out of his tent and kill him. ——— Therefore he has cut him round the ears with his sword after he has called him, but Aris escaped in the water in the dark, and because he had been lying flat on his stomach they could not see him, so they said to one another, turning back, "He's had it." ["*Hy heves al wel.*"] For they thought he was so wounded that he must die.

The 28 do. before the ship's Council,

Because Jan Hendricxsz has said very willingly, without being asked, that together with Allert Jansz he was guest one evening to Jeronimus, who told amongst other propositions, that if the ship *Batavia* had not wrecked within a few days, they would have seized it, therefore asked the before mentioned Allert, in the presence of Jeronimus, if that was true. ——— Confesses that it was true word for word as Jan Hendricxsz had told, and he takes the same on his soul and salvation, and is ready to die on it, and that everything he has confessed before this is true.

WE UNDERSIGNED PERSONS of the council of the ship *Sardam* declare upon our Manly Truth in place of the duly attested Oath, that all these above mentioned examinations have been made in our presence, and have been confessed by Allert Janssen of Assendelft, gunner, under torture as well as by freewill. Today this examination and confession has been read to him again and he has been asked if all this was not true, confesses free and unbound and at liberty, that it has indeed so happened, and because we have heard the same with sober ears and have seen with own eyes . . . .

[Declaration to truth of evidence signed by Pelsaert, Jacobsz, Deschamps, Gerritsz, Jansz, Yopzoon, and marked by Visch. Pelsaert's summary of the crimes of Allert Jansz follows and is printed in full.]

BECAUSE ALLERT JANSSEN of ASSENDELFT, gunner, aged about 24 years, putting aside all humanity, has changed himself into worse than an evil tiger filled with all thinkable wantonness and cruelties, not only done, but still in mind to do, namely, that he, through his innate corruptness, on the ship *Batavia*, south of the *Cabo de bone esperansa*, has allowed himself to be persuaded by Jeronimus Cornelisz, under Merchant, together with the skipper, Arian Jacopsz, Jan Evertsz, High boatswain, and still another 10 to 12 evil-minded men who also were roused to seize the ship *Batavia* according to his own confessions by examination, and who were working to like purpose with apt means to execute their plans—that is, that the skipper Ariaen Jacopsz ordered the High boatswain to smear the face and the whole body of the wife of a certain undermerchant, named Lucretia Jansz, whom he very much hated, with dung and other black substances, which was done on the night of 14 May, at which Allert Jansz was one of the principal accomplices, which shameful fact has been taken very hard by the Commandeur. Therefore when the Commandeur should put in chains the conspirators, who numbered 8,[103] that seemed to them a very apt opportunity to run into the Cabin in a rioting manner, and they would then have thrown the Commandeur overboard from the gallery; and they would have nailed the soldiers' hatch until they were masters of the ship, after which they would have murdered all except 120 Men whom they would have chosen out of the soldiers as well as the crew; and then they would have sailed with the ship to Mauritius to victual, and from there they would have gone pirating on the Company until they should altogether have become completely rich—though God the Lord did not wish to allow that extraordinary bad evil, but rather let the ship be wrecked. ——— The forementioned Allert nevertheless has behaved himself very insolently when the ship was wrecked, by getting drunk as well as doing harm to many people who were still aboard and who could not get off immediately. Moreover, coming from the ship, he has willingly let himself be seduced here on the islands near the Wreck by the godless seducer and murderer Jeronimus Cornelisz, to several murders wherein he has killed tyrannically without any compassion or grace towards his brethren and friends, as well as helping to kill them, as appears below more fully in the following. ——— Still further, together with the other evil-doers, he had resolved to seize the first Yacht that should come to rescue them, and to murder all who would not have been of service to them.

On the 10 July, Allert Jansz, together with Jan Hendricxsz, has

[103] Jan Evertsz, Allert Jansz, Rychert Woutersz, Cornelis Jansz alias *Boon*, Dirck Gerritsz, Jan Jansz Purmer., Abraham Hendricxsz, Harman Nannings.

helped to kill, by the order of Jeronimus Cornelisz, a sick English soldier named Jan Pinten.

Item, on 14 July, the before mentioned Allert has been fetched by Jeronimus personally out of his tent, and he has been ordered together with Andries de Vries, to cut the throat of Hendrick Claasz of Apcou, carpenter, because he was sick; which they have done.

Item, on the 21 July, being the same night that the predikant's family was murdered, the forementioned Allert has been called by Davit [sic] Sevanck, who ordered him, together with Cornelis Pietersz of Utrecht to call out of his tent Aris Jansz of Hoorn, under barber, and then to kill him. Whereon Allert Jansz has gone and called, "Aris, come outside, we have to catch 4 small birds for the Merchant." The foresaid Aris, though he was very much afraid, went with him, but when they came to the beach, Allert struck him around his ears with his sword, also Cornelisz Pietersz [struck him], but through the bluntness of their swords they only wounded him slightly, and he escaped in the darkness in the water by lying flat on his stomach so that they could not find him; at last that night he escaped with a small little yawl [skiff] and saved his life.

Item, on the 24 July, Jeronimus has ordered Allert, by word of mouth, to take to the beach a cabin boy, Andries de Bruyn of Haarlem; who said to him, "Come, Andries, we will go and look for birds," but has cut his throat there with a knife.

Also, being still at Sea south of the *Cabo* [and] with secret permission of the skipper Ariaen Jacopsz, he has slept in the Constable's cabin with Zwaantien Hendricx, servant, and had carnal knowledge of her.

To all which above mentioned gruesome murders he has very willingly let himself be used, as well as those he still intended to to, had God Almighty not prevented —— including the seizing of the ship *Batavia* and the yacht *Sardam* —— moreover still daily mocking at God, being one of the principals who forbade the praying and the preaching of His holy word, and who has very scoffingly put a stop to that, although he says that Jeronimus had ordered him so, with still more misdeeds apparently kept hidden, being Criminal Offences of evil consequence which cannot be tolerated by God or man, because nature sufficiently teaches that such evil-doers may not be left unpunished as an example to others.

—— Therefore the Commandeur *Franco. pelsart* and we undersigned persons of the council of the ship *Sardam*, having given the greatest thought to the matter, after long examinations and searching, exchanged the same (and weighed them the more because no hope of improvement in him can be expected, as he has already killed a man in Holland), we have sentenced the foresaid Allert Jansz of Assendelft, in order to turn away from us the wrath of God and to cleanse the name Christian of such a villain. ——— Thus we sentence him herewith, that, on Monday the first of October, he shall be taken to Seals Island to a place there made ready to execute Justice, and there first to cut off his right hand and after that to punish him with the Cord at a gallows till death shall follow, with confiscation of all his kit, monthly wages, and all that he may have to claim here in India against the General East India Company our Lord Masters. Thus done and attested on the Island *Batavia's* Graveyard, this 28 Sept. Anno 1629.

[Signed by Pelsaert, Jacobsz, Gerritsz, Jansz, Yopzoon and marked by Visch.]

TODAY the 24 Sept. on the Island *Batavia's* Graveyard, has been resolved by the Commandeur *Fransco. Pelsart* and the Ship's council, to examine Andries Jonas of Luyck, soldier, on his great murders, so understood to have done, and if necessary to bring him to torture—date as before.

ANDRIES JONAS of LUYCK, soldier, aged about 40 years, asked how many people he has murdered or helped to murder here on these Islands near the Wreck of the perished ship *Batavia* ——— confesses, that one day, being 9 July last, when the provost Pieter Jansz, as well as 14 other people sailing on 2 small rafts to the High Island, were murdered as well as drowned—whereof Pauwels Barentsz, Bessel Jansz, sailors, thought to save themselves here on the island, but were ordered by Jeronimus to be killed—then had the before mentioned Andries, after Jan Hendricxsz had struck Pauwels Barentsz, pierced him right through the throat until he died.

Item, confesses also that one day, being the 18 July last, he was ordered by Jeronimus, together with David Zevanck, Coenraat van Huyssen, Jan Willems Selynsz, Lucas Gillisz, Rutger Fredricx, Mr Frans Jansz, Jan van Bemmel, Cornelis Pietersz of Wtrecht, to sail with the little yawl to Seals Island; so then Zevanck has asked Andries Jonas at night, "Have you got a sharp knife on you?" He said, "Certainly I have a knife, but not very sharp." Whereon Zevanck handed him his own knife and said to him, "Cut the throats of the women with it." So without any objection Andries has gone to Mayken Soers, who was heavily pregnant, and, taking her by the hand, led her a little apart and said to her, "Mayken, love, you must die," and threw her underfoot and cut her throat. ―――― That being done, he saw that Jan van Bemmel was busy killing Jannetgien Gist (the wife of Jan Hendricx from the Hague) and has come to his help and has stabbed her to death with a knife. The other women, Laurentia Thomas, wife of Gabriel Jacobsz, corporal (who was killed on 15 of this month [July] together with the others on Seals Island) and Geertie Willemsz, widow, together with still another 15 Boys, were killed by the others, Sevanck as well as his accomplices, that night; except 3 boys who hid themselves in the bushes.

He, further asked, because we were very certain that he also had gone to the predikant's tent and been present when his family was murdered, whom he had killed or helped to kill ―――― Confesses, that at night Jacob Pietersz Cosijn had come to him and said, "Andries, you must help by taking a walk; as we go, we'll help along the predikant's folk. Have you a knife with you?" Andries answered, "Yea," and so he has gone to the tent, with Jacob Pietersz, where Davit Zeevanck,[104] Jan Hendricxsz, Wouter Loos, Mattys Beer, Leenart Michielsz, Cornelis Pietersz and Andries Liebent already stood round; so he saw that Wybrecht Claasz, who was called out, was killed by Jan Hendricxsz, whereon Zevanck with all the others went into the tent, and the foresaid Andries, with Jacob Pietersz, stayed outside, so he says. ―――― Therefore, to draw from him the straight truth we have brought him to torture. ―――― After suffering pain, persists that he has not been in the tent, even less wounded or killed anyone. To be more certain, we have brought him again to torture. ―――― Denies as before, to have been in the tent.

On 27 do. before the ship's Council,

Andries Jonas, again asked whether he has killed or helped to kill anyone, confesses of freewill that in the night when the Predikant's family was murdered, being 21 July last, he was called by Zevanck, who said to him that he had to call Mayken Cardoes out of her tent and cut her throat; whereon Andries Jonas has gone without any objection or reluctance, and has called the foresaid Mayken outside, saying to her that she must go for a walk with him; whereupon she asked him, "Andries, will you do any evil to me?"

---

[104] Pelsaert's constant misspelling of Zevanck's name is psychologically interesting. As an assistant, the man was one of his own staff, personally known to him, and his brutality presumably deeply shocked Pelsaert.

Whereon he said, "No, nothing at all," but having gone a little way he threw her underfoot and sought to cut her throat with the knife, but she gripped the knife in her hand so that it was stuck, and he could not carry out his intention because of her struggling; meanwhile Wouter Loos came running, who battered in her head at once with an axe or adze, until she died, and he then dragged her into a hole in which the predikant's folk had been dragged. ——— Confesses also that he has been very willing in murdering, and he does not now know how he had wandered so far from God. ——— Further asked whether, if they had been able to carry out their plan to overpower the other people on the High Island, he would have taken part in seizing the first-coming Yacht ——— confesses, that he would have taken part in it just as any other, for they were led into thinking that they would all be rich for life.

WE UNDERSIGNED persons of the council of the ship *Sardam*, declare on our Manly Truth, in place of the duly attested Oath . . . .

[The declaration is similar to those previously made. Dated 28th September, it is signed by Pelsaert, Jacobsz, Deschamps, Gerritsz, Jansz, Yopzoon, and marked by Visch. On the remainder of the page, originally left blank, a note in small writing has been added to one side.]

Andries Jonas, on today the 2 of October on Seals Island, with the noose on his neck, ready for death, confesses, to unburden his conscience, that when he was sleeping one night, being   July, a boy came creeping into his tent on hands and knees because he had seen that some were being killed that night, which Jacob Pietersz Cosijns saw; who waked Andries and said, "Andries, drag that boy outside and help him forth;" which the foresaid Andries has immediately done, and cut his throat outside the tent; and because we, the undersigned, have heard him confessing this same willingly and unasked, we have, in order to certify the truth, signed this with our own hands, date this 2 Oct. 1629.

[Signed by Pelsaert, Jacobsz, Gerritsz, Yopzoon, and marked by Visch.[105] Pelsaert's summary of the crimes of Andries Jonas follows.]

BECAUSE ANDRIES JONAS of LUYCK, soldier, aged about 40 years, here on the islands near the Wreck of the perished ship *Batavia* has let himself be turned aside from the Way of human or reasonable Creatures and has let himself be used willingly, through an innate

---

[105] As Jacobsz signs this, it is obvious that Jansz was either absent or detailed as officer in charge of hangings. Apparently Gijsbert Bastiaensz did not hear this confession; possibly Jonas was not of his church.

corruptness, by the godless Epicurean[106] villain, Jeronimus Cornelisz, undermerchant, to several murders, which he has committed very tyrannically, without any compassion, on pregnant as well as other women, and on Men whom he has killed and helped to kill, as appears from his confessions in full as mentioned below, given under torture as well as of freewill. —————— Furthermore, has decided, together with other evil-minded people, to seize the first Yacht that should come to rescue them, and to murder all who would not have been of service to them, namely, when they had mastered the people and killed those on the High island who had escaped the murdering; at the sorties and fights against them, he has three times shown himself very willing, and has helped to fight them more savagely than acknowledged enemies. —————— His murders start

On the 9 July, when Pietersz Jansz, provost, with still another 14 people, women as well as men, had made two rafts on Traitors Island, with which they had the intention to sail to the High Island, and to prevent that, it has been decided by Jeronimus and his council to drown or kill them, to which purpose a little yawl was manned and was sent out. At last they were chased away from the rafts, some have been killed, others drowned, while 4 to 5 men escaped and thought to save their lives here on the island; but then it was ordered by Jeronimus that they had to be killed without grace. So the before mentioned Andries Jonas has stuck a pike right through the throat of the sailor Pauwels Barentsz, who had been thrown underfoot by Jan Hendricxsz, until he died.

Item, on the 18 July, Andries Jonas has been ordered by Jeronimus to go, together with Davit Zevanck and another men, with the little yawl to Seals Island, in order to kill there the remaining 4 women and about 15 boys who had not been killed on the previous murder on 15 July. —————— Therefore Zevanck has asked whether he had a knife; Andries Jonas answered that he had a knife but it was not very sharp. Whereupon Zevanck handed him his own knife, saying, "Cut the throats of the women." —————— So willingly, without delay or objection, Andries has gone to Mayken Soers, who was pregnant, has taken her by the hand and led her a little to one side and said to her, "Mayken, love, you must die," and thrown her underfoot and cut her throat; that being done, he saw that Jan van Bemmel was trying to kill Janneken Gist (the wife of Jan Hendricx from the Hague), therefore he went to help the

---

[106] A follower of the philosophy of Epicurus, who taught in Athens that pleasure was the highest good or practice of virtue. Obviously Pelsaert is horrified by the treatment of the women and boys and is no longer able to restrain his pen.

before mentioned Jan van Bemmel and stabbed Janneken to death with his knife; the other two women and the boys were killed by the others, except 3 boys who had hidden themselves in the bushes.

Item, on the 21 July at night, Andries Jonas was called by Jacob Pietersz Cosijn, who said to him, "Come, Andries, you must help in a pleasant outing; we will put the predikant's folk out of the way." Whereon Andries took a knife with him, and together they have gone to the tent where he found others who were chosen for that deed, namely, Davidt Zevanck, Jan Hendricxsz, Lenert Michielsz, Mattys Beer, Cornelis Pietersz, Wouter Loos and Andries Liebent, and saw that the young maid Wybrecht Claasz was called out of the tent, whom Jan Hendricxsz killed, and Zevanck and all the others went into the tent and murdered the Mother with her 6 children, but Andries Jonas and Jacob Pietersz remained outside because the tent was filled with people. ——— That being done, Zevanck said to Andries Jonas, "Go and call Mayken Cardoes out of her tent and cut her throat." Whereupon he has gone immediately and called, "Mayken, are you asleep? Come, we'll go for a walk." ——— Coming outside, the woman asked, "Andries, will you do me evil?" He said, "No, not at all," but when he had led her a little way, he threw the woman underfoot and sought to cut her throat, but she gripped the knife and it stuck in her hand so that he could not carry out his plan because of her violent struggling. ——— Meanwhile Wouter Loos came running with an adze or axe and battered her head in until she was dead; then he, Andries Jonas, dragged her into the hole into which the predikant's folk had been dragged.

To all which forementioned murders he has let himself be used with great willingness, as well as the ones he still had the intention to do, had not the Almighty God prevented it, while he was furthermore daily mocking at God, being one of the principal who forbade the praying and the preaching of His Holy Word and very scoffingly put a stop to it, although he says that Jeronimus had ordered him so; with still more misdeeds that have apparently remained hidden, Criminal Offences, of very evil consequence, which cannot and may not be suffered by God or Man, as nature teaches us sufficiently . . . .

[The sentence on Jonas differs from the previous ones only in that he is not condemned to lose a hand. It is signed by Pelsaert, Jacobsz, Gerritsz, Jansz, Yopzoon, and marked by Visch. Dated 28 September 1629.]

TODAY 20 Sept. 1629 on the Island *Batavia's* Graveyard, has been resolved by the Commandeur *Fransco. pelsart* and the ship's council, to examine Rutger Fredricxsz of Groeningen, locksmith, on his great murders so understood to have done, and if necessary to bring him to torture. ——— Date as before.

RUTGER FREDRICX of GROENINGHEN, locksmith, aged about 23 years, has been asked how many people he has killed or helped to kill. ——— Confesses that one morning, being 5 July last, he has been ordered by Jeronimus Cornelisz to go with the biggest Raft, with David Zevanck, Mattys Beer, Coenraat van Huyssen, Lenert Michielsz, Wouter Loos, Cornelisz Pietersz and Jan Hendricxsz, to drown Hans Radder, Jacop Groenewaldt, trumpeter and Andries de Vries, assistant. They have gone to Traitors Island and Rutger has helped to bind the hands and feet of the trumpeter Jacop Groenewalt and has dragged him so into the Sea; but Andries de Vries, being bound, was untied and spared for the time being. ——— He has been further asked whether he had not killed any others. ——— Denies having wounded or killed any one further. ———Therefore, because we are sufficiently certain that he had willingly committed more murders because he called out daily over the island, "Is anyone to be boxed on the ear? I will do it for a tot,"[107] we have brought him to torture, to draw out of him the straight truth. After having suffered pain, confesses that one day, being 9 July last, when the provost Pieter Jansz with 14 others were going to the High Island on 2 rafts and were killed by drowning—from which Pauls Barentsz, Bessel Jansz, Claas Harmansz of Maagdenburgh and Niclaas Winckelhaack thought to save themselves here on the island, but it was ordered by Jeronimus that they should be killed—then Rutger has struck the mentioned Bessel Jansz with his sword until he was dead. That being finished, he ran to Claas Harmansz of Maagdenburgh who was coming up out of the water, and killed him alone, without any help.

Item, also confesses that one day, being the 14 July, he, Rutger, together with Jan Hendricxsz and Lenert Michielsz, was called by Jan van Bemmel into the tent of Jeronimus who ordered them to kill Andries de Vries, assistant, giving them each a sword thereto,

[107] Here Pelsaert writes *mutsjen*, a more modern form than his previous *mutsken*.

and pouring each a beaker of wine. So have gone outside and have killed de Vries about Noon, publicly.

Jeronimus Cornelisz, being present, was asked if that was indeed true, if he had so ordered Rutger thus; confesses, "Yea," because he and the council had decided thus. But that he certainly believes that Rutger had done more than he has confessed, because he was always very willing to offer his services if any one had to be put out of the way. —— Further asked whether, if they had been able to carry out their plan to overpower the other people on the High Island, he would have helped to seize the first Yacht that should have come to rescue them —— confesses that he would have helped the same as any other.

WE UNDERSIGNED persons of the council of the ship *Sardam* declare on our Manly Truth in place of the duly attested Oath....

[The declaration is similar to those previously made and is signed by Pelsaert, Jacobsz, Deschamps, Gerritsz, Jansz, Yopzoon and marked by Visch. Pelsaert, however, made a slip and wrote the date as 28th October 1629 instead of 28th September. Pelsaert's summary of the crimes of Rutger Fredericx follows and is printed in full.]

Because Rutger Fredericx of Groeningen, locksmith, aged about 23 years here on the islands near the Wreck of the perished ship *Batavia*, has let himself be turned aside from the Way of all human or reasonable Creatures, and through his innate corruptness let himself be used by the godless Epicurean villain, Jeronimus Cornelisz, undermerchant, for the purpose of several murders, which he has committed without any compassion, although they were his own shipmates and brethren —— Who, bound through an oath, has killed and helped to kill [people] who had never done wrong to any one, being obedient to tyrants, they sought to kill out of their own wickedness all the people except a few. —— After having come to this, they had the intention to seize the first Yacht that should come to rescue them, and to murder all who would not be of service to them; namely, when they had overpowered the people on the High Island who had escaped from the murdering, and killed them; he has taken part in the sorties against those, and has three times shown himself very willing to help to fight them more savagely than acknowledged enemies. His murders as follows—

On the 3 July Rutger Fredricx has been ordered by Jeronimus Cornelisz, together with Davit Sevanck, Coenraat van Huyssen, Gysbrecht van Welderen, Daniel Cornelisz, Mattys Beer and Leenert Michielsz, to go with the biggest raft and drown Jan Cornelisz of Amesvoort, Thomas Wenzel, Hendrick Jansz of Oldenburgh and Andries Liebent; and on Traitors Island the foresaid Rutger has bound Jacop Groenewald, trumpeter, hand and foot, and [they] have been dragged into the Sea, where they suffocated or drowned, except Andries Liebent, who was spared.

Item, because Pieter Jansz, provost, with another 14 people, women as well as men, had made 2 rafts on the Traitors Island with which they had the intention of going to the High Island, it has on the contrary been decided by Jeronimus and his council to drown or to kill them; therefore he sent a manned yawl to chase them from the rafts, and some have been drowned and some killed. —— But 4 to 5 men escaped and they thought to save their lives here on the Island; but it was ordered by Jeronimus to kill them without mercy. —— So the before mentioned Rutger has struck Bessel Jansz with his sword until he died. —— That being finished, Claas Harmansz of Maagdenburgh was coming to the shallows and Rutger ran to him and killed him all alone, without any help.

Item, also on the 14 July, Rutger, together with Jan Hendricxsz and Lenert Michielsz, was called by Jan van Bemmel to the tent of Jeronimus, and Jeronimus ordered them to kill Andries de Vries, assistant; has given each one a sword, also has poured out for each a beaker of wine, and so they have gone, the three of them, to de Vries and have killed him publicly, at Noon.

All which above mentioned Gruesome murders, to which he has with great willingness let himself be used, as well as those he still had in mind to do, had the Almighty God not prevented it . . . .

[Like Jonas, Rutger Fredricx was not condemned to lose a hand. His sentence is signed by Pelsaert, Jacobsz, Gerritsz, Jansz, Yopzoon, and marked by Visch. It is dated 28th September, thus emphasizing the slip made in the date of the foregoing declaration.]

TODAY the 23 Sept. 1629 on the Island *Batavia's* Graveyard, has been resolved by the Commandeur *Fransco. pelsart* and the Ship's Council to examine Jan Pelgrom de Bye of Bemmel on his great murders which so understood to have done, and the beastly life that he has lived here on the island, and if necessary to bring him to torture. —— Date as above.

JAN PELGROM DE BYE of BEMMEL, aged about 18 years, and late cabin servant on the perished ship *Batavia*, but here on the Island the servant of Jeronimus Cornelisz, undermerchant —— asked, how many People he had killed or helped to kill, denies that he had harmed or killed anyone, because there were plenty of others only too ready for that. —— Therefore have brought him to torture, because we are sufficiently certain that he spoke lies; having suffered pain, he confesses that one day, being 18 July last, he has gone to Seals Island with Davidt Sevanck, who took him with him on his own request, because he had heard that the remaining Women and Boys would be murdered. —— He has killed a boy that night, when the word was given; that being done, he ran to Jannetgien Gist, wife of Jan Hendricxsz from the Hague, whom he struck many times with his sword, whereon Andries Jonas came running along and who thereupon stabbed her dead with his knife.

Confesses also that one day, being   July last, he was sent to get Jan Hendricxsz at night, by Jeronimus, who ordered him, together with Andries Liebent and Jan van Bemmel, to strangle Anneken Hardens, wife of Jan Hardens; therefore they have gone, the three of them. —— Meanwhile Gysbrecht van Welderen came to help them, who made a noose of her hair ribbon and Jan Hendricxsz strangled her so; Jan van Bemmel sat on her legs.

He further asked, why on the 16 August, when Cornelis Alderszschans,[108] youngster [*hooplooper*] was to have his head cut off, he begged so very much that he should be allowed to do it; confesses, that he had gone out on that day with the little yawl and, coming into the tent, Jeronimus said to him, "Jan, here is my sword, which you have to try on the Net-maker to see if it is sharp enough to cut off his head;" Whereupon he was very glad. —— Sevanck, hearing the same, maintained that he was too light for that. Meanwhile Mattys Beyr came, who asked if he might do it, which was granted him. So he took the sword out of Jan van Bemmel's hand and took it to Gillis Phillipsen in order to file it sharp. —— Meanwhile Jan was busy to blindfold the boy in the presence of Jeronimus who said to the boy, "Now, be happy, sit nicely, 'tis but a joke." —— Meanwhile Mattys Beer, who had the sword under his cloak, slew him with one blow, cutting off his head. —— Jeronimus, confronted with this, and asked if the same were true and if he had thus ordered him, says, Yea, because the said Jan van Bemmel was daily begging him that he should allow him to kill someone, because he would rather do that than eat or drink—when he was not allowed to cut off the head of the foresaid youngster, he wept.

[108] *Schans* means "poop". Probably this was a deck boy or cabin boy for the Great Cabin.

On the 26 do. before the Ship's Council,

The forementioned Jan van Bemmel being brought again, has been asked why he has lived so godlessly here on the island, daily calling out, "Come now, devils with all sacraments, where are you? I certainly wish I now saw a devil, and who wants to be boxed on the ear? I shall certainly manage it!" Confesses, that he has done so and that he had been ordered the same, because daily he had heard from Jeronimus that there was neither devil nor Hell, and that these were only fables.

Further asked, how many Women he has here known carnally, says that he has done his will with Tryntgiens Fredricx and her sister Zussien Fredricx, and has slept with them, also with Anneken Gunner [*Bosschieters*], all of whom he has known carnally.

Asked, how many further gruesome misdeeds he has committed, confesses at last that he was certainly very eager to kill someone, but the others were always before him; and he was also eager to help to seize the yacht that would come.

WE UNDERSIGNED persons of the council of the ship *Sardam* declare upon our Manly Truth in place of the duly attested Oath . . . .

[The declaration is signed by Pelsaert, Jacobsz, Deschamps, Gerritsz, Jansz, Yopzoon, and marked by Visch. It is dated 28th September 1629. Pelsaert's summary of the crimes of Jan Pelgrom de Bye follows and is printed in full.]

BECAUSE JAN PELGROM DE BIJE VAN BEMMEL, aged about 18 years, late cabin servant of the perished ship *Batavia* and also, here on the islands of Houtman's Abroholer [*sic*], the late servant of Jeronimus Cornelisz, under Merchant, has become, through his innate corruptness, entirely and wholly a disciple of his Master, the Godless seducer and murderer of men, and has followed in his footsteps in Murdering, as well as what he still had in mind to do, if he had been able to do so. —— Item, he has also had carnal knowledge here of several married women and done his will with them, of whom two were sisters; as well as his gruesome life, mocking at God and cursing and Swearing, also conducting himself more like a beast than a human being, which made him at last a terror to all the people, who feared him more than any other of the principal murderers or evil-doers —— moreover very eager and industrious to help to seize the first-coming yacht, yea, even on the day when the Yacht *Sardam* had come, he had asked the Capt. Wouter Loos, "Come on, say; won't we now seize the Yacht?" Whereupon the other, seeing that the plan[109] had failed, answered, "No, I have given up the idea." ———— All this is according to his confessions by examination; by torture as well as by his freewill confessed ———— appearing in full as well as hereunder, to be seen according to the variety of his murders, to wit—

Item, on the 18 July the forementioned Jan Pelgrom has gone, on his own request, together with Davidt Zevanck and still many others, to Seals Island, because he had heard it said and resolved that the 4 women and the rest of the Boys still remaining on do. island since the last slaughter, had to be done away with. ———— So Jan, when the sign was given by Zevanck, has killed a Boy, but because it was night, and dark, the name is unknown to him. That being done, he ran to Jannetgien Gist, wife of Jan Hendricxsz from The Hague, gunner, whom he stabbed several times with his sword. Whereupon Andries Jonas came running and stabbed her to death with his knife.

On the 30 July, the before mentioned Jan van Bemmel has been sent at night to get Jan Hendricxsz, who, when they came to the tent, was ordered, together with Andries Liebent, to strangle Anneken Hardens, wife of Hans Hardens, whereupon Jan was very glad, and he went quickly, but meanwhile Gysbrecht van Welderen came to help Jan Hendricxsz, who was making a noose of her hair ribbon, but Jan Hendricxsz strangled her and Jan van Bemmel sat on her legs.

Item, also on the 16 August, Jan van Bemmel having been out with the little yawl, coming in to the tent, Jeronimus said to him, "Jan, here is my sword, which you have to try on that Net-maker, whether it is sharp enough, and cut off his head." ———— Whereon Jan was very glad and took the sword in his hand. ———— Meanwhile David Zevanck came up and maintained that Jan van Bemmel was too light and that another should be chosen for that; Mattys Beyr, who heard, requested that he be allowed to do it, which was granted him at length, and thereon took the sword from Jan, who would not give it to him willingly, but he seized it out of his hand and went with the sword to Gillis Phillipsz in order to have it filed somewhat sharper, and then came back with it under his cloak. Meanwhile, Jan van Bemmel had already blindfolded the boy in the presence of Jeronimus who stood by, who said to the boy named Cornelis Aldersz, of Ylpendam, "Now, boy, sit happily, they are only joking with you." Whereupon Mattys Beyr cut off his head. Whereupon Jeronimus, Zevanck, and others

---

[109] To conquer those on the High island, and to let the yacht's boat come ashore, make the crew drunk, and take the yacht by surprise.

were laughing, but on the contrary, Jan van Bemmel was weeping, because had not been allowed to do it.

Item, has daily on the island run round like a man possessed, calling out, "Come now, devils with all the sacraments, where are you? I wish that I now saw a devil. And who wants to be stabbed to death? I can do that very beautifully," with such gruesome, more devilish blasphemies.

All the before mentioned gruesome deeds, and lust for murders, which, he has himself confessed, he would very eagerly have done but could never further succeed, as well as the unnatural blood scandal of having slept with two sisters, both married women, so shamefully mocking at God, which acts neither may nor can be suffered by God, Who orders the evil-doer to be punished so that he shall not fall into greater sin. Because we cannot see in him anything other than great corruptness and no hope of improvement according to the judgment of all people, as well as appears from his deeds. —— Therefore the Commandeur *Franco. pelsart* and we undersigned persons of the council of the ship *Sardam* ....

[Sentence as previously, but without loss of hand. It is signed by Pelsaert, Jacobsz, Gerritsz, Jansz, Yopzoon and marked by Visch, and dated 28th September 1629.

At this point Pelsaert begins a new page and returns to making daily entries until 13th November.]

The 28 do. towards evening, after his examination and own confessions have been read to Jeronimus publicly, before all the people who were on the island, and because he knew that the council was gathered to reach his sentence. —— Requested by means of the predikant, a delay of a few days, because he desired to be baptised and so that he could meanwhile have time to bewail his Sins and think them over so that at last he might die in peace and in repentance. —— Because of such an understanding for [the necessity of] the saving of his Soul, we have postponed the day of execution until the first of October, so that he may have himself baptised the day after tomorrow, being Sunday—which the predikant has announced to him, namely, that a few days were granted to him, but he did not know how many. —— Jeronimus desired to know how many days, so that he might adjust himself, but the predikant put him at ease for that day, and he behaved himself as if he had some solace and was more courageous.

On the 29 do. Jeronimus desired again to know how many days respite had been given to him; protested, that if he were not told, he could not come to peace. At last I let him be told, whereupon he said, "Tut —— nothing more? Can one show repentance of life in so few days? I thought I should be allowed 8 or 14 days." So that he began to rage, saying, "I see well, they want my blood and my life, but God will not suffer that I shall die a shameful death. I know for certain, and you will all see it, that God will perform unto me this night a miracle, so that I shall not be hanged," which was his tune all that day. —— Therefore I ordered the Guard that no one should hand him a knife or anything else with which he could damage himself. But at night he secretly ate something with which he thought to poison himself, for it started to work about one hour in the morning, so that he was full of pain and seemed like to die. In this great anxiety he asked for some Venetian *theriac*.[110] At last he began to get some relief, because apparently it had not been strong enough, but he had to be got out of his prison certainly 20 times during the night, because his so-called miracle was working from below as well as from above.

On 30 do. on Sunday, when the sermon was about to begin, I ordered Jeronimus to be fetched, so that he, together with the other condemned criminals,[111] would be able to hear the Word of God, but he answered, he would not come and would not have anything to do with the talks of the dominie. —— See how miraculously God the Lord reveals his godlessness before all people and again makes it public how before this he has forbidden all preaching and praying to the Predikant. —— When he saw that all his subterfuges and sinister practices to remain alive were of no avail, firstly, that he desired to be brought to Batavia to speak once again with his Wife; after that, under the pretext of desiring to be baptised to get some prolongment of his life; at last, when he saw that all his attempts were without avail, his *Epicurean* or *torrentiaenschen*[112] outlook, which he had kept hidden during that time as much as possible, namely, that he said that there was neither Devil nor Hell; also that he still tried to maintain, here in his prison, that all he did, whether it was good or bad (as judged by others), God gave the same into his heart, for God, said he, was perfect in virtue and goodness, so was not able to send into the heart of men anything bad, because there was no evil or badness in Himself; saying with that, that all he had done was sent into his heart by God, for he had not been able to do anything out of himself; and still more such gruesome opinions which he had tried to imprint into the minds of the people here on the Island.

[110] Venice treacle: an antidote to bites of poisonous animals, compounded of many drugs.
[111] *Patients*: i.e., those condemned to suffer; convicts, or convicted persons.
[112] Pelsaert spells Torrentian phonetically; later he refers to Jeronimus's having followed the teachings of Torrentius.

On 1st October, the Wind S.S.Wt. with great stormy showers, and it blew so hard that it was not possible to go to Seals Island and bring the evil-doers to death according to their sentences.

On 2 do. the Wind South, but a bit quieter, and we have taken the 8 condemned to Seals Island in order to be punished according to their sentences on the Gallows with the Cord. Coming there, they begged that Jeronimus should be hanged first, so that their eyes could see that the seducer of men died. ——— But Jeronimus could not reconcile himself to dying or to penitence, neither to pray to God nor to show any face of repentance over his sins. But they all shouted at each other, "Revenge," some evil-doers shouted revenge at Jeronimus, and Jeronimus shouted at them. At last he challenged them, as well as the council, before God's Judgment Seat, that he wanted to seek justice there with them, because he had not been able to get it here on Earth. And so he died stubborn. ——— Mattys Beyr confessed to the Predikant, near the gallows, that he had also murdered another four Men, with a Boy, in the presence of Jeronimus one night, but he could not name them. He had not told the same all this time, and he requested therefore that one should pray for him on account of his many sins. ——— Also Andries Jonas, who confessed beneath the gallows that he had murdered still another Boy than he had confessed to, namely, that on a certain night when some other Men were murdered, whereon the Boy out of fear and because he was ill, came creeping on his hands and feet in their tent, which Jacop Pietersz Cosyn had seen, who said to Andries Jonas, "Andries, you must help to put the boy out of the way." Whereon he had gone outside, dragged the Boy out of the tent and cut his throat with his knife. ——— Allert Jansz of Assendelft, and the others, died also very Godless and unrepentant. But he warned me, as also the others, that we should have to watch very well on the Ship because quite many traitors remained alive who would seize an opportunity to execute that which they had intended; without naming anyone, saying he did not wish to be called an informer after his death. ——— Jan van Bemmel could not compose himself to die; weeping and wailing and begging for grace, and that one should put him on an Island and let him live a little longer. Therefore on account of his Youth, one has begged for His life, which at last we have granted to him, to put him on an island or the continent, according to occasion occurring.

On 3 do. the Wind W.S.W. with hard gale, and was not possible to do anything at the Wreck on account of the great turmoil.

On 4 do. the Wind as before, with hard gale, therefore nothing has happened.

On 5 do. the Wind E.S.E., with fair weather, therefore went to the Wreck of the foreship in order to get a brass piece of cannon and one of iron, which were hanging on the Wreck,[113] and towards night we got the brass cannon loose and have brought it to the Island.

On 6 do. the Wind Southerly; in the morning I have sent the fore mentioned piece of cannon on board; and have not been able to work at the poop of the Wreck on account of the hollow breakers, but have sent the little yawl to an island in order to see if there was anything to salvage.

On 7 do. the Wind Southerly as before. Have not been able to do anything at the Wreck, but have sent aboard some goods that were here on the island.

On 8 do. the Wind S.S.W. Have not been able to do anything at the Wreck on account of the hard gale.

On 9 do. the Wind as before. But a little quieter, therefore I have sent the boat to the Wreck to get the other iron piece of cannon, which they have brought towards evening.

On 10 do. the Wind as before; in the morning sent the before mentioned piece on board. Have not been able to do anything at the Wreck because of the hard wind, but we have begun to make preparations to get the water whereto a few days ago I had ordered to burn away the Thickets on the High island—on the one hand in order to catch better the Cats[114] that were on that, on the other hand in order to see if one could find hidden pits [*putten*] as had been found on Wiebbe Hayes' island.[115] When they were burning off they have found a pit with water, but very stinking. ——— After that, again a pit with brackish water. The next day they found under some burnt shrubs, a small hole that an arm might enter, threw a stone in and noticed that it gave an echo of Water. So the skipper has ordered to get pickaxes and crowbars from aboard, with which they have made a hole suitable to reach the water, which is, praise God, very good water, although this island has been searched enough and run over by me as well as other thirsty men.[116] But it seems that God did not suffer that one should be able to find the same [then].

[113] Guns were jettisoned after the wreck; these apparently stuck.

[114] Wallabies. Obviously to eat. It would be interesting to know if they intended to salt down some for the voyage as was the custom when any quantity of fresh flesh or fish was available *en route*.

[115] Here is clearly shown the differentiation between the *two* high islands. We already know that "cats" were found by Wiebbe Hayes: thus is established the fact of these two islands being East and West Wallabi.

[116] Before they left for Java after the wreck.

On 11 do. the Wind as before. Today we have filled the empty water vessels with the above mentioned water and brought them to the ship. —— In the afternoon our folk have been fishing with the smallest yawl and they found a barrel of vinegar lying on a cliff [reef].

On 12 do. the Wind as before. In the morning I have sent the skipper with the boat to the above mentioned cliff to get the barrel of vinegar and to bring it on board, and that he should sail from there to some small islands which were lying one to 2 miles Westerly of the ship[117] in order to see if some drift goods had not been washed ashore there, and to be on the ship again towards evening if possible, but that he should sail carefully, even if he had to stay out the night. —— Before noon the weather was somewhat calmer and the Sea being smooth, I have gone with the smallest yawl, together with the divers, to the Wreck; they dived up 75 *reals* in loose money, which had fallen out of a chest; and at last they found still another chest with money, upon which lay a piece of cannon which, through a sudden wind and on account of the smallness of the little yawl, we had to leave with heart's regret.

On 13 do. the Wind South, with a hard gale. Have sent the smallest yawl aboard, so that as soon as the skipper comes with the boat, he should go there himself, in order to lift the foresaid money chest, with the first suitable weather; towards evening it began to blow harder.

On 14 do. the Wind S. and S.S.W., with a hard storm, so that I fear for the boat.

On 15 do. the Wind and the weather as before, so that it was not possible for the boat to come back; towards evening the weather began to take off.

On 16 do. in the morning, the Wind S.E. and E.S.E. with apparently beautiful weather. Therefore I went again to the Wreck with the smallest yawl, in order to see if one could lift the chest with the little yawl, but coming near found that it was still breaking so much that one could not get close and much has been washed away by the last storm. —— After noon, I sent the foresaid little yawl aboard with a note to the uppersteersman [Claas Gerritsz] that he must man the yawl and provision it with Bread, Water and Wine, and to send them with the understeersman

[117] If here Pelsaert refers to the *Sardam* and not the wreck, she must have lain well down *under* East Wallabi, which seems unlikely whilst watering; if so these islands must have been to the *south*-west of the anchored ship; probably Pigeon Island, etc. But if he meant the wreck (as seems more probable) there are numerous unnamed small islands, in this case *north*-west.

[Jacop Jansz] to the nearest Islands to seek for the boat or its crew.

On 17 do. the Wind Southerly. Have seen the Yawl sailing away from the ship in order to seek the boat, as they have been ordered.

On 18 do. The Wind as before. In the morning the yawl has arrived here because it had turned back, and next, the uppersteersman came in the afternoon, who told me that the yawl had come back last night, but that they had not found any boat or crew on the nearest islands. But that there was another big Island about 3 miles N.N.W. from the Ship, but towards which they had not dared to sail because it blew too hard, also mentioned that on Sunday 13th, two Hours before evening, they had seen the boat 2 miles to Sea N.N.E. of them, but because just at that time the wind began to rise, they immediately lost it out of sight. So that, by God's Truth, it is to be feared that it has drifted away unless it has run to the foresaid Island that lies N.N.W of the ship and there, through the hard storm, the boat could have been knocked to pieces. ——— Whereupon I have sent the steersman on board immediately, in order to strengthen the yawl quickly with a plank and to prepare it to go to Sea, and to have the understeersman go out again provided with Water, Bread, grapnels, ropes, and everything they may need in search for the boat. ———

On 19 do. the Wind Southerly. Towards noon we have seen the yawl sailing from aboard in order to fulfil the ordered voyage; towards evening it began to blow harder.

On 20 do. the wind S. and S.S.W., blowing very hard so that they could not send us from aboard the food or drink which I had written and sent for with the smallest yawl.

On 21 do. the Wind as before, with a hard storm so that our yawl could not return from the islands, nor could food be sent to us from the ship although we had nothing left.

On 22 do. the Wind as before, with hard weather, so that the yawl could not come from the Islands, nor could the smallest yawl bring us any food or drink from the ship.

On 23 do. the Wind Southerly but much calmer than yesterday, but, God's Truth, still no vessel, neither from the islands nor from the Ship, which should have brought us food. For now we have not had anything in two days to give to the people. ——— Towards evening, near Sunset, the smallest yawl has come from the ship, praise God, with bread and other Food, and it started to become very beautiful weather.

On 24 do. the wind S.West. In the Morning, I have sent the foresaid small yawl aboard to fetch water, which they had not brought us yesterday. ——— About noon we have seen returning the big yawl which I had sent on the 19th with the understeersman to search for the skipper with the boat, and in the afternoon the foresaid yawl came here with the uppersteersman, bringing tidings that they had been on an island with high dunes, about 3 to 4 miles N.N.West of the Ship, which was set all round with a reef except for a narrow opening, which they just struck, so that they could go in. But they have not been able to see that the skipper or the boat have been there. It is a dry great island without having found any fresh water, but there was a host of gulls [*meuwes*] and eggs, and in the middle of the island it had a valley with much Sand.[118] So that, by God's Truth, the boat must have been turned over by the storm on the 14, or must have been driven away, to wit, with the skipper Jacob Jacopsz of *Sardam*, Pieter Pietersz of Ouwemierop, quartermaster, Marten Claasz of Texel Gunner, Cornelis Pietersz of Bolswart, late under-trumpeter on the ship *Batavia*, Ariaan Theuwissen of Harderwyck late gunner on the ship *Batavia*—

May God the Lord have been merciful to their Souls. *Amen*.

On 25 do. the Wind S.West. I have gone with the smallest yawl to some islands and reefs in order to see if anything had drifted ashore. Found there nothing else but woodwork with which the islands seem to be strewn due to the great quantity that has been washed ashore on all places. I had the intention to go to the Wreck, but found that there was such a surf that it was impossible.

On 26 do. the Wind Southerly. After noon, have gone with the smallest yawl near the wreck of the foreship, but found that such a surf ran outside that we could do nothing other than gather some iron hoops and other ironwork into the little yawl, and some lead which we got out of the forepart of the Wreck, with which we returned towards evening.

On 27 do. the Wind S.West. Early in the morning the big yawl has come hither from aboard, with the uppersteersman and the High boatswain,[119] because I had ordered him to come to examine some prisoners, which we have done before noon. But I have sent the yawl [back] to the ship, because it still blew too hard to do

---

[118] This is an excellent picture of North Island. I have seen the one reef opening clearly visible from the air; the sailors called the birds gulls, but the chances are that they were terns, which frequent these islands in hosts. There are large gull colonies also, but during September and October many of the islands have millions of terns nesting on bushes and on the ground.

[119] The uppersteersman was Claasz Gerritsz, as it has already been stated that Jacop Jansz held the rank of understeersman. The high boatswain of the *Sardam* was Symon Yopzoon, as appears from the order of signatures already noted (see page 157 and note 66) and the fact that Jacop Jansz has been stated to hold the rank of understeersman.

anything at the Wreck, with the foresaid Ironwork from yesterday and the firewood, with the order that it had to return immediately. Towards Noon the Wind began to run westerly and N.West, with which the water became so suddenly low [*slecht*][120] around the Wreck it can hardly be believed. ——— Therefore gave all possible signs with fires, flag-waving and other means as well, so that the yawl should return quickly. ——— Meanwhile I went with the smallest yawl and the divers, to the Wreck. Through strong showers, noticed that there still ran rather a big swell, therefore I remained lying outside with the little yawl for a long time, until through the ceasing of the rain as well as because of the fact that the weather became calmer, the water became very slack [*slecht*][121] so that we sailed around the Wreck. Found that the after part of the ship had been washed completely away and now had fewer sign-marks to show where we might find the money chest which we had seen on 12. But we looked for it so long that the divers found it. And they tied a rope to it in order to lift it, but it was too heavy for the light little yawl so that we stuck a buoy and went back to the Island in order to see if the big yawl had not come; but coming there, found not yet. ——— Therefore ordered the smallest yawl to go to Seals Island, because they could see them better from there and give better signals from there. At last towards evening the yawl came, half an hour before Sunset, and found that it was the fault of the quartermaster, who had been lying by the high island so long beyond his orders, and now it was too late to get the chest.

On 28 do. the wind S.S.West, nothing has happened on account of the strong wind and heavy breakers.

On 29 do. the Wind W.S.W. with hard weather as before. Have not been able to do anything at the Wreck. But have gone with the boat and the yawl[122] to the islands about. Got some wood and iron work which we have sent on board with the boat with the uppersteersman and High boatswain.

On 30 do. in the morning the Wind Southerly. Was one hour very calm; therefore I went with the smallest yawl and the divers to the Wreck, but found outside that the swell ran still so hard and that far outside the Wreck was [such] a surf that we could not come near, whereon it began to blow very hard from the S.S.West, so that we had to leave.

[120] *Slecht* can be taken here variably as "mean", i.e. low, or as "slack".
[121] Ibid.
[122] It is here noticeable that Pelsaert has slipped into calling the largest of the remaining ship's craft the *boat*, and the next in size (obviously one of those built at the islands) the *yawl*.

On 31 do. the Wind S.S.West with hard gale; in the morning, ordered the yawl to be loaded with firewood and to be sent on board again.

THE 1ST NOVEMBER, the Wind as before but a little quieter. Therefore by means of fire signals have requested the yawl from the ship, in order to see if the chest with money could be got out of the Wreck, but have seen no sign of ditto yawl.

On 2 do. the Wind Southerly, early in the morning have given them fire signals again, in order to get the yawl from aboard, so that do. yawl has come with the uppersteersman before Noon, but because the wind was so strong, have not been able to do anything at the Wreck. —— Therefore the steersman has again been sent aboard towards evening, with the yawl, in order to fetch the rest of the water from the High Island.

On 3 do. the wind Southerly as before, with strong Wind, so that we have not been able to do anything at the wreck; but sent the smallest yawl to the foremost part of the Wreck in order to see whether anything advantageous could be done, but have found nothing.

On 4 do. the wind S.S.East, but a little quieter and beautiful clear weather, so that again we have made signals with smoke to get the boat from aboard. Meanwhile I have gone with the smallest yawl, before noon, to the Wreck, but as soon as we have gone from land, we noticed North East of us several columns of smoke, as well as the main Coast of the Southland[123] which we could see perfectly, on which this smoke was, though before this the land had been seen by none here. —— This makes me imagine and firmly believe that the skipper with his crew have been stranded with the boat on this land, and because it is clear weather have given smoke signals, so that I hope that we shall find them still alive by the grace of God. —— In the afternoon the yawl has come back from the ship with the steersman, and so we have gone

[123] In 1956 I read a paper, "The Reports of Francisco Pelsaert", before the Western Australian Historical Society (published in *Early Days*; Journal and Proceedings of that Society, vol. v, part 2, pp. 1-18), in which I mentioned this statement. At the conclusion I was approached by Mrs Constance Norris, who told me that her father, the late Joseph Wright of Geraldton, had once seen what he presumed to be the Abrolhos Islands when he was fishing at the mouth of the Chapman River a few miles north of Geraldton, on a particularly clear day. This phenomenon had impressed him. It does give substantiation, in reverse, to Pelsaert's statement. I myself have frequently seen, at early morning or evening, the island of Rottnest, near Fremantle, elevated to a surprising degree by mirage. Presumably some similar trick of light was responsible for both the abovementioned appearances, as approximately 30 miles lie between the Abrolhos Islands and the mainland.

immediately to the wreck with the divers, but have not been able to find the money chest. Therefore we came back having done nothing.

On 5 do. early in the morning, the wind N.Wt., with beautiful clear weather, therefore I have gone in turn with the yawl and the smallest yawl, to the Wreck, and have ordered them to dive with great diligence in order to find the money chest, which, by God's Truth, notwithstanding all possible diligence, the divers have not been able to find; but they fished up the Box [*Casse*] with the Tinsel, as well as 4 silver Moorish fruit-dishes, with a ditto hand-basin [*lampetschotel*], weighing all together, by guessing Silver Marks. ——— Have returned towards noon because the Sea began to rise, and moreover it became lowering till a short time after Noon; then the Sun was shining brightly, have gone thither again with the yawl and the smallest yawl. ——— But after much searching have found nothing.

On 6 do. the Wind N.N.W. and N.W. with a topgallant gale and dark weather, with this wind it is now unsheltered [*opperwal*] at the wreck, then the Sea, to be contrary, rises very hard with breakers.

On 7 do. the wind S.Wt., also calm. Have gone again with the divers with the smallest yawl to the wreck, although after much searching have found nothing; therefore have begun to take our goods from the island on board.

On 8 do. the wind South. Have not gone near the wreck on account of the strong wind and surf, but continued to take the salvaged money and other goods, on board.

On 9 do. in the morning the wind S.S.E. but towards noon it usually shoots Southerly; today on account of the strong wind we could not go to the wreck but have sent a yawl with 4 chests of money and other goods, on board.

On 10 do. in the morning the wind S.E., but towards noon Southerly with a strong persistent wind. Today have gone on board with the other 3 chests of money and the other goods, in order to get ready for the voyage because there is no hope left of doing more at the Wreck.

On 11 do. the Wind S.S.East with a hard gale. This day spent in getting water because it blew too hard to get some woodwork from the Island *Batavia's* Graveyard.

On 12 do. in the morning the Wind South with small gale, and during the day it began to run to the North West with variable moderate winds and at last calm. ——— Therefore I have sent the small yawl again to the Wreck with the divers in order to see if anything could be found. ——— Towards evening they came back with 2 silver dishes and a carpenter's chest which they had fished up, declaring upon their Manly Truth that nothing more could be found, even if one remains lying here indefinitely.

On 13 do. the wind S.S.West with calm and beautiful weather. Have resolved today that, God willing, wind and weather so permitting, we shall go under sail on the 15th and make our voyage as fast as possible to Batavia; also one shall do justice to the following persons, who have behaved themselves on the Islands not altogether guiltlessly—but from fear of death have smirched their hands with human blood, to wit, Salomon Deschamps undermerchant, Rogier Decker late cabin-servant, Lucas Gillissen [sic] from the Hague, cadet, Abraham Gerritsen of Amsterdam and Claas Harmensen of Campen, as appears out of the following resolution and sentences ———

TODAY 13 November 1629 it has been resolved by the Commandeur and the Ship's council of the Yacht *Sardam,*

BECAUSE WE BY GOD'S TRUTH have spent here near the Wreck of the perished ship *Batavia* a little less than 2 months, and that against our will or intention, on account of the hard wind and weather, and although we have not passed by any opportunity of calmness and little surf, and have taken the opportunity to search with the divers for Cash and other wares in the wreck, so that with several efforts we have found 10 money chests, and because there have been 12 in the ship,[124] therefore, according with the explicit order of the Hon. Lord Gov. Gen., did not want to give up lightly. But are wholly convinced that nothing more is to be found ——— which we are now, seeing that all has been Searched through and Dived over, so that the Commandeur has proposed whether one should wait here again for a few days of calm weather, which usually comes one day in 15 to 20, to see if anything can be found (on that one). Because we think we are fully aware that all further searching is only time wasting and to remain here is only to the detriment of our Lord Masters, to sail as soon as possible to Batavia. ——— So has the Council concluded now that we have studied the matter most earnestly for the Gen. East India Comp., having taken into consideration that so much Cash and goods and further, more than 100 Men, remaining here on the basis of an uncertain hope, cannot but be a great loss and disservice. ——— Therefore resolved that tomorrow morning, God willing, wind and weather so per-

---

[124] One they had been unable to lift because of the cannon on it; the other had been broken open by Jean Thiriou after the wreck (see p. 243).

mitting, to go under Sail to Batavia. But first of all shall sail to the main Southland, East North East from here, in order to see [if we are able to find] the skipper and other 4 Men who were with him in the boat and who were driven away with hard Winds. Because on the 4th of this month we have seen several smoke columns, wherefrom one can presume that they have made the same as a sign.

Further also, Wouter Loos of Maastricht, soldier, after the capture of Jeronimus Cornelisz, under Merchant, has been made Captain of a troop of Murderers before our arrival and has let himself be authorized for that, and has made people swear with signatures and Oaths, to be true to him in everything, in manner [*forme*] as Jeronimus had done before his capture; whereupon on 17 September he has made the plan to go and fight against the defensive people on the High Island, in order to overpower them, although after 2 hours of fighting they did not advance any further than that 4 men have been shot very badly with their muskets [*musquetten*], of whom one named Jan Dircxsz of Emden, gunner [*bosschieter*], has died on 28 do. —— Furthermore, he has with great willingness let himself be used to several Murders, as appears out of his examination and own confession in full, as well as done his will with several Women. Towards which complete knowledge we have come very slowly, but we are fully certain of this. Therefore the Commandeur has proposed, because such Criminal Offences have been committed by him that may not or cannot be left unpunished before God and our High Authority at Batavia, whether [it is permissible] one shall punish with death the said Wouter Loos here, as an Example to others, or whether one shall put him on the main Southland in order to live with the Inhabitants of that Land, if God so please that they will let him live, in order to live a certain time with them and to look into the opportunities of the Land until the time ships might come on 25 or 26 degrees, so that he might still be rescued. Therefore the council [has decided] after we have taken notice of the same with due seriousness and after we have weighed and debated the case of the foresaid Wouter Loos, to sentence him, preferring grace in place of rigour of the Justice[125] and also the service of the Gen. East India Company, that he, together with Jan Pelgrom de Bye van Bemmel, who on 28th Sept. past, was sentenced to the gallows and who on account of his Youth obtained by entreating to be put on an Island, shall be put with a small yawl on the foresaid land as scoundrels and death-deserving delinquents, in order to make shift with the

---

[125] Cf. the English phrase "to enforce with the utmost rigour of the law."

The hangings on Seals Island as illustrated in the Lucas de Vries 1649 edition of *Ongeluckige Voyagie*.

A page from Pelsaert's Journal, showing part of the declaration to the truth of the evidence set down at the trial of Mattijs Beer, signed by the full Ship's Council of the Sardam *as well as by the undermerchant Salomon Deschamps. The note in small writing was added after Beer made further confessions "standing with the noose on his neck ready for death". It is signed by four of the Council, and by the Predikant Gijsbert Bastiaensz.*

foresaid small yawl and meanwhile to become familiar with the people there and to get to know and find out what there be of material in those lands, be it Gold, Silver, or anything of value, and if at any time some ships come to that Coast, or yawls come ashore, that they may then be rescued by those and report the opportunities of those lands.

Secondly, because the under mentioned persons have behaved themselves on these islands not guiltlessly, but through all too great fear of death have not restrained the murdering scoundrels, closing their eyes and dissimulating instead of maintaining and setting against the others Justice, their [own] honour, God, and salvation, but on the contrary have smirched their hands with the shedding of human blood, although they have been forced to it.

—— Therefore, after having taken their case with all consequences, well examined, debated and weighed —— We have unanimously found good to sentence some according to their misdeeds, with these underwritten punishments most nearly accompanied by death, as appears from the following sentences in full —— To wit, Salomon Deschamps, under Merchant, three times to keel-haul and to be flogged with 100 strokes, Rogier Decker of Haarlem, three times to keel-haul and to be flogged with 100 strokes before the mast, Abraham Hendricx[126] of Amsterdam, 3 times to keel-haul and to be flogged with 100 strokes before the mast, Lucas Gellisz from the Hague, cadet, 3 times to be dropped from the Yard and to be flogged with 100 strokes before the mast, moreover to confiscate 6 months wages to the credit of the Gen. East India Company —— Claas Harmansz of Campen, to be dropped 3 times from the yard and to be flogged with 100 strokes before the mast. —— Thus done and attested on the yacht *Sardam, datum ut supra.*

          FranCo. Pelsartt
          Claas Gerritsz
          Salomon Deschamps
          Sijmon Yopzoon
          This is the mark of
          Jan Willemsen ⚓ Visch[127]

[126] Pelsaert meant Abraham Gerritsz, cabin boy, as he wrote before, and as can be seen from the examinations that follow. Abraham Hendricx was a gunner who broached a cask of wine, the episode used by Jeronimus to spring the island mutiny; and mentioned by Pelsaert in his summary, at the end. The similar Christian name of course caused the slip—it is noticeable that Pelsaert makes several mistakes at this time. A. Gerritsz had been left by the ship *Leyden* at Sierra Leone.

[127] These signatures are particularly interesting. Jacob Jacobsz was now missing, and Jacop Jansz presumably on duty as officer of the watch. The extraordinary

> TODAY, the 24 Sept. 1629 on the Island *Batavia's* Graveyard, has been resolved by the Commandeur *Franco. pelsart* and the Ship's Council, to examine Wouter Loos of Maastricht, soldier, alias Captain, on his committed murders and the beastly life which he has led here on the islands, and to bring him to torture if necessary ——— Date as above.

WOUTER LOOS of MAASTRICHT, soldier, aged about 24 years, who on 2 Sept., after Jeronimus Cornelisz has been captured on the High Island, has been chosen and accepted by the rebel troop in his place as Captain, to which, on 8 do., he made them Swear, confirming his authorization with signatures and Oaths of all the persons, to be obedient to him in everything, whereupon he has resolved on the 17 of the same [*stanty*] to go and fight the above mentioned escapees and to overpower them if possible. ——— But after a long fight they did not advance any but that 4 men were badly wounded through musket shots, on account of which appears as inevitable that some will die. Therefore having asked him to what purpose he has fought against these folk ——— Says, because his folk were murmuring and no longer desired a ration of Water, but desired [either] to die or to become Masters of that Island. Has been persuaded by them, but maintains that he is very sorry he has done such.

Furthermore, as we are still informed that he also has been in the Predikant's tent when his family was murdered, and that he also has apparently done his share[128] in killing with the others. ——— He, being asked whom he has killed, Confesses that he was lying in his tent that day, towards evening, and that Davidt

---

feature is the signature of Salomon Deschamps attached to his own sentence. Hitherto he has only been called on to sign the declarations of truth following the given evidence, but not the sentences. The *datum ut supra* is 13th November, the same date on which Pelsaert earlier noted (see page 221) that "also one shall do Justice to the following persons . . .". It seems unbelievable that these sentences were carried out at the islands because the culprits were re-condemned and the majority executed at Batavia (see Appendix V). Bastiaensz, however, remarks in his letter that "some were punished on the ship" (see Appendix IV).

The document that follows these sentences begins on 24th September on *Batavia's* Graveyard but ends on 14th November on the yacht *Sardam*. Apparently from the beginning Pelsaert regarded the case of Wouter Loos as unresolved.

[128] Pelsaert writes *debuoir*. Elsewhere he uses the French *devoir*. This appears to be a confused word: possibly he also had *début* in mind.

Zevanck has called him outside, saying that the Predikant's family must be helped along at night, and that he had to keep himself ready for that towards that time. Whereupon he said, according to him, "There are plenty of folk, why should you take me?" But nevertheless has gone, together with Zevanck and 5 or 6 others to the Predikant's tent at night, and, coming in, Zevanck took the lamp, and said, "Here has been [reported] hidden Goods of the Company that we will search for, and we will get them." Meanwhile the lamp was blown out, and Wouter Loos took the kettle with seal's meat which hung above the fire and brought it to the tent of Annetgie Gunner [*Bosschieters*]. —— Coming back, he found that all the people had been murdered. Yea, the party having dragged them away, were then busy with the plunder; but says that he touched none nor did anyone harm.

Because he has been in the tent, nonetheless denies to have killed or helped to kill anyone, therefore he has been brought to torture in order to get the straight truth out of him. After suffering pain, denies as above, having laid hand on anyone, only that he took away the kettle. But confesses that when Hans Radder and Jacop Groenewald, trumpeter, were to be drowned, he has helped to tie their hands and feet, and so they have been dragged into the Sea.

Further asked how many Women he has known carnally here on this Island, confesses that he has slept a few times with Tryntgie Fredricx and Annetgie Gunner [*Bosschieters*] and has done his will with them. Also asked whether he has been with Lucretia Jansz in the tent after he has been made Captain a few days after the capture of Jeronimus. —— Says, that he will die the death if he has touched her dishonourably or has seduced her.[129]

On the 27 October again examined before the ship's council ——

As has come to our ears through Judith, daughter of the Predikant, that Wouter Loos has said or boasted before this that he has killed with an adze Bastiaan Gysbertsen, assistant, her eldest brother (when her mother, sisters and brothers had been murdered). Whereon, having taken strict notice and got further information, found has said this to still other persons. —— Therefore have brought him before us again in order to get the straight truth, drawing out of him with torture or freewill confession, that which we would have liked to know, either with threatenings or other means. —— Then found him still obstinate, so that have

[129] The above examination was made before the executions; the one that follows, after. Note dates.

brought him to torture ——— And asked, if he has boasted such to several. Secondly, he had been in the tent with an adze together with the other Murderers and apparently has committed his utmost share in murdering. ——— Confesses at last that he has beaten the eldest son underfoot with an adze, until he was dead, and that after that he has brought the kettle with meat which hung above the fire into his [own] tent.

Confesses also that a short time after the passing of the above mentioned, he went walking with Davidt Zevanck near the foresaid Predikant's tent and that he saw Andries Jonas was busy cutting the throat of Mayken Cardoes but he could not properly overpower her; therefore he, Wouter Loos, ran to them with a stick and has beaten in the head of the foresaid Woman, Mayken Cardoes. The which accords with the confession of Andries Jonas made of freewill before his death, saying that he had the intention to kill her. But that Wouter Loos ran to help him and beat her head in.

Declares further, that on 5 August, being on the high island, Jeronimus Cornelisz and Zevanck, who were going for a walk together, ordered that he must go and stab Jan Willemsz Selijns, cooper, because they feared that he might run over [to the other party]. Whereupon Wouter Loos went towards Jan Willemsz with the intention to execute what he was told, but coming near him, he was so confused in his mind and in such an upheaval that he could not do it, and warned the foresaid Cooper immediately that such had been ordered him, but that he would plead for him because he [Wouter Loos] was a great friend of Jeronimus.

WE UNDERSIGNED persons of the Council of the ship *Sardam* declare on our Manly Truth in place of the duly attested Oath . . . .

[The declaration is similar to those previously made. Signed by Pelsaert, Gerritsz, Deschamps, Yopzoon, and marked by Jan Willemsen [*sic*] Visch with a blotted sign. Dated 14th November, on the Yacht *Sardam*.[130] Pelsaert's summary of the crimes of Wouter Loos, and the sentence passed on Loos, follows and is printed in full.]

BECAUSE WOUTER LOOS of MAASTRICHT, soldier, aged about 24 years,

[130] All now aboard the *Sardam* ready to sail. Once more, it is an extraordinary fact that Deschamps, himself condemned to suffer the day before, 13th November (see note 127) is nevertheless called to witness this declaration—possibly because he had been present (himself unsuspected of murder) when the trial of Wouter Loos began on 24th September. Yet in view of the earlier signature to his own sentence, included amongst those of the others, it seems more likely that Pelsaert was indeed hard pressed for intelligent councillors and still retained some faith in the assistant.

but on 2 September, when Jeronimus Cornelissen was captured on the High Island by the defensive people, has been chosen and accepted by the whole mutineering troop in his place for their Captain, to which on 8 do. he made them Swear, confirming his authorization with signatures and Oaths of all the persons, to be obedient to him in all. Whereon he, the 17 Sept., has made the plan and has been persuaded by the mutineers [*muytmakers*] to go and fight the others who were on the High Island, in order to see if they could not overpower them. —— But after long fighting they have not advanced against them but that four of their men were very Badly wounded by muskets, of whom one, named Jan Dircxsz from Emden, gunner, has died on 28 Sept.; and apparently would have caused more disasters if it had not pleased God that we arrived here with the Yacht at the same time, or in the very hour, when they were fighting, and thus all their design has been destroyed.

Moreover, here on the Islands near the Wreck of the perished ship *Batavia*, the foresaid Wouter Loos has let himself be drawn aside from the way of humanity and of reasonable Creatures, and, through his Innate corruptness has let himself be used by the Godless, Epicurean villain, Jeronimus Cornelisz, of whom he was a great favourite, to the murdering of people, as appears from his confession as well as his examination by torture, as well as freewill confession in full, as well as mentioned underneath[131] —— To wit ——

That on the 5 July he has been ordered by Jeronimus to go, together with Davidt Zevanck, Coenraat van Huyssen, Jan Hendricxsz, Lenert Michielsz, Cornelis Pietersz of Wtrecht, and Rutger Fredricx, to go with the biggest Raft and drown Hans Radder and Jacop Groenewaldt, upper trumpeter, whom they have taken to Traitors Island, and Wouter Loos has helped to bind them hand and foot, and so they have been dragged into the Sea and suffocated.

Item, on the 21 July, towards evening the foresaid Wouter Loos has been informed by Zevanck that he must hold himself ready that night in order to help along the Predikant's family; towards evening, when it was time, he was called by Zevanck; wherefore he searched on the way for an adze, with which he went, together with Jan Hendricxsz, Mattijs Beer, Cornelisz Pietersz from Utrecht, Jacop Pietersz, Andries Jonas and Andries Liebent, to the foresaid *dominie's* tent, where Zevanck, entering, spoke, saying that Company's goods were hidden there, which he wanted to

[131] One of Pelsaert's most confused passages.

take out. —— Meanwhile, [they] blew out the lamp and began to beat about the troop with adzes and axes, so that Wouter Loos battered in the head of the eldest son, Bastian Gysbertsz, assistant, with an adze, until he was dead.

On the same night, after what passed as above, Wouter Loos went for a walk with David Zevanck, near the tent; when he saw that Andries Jonas was very busy cutting the throat of Mayken Cardoes, whom he had thrown underfoot, but that he could not execute his intention on account of her violent struggle and because she had taken the knife in her hand. —— Therefore the foresaid Wouter Loos ran with a chopper or stick towards her and battered in the head of the foresaid Mayken Cardoes, the which Andries Jonas confessed of freewill before he died.

Item, has also confessed that, being with Jeronimus and all the others on the High Island on the 5 August, he has been ordered by the foresaid Jeronimus that he should go and kill the cooper Jan Willemsz Selijns, but coming near him, his conscience reproached him in such a way that instead of killing Jan Willemsz he warned him of what he had been ordered. But that he could not do it, so that he has begged Jeronimus for [the life of] foresaid Jan Willemsz, because he was very much in favour [*omdat hy groot exces by hem hadde*] with Jeronimus; out of which it is very easy to observe what [a] favourite he has been with Jeronimus, and apparently has committed more with his tongue, by means of advice, than with his hands.

Item, also has had carnal knowledge here on the Island, of several married Women, and has done his evil will with them.

All which gruesomeness as the murdering of people and the raping of women as well as his intended determination, when he was made Captain following in the footsteps as successor of the villain Jeronimus Cornelisz, to go and fight the poor defensive people, when they wounded 4 very badly, of whom one has died, as said before, on the pretext that they wanted to be Master of the Water; but on the contrary no water was ever refused to them, but had offered all friendship with letters, which he has torn to pieces,[132] and has held them as enemies, as the said Wouter Loos has declared them to be in his authorization; being Criminal Offences of very evil consequences which are worthy of many deaths and which cannot or may not be tolerated by God or man, because nature (I leave aside God's commandments) teaches us sufficiently that one should punish the evil as an Example to others—

[132] See letter of the predikant Gijsbert Bastiaensz (Appendix IV), episode on 17th September, as above.

Therefore the Commandeur *Franco. pelsart* and we undersigned persons of the council of the ship *Sardam*, having given every thought to this matter, after long examination and searching, and having debated and weighed the same —— have preferred grace in place of rigour of the Justice to foresaid Wouter Loos, and have sentenced him as we sentence hereby, that he shall be put here on the main Southland as a death-deserving delinquent, together with Jan Pelgrom de Bye van Bemel, who was sentenced on 28 Sept., to the gallows on account of his misdeeds, but has been begged[133] from death, in order to make himself [Wouter Loos] familiar with the Inhabitants of this land and to search [out] what is happening here, and to be rescued some time by ships that may happen to fall hereabout, and to be of some service to the Company, with confiscation of his monthly wages, or anything that he may have to claim in India against the Gen. East India Company, our Lord Masters. Thus done and attested on the yacht *Sardam*, this 13 November 1629.

[Signed by Pelsaert, Gerritsz, Deschamps, Yopzoon, and marked by Visch. Immediately after this, a new, single page of instructions, issued to the two men to be marooned, and dated three days later (16th November) has been inserted by Pelsaert in order to preserve coherence. Presumably it is a copy of the document handed to them. It is unsigned, but it takes the form of an order by the Commandeur. Particularly well and clearly written, with impressive flourishes, it is not always equally clearly expressed.]

> INSTRUCTIONS for Wouter Loos, and Jan Pelgrom de By van Bemel, both death-deserving delinquents, who, on account of various considerations, are to be put here on the main SOUTHLAND—

WITH a Sampan [*Champan*] or Yawl,[134] which they will retain with all its appurtenances, in order to make shift with such; and shall see that with this Southerly wind which here now blows along the coast they can reach up to 25 to 24 degrees, by guessing,

[133] The use of this expression, and the reason earlier given (i.e., his youth, see page 213) helps to strengthen the impression conveyed, at the time of Jan Pelgrom's reprieve, that Pelsaert personally "begged" the youth's life from the other members of the ship's council.

[134] Nowhere else does Pelsaert use the word *Champan*; it can be presumed that this was one of the flat-bottomed *schuiten*, or yawls, made at the islands, but considered safe enough for the men to "make shift with" along the coast.

the which is about 50 Miles from this place.[135] In order to consider, observing good weather and opportunity, [whether] to put ashore there or here, to make themselves known to the folk of this land by tokens of friendship. Whereto are being given by the Commandeur some Nurembergen,[136] as well as knives, Beads, bells and small mirrors, of which shall give to the Blacks only a few until they have grown familiar with them.

Having become known to them, if they will then take you into their Villages to their chief men, have courage to go with them willingly. Man's luck is found in strange places; if God guards you, will not suffer any damage from them, but on the contrary, because they have never seen any white men, they will offer all friendship. —— Meanwhile, shall observe with all diligence what material, be it Gold, or Silver, happens there to be found, and what they esteem as valuable. So that, having come to perfect friendship with them, [you] may be able to ask, by signs and by learning their language, that a look out should be kept for ships, or for people coming from the side of the Sea, in order to obtain from them more of such goods as iron, Copper, or Nurembergen, of which you have with [you] several samples which without doubt will please them greatly.

The time that the ships make the Southland there, is in *April, May, June, July*, wherefore must look out keenly at that time, and seeing any, give suchlike signs as shall appear to be done with purpose, be it with smoke or otherwise.

Above all, keep God in mind, never forget Him; and without doubt He will keep you close in His shadow and will yet vouchsafe, at the last, a good outcome. —— Thus done on the Yacht *Sardam* this 16 November 1629.

---

[135] Estimates here given make it quite clear that Pelsaert's *myle*, or mile, cannot be approximated to mean the same distance as one minute. On this date, 16th November, as will later be seen, they had decided that they were on approximately 27° 51'. Taking Pelsaert's mile to equal 3 English miles, his 50, i.e. 150, North would give the position of approximately 25° 20'. He is using round figures, and also giving positions "by guessing", thus precision is not to be expected. The significance of "25 to 24 degrees" used here, lies in the fact that on the first trip north he had actually seen natives about 24°, on 14th June. Probably he could not at this juncture recall the past position on that day more accurately: it is obvious that he means that if the marooned men cannot find natives at this spot, they should travel about 150 or more miles North.

[136] At this time cheap wooden toys and trifles from Nuremberg were sold all over Europe; cf. the more recent Brummagem.

[Pelsaert next records some judgments passed on men and boys who took part in the events on *Batavia's* Graveyard. These judgments are here printed in full.]

BECAUSE BY GOD'S TRUTH, many, Yea, the most of people who have been here on the Island *Batavia's* Graveyard, have behaved themselves not guiltlessly, but have gone too far in many errors, of whom some, who after examination as well as by own confession have gone too far, [are] as follows. Firstly ──

Salomon des Champs of Amsterdam, undermerchant, who, considering his office, by which he has bound himself to the Hon. Lord Masters, has acquitted himself very weakly in fostering the interests of the Hon. Company and the saving of the poor people who have been so Pitifully murdered. But has permitted the evil to take its course without saying anything against it, shutting his eyes and dissimulating in order to prolong his own life. ──
Moreover on the 20 July at night, that he was fetched out of his tent by Jacop Pietersz, who took him into Mayken Cardoes' tent, where Davidt Zevanck, Jan Hendricxsz and Cornelis Pietersz of Wtrecht were, who said to him that they were not certain of his faithfulness, therefore took a Young Sucking child from the lap of the foresaid mother Mayken Cardoes, who was in the same tent, and said to him, "Deschamps, there is a Half dead child. You are not a fighting Man, here is a little noose, go over there and fix it so that we here on the Island do not hear so much wailing." Then he, Deschamps, without protest, has taken the child outside the tent and has strangled it, which is an act of very evil Consequence, Yea, is a Crime, which should be punished with all severity, because an Officer wishing to maintain his honour, oath, and Salvation, must punish others [for lack] of this and must seek to prevent more disaster and must not besmirch himself with gruesomeness. Nevertheless, the Commandeur and the ship's council of the ship *Sardam*, on several considerations, as well because the child had been poisoned by Jeronimus Cornelisz with *Mercurium sublimatum* and could neither live nor die. Secondly, because he has been forced to it, as otherwise he would apparently have been killed; do not wish to proceed to the extreme with the foresaid Deschamps, but using grace in place of rigour of the Justice ──
Have sentenced him as sentence him herewith ── That tomorrow he shall be keel-hauled 3 times and after that be flogged with 100 strokes before the Mast as an Example to others. ──
As well—

Rogier Decker of Haarlem, aged about 17 years, Cabin servant, and late servant on the Ship *Batavia* to Jeronimus Cornelissen, undermerchant, who has let himself be denuded of humanity and brotherly love and allowed himself to be driven by his late Master, Jeronimus, on the 10 August, to a tyrannical Murder; to wit, that on the foresaid day, when he was frying some fish in his tent, Jeronimus himself came to him and called him out of the tent to his, and poured him a beaker of wine, saying to him, "Here is a dagger. Go, and with this stab to the heart Hendrick Jansz of Purmerent, carpenter, who goes walking there with Deschamps." To which the foresaid has consented without any protest, and has gone outside and has stabbed to death the foresaid Hendrick. ———— The which is a Criminal Offence that should be punished with death, as it is very tyrannical to shed the blood of an innocent Man on a loose word. Nevertheless, the Commandeur and the ship's council, using grace in place of rigour of the Justice, on account of his Youth, as well as on account of fear that they would have killed him if he had refused such ———— moreover, have not been able as yet to find that he has let himself be used in any other ill-doing. Have sentenced him as sentence him herewith, that tomorrow he shall be keel-hauled three times, and after that be flogged before the Mast. ———— Also ————

Abraham Gerritsz of Amsterdam, Boy, aged about 15 years, who had run away from the ship *Leyden*[137] in the Sierra Leonas, and who had been taken from shore by the Commandeur, who, on 15 July, being on Seals Island when a party of Boys and Men were killed, was told by Davidt Zevanck, "Boy, you must help lustily to kill, or be in a fix yourself;" he has been very willing in the same, and with his knife cut the throat of a Boy named Frans Fransz of Haarlem, which is a Criminal offence of evil consequence which neither can nor may be tolerated, but as an Example to others he deserves to be well punished with death. Nevertheless, the Commandeur and the ship's council, using grace in the place of rigour of the Justice on account of his Youth as well as of his having done this out of fear ———— have sentenced him as we sentence him herewith, that tomorrow he shall be keel-hauled three times, and after that shall be flogged with 100 strokes before the Mast. ———— Also—

Lucas Gellisz from the Hague, cadet, who having donned the appearance of the scoundrels here on the Island, has followed their

[137] Immediately after he sailed from Batavia in the *Sardam*, Pelsaert met the *Leyden* in the Straits of Sunda, on 15th July, the very day of the murdering as here mentioned. See *Leyden* story under Journal date 15th July (p. 134, note 30).

Course in evil, with words and deeds ——— To wit, that on 9 July, when Pieter Jansz, provost, was being killed with his [party], he has let himself be used in the yawl and kept steady the Raft from which they threw the people into the Sea; as well as on the 20 July, when Passchier van den Ende, gunner, and Jacop Hendricxen of Amsterdam, carpenter, had their throats cut at night, he, together with Jan Hendricxsz and Lenert Michielsz, was ordered to go and execute the same. Then, because Jan Hendricxsz had cut both their throats, he could not help with it, but he has given him his knife, which Davidt Zevanck, who was present, ordered him to do, because Jan Hendricx stabbed to pieces 4 knives on Jacob Hendricxsz foresaid, before he could kill him. ——— Moreover, Lucas foresaid, on the 5 August when he was on the High Island together with all the others and Jeronimus and his council had decided that Mr Frans Jansz of Hoorn, upperbarber, was to be murdered, because they feared that he would change sides, then Lucas, together with Lenert Michielsz, Mattys Beer and Hans Jacops, were ordered by Zevanck to kill the foresaid Mr Frans under pretext of going in search of seals; so Lucas, after Lenert Michielsz has pierced him right through with a pike, Hans Jacopsz has battered in his head with a morning-star, and Mattys Beyr has cleft his head with a sword. ——— The foresaid has also stabbed Mr Frans in his body with a pike to show good faith. Which Gruesomeness he could just as well have omitted. Because the man was already so hacked and stabbed. But on the contrary has wanted to show that he was one of their humour and mind. Which neither can nor may be suffered, but as an Example to others deserves to be very heavily punished. Nevertheless, the Commandeur and the council, having considered the matter and having debated the same, prefer grace in the place of rigour of the Justice; have sentenced the foresaid Lucas Gellisz as sentence him herewith, that he shall be dropped from the yard arm three times, and be flogged with 100 strokes before the mast. ——— Moreover, with confiscation of six months wages to the profit of the Gen. East India Company, our Lord Masters. ——— Also—

Claas Harmansz of Campen, Boy, aged about 15 Years, who on the 18 July, when the Women and the remaining Boys were murdered on Seals Island, has hidden himself, together with 2 other Boys named   in the shrubs and dared to appear after several days. Whereupon Jeronimus Cornelisz ordered Jacop Pietersz to get the foresaid 3 Boys and to have them drowned on the way [back]. So Jacop Pietersz said to the foresaid Claas Harmansz, being in the little yawl, "Boy, throw the other 2

Boys overboard, or the same will happen to you." To which the foresaid Claas has consented, and has thrown the other 2 Boys overboard. —— Which is a cruelty that should be punished as heavily as possible. —— Nevertheless, the Commandeur and the council, seeing that it is a Boy who was ordered, being in a yawl where there was no escape, or else he would have been thrown overboard himself, do not wish to proceed to the extreme with him. But using grace in place of the rigour of the Justice, have sentenced him as we sentence him herewith, that tomorrow he shall be dropped 3 times from the yard arm, and after that shall be flogged with 100 strokes before the Mast. —— Thus done and attested on the Yacht *Sardam*, this 12 November, Anno 1629, lying at anchor under the High Island, 2 miles from the Wreck.[138]

[Signed by Pelsaert, Gerritsz, Deschamps, Yopzoon, and marked by Visch. For the next entry, 14th November, which begins again the daily record, Pelsaert does not start on a new page, but the flourishes with which he writes his own name and embellishes the mark of Visch, as well as the wide space left before recommencing the daily entries, appear to express relief at the ending of the examinations, as he then intended (they were resumed at the request of the untried prisoners) and the opening of a new chapter.]

ON 14 NOVEMBER the Wind S.S.West, have fetched the rest of the Folk from the Islands, in order to go under Sail tomorrow, and this day nothing particular has happened.

On 15 do., the Wind S.S.West, with apparently beautiful Weather. Therefore, have weighed our anchor in the name of God, and have gone under Sail, away from these disastrous Abrolhos, to the continent, Course, E.N.East, in order to search there for the skipper and 4 other men, who on the 14 of the past [month] have strayed from the ship through storm, and from there to expedite our journey hence to Batavia as speedily as possible. —— The place where the ship or the Wreck lies, is on the latitude of 28 degrees, 37-40 minutes, and where we were with the Yacht under the High Island is on 30 to 32 minutes N.N.West of the Wreck. Although the steersmen, after the wrecking of the ship on the [reef], have taken from the Islands the latitude of 28 degrees 8 minutes, and 28 degrees 20 minutes, the which has caused not a little misunderstanding in search of this place, and

---

[138] This document, following after the Instructions for Wouter Loos and his trial evidence, bears an earlier date than that of the sentences already noted, on the men concerned. Pelsaert went aboard the *Sardam* on 10th November and appears to have held trials on 11th and 12th November. It should also be noted that Deschamps, though he signs his own sentence, does not have his wages confiscated.

also loss of time, moreover not without great peril in sailing to the same, had not the Almighty God saved us purposely several times. ——— We have found here that the Wind, during the period that we have been lying here, generally blew from the South, and the South South East—also, in the morning it veers to the South East, or East South East, but a Little, so that here at the Wreck it is always adverse [*een leger wal is*]¹³⁹ and there is continually a hard surf, and one has to observe precisely the moment of smooth [*slechte*] water, otherwise one would never have been able to do anything on the Wreck. For when we first came here with the Yacht, there was a piece of the poop and the foreship still above water, but now it has been altogether washed away, so that under water lies only the keel with a little of the hold of the Wreck, where the pieces of cannon [*geschuts*], anchors, ropes, and suchlike heavy goods are lying, incredibly matted together, and cannot wash out.

Hereabout, it is very rich in fish, three kinds of fish but they are quite different in taste and form than on other Coasts. They are all low-lying Coral islands and Rocks, except 2 to 3 big Islands, on one of which they had found, long before we came here, 2 pits with Water. But these pits have become very brackish or salt during the time that we have been here, so that it is undrinkable; and on the other, where the Yacht was lying at anchor, we also, by burning off the shrubs or small bushes, have found 2 pits with Water, which were found very accidentally, or by luck, because there was, as I have mentioned before on the   of the past [month], only a small hole on the surface, big enough for a man's arm, and underneath quite a Cistern, or Water basin, under the earth; which on the surface we made so big with Crowbars and sledge hammers, that one could easily scoop out the water. ——— Moreover, on these islands there are large numbers of Cats, which are creatures of miraculous form, as big as a hare;¹⁴⁰ the Head is

---

¹³⁹ Lit., on the shore or lee side of a ship: idiomatically, "to find oneself in adverse circumstances". Here the latter makes better sense and would appear to convey Pelsaert's meaning.

¹⁴⁰ *Catten*: cats. This is the name given to the wallabies by Pelsaert and the others. This description of his is famous, having already been translated by Professor Heeres in *The Part Borne by the Dutch in the Dicovery of Australia 1606-1765*. It is the first description of an Australian marsupial, and a very accurate recording. It can be noted that Pelsaert began the myth that the young grew at the nipples; an idea that lingered for 300 years. His descriptions of the two large islands and the wells and "cats" are of themselves sufficient evidence to establish the Wallabi Group as the wreck site; the *Sardam* lay under one of the large islands two (six) miles from the wreck. Wallabies are found nowhere else in the archipelago.

similar to [that] of a Civet cat, the fore-paws are very short, about a finger long. Whereon there are five small Nails, or small fingers, as an ape's fore-paw, and the 2 hind legs are at least half an ell[141] long, they run on the flat of the joint of the leg, so that they are not quick in running. The tail is very long, the same as a Meerkat;[142] if they are going to eat they sit on their hind legs and take the food with the fore-paws and eat exactly the same as the Squirrels or apes do. Their generation or procreation is Very Miraculous, Yea, worthy to note; under the belly the females have a pouch into which one can put a hand, and in that she has her nipples, where have discovered that in there their Young Grow with the nipple in mouth, and have found lying in it [the pouch] some Which were only as large as a bean, but found the limbs of the small beast to be entirely in proportion, so that it is certain that they grow there at the nipple of the mammal and draw the food out of it until they are big and can run. Even though when they are very big they still creep into the pouch when chased and the mother runs off with them.

Also some grey turtledoves[143] are here on these 2 Islands, but of other creatures or fruits nothing but bushes; no, or very little grass. ——— This and all the foresaid has been experienced and has happened here at these Abrolhos. Therefore shall turn to the main Southland, whereto we are sailing. And about Noon, came near the land, where we sailed at about half a Mile from the beach with small sail, in order to see if we could see any people or signs, until the afternoon when we saw on the heights a little smoke rising, but it blew away immediately; however, anchored there at 21 fathoms, clean sand ground, in order to see if it was the skipper with his [men]; but the smoke remained in the background and no one appeared on the beach; from which we came to the conclusion that it had been made by the Inhabitants who did not dare to show themselves; remained lying at anchor, because it blew very hard, until—

[141] The Dutch ell was about ¾ yard. See *Jahangir's India*, p. 3, note 6.

[142] Meerkat, accurately *Cynictis penicellata*, a South African carnivore, covered with reddish fur, head and body a foot and a half long; bushy greyish tail a foot long. A name also given to "Madagascar cat" or lemur, which seems the more likely comparison.

[143] Undoubtedly the Brush Bronzewing, *Phaps elegans*, still abundant on the Wallabi Islands. As pointed out by A. H. Chisholm in *Strange New World*, p. 54, this is the first mention of a land bird in Australia. It is more likely, though, that the terns, numerous during the months of August, September, and October, were the "fowls" of the predikant's letter (see Appendix IV); which produced "eggs in basketsfull". It is a matter of surprise that Pelsaert does not himself mention the prevalence of sea birds.

On 16 do. in the morning, when we weighed our anchor again, the wind S.S.East with a topgallant gale, sailed again with small sail, close along the shore a *Cartoue*[144] shot from the surf; towards noon noticed the small Inlet where on 8 June when with the boat we were searching for Water, we thought to run in. But through the North-west storm which fell upon us, were in great danger of sinking, and God so miraculously saved us. Here saw several smokes rising up, and were altogether gladdened that our own folk might be there. Therefore I have immediately sent the yawl to the land in order to get sure information about this place and the smokes; who found around a steep corner, there where we thought would be Water, running water, which was brackish on the side to the Sea, but Higher up was Fresh. They also saw many footprints of people and small footpaths running to the Mountains, with many smokes, but the Blacks kept themselves hidden and did not show themselves to anyone. ——— Before this, when we were searching about here with the boat, we were also close under the land, but at this place have seen neither people nor smoke. ——— At this good opportunity, I have ordered the two sentenced delinquents, to wit, Wouter Loos and Jan Pelgrom de By van Bemel, with a Champan provided with everything, to sail to this land. God grant that it may stretch to the service of the Company and may God grant them a good outcome, in order to know once, for certain, what happens in this Land. ——— This small Inlet is situated on the latitude of 27 degrees 51 Minutes. In the afternoon, because there was no hope of finding any sign of the skipper, have set sail, our Course N.West two points outside the coast, because it began to blow stiffly; and towards evening we went towards West North West. ———

On 17 do. at Noon, the Southern Latitude of 26 degrees, 40 minutes, Course W.N.West, the wind South with a topgallant Gale.

On 18 do. at noon, the Southern Latitude of 25 degrees, 49 minutes, Course W.N.West, the wind S.S.West, with a topgallant gale.

On 19 do. the W [*sic*] Southerly, with a weak topgallant gale, at noon had no latitude, this 24 hours have sailed, by guessing, 30 miles, held W.N.W. Now have taken our Course N.West.

On 20 do. the Wind S.E. with a weak topgallant gale, course N.West, this noon had no latitude, but by guessing, have sailed 30 miles.

On 21 do. the Wind S.East, with a weak topgallant gale. Course N.West, this noon, had not latitude, but by guessing, have sailed

[144] Or *cartouw*: cannon firing a ball of 48 pounds. See p. 82, note 49.

30 miles. Holds here a very dark overcast sky with a dry South Eastern Wind.

On 22 do. in the morning our Course North, and have taken North to East in order to get in view the Cocus [*sic*] Islands. The Wind S.East with a Topsail gale. This 24 hours have sailed, by guessing, 36 miles; at noon had no latitude through dark sky.

On 23 do. at noon the Southern Latitude of 15 degrees 30 minutes, the Wind E.S.E. with a topsail gale, this 24 hours by guessing sailed 36 miles. Course Northern and Northern by Eastern.

On 24 do. at noon the Southern Latitude of 15 degrees 30 minutes, the Wind E.S.E. with a topgallant gale. This 24 hours sailed 37 miles. Course Northern and Northern by Eastern.

On 25 do. the Wind East with a topgallant Gale, at noon had no Latitude, but by guessing, this 24 hours sailed 30 miles; held North.

On 26 do. the Wind East as previously from the 25th, until the first quarter in the night, when it shot north north east, with a hard storm, so that could not carry any sail; but let it drift. It was raining the whole night and today until noon. Therefore had no Latitude. In the afternoon the wind took off and ran northerly, hoisted the topsails and ran over eastwards, until we saw some seaweed floating from the Cocus Islands, until night when it began to blow very hard so that in with the topsails till—

On 27 do. in the morning, the Wind North East, but again a hard Gale, and ran N.N.W. with a topgallant gale, the Wind shooting hard from the Northerly side. At noon had latitude of 12 degrees 3 minutes. Found us now past the Cocus Islands where we have drifted close by, but have not seen them.

On 28 do. in the morning the Wind has run East, so that we could sail Northern and N.N.East, with lovely weather and smooth water; at noon had the latitude of 10 degrees, 58 minutes; this 24 hours have held N.N.West.

On 29 do. in the morning the Wind shot S.East. So that we can now easily sail our Course North East towards Sumatra; at noon had the latitude of 10 degrees 2 minutes, have held this 24 hours N.E. to Northern, and sailed 17 Miles with beautiful, calm and lovely soft weather.

On 30 do. the Wind S.E. and S.S.East with beautiful and lovely weather, with smooth Water and Little Wind. At noon the latitude of 8 Degrees 40 Minutes, Course, North East, guessed to have sailed 37 miles.

ON 1ST DECEMBER, the Wind and Course as before, with beautiful lovely weather still, and smooth water. At noon had the latitude of 7 degrees 52 minutes, so that guessed sailed 17 Miles.

Resolution by the Ship's Council of the *Sardam* to punish the mutineers, dated 29th September 1629, on the island named *Batavia's* Graveyard. Here, clearly, the position of the wreck is given as 28½ degrees south latitude. This is the first statement of its position to be made by Pelsaert after the discovery of the wreck.

Instructions to Wouter Loos and Jan Pelgrom de Bye: Pelsaert's copy of a document handed by him to the young mutineers on 16th November 1629 when they were marooned on the mainland of Australia.

On 2 do. the Wind S.S.East, Course North East, with soft Breeze, as before, at noon had the latitude of 7 degrees, this 24 hours have sailed 18 Miles, from now on have held our Course N.E. to Easterly.

[On 2nd December Pelsaert, with the above entry, comes to the end of a page and inserts eight pages of further examinations and sentences carried out and pronounced during the trip north. (These are reproduced following this note.) They carry no date other than the final one, 30th November, which suggests that two days, 1st and 2nd December, had been spent in copying them out clearly from his notes, which was probably his custom so far as evidence was concerned. Following these inserted pages he later resumes his diary of the voyage under the date 3rd December.]

BECAUSE the under mentioned delinquents, the same as the others previously sentenced, have, on the islands near the perished ship *Batavia*, gone too far in obeying the villain Jeronimus Cornelissen, forgetting their Oath and the fidelity by which they were bound to the Gen. Company our Lord Masters, but on the contrary, quitting the same, have taken as their duty, with signatures as well by swearing of oaths, to be obedient to such a one, of whom they could sufficiently see that his procedures could neither exist nor be acceptable to God or Worldly Power; moreover, have behaved themselves very insolently and inhumanly after the loss of the ship ──── Wherefore some have been kept a very long time in bonds, in order to bring them thus to the Hon. Lord Gov. Gen. at Batavia ──── Then because they Urgently besought and also the community have begged for them, that the faults or offences committed by them may be allowed to be purged by due punishment here on the ship, begging for grace and to spare their lives: SO HAS the Commandeur called together the council here-over, whether one could finish same here on the ship absolutely, without falling into disgrace with the Hon. Lord Gov. Gen. or whether one should leave open their case until Batavia, in order to give the Hon. Lord Gov. Gen. the opportunity to do therein as pleases him. Which has been seriously considered by the council and after long debates ──── At last resolved and found good, seeing that all principal offences have been dealt with before this for security of the Company's ship and goods, and as evil-doers have been executed, that those of lesser importance shall be purged here, in order not to trouble further the Hon. Lord Gov. Gen. in his many duties, as we fear that the Javanese war[145] is causing him enough heartburning [*harten leet*], although hope such is not so ──── to

[145] Against the Susuhunan of Mataram, which had been dragging on for more than ten years, but had actually ended on 2nd October. (See p. 72.)

sentence and condemn here on the ship, the following persons ——— To wit ———

DANIEL CORNELISSEN of LUYCK, cadet, aged about 21 Years, who, on the 4 July, at the first drowning of people, has let himself be used willingly, together with Davidt Zevanck, Coenraat van Huyssen, Gysbrecht van Welderen, Lenert Michielsz, to go with the biggest Raft and drown Jan Cornelissen of Amesvoort, Thomas Wensel, and Hendrick Janssen of Oldenburgh, whom they have bound hand and foot on the raft, and he, Daniel, has thrown overboard the foresaid Hendrick Janssen of Oldenborgh, alias Zany. Moreover, on the 5 July, when Egbert Roeloffsz and Warnar Dicxsz, carpenters, were killed, he, Daniel, has pierced the foresaid Warnar, together with several others, with a sword; of which he boasted later, saying that it went through him as easily as butter.
——— So that the foresaid Daniel was considered to be one of the followers of Jeronimus Cornelisz and Coenraat van Huyssen, with their accomplices, and so, certain of his willingness, on 23 July they have sent him to the High Island where the escaped and defensive were,[146] with a letter translated into French, in order to Corrupt to treason certain French soldiers, as appears in full out of the same Letter, being handed to us. Then the same, marking the false Intention, have held Daniel prisoner until the time that we arrived with the Yacht, and thus has been delivered over to us. ——— Which are all Criminal offences not to be suffered without great fear of falling into disgrace with the Hon. Lord Gov. Gen. if he be not punished to the extreme with death. Nevertheless, the Commandeur and the council, leaning on the Clemency of the Hon. Lord Gov. Gen. who prefers grace in the place of rigour of the Justice, Have therefore not wanted to proceed with him to the extreme by reason of several considerations, But have sentenced him as they sentence him herewith, that with this apt opportunity he shall be keel hauled 3 times and after that be flogged before the mast with 200 strokes, with Confiscation of all his earned monthly wages, which he has earned since [leaving] the Fatherland to the profit of the Gen. East India Company our Lord Masters. ——— Also ———

HANS JACOB HEILJLWECK of BASEL, cadet, aged about 23 Years, who on the 15 July[147] has let himself be used on Seals Island, together with other villains, at the time when the first party of 18 Men

---

[146] The island of Wiebbe Hayes; here Pelsaert is again making the distinction between that and the island the yacht *Sardam* anchored beneath.

[147] Pelsaert has written first 18 July and changed to 15; the first was the date of the second foray to clean up the "remaining Boys" and women.

were killed there; that he, together with Davidt Zevanck and his accomplices, being there and the sign for murder given, Coenraat van Huyssen, the assistant Cornelis Jansz of Amsterdam ———[148] Coenraat van Huyssen seized the foresaid Cornelis Jansz and struck him over the shoulder with his sword, then he [Jansz] outwrestled him, so Hans Jacops came and pierced the breeches of the assistant, while running, with a pike, having the intention to pierce through him, but he escaped on a small raft or some timber which lay there. After that he has dragged into the Water all the dead to the number of 15 or more.

Further, on the 5 August in the morning on the High Island[149] Wouter Loos and the foresaid Jans Jacopsz were ordered by Jeronimus and Davidt Zevanck to go and kill Jan Willemsz Selyns, cooper, but when Wouter Loos came near the cooper, his conscience smote him, so that he could not do it. But warned Jan Willemsz that he should take care, for they were ordered to kill him. In the afternoon of the same day Mattys Beer, Lenert Michielsz, Lucas Gillisz and Hans Jacops were ordered to go and kill Mr Frans Jansz of Hoorn, the which they accepted greatly willing, and having led him a little out of the way under the pretext of searching for seals, Leenert Michielsz first stabbed him with a pike right through his body, after that Hans Jacops smote his head with a Morning star, so that he fell down, and Mattys Beyr has Cleft quickly with a sword. ——— All which Criminal offences as above should be punished with death. But the Commandeur and the council have considered and debated the matter earnestly, not wishing to go to the extreme, but using grace in place of rigour of the Justice, Have sentenced the foresaid Hans Jacops as sentence herewith, that with the first opportunity he shall be keel-hauled 3 times, and be flogged before the mast with 100 strokes, with Confiscation of 6 Months' wages to the profit of the General East India Company our Lord Masters. ——— Also —

CORNELIS JANSEN of HAARLEM, alias Bean [*Boon*] sailor, aged about 18 Years, who through his innate and incankered corruptness has let himself be used on 14 May 1629[150] on the ship *Batavia* south of the *Cabo de bone esperansa* by the High Boatswain Jan Evertsz of Monickendam, to the shameful deed done that night by them on

[148] Pelsaert finds himself confused, and begins again. His weariness or ill health is now visible in less even handwriting, as well as in lack of concentration.

[149] This is the other high island, not the island of Wiebbe Hayes; see murder of Frans Jansz, p. 175, note 87.

[150] Pelsaert's anger at the outrage on Lucretia Jansz is noted here, in his emotional words and general attitude to Cornelis Jansz whom he appears to feel was particularly implicated.

do. ship, to a woman; to wit, he, the foresaid Bean or *Boon*, together with Ryckert Woutersz of Harling, gunner, Jan Jansz Purmer of Amsterdam, gunner, Harman Nanninx, quartermaster, Dirck Gerrits of Harderwyck, Allert Jansz of Assendelft, gunner, Abraham Hendricx, gunner, towards night, between light and dark, have seized Lucretia Jansz, widow[151] of Boudewyn van der Mylen, when coming out of the Cabin from table, and have thrown her there on the steer-deck [*sturplecht*][152] and have dragged her from there into the Gallery, and have smudged her face as well as under her Clothes with black dung and other filth until they had cooled their evil lust; with still other wanton deeds which they have committed on do. ship, who, through the evil procedures of the skipper and other officers, were not easily at that time to be cured from that faction, because, by God's Truth, it was their plan to seize the ship. —— Hereupon the ship has been wrecked.

—— And so the foresaid Cornelis Jansz has not only gone beyond himself in wanton drunken drinking, and given himself to suchlike acts, but also with other scoundrels, has ordered that old wine [vintage] be poured and served there [in the Cabin], chasing out of it [those] who Belonged there. Also sticking knives in his Hat and the pleats of his Breeches, and if any spoke against his opinion Threw a knife at him, to cut. —— Moreover, has also let himself be found in the plundering of the Commandeur's Coffer,[153] from which he desired his share, the which has been given him. Whereunder was a gold Medallion with the visage of his princely excellency[154] cut out in Agate and embellished, which he kept until the following day, then he put it in his hat with still other valuables and threw it into the Sea, saying, "There lies the rubbish, even if it is worth so many thousands." —— These and more suchlike scoundrelly acts, which here come too long to narrate, have been committed by him and ought to be punished to the extreme, Yea, even with death.

Nevertheless the Commandeur and the council, after his offences have been well-weighed and the consequences considered, prefer grace in place of rigour of the Justice. —— Therefore, have sentenced him as they sentence him herewith, that with the first

---

[151] In this assessment Pelsaert displays his knowledge of van der Mijlen's death; in their evidence the men tried earlier would not have known of this fact, although it was known in Batavia.

[152] *Stuurplecht* in modern Dutch means quarter-deck; but at this period the rudder was still moved by a whipstaff, from this deck; in addition the gallery overhanging the sea, a new device, projected from this deck.

[153] Box specially for valuables. Another reason for Pelsaert's particular feeling against this man.

[154] Prince Frederick Henry, the stadtholder.

opportunity or apt weather he shall be keel-hauled 3 times, after that flogged with 150 strokes before the mast, with Confiscation of 18 months' wages to the profit of the Gen. East India Company our Lord Masters. ——— Also —

JEAN THIRIOU of HEYDELBERGH, soldier, aged about 38 years, who after the wrecking of the ship *Batavia* has offended very insolently and gone beyond himself, by remaining on the same ship when he was ordered to go ashore, because that day all the people, if they had so desired, had been very well able to get ashore, but some had their eye on drunken drinking, others went on plundering, and the foresaid Thiriou also remained on board for that purpose, and he has dared the next day to chop open with an adze, one of the Company's Money Chests which had been brought above for salvage; and at last he was driven away from it and, through the carpenter Hendrick Jansz, a piece of plank has been nailed on. Whereupon others have come, who prised off the nailed plank, and so the whole Chest was for the most part emptied, and at last, in drunkenness, have thrown the money at each others' heads. ——— Whereof he, the foresaid Thiriou, has been the principal instigator or leader, causing the whole Chest to be broken up, because he had no want of disciples in evil to follow him; and nothing [of it] has been found, to the great detriment and damage of the Company. Which is a matter that ought to be punished with death, that in place of protecting the goods of their masters they destroyed the same wantonly, the which deserves to be punished to the extreme, Yea, even with death. ——— Nevertheless, the Commandeur and the council, after having weighed his offences and considered the Consequences, prefer grace in place of rigour of the Justice. ——— Therefore have sentenced him as they sentence him herewith, that with the first opportunity or apt weather, he shall be 3 times keel-hauled, after that to be flogged with 100 strokes before the mast, with Confiscation of 6 Months' wages, to the profit of the Gen. East India Company our Lord Masters. ——— Also —

ANDRIES LIEBENT of OLDENBURGH, soldier, aged about 19 Years, who on the 21 July on the Island *Batavia's* Graveyard, has been ordered by Davidt Zevanck to keep himself near at hand at night together with the murderers, in order to help murder the family of the Predikant, which he has not refused, but with an axe in the hand, as was the weapon of all, was found near the tent; then, because he came late, and Davidt Zevanck was already busy with his [men] inside with the murdering, the foresaid Andries remained outside because the tent was too full of people, but when they began murdering, he took some meat out of the kettle of seals' meat that hung boiling above the fire and wrapped it in a cloth and off with it.

Also, on 30 July, together with Jan Hendricxsz, he has been called by Jeronimus into his tent, who ordered him to go and strangle Anneken Hardens, wife of Hans Hardens, to whom they have gone; meanwhile, Gysbrecht van Welderen came to help, who made a halter out of her hair snood and Jan Hendricxsz strangled her, and he, Andries, sat on her legs.

Moreover, he has at last become one of the principal mutineers, grumbling that they did not any longer want rationing of Water, but desired either to fight against the defenders, or to die, so that he has exceeded in words as well as in deeds, as by his Clothes, embroidered with much gold *passementerie*, wherein he has Consumed the Company goods in a very unlawful manner. ——— All which offences are of such evil consequence that they ought to be punished to the extreme. Nevertheless the Commandeur and the council, after having viewed the affair in ripe deliberation, and weighed seriously, prefer unanimously on account of several considerations, to give grace in place of rigour of the Justice.—To wit, have sentenced him as they sentence him herewith, that he shall be dropped 3 times from the yard [*reede*], and to receive 100 strokes before the mast. ——— Moreover, with confiscation of 6 months' wages to the profit of the Gen. East India Company our Lord Masters ——— Also ———

HANS FREDRICK of BREMEN, soldier, aged about 18 Years, who on the 5 July has gone beyond himself in a very unchristian way, showing himself to be one of the willing followers of the murderers. To wit, that when Egbert Roelofs and Warnar Dircx, carpenters, were killed on the island *Batavia's* Graveyard, the foresaid Hans Fredrick has also given 2 to 3 hacks to Warnar. ——— And because he has been ill a long time, Yea, most of the time, he has never been able to have a hand in it, much to his regret, although he has been reckoned amongst the armed in the Jonker's[155] tent. But has let himself be used very willingly in the fight against the defenders. Which above mentioned good-willing readiness he has shown, first when was still healthy, in helping to hack [Warnar] to death, an offence of very villainous evil that should be punished to the extreme. Nevertheless the Commandeur and the council,

---

[155] *Joncker*: young lord; member of exclusive aristocracy. Refers to noble birth of Coenraat van Huyssen and others.

having viewed and weighed the affair with ripe deliberation, unanimously prefer grace in place of rigour of the Justice. —— To wit, sentence him as sentence herewith, that he shall be dropped 3 times from the great yard, and be flogged with 100 strokes before the mast. Furthermore, with confiscation of 6 months' wages to the profit of the Gen. East India Company our Lord Masters. —— Also —

OLIVIER VAN WELDEREN of NIMWEGEN, cadet, aged about 22 Years, who, on the Island *Batavia's* Graveyard, although he has been ill most of the time, has committed himself with deeds as well as words, and has gone beyond himself. To wit, that on the foresaid island, he has slept with Sussie Fredricx, married Woman, and has done his will with her because she was in such a situation [*conjonctie*] that if she wanted to save her life she could not refuse. —— Secondly, he, Olivier, being the elder brother of Gysbert van Welderen, one of the principal murderers and scoundrels who had the intention to seize the ship *Batavia*, the foresaid Olivier was feared. Moreover, not content that he had done his will with her several times ashore, as here on the ship, has boasted of this, belying the Woman that she had offered herself to him, and besought it, which is a matter of evil consequence, which in an upright ship cannot or may not be tolerated, but as an example to others should be punished. —— Therefore the Commandeur and the council, after they have considered this matter, sentence the foresaid Olivier as they sentence him herewith, that he shall be dropped 3 times from the yard, and be flogged with 100 strokes before the Mast. —— Also —

JAN RENOU of MIOMBRY, soldier, aged about 22 Years, one of the defenders. Nevertheless, nearly forgetting the state of misery in which he had lived, immediately after our arrival, has gone very much beyond himself with words. To wit, that Sussie Fredricx, together with Anneken Gunner [*Bosschieters*] on the 20 Sept., having gone to the High Island,[156] had to remain there for 2 days through bad weather or hard wind. In which time the foresaid Jean Renoue has come into a tent where there were about 10 to 12 persons, saying, "Here is some news. Wiebbe Hayes has slept today with Zussie." Mentioning the place where it happened. "After that the trumpeter Cornelis Pietersz has also come there, and also done his will with her; after that I have gone there myself and have also done it 2 times;" mentioning the places and opportunity where the same

[156] The island of the defenders, i.e. Wiebbe Hayes's island.

would have happened altogether on one day. ——— Moreover, saying that she had done him some evil. Which lies or tales have spread immediately, so that it has daily been cast at the Woman that she had done so. Therefore have taken notice of this matter and have examined the foresaid Jean Renoue, who belies the same and that he has ever said it, but because there are 8 to 10 trustworthy witnesses who have heard him saying it, found his denials and oaths to be lies. ——— Which is a matter of very evil consequence, to defame someone with lies, and which he, in order to make them more credible, asserted not only that others had done their will with the Woman, but boasted of himself having gone there for the same. Thus the Commandeur and the council, after having considered the matter, have sentenced the foresaid Jean Renoue as they sentence him herewith, that he shall be dropped 3 times from the yard and be flogged with 100 strokes before the mast, as an example to others. ——— Also —

ISBRANT ISBRANTSEN of PURMERENT, assistant, aged about 20 Years, who on the 24 July, was ordered together with Reynder Hendrix, steward, and Gerrit Willemsz of Enchuysen, sailor, to go with Jacop Pietersz Cosyn of Amsterdam, lance-corporal, in the little yawl and to help rowing, with the order of Jeronimus to the foresaid Jacop, that he had to get 3 Boys who had kept themselves very subtly hidden at the murdering of the folk on Seals Island, and who had shown themselves again some days ago, and that he should drown 2 of the same, but spare one, who must throw the others overboard; the which Jacop Pietersz has done, and has got the Boys. ——— Being on the way, he secretly ordered Claas Harmansz, one of the 3, that he should get the Boys to sit on the gunwhale of the yawl and then push them overboard, the which Claas did with one. But the other, seeing that the same thing would be done to him as to his mate, wrestled and would not sit on the gunwhale. Whereupon Jacop Pietersz ordered Isbrant, who was sitting next at the oar, to help the Boy, the which Isbrant did without any protest. He seized him by one leg, as well as Claas Harmensz, and threw him overboard. ——— And because the foresaid Isbrant has not committed himself in anything else, before or after this, SO the Commandeur and the council did not wish to proceed to the extreme, out of several considerations, but have sentenced him as they sentence him herewith, that [he] shall be dropped 3 times from the yard, and shall be flogged with 50 strokes before the mast.

Thus done and attested on the Yacht *Sardam* this 30 November Anno 1629 ———

FranCo. Pelsartt
Claas Gerritsz
Salomon Deschamps[157]
Sijmon IJpzoon
This is the mark of
Jan 𝘈 Willemsz Visch

On 3 December in the Morning with daylight, have, God be thanked and praised, seen the Princen Islands and to the East, cape of Java [Java Head], and had the island Cracatour [Krakatoa] E.N.East of us, the Wind S.E. so that we could sail no higher than E.N.E; with the day, it became calm, and towards noon the Wind ran South and we near enough went over, in the night got close to the Coast of Java.

On 4 do. in the morning, when we found ourselves next to Angier, [Anjor] but it became very calm until the afternoon, when the Wind ran S.W. with a beautiful Breeze, but the Current ran so hard round to the West, that we gained only 3 miles the whole day, until at night when the Flood came, with which we have drifted past Bantam, and found ourselves —

On 5 do. in the morning near Man Eaters Island, with a beautiful land Wind, and have at last, God have thanks and praise for our safe journey, arrived in the roads of Batavia this afternoon.

---

[157] It should be noted that Deschamps, a fortnight after his presumed keel-hauling and flogging, is still on the council and signing the final trial document.

DECLARATION In Short, the Origin, Reason, and Towards what Intention, Jeronimus Cornelissen, undermerchant, has resolved to murder all the People, with his several plans, and in what manner the Matter has happened from the beginning to the end.

JERONIMUS CORNELISSEN, having made himself a great friend and highly familiar with the skipper Ariaan Jacops, moulded their similar intelligence and feelings into one, the skipper being innate with prideful conceit and Ambition, so that he could not endure the authority of any over him. Moreover, he was mocking and contemptuous of all people. Further, he was inexperienced or inept in getting on with people, in so far as it did not concern sea-faring. But Jeronimus on the contrary, was well-spoken and usually knew how to give the polish of Truth to his lying words; he was far more sly and skilled in getting on with people, because in Holland, or more exactly at Haarlem, he had been a disciple or Partner of Torrentius, whose opinion of the World, or type of belief, was still imprinted on him. Yea, he did not profess to any religion. So that Jeronimus was the tongue of the skipper and served as pedagogue to insinuate into him what he should answer if I wanted to speak to or admonish him; according to his own freewill confession. —— At the *Cabo debona Esperansa* the skipper and Jeronimus, taking Zwaantie, went ashore without my knowledge when I had gone inland in search of beasts. Furthermore, they behaved themselves on the Yacht *Sardam*, and after that on the ship *Bueren*, very beastly with words as well as deeds, so that they felt obliged to complain about this. —— Therefore the next morning in the Cabin in the presence of Jeronimus and more others, I spoke to the skipper about this evil-provoking which he had begun, with admonishing and threatening, and said that if he did not cease, should have to take other measures even before we arrived at Batavia. He excused himself that on the one hand he had been drunk, on the other hand that he did not know that one would take a thing like that so seriously. —— The same day, a short time after this happened, the skipper went above to Jeronimus and said, "By God, if those ships were not lying there, then I would treat that miserly Dog so that he could not come out of his cabin for 14 days (and were I a bit Younger, then I would do something else), then as soon as we lifted our anchor, I would very quickly be able to make myself [master] of the ship." Whereon Jeronimus at length asked, "How would you be able to do that, the steersmen have the [night] watch, and you have only the day watch?" He answered, "I should manage it, even if I had to do it in my own watch, and I shall very quickly be Master of the ship," while he repeated several times, "If I were Younger, I would do something else." Whereupon Jeronimus at length asked, "What would that be, if you were Younger?" But he would not give an answer for the time being; but a few days after that they came back to the same proposals, and he told all the above mentioned again to Jeronimus, "If I were Younger, I would not take counsel with myself so long." Whereupon Jeronimus protested strongly that if he would not tell why, he would doubt his perfect Friendship. At last he gave it away that he meant to make himself Master of such an excellent and rich ship as never before in his life had sailed out from Amsterdam, in order to try his luck therewith for one or 2 years. They all of them together would become so rich that *Kamphaan*[158] would not stand comparison to them. To which plan Jeronimus immediately agreed and approved as good; he asked him if one would be able to do this without great peril, whereupon the skipper answered, "I shall get most of the officers on my side and the principal sailors, and as far as the soldiers are concerned, we shall nail up their sty [*kot*] at night, until we are Masters." And it was thus decided to throw overboard or kill, as the opportunity presented itself to them, the Commandeur with all the people [other than] 120 stout men.

Whereupon a short time after that I became very ill, so that they hoped, and I did not think otherwise, than that I should have died; but after 20 days lying down, I began, Contrary to their opinion, to get better, and on 13 May I was up for the first time, through which the skipper and Jeronimus saw that their easily accomplished plan had failed, and that they would have to think of a means not only to create a disturbance, but also to put to the test the reliability of those who would bring the matter to execution. ——— That is [to say], the skipper had also taken a great hatred to a Woman named Lucretia Jansz, whom he had tried to seduce for a long time and not succeeded, and therefore he was very embittered towards her and had chosen her servant Zwaantie Hendrix with whom to spend his time and do his will, who readily accepted the Caresses of the skipper with great willingness and refused him nothing, whatsoever he desired; through which the love on both sides became so intense that without taking any

---

[158] The name of a V.O.C. ship. References to it appear frequently—sailing dates, cargoes, etc.—in various contemporary writings, but considerable research, in both Holland and England as well as in Australia, supplied no clue to this comparison.

thought of his honour or the reputation of his office, had sworn, according to the confession of Jeronimus, that if any one made even a sour face at the foresaid Zwaantie, he would not leave it unrevenged.

At last, when they were away from the *Cabo*, he took from her the name and yoke of servant, and promised that she should see the destruction of her Mistress and others, and that he wanted to make her a great Lady. ——— At last the skipper and Jeronimus, in the presence and with the knowledge of the foresaid Zwaantgie, decided after long debates and discourses, what dishonour they could best do to the foresaid Lady, which would be most shameful to her and would be supposed the worst by the Commandeur. In order therefore that confusion might be sought through her and through the punishment of those who took a hand it in, Jeronimus proposed that she should be given a cut over both cheeks with a knife, which could be done by one person, and few would perceive that they [skipper, Zwaantie and himself] had been the instigators of it. The skipper was of another mind, that it would be better that many should have a hand in it, then the Commandeur could not punish the many, or there would be a big outcry, and if the Commandeur should let it go unnoticed, then there was time enough to give her cuts on the Cheeks. At last they decided that they would give the Burden of this job to the High Boatswain, who had consented to everything, including the seizing of the ship, as well as all they might order him to do. That is to say, that at night, through some men chosen for it by the High Boatswain, they would smear with Dung, blacking and other Filth, the face and the whole body (which they Did 14 May in the evening between light and dark), the which was taken very violently and to the highest degree, by the Commandeur, and although he was still very ill, he thoroughly investigated who had been the culprits. For he more especially suspected, from many Circumstances of which he had become aware during his sickness, that the skipper had been the Author of it.

This has been the true aim which they thought to have brought off: to let it be spread by the High Boatswain that the people would be punished or brought to grief for the sake of Women or Whores, which the skipper would never permit to happen, so long as he lived. In the meantime, some who had had a hand in this, came to discussing their wish to seize the ship, and that now had occasion and opportunity. So when the Commandeur should put the culprits of this act into chains, they would jump into the Cabin and throw the Commandeur overboard, and in such a way they would seize the ship, towards which they also had some of the soldiers in their following. But have not been able to come to the complete number of those who have known of this, because they did not know one another.

Hereon the ship happened to be wrecked; and through some displeasure that the skipper had given to Ryckert Woutersz, one of the principal Accomplices, told in public when he got ashore what They had intended to do, by complaining very much about the skipper, and that he, for his part, had slept for some days with a sword under his head, and therefore had now been very badly rewarded by him [the skipper].[159] Jeronimus Cornelisz, who was still on the ship, and on account of the hard surf could not get off because he could not swim, remained so on the ship for 8 days like a hidden top-mast [*als blinde marsse*][160] (after we had gone with the boat in search of Water.) —— At last, coming ashore, understood that everything had become known about the seizing of the ship *Batavia*. —— Therefore from that time practising devilish shifts in such a manner as to prevent going to Batavia, acting very subtly and gradually, so that in the first 20 days it could not be perceived, except on 4 July, when a soldier named Abraham Hendricx of Delft, had tapped a Wine barrel several times and drank himself drunk, and had also given some to a gunner Arian Ariaansz, so that he also became drunk. Whereupon Jeronimus proposed to his council, which he had called together, that they were worthy of death without grace or delay, and must be drowned forthwith. —— The council consented in so far as it concerned Abraham Hendricxz because he had tapped the barrel, but in so far as it concerned the other, Arian Ariansz, it was given to him, and because he had some insight, they made difficulties and would not vote to sentence him to Death. Whereupon Jeronimus burst out, and said, "How can you not let this happen? Nevertheless, you will soon have to resolve on something quite else." At which words each one became afraid and could not understand what he meant by that. —— But the next day he dismissed his council and chose for his new council such persons as accorded with his desires, to wit, Coenraat van Huyssen, cadet, who would also have been one of the Conspirators in the seizing of the ship *Batavia*; as second, Davidt Zevanck, assistant; the third, Jacop Pietersz Cosijn, *Lanspesaat*; with those, the day

[159] Doubtless Woutersz was referring to the departure of the skipper in the ship's boat, without him.

[160] A stowed mast, lit. a blind mast. A stowaway? But *blinde marsse* was also a small yard under the bowsprit to which the sail was attached, and possibly Pelsaert was comparing Jeronimus to this, as he hid himself in the forepart of the ship.

after they had been chosen, he began the murdering, To wit, 4 Men, whom he ordered to be secretly drowned, the which was successful as wished. Furthermore, resolved by apt means to do away with all others except 30 to 40 of the stoutest, although in the execution of the above there would be no little peril — Because if the good people had perceived that all their lives were at stake, they could certainly have made a stand. But they prevented such a thing, because they chose 20 to 24 of the most willing, whom they divided, with their weapons, into 2 tents, taking away all weapons from those who had any. After the success of this test with the foresaid 4 men whom they had drowned, they continued daily with their plan by secretly drowning as well as killing; and whenever some one asked where the missing were, they informed the folk that the others had been sent to the High Land.

But the pretence of this became known. Whereupon, out of fear, Everyone tried to escape on timber and rafts to the High Island 2½ miles from the Wreck, where some persons had gone in the first place, who, to make a given sign if they found Water, would make 3 fires, and who, after they had been there some days, had found 2 hidden pits with Water; and therefore at several places made 3 fires which had been observed clearly enough by Jeronimus and all the people. But because they were busy with the murdering, which began on 4 July and went on until 21 do., when the number had been reduced to 40, they had affected [not to see].

—— Meanwhile, during those days, about 45 persons had gathered together on the High Island, consisting of those who had fled and those who had been sent away previously. —— When Jeronimus and his council had thus far effected their intention, they announced that they would seize the first-coming Yacht; and was resolved that they would let the boat with the high officers come Ashore first, so that they might kill them easily; and at night, with that same boat, they would be able to overpower the Yacht; which according to their reckoning could not fail. They would then for the time being have gone pirating, and after that, when they had become rich enough, they would have sailed into the Straits of Spain. But first they must master the people who had fled to the High Island, and get rid of them, for Jeronimus maintained that if the Yacht came sailing straight in, they would be warned by those. —— Therefore they made themselves ready to fight with them; but they could not win against the defenders, and returned without success. A few days after that they again made themselves ready with all the folk[161] they had at that time,

---

[161] Pelsaert has written the word "men" above "folk", without crossing out the latter.

who only numbered 32; then again their party had no success.
——Therefore they made another cast [*wendent over den boegh*], to make peace and to come to accord with them, in order, under the cloak of Friendship, to surprise them by treason at an opportune time. Which agreement Jeronimus would bring about by the *domini* [*sic*]¹⁶² who went back and forth. To wit, that Jeronimus would give them cloth [*laken*] for clothes, and that they must give back the little yawl that some of those who had escaped had taken with them. Whereupon Jeronimus went to fetch the cloth, saying joyfully to his folk that they now quite certainly had those folk surely in his hands. —— The next day Jeronimus went back with 5 of the principal Murderers or followers, going ashore to the defenders with the cloth, which he handed out there, deceiving them with many lies, saying that he would harm none, that it had only been on account of the Water that he had fought against them, that there was no need to distrust him because some had been killed, for those had been mutineers and scoundrels who had deserved it. But that he had left most of the people on the Island *Batavia's* Graveyard, because he could not transport them in the 2 yawls.

Meanwhile, Davidt and the others who had come with Jeronimus, were engaged to buy over some of the stoutest, promising them six thousand guilders if they would take their side, also that they should have a share in the Jewels, painting as bright as possible the luck lying to their hands. —— Whereupon those put their heads together because it looked like Treason, saying that they would have to be careful: decided that they would capture them; the which they did, and started to tie them up, then one of them escaped. —— The Murderers (who had been standing with weapons on a small island by the High land), seeing that their principal leaders had been captured, began to make themselves ready to attack and rescue them. Therefore, to make more sure that they [the defenders] would not be hampered by prisoners, killed four of the principals and kept Jeronimus Cornelissen bound; in whose place another Captain was immediately chosen from the soldiers, named Wouter Loos, who, 14 days after this happened, being then 17 Sept., resolved to go again to fight the defenders. Although after 2 hours of fighting they did not gain any advantage than that they gravely wounded 4 Men with 2 muskets that they had; of whom one, later, has died. —— At the same time or hour that they were fighting, we appeared with the Yacht. —— Whereupon a great joy arose amongst the defenders,

¹⁶² Gijsbert Bastiaensz, the predikant.

whereas on the Contrary the hearts of the murderers were smitten with fear, seeing that their Chance had passed and their plan was ineffective. —— Hereon we, after the great joy which we had drawn from the smokes on the High Island,[163] hoping to find a large party of people alive, had to learn with hearts' grief that more than 120 persons, Men, Women, and Children, had been Miserably murdered, by Drowning as well as by Strangling, Hacking and Throat-cutting; and also had in mind to do still more, which they would have put into action if Almighty God had not been aggrieved and thwarted their plan and all their intentions.
—— Moreover, has stopped them, submitting them to their well-earned punishment and God's just condemnation for the villainies they have so long committed and the Very great lust they have had therein.

God the Almighty be thanked for the good outcome and the rescue of us all. *Amen.*

---

[163] Wiebbe Hayes's high island; Pelsaert noted in his diary entry of 17th September that there was no sign of life on the high island under which the *Sardam* dropped her anchor.

APPENDIXES

APPENDIX I

J. P. COEN'S ORDER TO PELSAERT[1]

181 — Ordre

For the Commandeur Francisco Pelsaert and the Council of the yacht *Serdam* [sic], going to the Southland, 15th July 1629.

Because the Commandeur and skipper together with 45 persons arrived here with the boat of the ship *Batavia* on the 7th of this month, bringing tidings of how the foresaid ship *Batavia*, coming from the Fatherland, sailed off course on the latitude of $28\frac{1}{3}$ degrees Southern latitude, and, by God's Truth, has been wrecked, and the remaining people, about 250 souls altogether, men, women, as well as children, left on certain islands or rocks [*klippen*], situated from 8 to 10 miles[2] from the continent, in the uttermost misery to perish of thirst and hunger—

We have decided to unload the yacht *Serdam* speedily, and send thither to succour the people in time, and to salvage as much of the money and goods of the before mentioned wrecked ship, bringing all hither as soon as possible.

You shall therefore set sail tomorrow in the name of God, and shall hasten your journey with all possible diligence in order to arrive most speedily at the place where you have lost the ship and left the people, being as has been said before, at the latitude of $28\frac{1}{3}$ degrees Southern latitude, called Houtman's shallows [*droochte*].

Having arrived there expediently, shall try to save as many people and also as much money and goods as can be found there and can be saved with all possible means.

In order to dive for the money and other goods, with the yacht shall go several expert swimmers and divers, namely, two Netherlanders and four from Gujarat.[3] Inspire them that they must do their duty, promising also that they shall be well rewarded by us, and try if it is possible to salvage all the money, so that the Company may receive some recompense to balance its great loss. Remember to bring hither the casket of jewels that before your departure was already saved on the small island along with the people.

In case you do not perceive any of our folk near the wrecked ship or on the small islands lying nearby, which we hope will not be the

[1] Translated by E. D. Drok from the Old Dutch in H. T. Colenbrander, *J. P. Coen: Bescheiden omtrent zijn Bedrijf in Indië*, vol. v, pp. 575-7.
[2] Using the measurement of approximately 3 English miles to one Dutch, as with Pelsaert, this gives 24 to 30. The Wallabi Group is approximately 30.
[3] *Guseratten*; these were Indians.

case, shall find out whether some have gone to the continent and try to discover the place, searching for the folk as much as possible and so far as you are enabled to do.

Having salvaged and saved everything you can lay hands on, shall apply yourself hither with all speed.

In case through bad weather, storm and hard winds, you are prevented from approaching the reefs where the ship has been wrecked, and do not see any instant means to salvage the money, shall not depart lightly therefrom, and turn hither without having fulfilled the purpose, but keep in mind that the sun comes round to the South, that summer is near and that calm and beautiful weather is to be expected day after day, wherefore shall remain there until better opportunity arises, watching for good weather and calm water in order to save, if possible, all the cash (and we have good hope of that) even if it should take three, four, or more months.

Unless on arrival there are still such a number of our people that you should be compelled to come hither sooner by lack of water, when shall consider everything to the best [interests] of the Company, especially marking, whether on the mainland [continent], either to the South or to the North, there is to be found a suitable anchorage and water, in order to transport thither the people and to shelter the yacht until the sun will have come South of the line, so that without doubt a more opportune time must come and means arise, to salvage the cash, which is an obligation to the Company and on which your honour depends. Meanwhile Your Hon. shall control the water carried aboard the yacht, and also gather as much as possible when it rains, so that the vessels may remain filled.

On the voyage, shall keep a detailed journal, taking good note of lands, shallows, reefs, inlets, bays, and capes, which you may encounter and discover; everything on its correct latitude, longitude, and position.

And that during the voyage good order and peace may be kept and proper duty maintained in saving the Company's people and goods, we have decided to command the Hon. Francisco Pelsaert, lately Commandeur on the ship *Batavia*, to have authority over this yacht and the management of the mentioned affairs, as we ourselves order him herewith; ordering and charging all officers and sailors on the yacht *Sardam*, also those who may be saved from the wrecked ship *Batavia* and brought hither, to recognise the before mentioned Pelsaert as chief over them and to acknowledge him and obey him, in such manner as if all were responsible to ourselves.

Done in the Castle Batavia, on 15th July 1629.

APPENDIX II

LAST LETTER OF FRANCISCO PELSAERT[1]

To the Lords High and Mighty
of the Chamber of Amsterdam ———

Honourable, brave, wise, provident,
very discreet Noble Lords ———

It is to me more than Grief that the Disaster of the woeful Happenings of the ship *Batavia* must be again related, also the remaining of it on the Abrolhos of Frederick Houtman, situated on the Latitude of 28 degrees 37 minutes, as well as the miserable State experienced by everyone, snare thrown around the neck by the Terrible surf of the reef on to which the ship was denavigated; then no Water could be salvaged from the ship, through which we have come to the extreme of want and been forced to resolve to go in search of Water with every boat; which we at that time have not been able to find at the near-lying Islands; at last to sail to the main Southland, which was 8 miles from the Wreck; there we have not been able to get ashore because of the daily high winds blowing out of the South South West, but through Storm and Wind were so driven to the North that it was beyond human power to come around; and at last with great Peril, Thirst and Need, had to resolve to sail to Batavia to advise the Hon. Lord Gov. Gen. of our woeful Happenings, and to request to be allowed to be sent thither in the shortest possible time with a Yacht, with Water and Provisions, to get the people and to salvage as much money and goods as might be possible; the which was allowed me by the Lord Gov. Gen., and departed on the 15th July, 7 days after our Arrival, although I was wholly ill and reduced to great wretchedness, with the yacht *Sardam* again to the Southland, where, after enduring many Perils, on 17th Sept. we Arrived west of the Wreck. ——— There, by God's Truth, our great happiness when we observed [there were] people, was changed into great grief when with great Anguish of the Heart we learnt that an undermerchant Jeronimus Cornelissen, who by his innate corruptness had allowed himself to be led by the Devil to the evil resolution that he had ordered his Accomplices there to kill 124 people, in order to expedite their plan to seize the First-coming Yacht that came to fetch them. Whereon in such Conjunction [of circumstances], as I found there, with so many corrupt and half corrupt people who had not yet given up trying their evil resolution, have been forced to hang the

---

[1] Addressed to the Directors at Amsterdam, as cover to his Journals and a personal assessment of the disaster. Translated by E. D. Drok from a photostat of the original document (ARAKA, VOC: 1630[II]).

Principal Leaders on the Gallows, punishing them with death earned a hundredfold, in order [to preserve] the Company's goods as well as ship's people as well as Cash, which very miraculously and with many Perils had been fished up, to wit, 10 money chests, all the jewels, and other goods as appears from the enclosed notice—with such hazards and Perils as cannot be put into Words—as has been described in full by me to the Hon. Lords by handing to the Lord Gov. Gen. Specx [my journal], which is being sent by him to the Noble Lords, wherein the Lords will see how the loss of the ship, with all the happenings to which by God's Truth it has been subjected right from the beginning out of Texel until at last to my immeasurable Grief it has been denavigated, is wholly because I so unwisely [trusted] the arrogant presumption of the skipper and steersmen, who still reckoned [*gisten*] to be 200 miles from Land. It is our honour that Zeal towards the service of the Gen. Comp.[2] has been greatly strengthened through continuous Grief and sorrow of the heart, which scarcely can be forgotten or ignored by me; and now for the first time I can clearly see and realise that a human being often finds that his Worldly welfare has fallen into the hands of 2 or 3 perfidious men.

At present the pack of all disasters has moulded together and fallen on my neck, yea, not quite possible to express with the pen, will moderate the same as much as possible, and though I have cried out my eyes, shall be able, by the Grace of God, to resume due service and Duty such as I have always endeavoured in service to the Company, as I did although I was exhausted, due to serious illness and poor health into which I had fallen at the *Cabo de Bona Esperansa*, until the ship happened to be Wrecked (so it ended) that I had to come to Batavia 400 miles with the boat in great Misery, with hunger, thirst and want, from where I immediately requested the Lord Gov. Gen. that he would send me again with a Yacht to the Southland in order to repair the great damage done to the Hon. Company in so far as in human power, as has been fulfilled, Praise be to God. —— Hoping that the great and uncommon wisdom and far-seeing Consideration of the Lords will in Consequence be drawn [to the above extenuating circumstances] and because I have arrived here only now at the [moment of] Departure of ships to the Fatherland, and because the time falls very short by manifold Occupations, which is the reason that I cannot write to the Lords Precisely as should be done. —— But because I have written all the happenings in full as told above, I pray the Hon. Lords will take the will for the deed.

Through shortness of time, it has not been possible to finalise the salvaged Books of the ship *Batavia* and to Copy them to be sent with these ships to the Hon. Lords, except the Muster-roll which the Bookkeeper Buiquoij is sending along with other Books in which the Hon. Lords will be able to see where and in what manner the people have died or have been done to death—which are still open, and are standing

---

[2] "Comp." was omitted and written in above.

not yet completely written up, being 113 persons that with a boat as well as with the yacht *Sardam* have arrived alive at Batavia, as well as 7 women and 2 children, altogether 122 souls.

May the Almighty God cease to do more detriment and damage to the Hon. Company. Amen.

The two enclosed bills are from Jacob Jacobsz of *Sardam*, lately skipper on the yacht *Sardam*, and from Pieter Pietersz of Ouwenuerop, quartermaster, who, sailing round with the boat near all the Islands of the rocks [*rudse*] of the wrecked ship *Batavia*, have been capsized by the strong Wind and drowned. And because the new freight of the yacht *Sardam* is not to be despatched earlier than next year, I therefore send the bills now in order that they will not get lost, and also that the Hon. Lords will be able to do Contentments [arrange compensation] to their Wives. ──────── On the back of the bills I have also made a note for what amount they will also be credited here in the new books which through lack of time I have not been able to send along.

Herewith

Honourable, Brave, Wise, Provident, Very Discreet Hon. Lords, I shall pray God that according to my humble Wishes, He will safeguard the Hon. Lords from further damage, and will bless them with a year of expansion and abundant trade and all that is necessary for their souls' salvation. *Done at Castle Batavia this 12th December 1629—*

Your most humble servant to the Hon. Lds.

FranCo. Pelsartt.

Appendix III

THE DAGH REGISTER REPORT OF 22ND MARCH 1636[1]

Verscheijde grove particulariteijten tot merckelijcke prejuditie vande Comp. is voornoemden Barent Pietersen[2] mede aenroerende tot laste van de Agrase residenten als daer sijn Salomon Voerknecht, IJsbrant Pietersen ende voornamentlijck Lodewijck Trijssens die tot verantwoordinge vandien, alsnu ook herwaerts gesonden, ende in verseeckeringh gestelt is.

Gelijck oock daer beneffens verhaelt heur gedebaucheert ende grousaem leven, onder anderen mede van[3] Francisco Pelsaert alhier overleden, voor desen mede tot Agra geresideert.

[*Translation*: [On account of] several great irregularities to the considerable prejudice of the Company, the abovementioned Barent Pietersen has now been sent hither and imprisoned, together with Salomon Voerknecht, IJsbrant Pietersen and especially Lodewijck Trijssens; has been pointed out they were in addition a burden on the residents of Agra and must account for this.

As also there, moreover, was related their debauched and gruesome living, among others of [or *by*] Francisco Pelsaert, here deceased, before this likewise residing at Agra.]

---

[1] Printed here firstly in the Old Dutch from H. T. Colenbrander's edition (dated 1899, p. 52), then in translation by E. D. Drok, who also used a photostat of the original document (ARAKA, VOC: 1031, 1637[1]).

[2] The Barent Pietersen mentioned had been uppermerchant at Agra, as was Pelsaert, and was accused of financial irregularities.

[3] E. D. Drok makes the following note: "Van could here be *by*, not *of* meaning *about*. It may here equal the Germanic usage of *von* whereby in the passive the agent is rendered by *von*." (See p. 72, note 27.)

Appendix IV

THE LETTER OF GIJSBERT BASTIAENSZ, PREDIKANT[1]

C O P Y
Of the Original Letter, by
GIJSBERT BASTIAENSZ
Written from BATAVIA, from here
to his Brethren concerning his perilous and
disastrous journey, going to
India in the year 1628.
God be with us; Amen.

With hearty greetings and all good wishings to my Brother Jan Bastiaensz, to Hugo my Brother-in-Law, to Sister Anneta, Sister Sara, the Treasurer Pandelaer, my Cousin Schepens, and all his, all the Predikants there, to Willem Reyersz Swanen-burgh, Janneken Maertens: in one word to all those whom thou knowest ought to be greeted by me: this little script has as purpose—although with great sorrow as if I am afraid to put the pen on the Paper—to inform you of my happenings on the journey. However, good time has passed since this event, and having yielded myself to the providence of the Lord who tries his children for their benefit; and again through the Grace of God having gained some strength and power, for I could hardly stand on account of weakness—this then is the dearly paid for content of my adventures on this great and burdensome journey.

We, as is known to you, have sailed from Texel on the 27th October, 1628, and on the same day we ran aground with the Ship, thinking that we should perish there with the Ship. But God the Lord this foreseeing, we got free, and continued sailing on the 28th of that month, firstly under the shore of England, and after that to the Siara-leonis, and thirdly to the Cape. What has happened during the journey in this time—only matters of small importance—will, D.V., be known at Amsterdam out of the Journal[2] which is in the hands of the Hon. High and Mighty Lords. Then after sailing from the Cape, it happened thus: There arose some trouble between the Skipper and the Commandeur and it was caused by two Women, of whom one was mis-handled on the Ship. Therefore many troubles have befallen the Ship. And we, wandering away from the other Ships, have sailed on to

---

[1] Translated from the Old Dutch by E. D. Drok from *Ongeluckige Voyagie van't schip Batavia*, de Vries edition 1649, p. 45 *et seq.*

[2] Journals kept on the voyage were thrown over by the mutineers; see evidence of Lenert Michielsz van Os, p. 186.

shallows near the Southland on 4th June, 1629, the second day of Whitsuntide, where on the same day I, with some others exclusive of my wife and children, have been set by means of a Boat or Sloop on an Island which after that time is named *Batavia's* Graveyard; and also to another Island, called the Traitors Island, they have taken some Barrels with Ships' Biscuit and other things; after that they searched for Water on one or two Islands in the neighbourhood; and not finding any, the Commandeur with his Council decided to go to Batavia with a Boat with about forty Men, which has happened; they left then another Sloop at the Traitors Island for the purpose that we should get Water by that means, either on an Island or from the Ship; but the Understeersman [Gillis Fransz] with other Sailors, having gone in the Sloop to find Water, have also gone with the Boat, and left us there sad and miserable: having no drink of Wine or Water in four or five days, so that we had to drink our own water, and also many died from thirst. After that God sent rain, and by means of rafts which they made, we got some Biscuit, Wine and Water; and the men who were still on the Ship came gradually from aboard, some of them were drowned, others came ashore where we were, amongst whom also was *Jeronymus Cornelisz*, Undermerchant of the ship *Batavia*, who has been elected Chief; and this Merchant in the beginning behaved himself very well; but after having been a while with us, he went astray in a most disgraceful manner and committed cruelties; first, he has made an agreement or secret plan with some whom he trusted and revealed to them his intention. It amounted to this: He said to them that the number of the people who were there together, about 200, must be reduced to a very few. He said that the Commandeur, before he went away with the Boat, had given him to understand this, and so he started what he had in mind: he ordered some to go to a land, two or three miles from the land where we were, to seek Water; for (so he said) the People could not live in such great numbers on the little Water they had. Those people coming back again from that land had got enough information that there was not any consolation there for any Human Beings; but the Merchant ordered them to say that there was Water and good food for the people; whereupon some others were ordered to go, and others went of their own accord to know truthfully if there was Water, and that [if so] they would start fires; but they did not find Water on that high land, but they came to another high land, and there they found Water, and then they made fires. Now, seeing that [the fires] continued, everyone said, there must be Water, the People would not otherwise be able to live, so that now and then some of the boldest Soldiers by chance came together where the Water was: then he with his Council and the Soldiers who were on his side started to put his plan into action. They had rafts; and on these they put 8 or 10 Men and on each raft they also put 2 or 3 of the boldest Soldiers who were still with us, and, not knowing anything, those were tied with ropes by the evil ones and thrown into the Water when it became Deep; and then they informed us that they had taken them to the high land where the Water was. They also took Men, Women, and Youths to an Island close by us, called Seals Island, pretending that they would take care of them; meanwhile the wickedest Murderers went along and murdered some of the People, some they walked into the Water, some saved themselves on rafts and other things and reached the land where the Water was; coming there and there finding the others, they related all that had happened to them, so they perceived what was going on, and they stayed there all together, about a 50 of them; they then remained away from us, and now, as the boldest Soldiers were gone, they started to murder pregnant women, to strangle Men and Children, for they showed themselves to be nothing other than highwaymen; the whole day long it was their catch-call, "Who wants to be boxed on the ear?" so we all of us together expected to be murdered at any moment; and we besought God continuously for a merciful relief. But the Murderers decided to spare me and my Daughter Judick, for there was one of the blood-council who often wished to Marry my Daughter; so they invited me and my Daughter Judick to one of their Tents, for an evening meal; the Daughter I took with me, we not knowing why—have murdered my Wife and Children, all together, on that night; I, coming home with my Daughter, have wept very much, as I had much reason for it. Next day some have come to me as I wept very much and said that I ought not to do so. Said, that does not matter; be silent, or you go the same way. O cruelty! O atrocity of atrocities! Murderers who are on the roads often take their belongings from People, but they sometimes leave them their lives: but these have taken both, goods and blood. And so, briefly, this being the most important thing, my Daughter and I, we both went along as an Ox in front of the Axe. Every night I said to my Daughter, you have to look tomorrow morning, whether I have been murdered. Many things which happened I pass over, except that my Children got a very meagre ration, so that they nearly perished from hunger and thirst; I ate Seals' skins; and I put some salt Water into the tot of Water I was given, so that it would last a little longer. They forbade me to pray and to preach. Most of the time I sat on the beach reading, and then I plucked some Salad or Grass that was there, and then I had neither Oil nor Vinegar; for two months I tasted neither Bread nor Rice. I have been so weak that I could not get up; I had to pull up and push off the little Boats with which they navigated; every day it was, What shall we do with that Man? The one would decapitate me, the other poison me, which would have been the sweeter death; a third said, Let him live a little longer, we might make use of him to persuade the folk on the other Land to come over to us—that was those fifty who were there together and who had found the Water; for they were afraid of those then; for they thought, if there comes a Yacht to rescue us, then they will be in our way; as has happened, too, as you will hear. Meanwhile, the case of my Daughter Judick, of which I started to tell you, has happened in this way: a certain Coenraedt van Huyssen from Gelderlandt, otherwise a handsome Young Nobleman, who also had become a member of the Council of those Murderers, besought my Daughter in Holy Wedlock. But said he would make a Betrothal with her and marry her legally[3] before all the World, that he would do at the first opportunity; many words were said about this matter, too long to narrate; for Judick and I deliberated thus, that it was better to be kept legally by one Man, in such a time, than to be mis-used as happened to the other Women. Therefore he made a betrothal vow with her and all that went with that. With Judick, I begged that she should go and live with him the next day, which also was consented to by van Huyssen; but the other Murderers, coming in front of the Tent, said that it had to happen that night and immediately, otherwise they were ready to kill us, and so it went on the whole evening; she has been with him in that respect, but she has not been abused, as she told me. What could one do against it? Now this is her luck, according to them, that van Huyssen was so kindly disposed to her, thus my Daughter has been with van Huyssen about five weeks, he also has protected her very well, so that no disaster has befallen her, otherwise than that she had to remain with him; the other Women were very jealous of her, because they thought that too much honour was accorded her. Meanwhile, I nearly perished of discomfort; my Daughter and I could hardly speak to each other secretly; van Huyssen hardly talked to me: sometimes my Daughter and I were a quarter of an hour together and then I told her—as I have said before—what she had to do if she should find me in the morning, slaughtered; and that also we must be prepared to meet God. This then was the position; and they went on murdering so long that only a few were left, about a thirty, me included; but they did not know what to do with those who were on the Land where the Water was, about a fifty of them, of whom I spoke before. To be short, they decided to go there in their small Boats in order to persuade those with sweet words and beautiful promises, to bring them into the net, or otherwise to overpower them with force; which happened. I also went along as a Soldier, hoping, as I said to my Daughter, to come into contact with these people. Coming on an Island opposite those people, they gathered immediately and derided us, saying, Has it gone so far that that good Man, the Predikant, has to come along? Then they went over in their little Boats. And so our Merchant offered them Peace, but trying to deceive them; the others said they would have nothing to do with the offering of Peace, for they knew very well that they tried to deceive them; and there were two of the Murderers who each had a Musket, and who tried to shoot the people, but those guns would not go off, and then the others scoffed at them. Then they started to talk friendship with each other; the Murderers had put it on paper; they asked me if I would take it over to the other party? I said yes; for that was what I longed for, as thus I could fulfil my intention without

[3] By the laws of Holland no marriage was legal without the consent of the parents of both parties.

any trouble arising; so I went thither and hither, and the good ones said they would keep me there until the next day, but the scoundrels then said they had to send me back; and that went again and again. But I had told them that they should say that I ought to stay with them a Month or two, because I was also their Predikant; and that they did. It was arranged that next day the Merchant should bring back some material and clothes to the People who were there where the Water was, and to talk more to the point with each other in order to establish Peace; and he appointed a certain time. The next day the Merchant, with van Huyssen, Zeevanck, and also three others, have come and brought some *Laken* [woollen cloth], some wine, and other things. The other Murderers, with a few good ones, as well as the Women, remained on the Island opposite them. After the goods of the Merchant had been divided, and after the Wine had been poured out, those on the side of the Murderers began to talk with the good ones; they were walking hither and thither and started to talk with the good Soldiers. Saying, that they would trust many things to them, and they wished the most important would listen to the Murderers, that they knew of big profits for them, offering them money. The good ones, who well understood the case and saw whither it was leading, had given promises to each other to catch them and kill them, because they were the most important of the Council. And so it happened: four killed, one got away, and the Merchant taken prisoner. This being so, I have been with the good ones, and have remained with them, who have given me food and helped me to my feet again. There was water also, Sweet as milk, in wells; they also made me a pair of clogs, in which I walked, and which I shall keep as long as God grants me life; for, whilst with the Murderers, I could not get anything at all, whilst all the time I was to be murdered at any hour; and now that van Huyssen, my Daughter's Betrothed, had been killed, I also was in great peril lest they violate my Daughter, or lest she be decapitated by the Murderers: the more, because the good ones called out, after they had killed those four, of whom I told above, Come over to us who are not Murderers. And they called, Judick, come to your Father; but one of those said to Judick, If you have any thought of going to your Father, we will cut you to pieces; and they said, It is all the doings of your Father that those people have been slaughtered. But my Daughter has been saved by God, so that after that time nothing bad has happened to her. Meanwhile, through the death and capture of the above-mentioned persons, the strength of the Murderers has been decreased. Then they went again to their Island, with the Women who were with them. Time would fail me to relate everything; how miraculously God has blessed the good ones who were together, with Water, with fowls, with Fish, with other Beasts, with Eggs in basketsfull; there were also some Beasts which they called Cats [wallabies] and with as nice a taste as ever I tasted. Of the guns and pikes they made, one is inclined to say how is it possible that Men can invent such things? They also showed me their friendship, kissed me, and would have carried me on their hands. While this happened, the Murderers have set up a new Government, and have come to us again on 17 September, 1629; then I have made up a script, that they should have peace with each other, and that they should not do any harm to the good ones. But they tore that in pieces and have come at us and have wounded four Men with their Muskets, of whom one has died; and as soon as they had again left the Land, so immediately we sighted the Yacht from Batavia, that came to relieve us; whereon the pious ones jumped with joy, and the good ones immediately went in their little Boat to the Yacht to warn them. This being done, those on the Yacht have been on their guard. For, as is now known to us out of the scoundrels, this has been the cause of all the misery: that they had in mind to seize the Yacht that came to save us and then sail away with all the Jewels and Money to a place of their liking. Also, inquiries have been made with regard to the Skipper [Ariaen Jacobsz], who has been imprisoned along with others, because (so men said) a number of them, especially Jeronymus, would have taken over and sailed away with the Ship *Batavia* had it not run aground. It is said that closer inquiries are being made into this second matter, namely, the running away with the Ship. In any case, it is very true regarding the Yacht; for they very well could have done it, but for the good folk on the high Land, who were in their way; for of that I could give good reasons, had I the time. Some of the Murderers went aboard, hoping it would turn out for the best; I also went aboard from the other Land, where the Merchant had been kept bound, together with him; they were all chained, and chained well. The following day, the other Murderers who were on *Batavia's* Graveyard were imprisoned by the Commandeur Pelsaert and those who were with him. The Commandeur and his Council, after having tried them, decided to hang some; but to cut off the right hand of Jeronymus Cornelisz, which was done. But if ever there has been a Godless Man in his utmost need, it was he; he had done nothing wrong (according to his statement). Yes, saying even at the end as he mounted the Gallows: Revenge! Revenge! So that to the end of his life he was an evil and Godless Man. The justice and Vengeance of God has been made manifest in him, for he had been a too-atrocious murderer. On board the Ship he had often shown his Godless wrong-headedness by Godless proposals. But I did not know he was Godless to such an extent. Of the others, some were punished on the Ship, some were brought to Batavia. This then, in large outline, is the whole story, which would have taken too much time narrated with all circumstances; for one could have written a very voluminous Book on it. So that when this is not written in good order and clarity there are two good reasons: firstly, I had not the time, for the Ships are ready to sail for the Fatherland; secondly, because we have just come out of such a sorrow that the mind is still a little confused, for I had not in mind to write so much. This then has as purpose to warn the Honourable High and Mighty Lords, at all occasions to have good, trustworthy, and Godfearing persons in their employment, especially Merchants and Skippers, everything depends on that; for it must be said that that is of the highest importance. All these disasters related above have happened between the time of 4 June 1629 and the 17 September 1629, inclusive; then the Yacht came to relieve us.

FINIS

APPENDIX V

FINAL SENTENCES ON MEN ALREADY EXAMINED AND SENTENCED ABOARD *SARDAM*[1]

MONDAY the 28th January Ao. 1630

ALL the Documents and Evidences as well as the criminal charges [*criminelen eijsschen*] by [*van*][2] the Fiscal Advocate, Antonie van Heuvel, against the gruesome Murderers of men from the Southland, having been handed over to the Hon. Ld. General [Specx] in the presence of the Hon. Lords Councillors of India (being assisted by the Honorable Council of Justice), as well as the Sentences of the mentioned Lords Councillors of India and the Council of Justice pronounced against the same; His Hon., after reading the previously mentioned exhibited Documents, as well as the personal Confessions of the mentioned Delinquents, has approved the advices given by the said Councillors: that the Delinquents, on account of their Abominable gruesome cruelties and suchlike unheard of Murders of men and raping of Women, Namely, Jacob Pietersz Cousijns, Steenhouwer, shall be broken from under upwards and the body put on a Wheel. Salomon Deschamps, Undermerchant, Daniel Cornelisz of Luijck, Soldier, Hans Jacops Heijlweck, and Lucas Gelissz from the Hague all four, to be punished with the Cord until Death follows, previously cutting off the right hand of Daniel Cornelisz.

Rogier Decker of Haerlem and Abraham Gerritsz, Boys, to draw lots which of the two shall be punished with the Cord, and he who shall draw himself free from Death, shall be severely flogged, with a Halter round his neck.

Andries Liebent of Oldenburgh, Hans Fredricxsz of Bremen and Olivier van Welderen, to flog them all severely, tied to a pole, and to exile them all for three Years in chains, Hans Fredricx shall have a Halter on his neck as well.

Cornelisz Jansz *Boon* ["Bean"] young sailor, to be flogged and marked with a brand, and to flog Claas Harmansz, Boy, with a Halter around his neck.

Isbrant Isbrantsz of Purmurent, Assistant, with a Halter round his neck, shall watch the execution of Justice.

And hereupon it is laid down that the Executions shall take place on Thursday.

[1] Translated by E. D. Drok from photostats of original document: ARAKA, VOC: 1011, O.B. 1631[I], Resolution of the Governor-General in Council.

[2] This is *van* used in exactly the same manner as noted in Appendix III, note 3. Can mean *of* or *by the*.

Furthermore, it has been found good by the Hon. Lord General and the Councillors of India to gratify the further persons who have shown themselves faithful and piously resisted the evil, each one according to his ability, with two months' wages, and the Soldiers who are not Cadets, to be given the mentioned rank, as well as 10 guilders per month, which will also be enjoyed by all the Sailors who earn less than 10 guilders per month.

And Wijbe Heijches [Wiebbe Hayes], sailed out as a Soldier, who has allowed himself to be used as a leader, to be gratified with the office and rank of Standard-bearer [*vaendrager*][3] with wages of 40 guilders per month, all with the promise of further advancement according to opportunity and merit.

---

[3] *Vaendrager* can mean standard-bearer, also ensign or cornet; is clearly the lowest commissioned rank.

Appendix VI

LETTER FROM RUBENS TO PEIRESC[1]

Il Sr. Rockoxio vive, sta bene e baccia a V.S. di vero cuore le mani. Io ho il disegno ed ancora il molo di quel vaso d'Agate che V.S. ha visto (il quale comprai duo mille scudi d'oro) ma non del concavo. Egli non aveva pero maggior grossezza che di una caraffa ordinaria di vetro alquando grossiero et mi ricordo d' haverlo misurato et si teneva giustamente una misura che chiamamo nella nostra lingua con un vocabulo assai inetto Pot! Questa gioja essendo mandata alle Indie orientali sopra una caracca venne in mano d'ollandesi sed periit inter manus repientium ni fallor, perche avendo fatto tutte le diligenze possibile nella Compagnia Orientale à Amsterdam non ho mai potuto sapere novi alcuni.

---

[1] Dated 18th December 1634. From "The Rubens Vase, Its History and Date", by Marvin C. Ross, *Journal of the Walters Art Gallery*, Baltimore, U.S.A., vol. vi, App. 11, 1943. For translation see Chapter V, p. 91.

Appendix VII

THE WHITE ANGEL

The house named De Witte Engel (The White Angel), once owned by Jan (or Hans) Meynertsz and his wife Steffanie Joosten, the parents of Lucretia Jansz, is still in existence. Lucretia was born at a house of this name, standing on the Nieuwendijk at Amsterdam, in 1602. After her father's death, her mother married again, and in 1608 her step-father, Dirck Crijnen, sold the house but retained a mortgage on it, which he still held in 1612.

Inquiries made in Amsterdam on my behalf by the Baroness van Lynden-de Clercq have disclosed that No. 113, the Nieuwendijk, was known by the name of De Witte Engel. The date 1635 is carved on an upper storey which, from appearances, could well be an addition. That year is also the presumed date of Lucretia's return to Holland, and could have some significance, if it were also the date of clearing the mortgage; in which case the building may have been renovated or remodelled.

Regarding this house Dr I. H. van Eeghen, Assistant Director of the City Archives of Amsterdam, has written to me: "At this moment there is not a house called the Witte Engel on the Nieuwendijk. The names of the houses changed often. . . . As you looked for a Witte Engel at the beginning of the 17th century, we tried to find one for you and succeeded. This was the house owned by Dirck Crijnen in 1608. From the old registers of taxation, we were able to make out that this house is at this moment numbered 113. There is no doubt about this. It must have been rebuilt, or in any case have got a new façade later in the 17th century. . . . When Lucretia's father Hans Meynertsz was buried on 16th August, 1602, there was only one child. So I think, as she was the second child, she must have been born after his death. I am certain that the mother moved into another house after she had married for the second time. In 1605 quite other people are mentioned as living in the Witte Engel on the Nieuwendijk."

As it is clearly established that Lucretia Jansz was born at No. 113, the Nieuwendijk, in 1602, that house must be the oldest known domestic building to be linked with Australia.

Appendix VIII

MORELAND'S ASSESSMENT OF PELSAERT[1]

"The most detailed account of the standard of life in Northern India during our period is that which was drawn up in 1626 by Francisco Pelsaert, the chief of the Dutch factory at Agra, on the basis of his seven years' experience of the country. The translation of his account which follows contains, it will be seen, strong expressions, which, when divorced from their context, may suggest the efforts of a sensational writer; but if his lengthy report is read as a whole, it will be found that he was a cool-headed and competent merchant, with a straightforward if occasionally colloquial style, and with a lively interest in his surroundings. He was very deeply impressed by the poverty and oppression he saw around him, and the occasional vehemence of his language must be accepted as indicating the strength of his sympathies with his poorer neighbours."

[1] W. H. Moreland, *From Akbar to Aurangzeb*, p. 198.

APPENDIX IX

THE SITE OF THE WRECK

[The following passage was originally a chapter in the main body of text. However, on 4th June 1963 the remains of the wrecked *Batavia* were discovered on the reefs of the Wallabi Group of the Houtman Rocks as the result of a search based on my opinions as here reasoned and expressed. Square-bracketed interpolations have been introduced to add a few facts arising from this discovery located on Morning Reef, little more than a mile to the east of Noon Reef.]

For more than three centuries the site of the wreck of the *Batavia* remained an open question. The fact that the full text of Pelsaert's Journals has never been translated into modern Dutch, let alone English, until now; the inaccessibility of the islands; above all, early assumptions drawn without sufficient research, led to the greatest confusion and many differing opinions.

Unfortunately, with the exception of one hitherto disregarded but nonetheless signficant figure used casually by Pelsaert when recording trials' evidence (to which attention will later be directed), the now fully translated Journals failed to specify any position more accurately possible for *Batavia's* wrecking than the untenable $28\frac{1}{3}$ degrees mentioned in *Ongeluckige Voyagie*, and the V.O.C. documents already quoted; and thereafter re-issued in all later references, as well as translated into English in the Heeres volume on Dutch discoveries in Australia.

However, despite the fact that the old navigators did remarkably well in fixing their positions (as also will be shown), it must not be forgotten that their instruments were crude. To this day an error of some miles by dead reckoning is not, even by naval authorities, considered a gross error. Therefore the one way in which to arrive at a reasonable conclusion is to consider all the evidence (now made available by full translation of the Journals) *other* than the nautical findings, and to fit that evidence to the actual scene as it exists today.

That scene is unlikely to differ greatly. In a paper on the geomorphology of the Houtman Rocks, Rhodes Fairbridge notes that particular region as being highly stable.[1] Also, a recent geological study of the islands by Curt Teichert[2] demonstrates that even the sand ridges and

[1] Rhodes W. Fairbridge, "Notes on the Geomorphology of the Pelsart Group of the Houtman's Abrolhos Islands", *Journal of the Royal Society of Western Australia*, vol. xxxiii, 1946-7, p. 2.

[2] Curt Teichert, "Contributions to the Geology of Houtman's Abrolhos, Western Australia", *Proceedings of the Linnean Society of New South Wales*, vol. lxxi, 1947, parts 3-4.

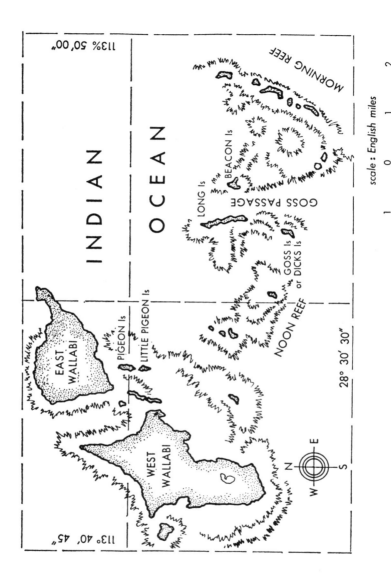

Author's map of the Wallabi Group of the Houtman Rocks.

broken coral deposits build up very slowly. There is nothing to indicate that during the past three hundred years the area has altered beyond recognition; what the eyes of the shipwrecked crew saw in 1629, the eyes of the seasonal crayfishers, who inhabit the islands for six months of every year, still see today.

Houtman first noted the archipelago in 1619. Enlarging on the advice of Brouwer and Coen, he again advised skippers, after leaving the Cape of Good Hope to

> ... run on an eastern course in 36 and 37 degrees Southern Latitude until you estimate yourself to have covered a thousand [i.e., 3000] miles to eastward, after which you had better shape your course north and north by east, until you get into 26 or 27 degrees, thus shunning the shoal aforesaid which lies off the Southland in 28° 46' ... and then, as before mentioned, from there hold your course north by west and north-north-west and you are sure to make the western extremity of Java.[3]

The *Batavia* was following the second course laid down, running north-east by north, when she hit the reef.

The archipelago lies approximately thirty-seven nautical miles, or minutes, off the coast of Western Australia, stretching from 28° 15½' to 29° 00½' S. Lat., and is divided into three distinct groups, with one solitary island to the north. Taking Houtman's 28° 46' as the point at which he sighted the reefs would indicate that he first saw the centre group, and from there sailed approximately the distance he gives (thirty miles, as his stated ten becomes when reckoned by Pelsaert's approximated usage of the term "mile") which would carry him past the northern island—a very accurate calculation. Although all the V.O.C. higher officers were warned of Houtman's discovery, the islands were not named in print until they appeared on the 1627 map of Hessel Gerritszoon[4] when they are marked as "Fr. Houtmans abrolhos"; on his map of the following year, they are simply "Houtmans Abrolhos".[5] On present-day British Admiralty charts they are named The Houtman Rocks; but the original name has been preserved by most travellers and writers, and the people of Western Australia invariably refer to them simply as the Abrolhos Islands, or merely the Abrolhos.

The term itself was once supposed to be a contraction of the Portuguese *abri vossos olhos* meaning "keep your eyes open".[6] In 1897 it

[3] J. E. Heeres, *The Part Borne by the Dutch in the Discovery of Australia 1606-1765*, p. 15.

[4] See *Caert van t'Landt van Eendracht, A° 1627* in J. E. Heeres, *op. cit.*, p. 9. The Land of Eendracht was so named after the ship of Dirk Hartog, who in 1616 had discovered the island that now bears his name, and the adjacent mainland. The scale of this map is given in "Duytsche mylen".

[5] C. Teichert, *loc. sit.*, p. 145. J. Forsyth (see note 9 of this appendix) says these islands are also marked on the little-known 1622 map of Hessel Gerritsz.

[6] J. S. Battye, *Western Australia: A History from its Discovery to the Inauguration of the Commonwealth*, p. 24, footnote 1.

was mentioned by Pasco[7] as being the look-out's cry used by early Portuguese sailors and adopted by mariners of other nationalities to indicate perilous areas.[8] More recent research by Mr John Forsyth reveals that the word originally in use amongst the Portuguese meant "spiked obstructions". To Spanish seamen this sounded like their own "open (your) eyes"; accordingly they wrote *abre ojos* and gave it that meaning very early; with the result that the false etymology soon became world-wide and has remained current.[9] Since the Portuguese connotation is extremely apt there would seem little reason to reject it in favour of the older, more fanciful explanation.

The reefs and islands are in fact the southernmost coral islands of the Indian Ocean.[10] They were first surveyed by Commanders Wickham and Stokes in 1840. Although survey vessels have paid visits from time to time, Admiralty Chart No. 1723, drawn from the observations of those two officers, remains the one still issued and used today.

A century earlier, in 1740, de l'Isle published his first map of the world. On it is clearly marked *Route de Pelsart 1629*, a simple line drawn from the vicinity of Eendracht Land to Java. Wickham and Stokes of course knew of these maps, and had very probably read, or knew of, Thévenot's description of the wreck and journey north.[11] Discovering the Houtman Rocks to be three distinct groups of islands, the surveyors in 1840 named the most southerly the Pelsart Group, the centre, Easter Group (for the date they were there), and the most northerly the Wallabi Group after the small marsupials they found on the two largest islands but nowhere else in the archipelago. The large solitary island farther north they named North Island for obvious reasons. They also gave the name of Pelsart Island to the largest island of the southern group, and called the most southerly tip of that island, which (except for a chain or so of reef) is also the most southerly point of the whole archipelago, Wreck Point. In addition, on the manuscript surveys they made the following note at 29°S., 113° 56′E.: "Probably on this part of the reef Commodore Pelsart was wreck'd in the Batavia (1628)."[12] In his diaries, published later, Stokes wrote:

On the south-west point of the island the beams of a large vessel were

[7] J. Crawford Pasco, R.N., *A Roving Commission: Naval Reminiscences*, p. 116.

[8] A year later, in Muller & Co.'s Folio volume of Tasman's Journal and Explorations, with a biography by Professor Heeres, the professor noted (p. 97, footnote 1) that Abrolhos was "a Portuguese word for cliffs, rocky projections rising from the sea".

[9] John Forsyth, "The Visit of the Yacht *Grootenbroeck* to the Coast of the South-land in 1631", *Early Days: Journal and Proceedings of the Western Australian Historical Society*, vol. v, part 3, p. 19; also note (8) p. 24.

[10] C. Teichert, *loc. cit.*, pp. 145, 147. Lord Howe Island in the Tasman Sea, S.Lat. $31\frac{1}{2}°$, has a fringing reef on the west coast; Middleton and Elizabeth reefs, between 29° and 30° S.Lat., also in the Tasman Sea, are small bank atolls.

[11] M. Thévenot, *Relations de divers voyages curieux* (Paris, 1663).

[12] J. Lort Stokes, Hydrographic Department of the Admiralty, London, manuscript surveys made by Stokes and Wickham in 1840. Chart No. 1723.

APPENDIXES 279

discovered, and as the crew of the Zeewyk, lost in 1728[13] reported having seen the wreck of a ship on this part, there is little doubt that the remains were those of the *Batavia*,[14] Commodore Pelsart, lost in 1627 [*sic*]. We in consequence named our temporary anchorage Batavia Road, and the whole group Pelsart Group. It was the wreck of this Dutch ship that led to the discovery of this part of the continent of Australia, Commodore[15] Pelsart himself having crossed over to it in a boat in search of water.[16]

Thus for nearly half a century Lort Stokes's opinion was accepted; not until towards the end of the nineteenth century, when the guano deposits on the islands attracted exploitation, did doubts arise. Then a copy of *Ongeluckige Voyagie*[17] came into the possession of Mr Florance Broadhurst and was subsequently translated by Mr William Siebenhaar of Perth, the full text being published in the Christmas 1897 issue of *The Western Mail* under the title "The Abrolhos Tragedy: The First Complete Translation in English of the Original Dutch Account Published Eighteen Years After the Massacre". Professor Heeres's work appeared two years later, giving direct translations from those parts of Pelsaert's Journals that referred to the islands and the mainland (but not the mutiny or trials) and including all but one of the presumed nautical positions as stated by Pelsaert.

From then on speculation became widespread, for it was now obvious that none of the positions mentioned in the Heeres translation could possibly be accurate when checked against the Admiralty chart of the Houtman Rocks. It was also obvious that several islands, situated in particular relationship to each other and the wreck, were necessary to fit the story. However, in the fully translated Journals one other figure is mentioned, once only, and casually, in the heading to a summary of evidence which Pelsaert recorded on 28th September 1629.[18] This posi-

[13] The *Zeewyk* was wrecked on Half Moon Reef in 1727. Many relics have been found on Gun Island (see Malcolm Uren's *Sailormen's Ghosts*, and Frank H. Goldsmith's *Treasure Lies Buried Here*). The skipper of the *Zeewyk*, Jan Steijns, made a map that establishes the site of the wreck (see J. E. Heeres, *op. cit.*, p. 93).

[14] Pelsaert clearly states in his Journals that the *Batavia* was practically broken up before he left the islands in November 1629. There was scarcely likely to be a "wreck" sufficient for anyone to note a hundred years later.

[15] Here is one of the many errors that led to Pelsaert's being regarded as a mariner.

[16] J. Lort Stokes, *Discoveries in Australia, 1837-43*, vol. ii, p. 138.

[17] This is the Jan Jansz 1647 edition, a small vellum-bound volume printed in hand-set black-letter type on excellent hand-made paper, illustrated with copper-plate engravings. On the fly-leaf a purple ink stamp proclaims the copy in the J. S. Battye Library of West Australian History to have been the property of "Broadhurst, McNeil and Co., Guano Contractors, Houtman's Abrolhos, W.A." In faded ink writing is also inscribed, "Presented to the Victoria Public Library by F. C. Broadhurst, whose firm have been working the guano deposits on the Abrolhos Group since 1883. Geraldton, 8th July 1903." The date July 1895, below Mr Broadhurst's signature on the inside cover, is the date he acquired the volume.

[18] ARAKA, VOC: 1010, p. 250 verso: Francisco Pelsaert, MS. *Sardam* Journal.

tion of 28½ degrees was passed over by Heeres, who omitted the trials as irrelevant to the discovery of Australia. The summary is included in the 1647 edition of *Ongeluckige Voyagie*, but the position wrongly given as 28 degrees, a latitude so far north as to be clear of the islands and not worthy of consideration.

Having read only the above mentioned published works and many lesser published references, I first visited the Abrolhos Archipelago in 1949, when I spent a week on Pelsart Island, in the Pelsart Group. Evidence of the eyes immediately indicated that the islands mentioned in *Ongeluckige Voyagie* are certainly not there; despite various valiant attempts to manipulate the story to fit that group.[19] Pelsart Island is no more than fifteen feet above sea-level. A beautiful isle, seven and a half miles long and at its widest no more than 600 yards across,[20] in the spring it becomes the nesting place of countless thousands of seabirds. It is too large to be considered as the small isle seen at daylight on the morning of the wreck and later named *Batavia's* Graveyard. Neither can Middle Island, at one point rising to eighteen feet but no more than 1000 yards long and 550 yards across[21], reasonably be regarded as a "high" island.[22] All other islands of the group are considerably lower than the two cited. In addition, study of the chart revealed that nowhere else is there an anchorage of twenty-seven fathoms to match that of the yacht *Sardam*, which came in to the rescue sailing on a south-west course[23] and anchored at that depth

[19] Indeed, the fantastic assumptions were many. In the *Perth Gazette* for Saturday 15th April 1847 appears the following: "*Curious Discoveries on the Abrolhos Islands*—During the late occupation of these Islands by the Pelsart Fishing Company, numerous discoveries have been made—relics of the wreck of Houtman and the visit of Admiral Pelsart. They consist of part of a sword on which is the name of 'Houtman', an officer's epaulette, belt bucklets, skeletons, coins etc. The discovery of the first skeleton was made by Mr Willis, on the spot where he had spread his blanket, and in the morning finding his pillow harder than was exactly pleasant, looked for the cause, when he found his bed composed of human bones. Mr Willis also discovered water on a third Island, contained in a well in the rock, by the side of which in the rock was an iron bolt, firmly fixed, most probably left by Houtman; this Island has been appropriately called 'Bolt Island'; also a large round hole, with a great quantity of bones in it. On one of the Mangrove islands, skeletons were found, also a quantity of Dutch bottles, evidently thrown away as they had been emptied during a carouse. The coins bear the date 1716 and are of copper, these must be relics of Houtman's party, who was wrecked in 1727; but the skeletons most probably are those of the mutineers who were shot by Admiral Pelsart." The confusion of Houtman's original discovery with the wreck of the *Zeewyk*, indeed the whole paragraph, is a very good example of the legendary nature of much early comment.

[20] C. Teichert, *loc. cit.*, pp. 159, 160.

[21] Rhodes W. Fairbridge, *loc. cit.*, p. 19.

[22] In *Discoveries in Australia, 1837-43*, vol. ii., p. 151, Lort Stokes mentions finding a well on Middle Island with good water that rose and fell with the tide, and states that he thought it the well mentioned by Pelsaert. This opinion contributed to early beliefs in favour of the Pelsart Group.

[23] Pelsart's Journals, 16th September 1629.

"2 miles" (i.e., 6) from the "high" island, the next day sailing on to lie sheltered "under" the high island itself. When eventually the full translation of the Journals was completed we found that, after the skipper of the *Sardam* was lost on 13th October 1629, a search party landed on "an island with high dunes, about 3-4 [9-12] miles N.N.West of the ship [*Sardam*]".[24] The description which follows[25] tallies with Lort Stokes's own description of solitary North Island, which is situated eleven to twelve miles north-west by north of the anchorage under West Wallabi in the Wallabi Group. Pelsaert also states that the *Sardam* lay at anchor "N.N.West of the Wreck".[26] Thus all claims in favour of the Pelsart Group became discredited. Had the *Batavia* struck at Wreck Point, as hastily presumed by Stokes, or at any other point on the great Half Moon Reef of the southern group, as a ship sailing her course must have done, there is no island with high dunes lying to the north-north-west—nothing but more reefs or the open sea.

But before this fact from the Journal was known to me, personal discussion with local fishermen and attention to the chart suggested the Wallabi Group to be my proper objective. From time to time various writers have advanced ingenious theories concerning the Easter or Centre Group, but, once again, the chart and descriptions given by fishermen offered sufficient obstacles to belief. Reefs discourage any ship of size from entering the "lagoon" on a south-west course, nor is an anchorage of twenty-seven fathoms available in the necessary position. Moreover, Rat Island, the solitary isle of substance, is not a mile long and less than half that distance in width; it rises no more than thirteen feet above sea-level. The rats that inhabit this island are certainly not the "cats" of Pelsaert's Journal, so accurately described by him and universally accepted as being the wallabies after which Wickham and Stokes named the northern group, as they likewise named the two largest islands of the group, on which alone the creatures live (East and West Wallabi). Stokes even wrote in his *Discoveries*, "As there is no record of the Dutch having visited the northern group, it is impossible to say whether wallaby were then found on it or not. How they could have got there is a mystery. . . ."[27] It is therefore clear that Pelsaert's Journal was unknown to Stokes, or this group might have been correctly named for Pelsaert instead of the most southern.

The gentle little animals now named tammars[28] are in fact a unique

[24] Our first translation gave this as "wreck"—see my article "The Wreck of the Batavia", *Walkabout Magazine*, vol. xxi, no. 1, p. 36, January 1955. The correction alters (to advantage) the distances then cited, though it is still possible that Pelsaert meant the wreck.
[25] Pelsaert's Journals, 24th October 1629.
[26] Ibid., 15th November 1629.
[27] J. Lort Stokes, *op. cit.*, vol. ii, p. 155.
[28] *Macropus (Thylogale) eugenii houtmanni* is the classification given by John Gould: that is, belonging to the wallaby species of the kangaroo genus, named after Prince Eugene by Desmarest, the French scientist to whom an early specimen of wallaby was sent, and finally differentiated by Gould as peculiar to the Houtman

variety of the marsupial family. Teichert offers the opinion that their presence is an indication that the islands were once joined to the mainland, but so long ago that the animals developed the characteristics that now differentiate them from the usual mainland tammar.[29] However that may be, they do not exist on any other of the Abrolhos Islands and have not done so within recorded memory. Certainly in 1629 the crew of the *Batavia* found them only on the two "high" islands. The sailors also eventually discovered water on both those islands, in "wells" or natural holes, which will be discussed later. These, too, exist today. In addition, the two islands both rise to approximately fifty feet above sea-level. These three features, the animals, the water-holes, and the height, which together pertain *only* to the two large Wallabi islands of the Abrolhos archipelago, lead to the obvious conclusion that the *Batavia* was wrecked somewhere in the vicinity of this group.

Further evidence comes from the course followed by the *Sardam* when returning to the rescue. At one stage she was blown as far south as 30°. Sailing west, they sighted the continent on 3rd September and saw that the land appeared to stretch south-south-east for about "four" (i.e., twelve) miles, where "the horizon ended"—very probably curving in from Green Head, or North Head, if they had not gained height. They ran north up the coast, and the following day at 28° 50′ noted a change in the lie of the land which would coincide with the alteration of angle north of Point Moore, where Geraldton stands today. A south wind carried them west in the afternoon, and towards evening they saw ahead to the west "some shallows" and about "a musket shot away" found a fine sandy bottom at twenty-five fathoms. Today's chart shows "fine shell sand" at twenty-five fathoms off the small islands north of Pelsart Island, in the southern group, slightly south of the latitude given. Or if they ran farther north, it would be Hummock Island that they saw; whichever it was, they turned away, sailed E.S.E. for a short distance, and anchored in twenty-seven fathoms. On 5th September they tacked about for some time and appear eventually to have seen Pelsart Island:

> ... this reef or shallow stretched out S.S.W. and N.N.East, found along here 27-28 to 29 fathoms sand ground; at 11 hours before noon

---

Rocks. Tammar is the native name for the species, brought into use by the late Mr L. Glauert, Past Director of the Western Australian Musem, who gave me the following note: "One of the smaller members of the kangaroo family grouped as wallabies, but lacking the extremely developed hind limbs of the kangaroo, thus approaching the quokka of Rottnest Island, and like it having a more rat-like face, the ears being smaller. The colour is brownish grey intermixed with longer black hairs and having practically no pattern. It stands about 18 in. to 2 ft erect. The Wallabi Island tammar differs slightly from its relative on Garden Island and the mainland by distinctions that require a specialist's knowledge to perceive." The mainland quokka haunts swampy country, the tammar prefers more open country. There are swamps on Rottnest, but not on Garden Island or the Wallabi Islands.

[29] C. Teichert, *loc cit.*, p. 185.

the continent[30] had disappeared from our sight; at noon had the Southern Latitude of 28 degrees 59 minutes, and the corner of the reef was W.S.West from us, with dirty steep ground with depths from 50 to 60 fathoms.

This seems extraordinarily close reckoning; the position given is in fact exactly that of a ship lying one minute north to the east of Wreck Point (as it was named by Lort Stokes). It is also significant that, although they were then searching for a locality they knew, there is no suggestion that this point appeared familiar. The first set of soundings are also more or less exact, and greater depths are reached almost immediately Wreck Point is passed, sailing west. The general picture, if not the precise order of finding, is surprisingly correct.

After they had taken the position at noon a calm fell, but a current carried them west. The breakers were left behind, but during the stillness of the night they drifted in so close that they could hear the roar of the breakers. Along Half Moon Reef that is a sound that never ceases. By morning the rocks were out of sight, but about 10 a.m. the wind came up from the W.N.W. and they turned towards the rocks and had the latitude 28° 44' at noon—accurate findings again, for these would be the western reefs of the Easter Group. "This shallow stretches further out S.E. and N.West," as Pelsaert puts it.

This tacking about continued for several more days in an endeavour to approach the islands at exactly 28° 20', at which position they expected to find the wreck of the *Batavia*. But winds and currents were adverse; on 13th September, having arrived at "the most Northerly point of the Abrolhos", Pelsaert resolved to

... keep bearing beneath the extreme [i.e. most northerly] shallow, and tacked slowly towards that again, the wind S.S.E., Course East; coming in a little, immediately had clean Sand ground at 30 to 35 fathoms; at noon, the latitude of 28 degrees Southern Latitude; shortly after saw again the main Southland.

This would be just north of Port Gregory. High winds next held them up, but at last on 16th September they sailed south, then southwest, and Pelsaert was able to write

... towards evening saw the rocks of our wrecked ship *Batavia* and I recognized[31] [lit.: I was recognized] the High Island, although the Steersmen[32] sustained that it was the other land; 2 hours in the night anchored again on 27 fathoms clean Sandy ground.

[30] Pelsaert writes *vastelandt,* by which he means the continent. The order of writing is here confused: this sentence should obviously have preceded the reference to the sighting of the reef.

[31] In Tasman's Journals, p. 96, footnote 2, ed. Frederik Muller 1898, *ende wierdt ick verkendt* is translated as "and I was recognized from" the High Island. But in *The Part Borne by the Dutch in the Discovery of Australia 1606-1765*, p. 60, Heeres corrects this to the more logical "and I was sure I saw the high Island".

[32] Claas Gerritsz, uppersteersman from the *Batavia*, and Jacop Jansz, understeersman from the same vessel.

The following morning they found they were still about 2 [6] miles from the high island with wind North. But as they approached they "saw smoke on a long island [West Wallabi] 2 [6] miles West of the Wreck, also on another small island close by the Wreck".

This description gives what is really a clear picture of sailing in to the Wallabi Group *from* the north-east, as I have myself experienced it; on the occasion of my visit we went fishing in almost the exact position from which I believe the *Sardam* crew first sighted the islands from the eastern side.

Pelsaert was amazed to find no one on the "Highest island" (he here uses the superlative) where he landed. But later in the day he entered the fact that a soldier named Wiebbe Hayes had been sent with his party to "a long island" in order to search for water (which they found) and thereafter he several times refers to "the island of Wiebbe Hayes" as distinct from the "High island"; although sometimes the former is also called "the High island". In his letter the predikant Bastiaensz[33] also mentions two main islands, apart from the smaller ones named by the mutineers.

Still further evidence of the Wallabi Group being the correct group comes from the record of the visit paid by the understeersman of the *Sardam* to "another big island". On 24th October 1629 Pelsaert writes that they reported

> ... that they had been on an island with high dunes, about 3-4 [9-12] miles N.N.W. of the Ship, which was all set round with a reef except for a narrow opening which they just struck, so that they could go in.... It is a dry great island without having found any fresh water, but there was a host of gulls and eggs and in the middle of the island it had a valley with much Sand.

Compare this with Lort Stokes's description of North Island which he writes lies ten miles north of East Wallabi:

> The island was about a mile across, and nearly circular. It was surrounded by a range of hills, with a flat in the centre, covered with coarse grass, where a great many quails were flushed, affording good sport, but not a single wallaby.[34]

The main features mentioned by both men are clearly visible from the air, notably the single opening in the formidable reef barrier, the one that the *Sardam* sailors were lucky enough to strike immediately. *There is no other "island with high dunes" in the archipelago that fits Pelsaert's description and can also be shown to lie from nine to twelve miles N.N.W. of a ship at anchor under any "high island" other than East or West Wallabi*; despite the fact that from time to time writers, and others, have exercised considerable ingenuity endeavouring to identify islands in both the Pelsart and Easter groups with the "high island" under which the *Sardam* lay.

[33] See Appendix IV.   [34] J. Lort Stokes, *op. cit.*, vol. ii, p. 163.

APPENDIXES

Finally, Pelsaert makes a general observation as he leaves, on 15th November: "They are all low-lying Coral islands and Rocks except 2 to 3 Big islands. . . ." This remark obviously includes North Island. Moreover, it would still remain valid had any members of his crew ever sailed southwards in one of the small boats (of which there is no evidence) to one of the other groups: there are no other islands of the archipelago that warrant the term "big", as do the large islands of the Wallabi Group and North Island. In addition, Pelsaert himself failed to apply such a term to the next in size, Pelsaert Island, when he skirted its shores in the *Sardam* on 5th September 1629.

It remains therefore to see if in other more precise details the locality also fits the story, and, if so, whether a reasonably definite wreck site can be deduced.

At the beginning of the Journal detailing the wreck and the open boat voyage to Java, Pelsaert gives the wreck as being "situated on the Latitude of $28\frac{1}{3}$ degrees". Throughout the search made in the *Sardam* this is the position they always tried to reach. This position must have been estimated by Ariaen Jacobsz, skipper of the *Batavia*, soon after the wrecking, and checked by Claas Gerritsz, his uppersteersman; possibly also by the understeersman Jacop Jansz. When Pelsaert returned with the *Sardam* and eventually located the wreck, he appears to have been so overcome by the horrors of the mutiny that he made no specific note regarding any amended calculation. But on 28th September in the heading to his summary of the trials he writes:

> . . . on the island named *Batavia's* Graveyard, situated in the vicinity of the Wreck of the lost ship Batavia, in the Latitude of $28\frac{1}{2}$ degrees Southern latitude about 9 [i.e., 27: in fact, about 37] miles from the main Southland.

This $28\frac{1}{2}$ (instead of $28\frac{1}{3}$) must be a slip (although it is very firmly written), or else (what seems to me more likely) it is in fact a position that had been fixed by Jacop Jacobsz, the skipper of the *Sardam*, and on the date given was accepted as being correct. However, before they finally left the islands a new official check was apparently made and specifically noted by Pelsaert on 15th November, the day of departure:

> The place where the ship or the Wreck lies is on the latitude of 28 degrees 37-40 minutes[35] and where we were with the Yacht under the High Island is on 30 to 32 minutes, N.N.West of the Wreck[36]

[35] Pelsaert's 37-40 minutes, or "37: a 40" (as the writing is not clear) is given by J. E. Heeres (*op. cit.*, p. 60) in his English translation as "36 or 40". In the Dutch version the figures are correct, but Heeres places a grave accent: "à". In the next sentence Pelsaert's "a" ("30: a 32 minutes") is quite clear. E. D. Drok considers that here and elsewhere Pelsaert's "a" is equivalent to the French "to", and was quicker to write than the Dutch "tot".

[36] Earlier, on 13th November, at the end of sentences passed aboard the *Sardam*, Pelsaert writes "on the Yacht *Sardam* . . . lying at anchor under the High Island, 2

although the steersmen, after the wrecking of the ship ... have taken from the Islands, the Latitude of 28 degrees 8 minutes, and 28 degrees 20 minutes,[37] the which has caused not a little misunderstanding in search of this place and also loss of time.

These latter figures show how great was the amount of approximation in all cases. The final corrected position of the wreck can reasonably be presumed as having been made by Claas Gerritsz and Jacop Jansz (it must never be forgotten that Pelsaert himself was a merchant, not a navigator), since by that time Jacob Jacobsz, master of the *Sardam*, had been "blown away" and lost whilst searching small islands "Westerly of the ship",[38] on Pelsaert's orders, for flotsam.

The first position of 28° 20′ lies on the great reef just south of solitary North Island, and is thus an impossible site by reason of the many islands needed to fit the story; that of 28° 8′ is obviously worse. The amended version of 28° 37′ to 28° 40′ stretches from the centre of Middle Channel (entirely free of reefs) lying south of the Wallabi Group, to a point on the northern fringe of the Easter Group; also an impossible site by reason of the aftermath of the wreck which requires small islands to lie close by the *Batavia* driving on a N.E. by N. course.[39] Accepting, therefore, the point of 28° 37′ as the most correct of those officially given by Pelsaert (and not forgetting the 28° 30′ casually recorded in the Journal on 28th September), what can one find? It becomes clear that a ship sailing at night on a course northeast by north could skirt Evening Reef and strike Noon Reef or Morning Reef in the latitude of 28° 30′.

This latitude is not without possible significance. In 1627 J. P. Coen had returned to Batavia as Governor-General for a second term. On arrival he had written to the Directors at Amsterdam.

... we continued our voyage with the *Galias*, and in the afternoon of the 5th of September in 28½ degrees S.Lat. came upon the land of *d'Eendracht*. We were at less than half a mile's distance from the breakers before perceiving the same, without being able to see land. If we had come upon this place in the night time, we should have been in a thousand perils with our ship and crew. In the plane charts the reckonings of our steersmen were still below 300 and 350 [i.e., 900 and 1050] miles from any land, so that there was not the slightest suspicion of our being near any, although the reckoning of the chart with increasing degrees showed only 120 [360] miles, and by

---

[i.e., 6] miles from the Wreck". This slightly shortens the distance; again showing the markedly approximate nature of the reckoning.

[37] These two were taken under Ariaen Jacobsz's command.

[38] *Sardam* presumably, but *Batavia* would fit the situation better. Pelsaert generally refers to the *Batavia* as "the Wreck". But all references to the "ship" are ambiguous: cf. his use of both on 15th November.

[39] But Pelsaert chooses to mention only 28°37′ in his last letter to the V.O.C. Directors at Amsterdam.

the terristrial globe only 50 [150] miles distant from the land. But to this little attention had been paid. It seems certain now that the miscalculation involved in the plane chart from Cabo de bon' Esperança to the Southland in 35 degrees latitude gives an overplus of more than 270 [810] miles of sea, a matter to which most steersmen pay little attention, and which has brought, and is still daily bringing, many vessels into great perils. . . . We would request Your Worships to direct attention to this point, and have such indications made in the plane charts as experts shall find to be advisable; a matter of the highest importance, which if not properly attended to involves grievous peril to ships and crews (which God in his mercy avert).

In this plane chart the South-land also lies fully 40 [120] miles more to eastward than it should be, which should also be rectified.[40]

These instructions would unquestionably have been handed to Ariaen Jacobsz before sailing from the Texel in October 1628. Therefore it seems to me unlikely that he and his steersmen would deliberately place their "shallow that must be lying quite a distance from the unknown country" in *exactly* the latitude mentioned by the formidable Jan Pieterszoon Coen, despite his mistaking the Abrolhos reefs for the mainland and the fact that they themselves saw no sign of the Southland (though it is obvious that Pelsaert was from the start very sceptical regarding Ariaen's contention). Actually, the land of the *Eendracht* lay in 25°;[41] which again serves to show how exceedingly uncertain were all supposed positions on the Southland coast at this time. Moreover, room must always be allowed (in the seventeenth century no less than today) for human error—and the manipulation of damning evidence. I incline very much to the view that when after the wreck Ariaen Jacobsz declared the reef to lie in $28\frac{1}{3}$ degrees, or in 28° 8', he made a deliberate error, determined to avoid Coen's specified 28° 30' at all costs.

My reason for this is that immediately afterwards Ariaen navigated a small boat to Java with great skill, and that his findings, as recorded by Pelsaert in his Journal, were then extraordinarily accurate. In addition, the *Sardam* positions already quoted were fairly accurate also; whilst there is the one definite entry by Pelsaert (made when the *Sardam* skipper Jacob Jacobsz was still alive) which places the wreck in the latitude of $28\frac{1}{2}$ degrees. Therefore, the final amended positions of 28° 37' to 28° 40' show that Claas Gerritsz and Jacop Jansz were either poor mathematicians or else that they too had no desire to correct their original error (made in company with Ariaen Jacobsz). They knew, before leaving Batavia, that Ariaen had been arrested for carelessness in losing his ship; probably they also were appalled by the mutiny, perhaps nervous and shamed (as was Pelsaert) by the time lost in searching for the wreck. It was doubtless more politic to avoid

---

[40] J. E. Heeres, *op. cit.*, p. 52.
[41] Also the coast is high and clearly visible at one and a half miles; cf. Pelsaert's Journals, 12th June.

that significant 28½ degrees, having already "paid little attention" to longitude and over-run the *Batavia* some 200 [600] miles[42] to the east, exactly as Coen warned against. Yet of these two possible reasons for wrong amendment, poor reckoning is probably the more correct: although Ariaen's findings off the coast of Australia can be closely checked, the amended reckonings of Gerritsz and Jansz are no nearer to reality than those originally advanced for the wreck of the *Batavia*. Therefore, seeing that the courses followed by Ariaen Jacobsz in the open boat and Jacob Jacobsz in the *Sardam* can be traced today with fair accuracy, it would not be unreasonable to presume that Ariaen Jacobsz either did not himself check the original findings made after the wreck, or else preferred to allow an error on the part of his steersmen to stand; and that the first casual mention made on 28th September by Pelsaert on his return, of 28½ degrees, is in fact the correct position, given by Jacob Jacobsz.

To return to the wreck. Would it be possible for a ship to strike Noon Reef or Morning Reef without warning? Coen's opinion of that dangerous likelihood has been cited. It was moonlight when in May 1952 I paid my visit to the Wallabis—the conditions were practically the same as when the *Batavia* struck in June 1629. Even on a clear night, a haze hovers; though the moon be full, the isles are mysteriously lost to view. In morning light they are scarcely more discernible, except that, approached from the east, the hump of West Wallabi floats on the sea like a high hat. Distances are enormously deceptive. West Wallabi, reputedly nearly as high as the southern tip of East Wallabi, certainly does not appear so. During the time of my visit the tricks played by light were very marked: Pelsaert comments on this varying visibility in those parts of his Journal that cover salvaging operations. Lort Stokes writes, "It seemed as though nature had determined to entertain us with a series of dissolving views. . . ."[43] The whole atmosphere of the Wallabis is one of elusive form, the spray cast up on the great reefs acts like gauze in a theatre, everything is remote and mysterious, sometimes enlarged, sometimes diminished, never altogether clearly defined. Having seen the islands, it is not difficult to imagine an unforeseen wreck on Noon Reef or Morning Reef, at night, in moonlight; moreover, the Indian Ocean does not strike here with the same direct impact as on the outer reefs of the other groups, or those beyond West Wallabi; only when the wind blows hard (as Pelsaert found) do the breakers roar and pound; whereas even on a still night, as he noted when in the vicinity, the roar of Half Moon Reef is considerable.

Pelsaert also notes that the tide began to ebb rapidly after the ship struck and, after his return, he describes on 27th October an abnormally low tide in the afternoon, associated with a change of wind. Fairbridge comments that in the months of June, July, and August maximum tides are generally in daylight, but that from October to

---

[42] See Pelsaert's letter (Appendix II).
[43] J. Lort Stokes, *op. cit.*, vol. ii, p. 152.

January the best low tide is usually in the morning; in the opposite season it is generally in the late afternoon, with high tide in the early morning; but Fairbridge stresses that abnormalities are frequent because the controlled movements of the tide are often modified by the prevailing wind and barometric conditions. Pelsaert also writes, on 15th November:

> We have found here that the Wind . . . generally blew from the South or the South South East . . . also, in the morning it veers to the South East or East South East but a Little, so that here at the Wreck it is always adverse [*een leger wal is*] and there is continuously a hard surf, and one has to observe precisely [the moment of] smooth [*slechte*] water, otherwise one would never have been able to do anything on the Wreck.

Fairbridge states that in July

> The normal south-westerly winds, which blow for much of the year in this region, would generally back steadily to south, south-east and east, when there would be a day or two of calm and sunshine. . . . Then it would back quickly to north and blow a gale from the north-west for several days; and then the process would be repeated at longer or shorter intervals.[44]

This pattern emerges distinctly from the pages of Pelsaert's Journals.

Teichert, in his notes on tides, stresses unusual tide behaviour throughout the archipelago, and puts forward the opinion that the spring rise and fall on the mainland coast due east of the Wallabi Group is considerably higher than the $1\frac{3}{4}$ feet marked on the charts, being in fact in excess of three feet and probably nearer five.[45] Pelsaert mentions that on 4th June they "had sailed there by high tide" two hours before daybreak, which at that time of year would be about a quarter past six.[46]

At daylight after the wreck two small islands were seen close by. Ariaen Jacobsz, sent to investigate these with the ship's boat, reported that he believed they remained above water at all times, but that he had been unable to get alongside because, although in many places the water was several fathoms deep, in others the reef was all but dry. This tallies with the condition of Noon Reef as described in the *Australia Pilot*; a great reef "nearly 4 miles in length . . . it has also numerous small islets and rocks on it, and encloses a lagoon."[47] As light gained Pelsaert saw 'an island that by guessing lay at least 3 [i.e. 9] miles from the ship"[48], but meantime action became necessary. The majority of the ship's company were landed on the larger of the two

[44] Rhodes W. Fairbridge, *loc. cit.*, p. 4.
[45] C. Teichert, *loc. cit.*, p. 150.
[46] Sunrise at Geraldton, W.A., in early June at 7.10 a.m. Nautical twilight approximately 55 minutes earlier. Wrecked about 4 a.m.
[47] *Australia Pilot*, vol. v, 2nd ed., 1923, p. 325.
[48] See opening entry of Pelsaert's Journals (p. 124).

specks, later christened *Batavia's* Graveyard by those who remained there until the *Sardam* returned. The second was dubbed Traitors Island. The Predikant notes that from it the rescue party sailed away; doubtless the name was bestowed by Jeronimus Cornelisz as part of his campaign to discredit Pelsaert. A third island was named Seals Island by the castaways.

On 27th October, Pelsaert sent men to Seals Island from *Batavia's* Graveyard to signal with smoke to the *Sardam* lying at anchor under the high island, because it was easier for *Sardam* to see such signals made from Seals Island rather than from *Batavia's* Graveyard, although at various times smoke signals were also made from the latter. Pelsaert also writes on 25th September that from *Batavia's* Graveyard he could watch the divers at work at the wreck, fishing up a chest—accordingly he himself jumped into a skiff [*schuitje*] and went to inspect.

From the above evidence, I have come to the conclusion that *Batavia's* Graveyard is the island now known to fishermen as Dick's Island,[49] situated on the eastern extremity of Noon Reef in the Wallabi Group, in latitude 28° 30′.

[Discovery of the wreck itself on the *western* edge of Morning Reef, little more than a mile from the *eastern* edge of Noon Reef, and relics since found on Beacon Island, establish that island as the one named *Batavia's* Graveyard.]

Dick's Island is a limestone and coral "platform", with overhanging ledges to the south and east. It conforms with the extraordinary picture drawn by the contemporary illustrator of the story in *Ongeluckige Voyagie*, and which I venture to think may have been the result of eye-witness description by a survivor, given either to the compiler or the publisher of that book. Why otherwise should it have been so drawn? The formation is unusual to European imagination; in the other illustrations the other isles are conventionally treated, whilst the torture scene has no relation to the true facts of the trials, which were carried out in a tent ashore. Apart from such idle speculation, it would be possible for Pelsaert standing on Dick's Island to see clearly what was happening at a wreck on Noon Reef, while at the same time Long Island (as the fishermen call it) lies less than a mile north of Dick's, and to some extent would mask the latter to a ship at East Wallabi, a "high island". Long Island is low and sandy, therefore likely to be frequented by seals, although they are mentioned by Pelsaert as being present on other isles, and as late as 1843 John Gilbert notes that "all the islands in this group are very thickly inhabited by the seal; we would frequently come upon groups of 7, 8, and 9 lying asleep on the sandy beach. . . ."[50] Long Island has also many bushes for hiding be-

[49] Named after Mr Dick Burton, a Geraldton fisherman who once made it his base, finding that the small beach and lagoon afforded excellent shelter. This island is shown as Goss Island in my *Walkabout* article and on the end papers of my novel *The Wicked and the Fair*, but at that stage I had been misinformed.

[50] BLWA: John Gilbert, Letter to *The Inquirer*, dated 19th April 1843.

neath; another necessary feature. Therefore I believe Long Island to be Seals Island. [The discovery of the wreck does not impair this opinion.]

The high island under which the *Sardam* lay is unquestionably East Wallabi, both by reason of the positions already put forward, and because no vessel of any size could find, or dare to seek, anchorage under West Wallabi. Confusion has always hitherto arisen, as already shown, because there were *two* "high islands", often ambiguously referred to, and never at any time clearly differentiated, in *Ongeluckige Voyagie* or even in Heeres's translations. Thus the "island of Wiebbe Hayes", which is the "long island 2 [6] miles west of the Wreck" on which Pelsaert saw smoke on arrival in the *Sardam*, becomes West Wallabi, which is approximately four miles from Dick's Island (or *Batavia's Graveyard*), but looks to be farther.

It will be recalled that Wiebbe Hayes was a soldier who became leader of a party sent to seek water—though it is obvious from the evidence that Jeronimus expected them to perish. They very nearly did; only after twenty days did they presumably dare to taste the water they found in two pits [*putten*] or caverns, because it rose and fell with the tide.[51] They thought it must be salt, and doubtless the thirsty men feared madness. This rise and fall would be quite possible if the sandy floors of the caverns were an inch or so below sea-level, or if they were connected by crannies; this would also explain why the water became more and more brackish as it was used up, until by 15th November, as Pelsaert said, it became undrinkable. (This supply was rain-water, not rising from a spring, but collected in what geologists call "sink-holes"—crannies in the limestone into which the rain pours through various crevices, in time enlarging the original small basins into quite large "caverns".) In 1840 Lort Stokes discovered on West Wallabi "two caverns similar to that on East Wallaby Island, from which we got three tons of excellent water".[52] The *Australia Pilot* also notes this supply, situated half a mile west of the eastern point.[53] And Teichert writes, "There is one sink hole with good water . . . situated about 200 yards from the shore of the second bay south of the easternmost promontory of the island."[54]

On East Wallabi two "wells" are marked on the Admiralty Chart, but not the "cavern" mentioned by Lort Stokes as lying under Flag Hill, a limestone cavern fifteen feet deep in which he found brackish water.[55] However, an ancient fisherman, the late Captain Dines Jacobsen, told me that he knew of *three* water-holes on East Wallabi; and Pelsaert's men found three on the high island that was *not* "the island of Wiebbe Hayes", when, under his directions, they were burning off.[56] This was in order, firstly, to get more "cats" for eating, and secondly,

[51] Pelsaert's Journals, 20th September 1629.
[52] J. Lort Stokes, *op. cit.*, vol. ii, p. 161.
[53] *Australia Pilot*, vol. v, p. 323.
[54] C. Teichert, *loc. cit.*, p. 176.
[55] J. Lort Stokes, *op. cit.*, vol. ii, p. 155.
[56] Pelsaert's Journals, 10th October 1629.

to see if more "hidden pits as had been found on Wiebbe Hayes's island" could be uncovered. They discovered "a pit with water but very stinking. After that, again a pit with brackish water." But the next day they found a small hole, threw a stone into it and heard a splash; whereon the skipper of the *Sardam* (it was two days before he was sent on his fatal mission) ordered a crowbar and pickaxe to be fetched from the yacht. When the hole was enlarged they found very good water. I have been told that the best well on East Wallabi has been greatly enlarged at some time by pickaxes. It seems very probable that the sailors of the *Sardam* made a start in 1629! This precise evidence of the several water-holes is of itself sufficient to establish the identity of Pelsaert's two "high islands"; similar holes do not exist elsewhere in the archipelago.

From Dick's Island to West Wallabi is approximately six miles as judged by Pelsaert (four in fact).[57] There are several islets and numerous reefs that are on occasions dry, therefore it would have been possible for men on spars (another necessity of the story) to effect a journey from the latter to the former; but it would be much less easy in the case of East Wallabi. Yet if West Wallabi is the closer and the larger, why did Pelsaert, and later those who took Wiebbe Hayes first to East Wallabi, not go to the westerly island first? I believed that the tricky light of the locality had something to do with that, and soon formed my own definite opinion, which nevertheless had to wait for confirmation.

I had reached these conclusions regarding the principal islands and the wreck site after my visits to the Wallabis by fishing boat in 1952. But I still had no visual or even hearsay evidence that either a small island in the correct position to serve as Traitors Island, or a beach on Dick's Island, existed. And if the latter was to be reckoned *Batavia's* Graveyard, a beach there had to be; in his letter the predikant Bastiaensz tells how he "sat on the beach reading", and that he had to do duty for the mutineers by tying up "the little boats with which they navigated".[58] So far as I had been able to observe from fishing craft, Dick's Island rose like a mushroom from the sea, with a sharp ledge about six or seven feet high all round, similar to those that formed the shores of other islands in the group such as Beacon Island and Pigeon Island. [I discarded Beacon Island as a possible *Batavia's* Graveyard because fishermen told me it had no beach. But in fact there *is* a small beach; nor does Beacon rise sharply from the Sea.] None of the fishermen I met at the time had visited Dick's Island. It seemed to me that the only way in which a clear picture of the whole group could be gained was to see it from the air.

Eventually, through the courtesy of the Minister for Air, William McMahon, I was permitted to fly on one of the R.A.A.F. routine survey flights at the time being conducted from Pearce. Imagine my satis-

[57] Ibid., 17th September 1629 gives 2m.; in Summary 2½m.
[58] See Appendix IV.

faction to see clearly that the oval of Dick's Island is broken by a curve on the north-west, and that in the hook of this curve lies a small beach. [On Beacon Island the beach lies on the South, but is very small, with grey sand.] The formation suggests a ceaseless wash or current from Noon Reef; moreover there is a sand spit at the south-west end. Not only were barrels of wine and vinegar washed ashore on *Batavia's* Graveyard, but Jeronimus Cornelisz himself reached the island clinging to a mast. In addition, from the air a second small sand cay can be seen lying about a mile west of Dick's Island in a position suitable to be the second of "two small islands or rocks not so far from the ship" if wrecked on Noon Reef. [There is also a tiny island and some rocks close to the edge of Morning Reef.] Pelsaert saw "an island that by guessing lay at least 3 [9] miles from the ship"—the only one he then thought likely to be of any use. In fact Flagstaff Hill on East Wallabi (which I believe he saw) is rather less than five miles distant from Noon Reef or Morning Reef, but it presents an extraordinarily faraway appearance.

In 1954 the survey sloop *Warrego* visited the islands. Commander A. H. Cooper was kind enough to provide more details regarding Dick's Island. A report sent to me reads

> ... [from the island] the spray and surf on the west side of Noon Reef are in the line of sight between it and the south end of West Wallabi island. This has the effect of making West Wallabi appear far more distant than East Wallabi, and the 50 feet hill on East Wallabi appears to be a good deal higher than any other hill. From the southern part of Noon Reef the Wallabi Islands look almost like one long island, but two small gaps are visible. However, from the observer's low height of eye it could easily be assumed that these two gaps were connected by low-lying land.

In a covering letter Commander Cooper also said that the southern end of West Wallabi appeared to be far more distant than it is; all of which contributes to the belief that it was more or less invisible to Pelsaert's company in the flying spray of the storm after the wreck of the *Batavia*, and that accordingly they first sailed in the ship's boat towards East Wallabi, as appearing both closer and more hopeful. [From Beacon Island West Wallabi is scarcely visible.] Commander Cooper added

> I have the impression that East Wallabi is the island of substance, of height, whilst the other is low and flat and uninteresting. This notwithstanding the fact that both are supposed to be of roughly the same actual height.[59]

A note on a naval sketch map of the islands of Noon Reef, done at the same time, states that the one marked (c) (Dick's Island) is "about 250 yards long and 8 feet high. Surface of coral chips and sand, 50%

---

[59] Letter from Commander A. H. Cooper, R.A.N., dated 9th September 1954.

scrub covered."[60] Long Island (taken to be Seals Island) lies a mile to the north. To the west are several small islands, the nearest about a mile distant, being the same small island I had noted from the air. Reefs and shallows stretch away west and north-west to the two Wallabi Islands and other islets, but to the east lies the deep channel of Goss Passage, separating this cluster from Morning Reef and several more islets scattered over its formidable length: probably these are the "islands and reefs" to which Pelsaert sailed in a small boat on 25th October searching for valuable jetsam but finding only "wood-work" from the wreck.

Thus the evidence of the Journals (not forgetting the solitary entry of $28\frac{1}{2}$ degrees Southern Latitude) and the other records quoted, as well as the observations of naval surveyors and local fishermen which support personal impressions gained on my own visits, combine to substantiate my original conclusion that the ship *Batavia* was wrecked in the vicinity of Noon Reef, not far from Dick's Island, in the Wallabi Group. [The now discovered wreck lies rather more than a mile to the east.]

It is unlikely that any further documented evidence that might clarify this point still exists. It is, however, possible that some day relics may be found that will either confirm or destroy this theory: many guns were cast overboard [these have been found], and although the majority of chests were salvaged, Pelsaert stated that the one surmounted by a cannon was left submerged. For this Abel Tasman was ordered to search in 1644. Also, although Pelsaert makes it quite clear that the surrounding isles were meticulously scoured for every item of any value that might be carried back to Java, the bodies of the predikant's murdered wife and children remained buried in a common grave on *Batavia's* Graveyard; they had not been cast into the sea to the fishes along with the majority of the victims. Also, seven of the murderers were hanged on Seals Island. The latter were probably left hanging in the custom of the day. Although it is very likely that their bones soon disintegrated or were blown into the sea, some of the gallows timber may well have lasted three hundred years, buried in the sand; more probably it has been unsuspectingly used up by fishermen, hungry for wood; if indeed Pelsaert did not himself, in his recorded eagerness to salvage everything, have the corpses cut down and the timbers carried away aboard the *Sardam*.

---

[60] Sketch map showing islets in the vicinity of Noon Reef, Houtman's Rocks: photostat sent to me by Commander Cooper, 1954.

APPENDIX X

THE LANDINGS IN AUSTRALIA

The accuracy of Ariaen Jacobsz's reckoning during the open boat journey up the Western Australian coast can be substantiated. In his account Pelsaert states that they first sighted the Southland in the afternoon of 8th June in the vicinity of latitude 28° 13', "and saw shortly thereafter the continent, and guessed to be 6 miles N by W of our ship".[1] Heeres translated this: "and shortly after sighted the mainland, which we estimated to lie 6 miles north by west of our ship."

In fact Pelsaert is ambiguous: is the continent six (eighteen miles north by west of the boat they are in, or of the wreck of the *Batavia*? Or does he mean that the boat they are in (and taking their position from) is six (eighteen) miles north by west of the *Batavia*? Taking into consideration his usual mode of expression when estimating a position, I prefer the last. This point, however, is not so important as the extraordinary (and impossible) "N by W" direction.

In an article published in *Walkabout*[2] I went to some pains to sustain the opinion that Pelsaert had meant "N *to* W" rather than "N *by* W", this opinion being founded on his use of the Dutch *te* rather than his usual *ten*. And I backed this up by pointing out that the maps of Hessel Gerritsz (which Pelsaert must have seen) and that of Abel Tasman, 1644,[3] distinctly show that thirty miles *north* of the Abrolhos the mainland does lie *almost* west of the archipelago; indeed, in the latter chart there is a distinct gulf in the continental coast directly west of the islands.

However, greater familiarity with Pelsaert's handwriting has made me abandon the alternate meaning on which I pinned my argument. The *n* in his *ten* is frequently rudimentary, therefore the direction he gave was most certainly "north by west". Of course, the latter half of my argument is still valid; but on the whole I now think it more likely that Pelsaert made a slip and wrote W when he meant to write E. Certainly, five months later, when the *Sardam* sailed from the Abrolhos to the mainland, he gave her course as "E.N.East". Of course, in the previous September, searching for the wreck, they had tacked back and forth close to the mainland both above and below the islands,

[1] In J. E. Heeres, *The Part Borne by the Dutch in the Discovery of Australia, 1606-1765*, p. 56, this is given as *zagen oock korts daarnaar het vaste landt, ende gisten 6 mijlen N. ten W. van ons schip te zijn*. It is the same on the microfilm of the original Journal entry used by E. D. Drok and myself.
[2] "The Wreck of the *Batavia*", *Walkabout Magazine*, vol. xxi, no. 1, January 1955, p. 37.
[3] Abel Janszoon Tasman's Journal of His Discovery of Van Diemens Land and New Zealand in 1642, Map I.

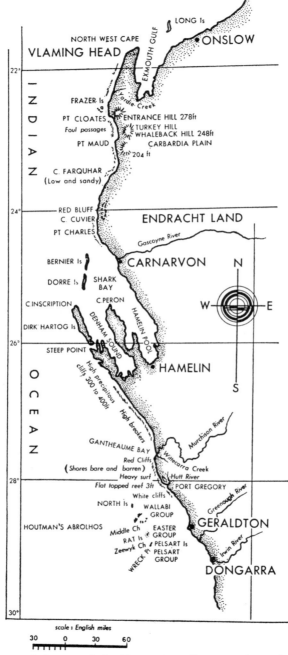

Author's map of the part of the Western Australian coast along which Pelsaert sailed.

and must therefore have been much better orientated than when they left the wreck in the open boat. Yet it is still possible that Pelsaert believed a gulf to lie west of the islands.

At this time all longitudinal assessment, made by Ile de Ferro[4] reckoning, was still extremely vague. Only once or twice in the *Sardam* record of the return trip to the islands does Pelsaert give longitudinal positions—these seem correct enough when based on the Ile de Ferro ruling. But there is no attempt by Houtman, Coen or Pelsaert to state the longitudinal position of the Abrolhos. The 1644 Tasman map, drawn from the information of all "the Company's discoverers" which would include Pelsaert, since Tasman never touched this part of the coast, still shows a blank space on the mainland directly opposite the islands, above which the land runs to the north-west.

Pelsaert writes that on the night of 8th June they lost sight of the land by necessity of standing out to sea, but regained it on the 9th, "a level Rocky land without trees, about as high as Dover in England". On Admiralty Chart No. 1723 the coast carries here the words White Cliffs. The comparison is inevitable, even when the cliffs are seen from the air. In fact, these cliffs lie three or four miles south of the above position, but during the night the voyagers were uncertain of their course and only guessed (as so very often) where they were. Moreover, the wind was "mostly N.W." and they were likely to lose height. Continuing for the 9th:

> Here we saw a small inlet as well as low dune land, where we intended to land, but approaching, noticed that there was a big surf and many breakers near the shore.

On the latitude 28° 13½' lies a small bay into which the Hutt River sometimes empties: the river has a wide sandbar, more often closed than open. A mile farther north, wide white dunes flank the Hutt Lagoon. Off shore is marked "Heavy Surf".[5]

Objections to this area being the spot mentioned by Pelsaert have been made by several writers, on the grounds of there not being a sufficiently well-marked "small inlet". However there is a distinct eastwards curve of the coast, and it is also possible that at that time the Hutt Lagoon was an open inlet. The mainland shores even today are by no means as stable as the island coasts, especially where there are windswept dunes. Also, the *Australia Pilot*[6] notes that with heavy westerly gales the sea washes over the low sandy beach into the lagoon. Since Pelsaert viewed the coast during a heavy north-west gale, the present lagoon might well have appeared to be an inlet.

[4] Ile de Ferro is one of the Canary Islands. Later in the seventeenth century the meridian of Ferro was reckoned as 20°W. of Paris. If the earlier starting point is used, the *Sardam* positions are within reason, whereas using the latter they are impossible. On 31st July Pelsaert gives the *Sardam's* position as latitude 29°9' and longitude 132° 8'.
[5] Admiralty Chart No. 1056, inset.
[6] *Australia Pilot*, vol. v, 2nd ed., 1923, p. 316.

> To this spot Pelsaert returned in the *Sardam* on 16th November:
>
> ... sailed again with small sail close along the shore at a distance of a Cannon [*cartoue*] shot from the surf; towards noon noticed the small Inlet where on 8 June when with the boat we were searching for Water, we thought to run in. ... Here saw several smokes rising up, and were altogether gladdened that our own folk might be there [the skipper and men of the *Sardam* who had been "blown away" on 13th October]. Therefore I have immediately sent the yawl to the land in order to get sure information about this place and the smokes; who found there around a steep corner, there where we thought would be Water, running water, which was brackish on the side of the Sea, but Higher up was Fresh. They also saw many footprints of people and small footpaths running to the Mountains, with many smokes, but the Blacks kept themselves hidden. ... At this good opportunity, I have ordered the two sentenced delinquents, to wit, Wouter Loos and Jan Pelgrom de By van Bemel, with the Champan provided with everything, to sail to this land. ... This small Inlet is situated on the latitude of 27 degrees 51 Minutes.

This correction of Ariaen Jacobsz's original position (of being in the vicinity of 28° 13′) fixes on a point crossed by cliffs of red rock, which I have myself seen from the air. It appears to me to be even more inaccurate than the 28° 37′-40′ given as possible corrected wreck-sites. However, arguments in favour of Gantheaume Bay being the "small inlet" have been from time to time advanced; more recently by Mr P. E. Playford[7] who has traversed the area in question during geological surveys and is convinced that a cove north of Red Bluff at approximately 27° 43′ is the spot. There is a beach north of this cove, and a fresh stream in Wittecarra Gully, as well as Meenarra Hill, a very conspicuous high point.

In conversation, Mr Playford put forward not only his own observations (made from the land) but also those made by George Grey in his Diaries.[8] Perusal of the latter, however, seems to me to strengthen rather than lessen the case for the Hutt River area. In the first place, Grey mentions that the Bay was "lashed throughout its whole extent by a fearful surf".[9] He, also, was in an open boat after shipwreck, and with some misgiving decided to land. His boat was broken to pieces, and this in March; nor does he make specific mention of bad weather as does Pelsaert; so that the area is not promising from the sea. Grey then describes finding the small fresh stream and, a mile or so inland, "came out upon one of the most romantic and picturesque looking estuaries I had yet seen".[10] There were many native paths; also black

---

[7] P. E. Playford, "The Wreck of the *Zuytdorp* on the Western Australian coast in 1712", *Early Days: Journal and Proceedings of the Western Australian Historical Society*, vol. v, part 5, 1959, pp. 5-41.

[8] George Grey, *Journals of Two Expeditions of Discovery in North-West and Western Australia during the years 1837, 38 and 39.*

[9] Ibid., vol. i, p. 411. [10] Ibid., vol. ii, p. 3.

swans. Shortly after, Grey found the mouth of the Murchison River. Pelsaert's landing party made no mention of seeing swans—that was left to Vlamingh in 1697, at the Swan River which he named.

Mr Playford also partly bases his contention on Heeres's translation of Pelsaert's words, which differs slightly from that made by Mr Drok, already quoted. Heeres translates:

> I therefore sent the pinnace ashore directly for the purpose of getting certain information regarding the place and the clouds of smoke we had seen; *the men in her*, after rounding a steep point, where we had suspected the presence of water, discovered a *running streamlet*, of which the water was brackish near the sea, but quite fresh higher up.

The italics are mine. The more literal translation by Mr Drok reads:

> Therefore I have immediately sent the yawl to the land in order to get sure information about this place and the smokes; who found around a steep corner, there where we thought would be Water, running water, which was brackish on the side to the Sea, but Higher up was Fresh.[11]

This gives me the impression that the landing party found the water on foot; Mr Playford imagines the "men in her"— i.e., in the pinnace or yawl—pulling round a "steep point" such as exists at his selected site at the south end of Gantheaume Bay. I envisage them walking up the Hutt River, which takes a sharp bend around a high ridge. This river is described also by Grey: "The estuary became narrower here [the estuary presumably being what is now called the Hutt Lagoon] and shortly . . . we came upon a river running into it from the eastward; its mouth was about forty yards wide, the stream strong, but the water brackish, and it flowed through a very deep ravine, having steep limestone hills on each side."[12] He noted earlier that native paths ran everywhere and that eastwards rose a "high range of rocky limestone hills". There is no mistaking this spot for any other, as Grey himself gave the Hutt River its name. Like Pelsaert, he mentions brackish water, whereas the Wittecarra stream receives no such comment. The hills (Pelsaert's "mountains"), now named Mount Victoria and Mount Albert, rise to 500 feet.

Another point in favour of the Hutt River location is the lie of the coast. On 9th June Pelsaert mentions that the coast "stretches here mostly N by W and S by E." Whatever else changes in a few centuries, the compass-determined general lie of land does not. And, if the Gantheaume Bay area is to be cited, the fact that after Bluff Point is

[11] *Daarom heb jck de schuijt dadelyck naar 't landt gesonden, om seker bescheijt van de plaats ende roocken te krygen, die daar om eenen steylen hoeck, daar wij vermoeden van water gehadt hadden, een afflopent water vonden, dat vooren aan de zeekant brack, maar om hooge zoet was.* (See J. E. Heeres, *op. cit.*, p. 62.)

[12] George Grey, *op. cit.*, vol. ii, p. 19.

passed the coast turns almost due north, then N.E. by N. and S.W. by S., must not be overlooked.

Taking all these matters into consideration, I remain in favour of the Hutt River area being regarded as the landing place of *Sardam's* men, as well as the spot at which Wouter Loos and de Bye were marooned. Ariaen Jacobsz's original fix of approximately 28° 13′ seems nearer the mark than the correction made by Gerritsz and Jansz on the *Sardam*. No further mention is made of the mainland coast in the continuing record of the *Sardam's* journey home to Java, for on 22nd November she altered course to North by East "in order to get in view the Cocus Islands".

However, in the record of the open boat journey farther up the coast in June with Ariaen Jacobsz as skipper, accuracy of reckoning prevails. They kept on as steadily as bad weather would permit, hoping always to land in order to search for water. On 12th July they had the latitude of 27°, but were unable to find an opportunity to land because of strong breakers. Pelsaert writes that the coast was "very steeply hewn without any foreshore or inlets as have other countries, but it seemed to be a dry cursed earth without foliage or grass." On latitude 27°, Admiralty Chart No. 1056 notes "High Sandstone Cliffs" and "High Breakers".

The Journal continues until at last on the morning of 15th July they came to

> ... the point where a large reef stretched about one [i.e., 3] mile to Sea; then we ran between the land reef and the sea reef, which we guessed to be at 23 degrees, and sailed thus along the Coast, alongside which stretches a reef, where between the land [and the reef] appears to be very smooth and still water; we did our best to get into it but found no opening till nearly noon, when we found an opening where there was no surf; ran into that, but it was very rocky and sometimes not more than 2 feet of water—This coast had a dune foreland about one mile [i.e., 3] wide before one comes to the High Land, therefore began to dig in this place.

These reefs are clearly marked on Admiralty Charts, but recent aerial photographs of the area supplied by the R.A.A.F. to the Commonwealth Bureau of Mineral Resources and made into "mosaics" by the Lands and Survey Department of Western Australia, give a much clearer picture, and one that fits Pelsaert's words.[13] From these it can be seen that the breakers of the "sea-reef" do not show as being clear of the "land-reef" until north of Point Maud, where, almost exactly on 23°, a formidable reef lies approximately three miles from the shore; but a wide passage offers no difficulty to a boat wishing to sail between the two reefs.

At first I believed that the *Batavia's* company sailed north inside the "sea-reef" until they found an opening in the "land-reef" that en-

[13] Original air photos by R.A.A.F., Minilya 2/50, 1/01. Yanrey 15/02, 14/95 etc.

abled them to reach the shore near Whaleback Hill, 243 feet. But reports from people I have interested in the matter and who have paid recent visits to that area, both by land and sea, suggest a spot north of Fraser Island as the more likely. In the first place, although I have evidence that water cannot be obtained by digging in the sands near Whaleback Hill, I am also informed by geologists that there is small likelihood of *rock holes*, such as Pelsaert mentions, being found in that vicinity. It is difficult to think that the *Batavia* company could miss the good Point Cloates landing, but Pelsaert gives no wind data on this date, and if it was rough they may have seen the point ahead bounded by strong surf (as the aerial photos, taken in June, show it to be) and preferred to search further. Certainly they cannot have landed at Point Cloates, because water is easily to be found by digging: a diary now in my possession, kept in 1889 by G. J. Brockman of Minilya Station near the present port of Carnarvon, describes a trip by boat and foot along this very shore. He was endeavouring to sink wells for stock, beachcombing and dry-shelling on the reefs as he went. He mentions getting good water at Point Cloates by digging; and I understand the whaling station that existed there until a few years ago drew all its supplies from sand wells.

Suppose therefore that the *Batavia* company avoided Point Cloates but ran in just north of Fraser Island and managed to land. They would have found there a large sand patch and a foreland of dunes nearly three miles wide, before higher land is reached. Just here the coast bumps out, whilst inland, as the mosaics show, a rocky range rises up to 350 feet; and behind, the land stretches away in a tableland.[14] Pelsaert writes that they landed and at once dug several holes in the dunes, but found salt water. In his diary G. J. Brockman writes: "I started out six miles [i.e., north from Point Cloates] to put a well down. . . . I got salt water in one well and stone in the other, so returned to camp."

A point six miles north of Point Cloates is directly opposite Fraser Island. Later, returning from Yardie Creek (his most northerly camp) Brockman mentions camping where "the stony ranges come within ¼ mile of the beach". Next he struck across "the big point to the large bay 7 miles north of Point Cloates; here I put a well down about 3 ft, but don't think it will stand being so close to the sea". The following day he "put a well down about a mile from the beach, got a large supply of good water". This, I imagine, is the present Beejoo Well. In addition, several more wells are map-marked in this area. It can be seen that these statements confine the place of Pelsaert's landing to an arid stretch between Point Cloates and Brockman's "big point", beyond which bulge, as the photographs and maps show, the ranges lie close to the shore, with no wide "dune foreland".

Pelsaert continues: "A party of folk therefore went to the High

[14] Shown also on 1944 W.A. Ordnance Maps No. 1237 Yanrey, F50/9 and 12, Zone I, and Original Plans P/1032, P/1034, Lands and Surveys Department, W.A.

land where they found by chance some small holes in a rock that were full of fresh water that the rain had left there." Great luck, indeed; because, having the following morning continued to search for "more such holes in the range", they discovered that "beyond the heights the country was flat again, without trees, foliage or grass, except for high anthills thrown up of earth, which in the distance were not unlike the huts of people".

Normally this area is a spinifex plain; there must have been a drought in 1629; or possibly it had been burnt out by summer lightning. Mr Murray Johnstone, a geologist on the staff of W.A. Petroleum Ltd, told me that he has seen the plains in this vicinity lying stark and dry after such fires. Also, that north of Point Cloates and well inland, there are innumerable anthills.

The desperate party from the *Batavia* camped for the night by the rock holes and scooped some twenty gallons into their casks. After their disappointment they decided to set sail for Java. They had seen a few natives, whose presence meant the existence of water; but the blacks had run off when approached and further search seemed vain.

They continued therefore to sail north inside the reef until they found another opening. They were then in the latitude of 22° 17'. Pelsaert writes that he had the intention to "run to the river of Jacop Remmessens", but that the wind and the currents forced them from the coast. Probably also the steering of Ariaen Jacobsz, who had always intended to sail to Java or Malacca and had no intention of returning to the wreck at this stage. A course was thereupon set for Java. Eleven days later they sighted land, in the evening reaching the island now called Nusa Kambangan. They had made an epic trip; it was a triumph of navigation for Ariaen Jacobsz, whatever his other shortcomings.

For more than two centuries mystery surrounded the "River of Jacop Remmessens". A watercourse in the same area is marked "Willems Rivier" in the 1618-28 maps of Hessel Gerritsz, cartographer of the V.O.C. This has been variously identified as the Ashburton River and the opening into Exmouth Gulf, since it appeared on the maps after the visit of Willem Jansz, uppermerchant on the *Mauritius*, to an "island" in lat. 22° S., in 1618.[15] But on Keppler's map of 1630[16] appears "Jac. Rommer Rivier", and on Calvert's reproduction of the Tasman map of 1644[17] *both* rivers are shown close together, the last-mentioned being the more southerly. They may well have been one and the same. As far as Jacop Remmessens's river is concerned, the Dutch historian P. A. Leupe states that he found a steersman

---

[15] T. D. Mutch, "The First Discovery of Australia", *Journal of the Royal Australian Historical Society*, vol. xxviii, 1942, part 5, pp. 44-6.

[16] J. E. Heeres, *op. cit.*, p. 10.

[17] A. F. Calvert, *The Discovery of Australia*, 2nd ed. (1902), map facing p. 136 (reproduction of Tasman's map—see note 3 above).

named Jacob Remmetz on the *Vrede* in 1619,[18] but I have discovered nothing further about this ship. On the other hand, although Professor Heeres makes no reference in *The Part Borne by the Dutch in the Discovery of Australia* to the following statement made by him in Muller's edition of Tasman's Journal, it seems to me to be well worth consideration: he writes that "as early as 1615, certainly before January 30, 1616, a vessel named *Mauritius de Nassau*, sailed from a Dutch Port, under the command of Jan Remmetszoon, of Purmerend."[19] This ship had instructions to direct a course to the supposed Southland and to see if there existed an opening into the South Seas. If not, Remmetszoon was to run on to the East Indies. But, "Nothing is known of the result of this expedition which might possibly have led to fresh discoveries."[20]

This voyage was not originated by the V.O.C. but if Remmetszoon did discover a river, the fact might easily have become generally known. And, allowing for the usual carelessness in nomenclature, there seems little difference between Jan Remmetszoon and Jacob Remmetz or Remmessens. Pelsaert's definite statement regarding the place where he expected to find a river clearly points to Yardie Creek. A sketch in the field notebooks of A. J. Bennett, who surveyed this area for the Lands and Surveys Department of Western Australia in 1912, shows a wide mouth.[21] On a typewritten list of information about place-names compiled by Chief Draftsman J. Hope during this period, Yardie Creek has set against it: "The Jacob Remmessens River of the Dutch, 1628, and the river Guillaume of the French 1801-3. Its appearance from the sea is that of the mouth of a large river." Added by hand in red ink is the note: "Hence the error".[22] This error appears to have been corrected now. In 1913 a map compiled by C. Y. Dean shows the name Jacob Remmessens River bracketed with Yardie Creek for the first time on one of the Public Plans of Western Australia.[23]

Of Yardie Creek, G. J. Brockman (who had seen the dramatic landscapes of the Kimberleys) writes in his diary: "The tide being high we were able to cross the Bar and sailed up a mile, with precipitous rocks on each side from two to 300 feet above water. . . . This is really a grand sight, I have seen nothing like it anywhere."[24]

Mr Murray Johnstone told me that a bushman's tale declares that high on these rocks can be seen a carved inscription, reputedly in

[18] P. A. Leupe, *De Reizen der Nederlanders naar het Zuidland op Nieuw Holland*, p. 58.
[19] Abel J. Tasman's Journal, p. 92.
[20] Ibid., p. 92.
[21] LSDWA: A. J. Bennett, Field Survey Book No. 60, p. 60.
[22] LSDWA: Original unnumbered and undated list of place names compiled by J. Hope. (File No. 98/300.)
[23] LSDWA: Original print, Public Plan 95/300, No. 3, signed C.Y.D. (C. Y. Dean), dated 27th Augst 1913.
[24] G. J. Brockman, MS. Diary 2nd February 1888 to 13th August 1889 (in possession of H. Drake-Brockman): entry dated 31st March 1889, p. 83.

Dutch. If this should prove to be true, more may yet be learnt about Jacob Remmessens.

However that may be, the fact remains that Francisco Pelsaert himself slept for one night on the continent of Australia, probably within a few miles of Point Cloates. He was the first European of distinction to do so. And, if one disregards the two men marooned farther down the coast, the sailors from the wrecked *Batavia* who were in his party, have also their share of this historic honour. As far as I can discover, no earlier landing party ever dared to risk a night ashore.

Appendix XI

HENRIETTA DRAKE-BROCKMAN'S ACCOUNT OF THE WRECK EXPEDITION

[In June 1963, a wreck was discovered on the reefs of the Wallabi Group of the Houtman Abrolhos. One month later, a major expedition to the site was undertaken, and Henrietta Drake-Brockman accompanied it. Shortly afterwards, she wrote a letter to her family, expressing her mounting excitement as piece after piece of evidence had come to light, confirming the accuracy of her years of painstaking research, and that this, indeed, was the *Batavia*. The results of what came to be known as the Batavia Expedition necessitated last-minute changes to *Voyage to Disaster*, and Henrietta Drake-Brockman returned to Perth to revise the chapter entitled "The Site of the Wreck", which was then published as Appendix IX.

Henrietta Drake-Brockman's original letter, typewritten, and annotated in her own handwriting, is held in the National Library of Australia. The following version has undergone minor editing, to correct typographical errors and to delete personal references.]

Perth, 15.8.63

Dear Family

The *Batavia* Expedition was really exciting. Dick Drok and I were motoring up, leaving 11 p.m., on July 31st, when a radio came from the army ship *Lerida* that we had to be in Geraldton by 8 a.m. on 1st August. So we set off about nine and drove all through the night. Reached Geraldton—320 or so miles north—just as the faintest light showed. Toured wharfs looking for our ship, and found her, but all fast asleep. So took a turn round the wharf and went back about 7 a.m.

We eventually left at 10 am, after all our rush! 47 miles to the Wallabis—a pleasant enough trip with lunch aboard. These little army ships are rather quaint, run stores, and repairs—all dressed as soldiers (when in uniform!). Skipper a 2nd Lieutenant; rest, except for galley-man, N.C.O.s with one warrant officer. All terrifically interested in the venture, and I spent some time reading bits from the Journals' galley prints—which thrilled them too. They have three divers, left at the islands, but met on return journey, all under twenty and S.A.S.—a commando unit.

We anchored off the navy ship, which, though slightly larger, was not as neat a vessel as *Lerida*.

We came in to the anchorage by the northern passage instead of Goss, as I went last time, and it was quite strange. It is a very noticeable fact, how greatly the apparent heights of the islands vary from different angles and from day to day.

There were various small boats bobbing round and men in black rubber skin suits, and then Hugh Edwards and Max Cramer dashed up in style in the *Batavia* boat—aluminium, donated by de Haviland, and a very smart piece.

Beacon Island is hammer-shaped, as on the map I made [see page 276]—very low, covered in a yellow-daisy-flowered plant, with some shrubs. And there, to my irritation, was the "little beach" of the Predikant, quite clear though rather grey in contrast to other coral strands, on other islands; and I cannot think why the fishermen said there was NO beach on Beacon. Otherwise I would have been 100% right, rather than merely 90%—Beacon was always the obvious island, if *Batavia* was dead on course, as apparently she was.

We went out that afternoon to the site, not the three miles Pelsaert said from the island but about two. Had to tour round the reef, though, to get there—a debatable point is whether Jacobsz went straight in, over the breakers, which we mostly thought he did—particularly David Johnson, the fisherman whose guests we were—we went out in his boat, first saw where the several guns they had lifted from the deep were, by a float (petrol drums) waiting to be picked up.

There were three very dramatic moments for me: first, the sight of the great anchor on the reef under water; secondly, the first moment the eleven foot gun broke the surface of the ocean after 334 years; and thirdly, the moment the skull, with its hanging jaw, came leering and ghastly from the sand.

Dick and I went over immediately, at the wreck, with the skin men. The water was gloriously clear, and I did not once think either of sharks or the coldness—too excited! Many of the guns had already been shifted but there were plenty still lying on either side of a sort of trough the hull must have made. And there was the giant pick, really beautiful, the shaft covered with short soft russet weed, the sun dapples and beams lighting it. Indeed, the diffused light underwater is extremely pleasant, and the fish swimming by unperturbed, so elegant—indeed, everything on the reef edge was—the great flat rounds of the cabbage leaf coral, a russet green—the corals here are not as bright as those in the Dampier archipelago—though some of the stag-horn is bluish. They said there were seven smaller anchors—those kedges, I suppose, with which they forlornly tried to wind *Batavia* from the reef. But the lovely large one must be at least twelve feet long—the next time I went down, one of the camera men took one of me hauling myself down the shaft. Do hope it comes out (TV) but expect it will look awful of me. I am hardly yet graceful at the game! But it was as splendid as I have always thought, and would be quite a good sport for me, despite age, if ever I could get opportunity.

They fished up all sorts of relics from the wreck—some of the pottery pieces are charming—one little brown one [would] need very little cleaning to go in one's lounge. Other items are in the press clippings sent you. The nautical instruments seem the most interesting to me. They also got half a leather belt with a knife or dagger in its case. Cannon balls, gunpowder canisters, sheets of bronze that evidently [had] been part of a box or chest, and very hardly touched by 300 years—not at all encrusted like the pewter coffee and other pots. Also a mortar in bronze, quite perfect (no pestle, alas) with Amor Vincit Omnia round the edge and date 1625.

A hundred silver coins of different countries and denominations. None later, when I left, than 1625. On pressure they doled me one out, and a very bad piece too. I wanted three—one for me, one for Dick, and one for Douglas Stewart, but no hope. Shall try again. Some were very good—and I could have had cleaned and mounted for me to wear as a lapel brooch.

To return to the first day: the navy set a charge to sunder two guns, and them we transferred to their ship, and set out to raise the cannons at the float. They started with the large one—there were two other embossed bronze ones—but though it rose from the water, it was too heavy for them, and their winch mast broke. So back went the cannon to the sea. And the navy boat to Geraldton—Dick had to go with them, too, to get back to school on Monday—too bad. We also had Mrs Johnson's collie-dog with us on the navy ship, and not the least strange part of raising the gun was the dog's excitement—thought it was a huge sea monster as it rose pallidly from the sea floor—and barked madly as it broke from the water.

The next day I did not go out to the wreck, but watched digging and sieving rock on shore—just before Dick left we two were ferried over to a tiny isle near the reef that he and I now think must be Traitors—the following day I was taken to the one they now call Seals—but I won't accept it at all—too far off, too difficult of access, no bushes at all. Seals are there now, we saw their souffle marks made shortly before, but they had gone. There is part of a thirty foot length of mast there—17 inch circumference on the part cut off and taken to Beacon for a chopping block. It could be the *Batavia* chopped mainmast, as it is in the direct line of drift. And it is certainly very old. They did bring up part of her timbers from under a ledge, though really only the shape of the ship remains—that trough is the 150 feet that I was told she was likely to be, incidentally.

Sunday everyone had a rest, except for digging up the skeleton. There were others under the house, but Johnson would not let them tunnel—a pity—as I feel sure that they would probably find the Predikant's family bones and so make identification sure. This could have been the eldest son—he was a big fellow, but still thin. Teeth broken—

shattered—so I really think he was hit with a dissel [adze], though the doctor insisted the head cut was a sword, a dissel would have cut the throat and shattered the teeth with the haft at one blow. De Vries is the only one stated to have been killed with swords—could be, as he lay not more than fifty yards from the sea, and the little cove there, if he ran into it, is not one that washes to sea—as I had imagined—they would have had to pull him in and cover him—he was no more than 3 foot or so, under. The men called him Charlie and made a lot of ribald jokes, but they talked and talked about him all evening, and I think were a bit shattered by his ghastly appearance until he was shifted—I heard a lot of talk next morning about nightmares; queer, isn't it?

At the end of Beacon, on the thin point, is a strange cell-like foundation, about two feet high, made of coral slabs, laid very professionally in walls. Max would have this was a "fort"—I said it might be a look-out to see what was coming ashore from the wreck, but was very skeptical until I heard it had been buried under scrub. I made them take me one day to *my* Seals Island, and there they found another such structure in a hollow, and larger. Pelsaert does say Jeronimus had a prison, and the Predikant that others were "imprisoned" on Seals Island—so perhaps? Both situations are so queer that it certainly does not seem likely that fishermen bothered to build them. Anyway, when I left they were all ready to believe that my Seals Island was indeed the right one on which the hangings took place etc.

Another day we went to West Wallabi, and undoubtedly found the spot where the fight took place between Wiebbe Hayes's men and the mutineers. Two small islands from which one group could shout at the others, the water in wells etc. I did not manage to see it close, as they went to the west coast instead of the east, as I begged, and after struggling more than a mile through thick scrub full of stinging nettles, and riddled with mutton bird holes into which I kept falling, Mrs Johnson (who was nearly in tears despite her younger years) and I gave it up and after climbing to the highest point to see the layout, stumbled back via the beach. This island has hundreds of carpet snakes, we were photographed wreathed in them, and a dozen [were] caught to take back to Beacon and Perth as pets. I liked them, myself, they felt lovely!

As we all sat round the two tables in the kitchen of the Johnsons' camp at night, pirates weren't in it. We were fourteen strong, twelve men, mostly dark and unshaven, so they looked villainous enough for anything, and Mrs J.—Petra—and me. She was about 35, had been a maternity nurse at King Edward's—as a matter of contrast, she is one of the quietest and gentlest young women I have ever met! Could, I suppose, be called an old-fashioned girl. Her husband [had an] interesting history which he told me one day when the others were diving and he and I alone in the boat. They have been married only three years, and this warm domestic atmosphere surrounding all the rest was piquant to say the least. She fed us very well, her large family, and one of the camera men was a first class cook, too. I was very sorry I had to leave after five days—all those proofs at home. It was a perfect holiday so far as I was concerned, and they all begged me to stay— especially Mrs Johnson, who really loved having me—a nice and unexpected sensation for me—and also said she couldn't bear all those men alone. I said she'd get used to it, but she said she was more accustomed to women and babies! For me, it was like old nor'west days again. And one of those so *Australian* occasions I like so much— from all walks of life, that party, but all perfectly at ease and enjoying it.

Some people still haver about the *Batavia* angle. But it is quite certain. Dick and I are. Every single thing fits like a glove. There is no single unrelated item or place. They are sure themselves, too, but still hope to find what they consider conclusive proof. But I don't know what they think they mean by that—they won't find the name painted on anything!

I am enclosing a rubbing off the one gun I saw in Geraldton—and there is the VOC plus A for Amsterdam.

[Handwritten postscript] Have now all come back, and equally certain it is the *Batavia*.

The book is now announced for November and the jacket chosen pleases me very much. It has been a ghastly ordeal—and still perhaps page proofs.

BIBLIOGRAPHY

OFFICIAL DOCUMENTS IN MANUSCRIPT FORM

Batavia and *Sardam* Journals of Francisco Pelsaert. ARAKA, VOC: 1010. The Hague, Holland.
Last Letter of Francisco Pelsaert, dated 12th December 1629. ARAKA, VOC: 1630^{II}.
Brieff Bouck, 25th September 1629 to 20th September 1630. Nederlandsche Comptoir im Jambij. ARAKA.
Bennett, A. L., Field Survey Book No. 60. LSDWA.
Dagh Register, Casteel Batavia, dated 22nd March 1636. Remark re Pelsaert's life at Agra. ARAKA, VOC: 1031 (1637^I).
Hope, J., Original typewritten list of place names. File No. 98/300. LSDWA. (The list itself is unnumbered and undated.)
Letter, Antonio van Diemen to Pieter de Carpentier, dated 30th November 1629. ARAKA, VOC: 1009, O.B. (1630^I).
Letter, Governor-General and Council to Directors, dated 15th December 1629. ARAKA, VOC: 1009, O.B. (1630^I).
Letter, Pieter van den Broecke to Directors, dated 16th December 1627. ARAKA, VOC: 1004 (1628^{II}).
Original Air Photos by R.A.A.F., LSDWA, Minilya 2/50, 1/01; Yanrey 15/02, 14/95 etc.
Original Plans, LSDWA, P/1032, P/1034, Litho/95/300.
Original print, LSDWA, Public Plan 95/300, No. 3.
Remonstrantie of Francisco Pelsaert. ARAKA, VOC: 4464, v18, pp. 1-3.
Resolution of Appointment of Francisco Pelsaert for Renewed Term of Office, dated 16th July 1620. ARAKA, VOC: 983 (1621^I).
Resolution of Governor-General and Council (death sentences), 28th January 1630. ARAKA, VOC: 1011.
Resolution of Appointment of Francisco Pelsaert to Jambi Expedition, dated 27th April 1630. ARAKA, VOC: 1011 (1631^I).
Resolution of Governor-General and Council dated 13th September 1630. Report, *inter alia*, of Pelsaert's death. ARAKA. VOC: 1011.
Resolutions of Heeren XVII at Amsterdam, dated 17th March 1632 and 31st August 1635, re estate of Francisco Pelsaert. ARAKA, VOC: 185.

PERSONAL CORRESPONDENCE, ETC.

Brockman, G. J., Diary, 2nd February 1888 to 13th August 1889. In the possession of the author, H. Drake-Brockman.
Letter from Professor Neville Burkitt, dated 16th May 1954.
Letters from Dr W. Ph. Coolhaas, dated 14th June, 13th September, 20th October 1960.
Letter from Commander A. H. Cooper, R.A.N., dated 9th September 1954.
Letter from Mrs Meilink-Roelofsz of the Kol. Arch., The Hague, dated 26th November 1953, re Boudewijn van der Mijlen.
Letter from Dr I. H. van Eeghen, dated 25th January 1960.
Letter from Mr Soendojo Wirjowinoto, dated 23rd July 1954, re marriage of Lucretia Jansz etc., at Batavia.
Photostat of *Sketch Map Showing Islets in the Vicinity of Noon Reef, Houtman Rocks*, enclosed by Commander Cooper in his letter dated 9th September 1954.

PRINTED WORKS REFERRING TO FRANCISCO PELSAERT, THE *BATAVIA*, AND THE ABROLHOS ISLANDS

Adamson, Bartlett, "Island of Death", *Sea, Land and Air*, April 1920, pp. 1-6.
Australia Pilot, vol. v, 2nd ed. London 1923 (with supplement to 1957).
Batavia: De Hoofdst ad van Neerlands O. Indien etc., Kerkzaaken, vol. iii. Amsterdam, 1783.
Battye, J. S., Litt. D., *Western Australia: A History From Its Discovery to the Inauguration of the Commonwealth*. Oxford, 1924.
Biographie Universelle, Ancienne et Moderne, ed. L.-G. Michaud. Vol. xlvi, Paris, 1826; vol. li, Paris, 1828.
Calvert, Albert F., F.R.G.S., *The Discovery of Australia*, 2nd ed. London, 1902. Also volume of *Plates* attached to the book.
Chisholm, A. H., *Strange New World*. Sydney, 1941.
Cohen, B. C., "The Discovery of Western Australia, with Some Early Medical History", *Medical Journal of Australia*, 13th June 1953, pp. 840-3.
Colenbrander, H. T., ed., *Dagh Register gehouden int Casteel Batavia, Anno 1636*. The Hague, 1899. Ditto, *Anno 1643-4*. The Hague, 1902.
Colenbrander, H. T., ed., *Jan Pietersz. Coen, Bescheiden omtrent zijn Bedrijf in Indië*. Vol. iii, The Hague, 1921; vol. v, The Hague, 1923.
Collingridge, George, *The Discovery of Australia: A Critical, Documentary and Historic Investigation Concerning the Priority of Discovery in Australasia by Europeans Before the Arrival of Lieut. James Cook in the "Endeavour" in the year 1770*. Sydney, 1895.
Collingridge, George, M.C.R.G.S., *The First Discovery of Australia and New Guinea, Being the Narrative of Portuguese and Spanish Discoveries in the Australasian Regions Between the Years 1492-1606, with Description of Their Old Charts*. Sydney, 1906.
Coolhaas, W. Ph., ed., *Jan Pietersz. Coen, Bescheiden omtrent zijn Bedrijf in Indië*, vol. vii. The Hague, 1952.
Coolhaas, W. Ph., "Een Indisch Verslag uit 1631, van der hand van Antonio van Diemen", *Bijdragen en Mededelingen van het Historisch Genootschap te Utrecht*, vol. lxv, 1947, pp. 7-283.
De l'Isle, Guillaume, Maps of the World, 1740, 1750-60, 1775.
Deperthes, J. L., *Histoire des Naufrages*. Nouvelle edition par J. B. B. Eyriès, vol. ii. Paris, 1815.
Drake-Brockman, H., "The Reports of Francisco Pelsaert", *Early Days: Journal and Proceedings, Western Australian Historical Society*, Perth, vol. v, 1956, part 2.
Drake-Brockman, H., "The Wreck of the *Batavia*", *Walkabout Magazine*, Melbourne, vol. xxi, 1955, no. 1.
Drake-Brockman, H., *The Wicked and the Fair*. Sydney, 1957.
Eyriès, J. B., *Histoire des Naufrages*, vol. ii. Paris, 1815.
Fairbridge, Rhodes W., B.A., D.Sc., F.G.S., "Notes on the Geomorphology of the Pelsaert Group of the Houtman's Abrolhos Islands", *Journal of the Royal Society of Western Australia*, vol. xxxiii, 1946-7.
Favenc, Ernest, *Marooned on Australia*. London, 1905.
Favenc, Ernest, *The Story of Our Continent*. Sydney, n.d.
Forsyth, John, "The Visit of the Yacht Grootenbroeck to the Coast of the Southland in 1631", *Early Days: Journal and Proceedings of the Western Australian Historical Society*, vol. v, 1957, part 3.
Foster, William, *The English Factories in India. A Calendar of the Documents in the India Office etc.* 1622-3, Oxford 1908; 1624-9, Oxford 1909.
Gandevia, B., "A Tragedy for Tradition", *Medical Journal of Australia*, 5th October 1957, p. 505.
Geyl, P. *See under* Pelsaert, Francisco.
Glauert, L., B.A., "The Development of Our Knowledge of the Marsupials of Western Australia", *Journal of the Royal Society of Western Australia*, vol. xxxiv, 1947-8.

BIBLIOGRAPHY

Goldsmith, Frank H., *Treasure Lies Buried Here*. Perth, 1946.
Gordon, W. J., *The Captain General, being the Story of the Attempt of the Dutch to Colonize New Holland*. London, 1888.
Grey, George, *Journals of Two Expeditions of Discovery in North-West and Western Australia during the years 1837, 38 and 39*, vols. i and ii. London, 1941.
Harris, D. D., F.R.S., *Voyages and Travels*, vol. i. London, 1744.
Heeres, J. E., LL.D., "De Gouverneur-General Hendrik Brouwer", *Oud-Holland*. Amsterdam, 1907.
Heeres, J. E., LL.D., *The Part Borne by the Dutch in the Discovery of Australia 1606-1765*. Leiden and London, 1899.
Heeres, J. E., LL.D., ed., *Dagh Register gehouden int Casteel Batavia, Anno 1624-1629*. The Hague, 1896.
Kingsley, Henry, *Tales of Old Travel*. London, 1869.
Lamb, John, "Australia's First Pirate", *New Nation Magazine*, 1st September 1931.
Leupe, P. A., *De Reizen der Nederlanders naar het Zuidland op Nieuw-Holland*. Amsterdam, 1868.
Lindsay, Lionel, "The Story of the Abrolhos", *Lone Hand Magazine*, 2nd August 1909.
Macco, H. F., *Geschichte und Genealogie der Familien Peltzer*. Aachen, 1901.
Major, R. H., F.R.S., *Early Voyages to Terra Australis*. London, 1859.
Mooy, J., ed., *Bouwstoffen voor de Geschiedenis der Protestansche Kerk in Nederlandsch-Indië*, vol. i, 1927.
Moreland, W. H., C.S.I., C.I.E., *From Akbar to Aurangzeb: A Study in Indian Economic History*. London, 1923.
Moreland, W. H., C.S.I., C.I.E., and Geyl, P., Litt.D., *Jahangir's India*. See under Pelsaert, Francisco.
Nieuw Nederlandsch Biografisch Woordenboek. Ed. Dr P. C. Molhuysen, P. J. Blok, Dr L. Knappert. Vol. v, Leyden, 1921.
Ongeluckige Voyagie van't Schip Batavia Nae de Oost-Indien Gebleven op de Abrolhos van Frederick Houtman, op de hooghte van 28 1/3 graet, by-Zuyden de Linie Aequinoctiael, Uytgevaren onder den E. Francoys Pelsert. Jan Jansz, Amsterdam, 1647.
Ongeluckige Voyagie Van't Schip Batavia, Na Oost-Indien: Ut-gevaren onder de E. Francois Pelsaert. Gebleven op de Abrolhos van Frederick Houtman, op de hooghte van 28.en een half graden by Zuyden de Linie Equinoctiael. Lucas de Vries, 1649, Utrecht.
Pasco, J. Crawford, Commander R.N., *A Roving Commission: Naval Reminiscences*. Melbourne, 1897.
Pelsaert, Francisco, *Jahangir's India. The Remonstrantie of Francisco Pelsaert*. Translated from the Dutch by W. H. Moreland, C.S.I., C.I.E., and P. Geyl, Litt. D. Cambridge, 1925.
Perth Gazette, 15th April 1847.
Playford, P. E., "The Wreck of the *Zuytdorp* on the Western Australian Coast in 1712", *Early Days: Journal and Proceedings of the Western Australian Historical Society*, Perth, vol. v, 1959, part 5.
Ross, Marvin C., "The Rubens Vase, Its History and Date", *Journal of the Walters Art Gallery*, Baltimore, vol. vi, 1943.
Scott, Ernest, *Australian Discovery by Sea*, vol. i. London, 1929.
Seaman's Recorder, vol. i, pp. 281-9. London, 1825.
Siebenhaar, William, "The Abrolhos Tragedy: The First Complete Translation in English of the Original Dutch Account published Eighteen Years after the Massacre", *Western Mail*, Perth, Christmas Number 1897.
Stapel, F. W., *De Oostindische Compagnie in Australië*. Amsterdam, 1937.
Stewart, Douglas, *Shipwreck. A Poetic Drama*. Sydney, 1947.
Stokes, J. Lort, *Discoveries in Australia, 1837-43*, vol. ii. London, 1846.
Tasman, Abel Janszoon, *Journal of His Discovery of Van Diemens Land and New Zealand in 1642 . . . to which are added Life and Labours of Abel Janszoon Tasman by J. E. Heeres*. Frederik Muller, Amsterdam, 1898.

Teichert, Curt, D.Sc., "Contributions to the Geology of Houtman's Abrolhos, Western Australia", *Proceedings of the Linnean Society of New South Wales*, vol. lxxi, 1947, parts 3, 4.
Thévenot, M., *Relations de divers voyages curieux*. Paris, part i 1663; part ii 1664.
Tijdschrift voor Indische, Taal-, Land-, en Volkenkunde. Ed. W. Stortenbeker jun. and L. J. J. Michielsen, vol. xviii, Zesde Serie, vol. i. The Hague, 1872.
Uren, Malcolm, *Sailormen's Ghosts: The Abrolhos Islands in Three Hundred Years of Romance, History and Adventure*. Melbourne, 1940.
Van Dam, Pieter, *Beschrijvinge van de Oostindische Compagnie*. Ed. F. W. Stapel. Vol. i, part i, The Hague, 1927.
Van Troostenburg de Bruijn, C.A.L., *Biographisch Woordenboek van Oost-Indische Predikanten*. Neijmegen, 1893.
Zadoks Josephus-Jitta, A. N., "De Lotgevallen van den Grooten Camee in het Koninklijk Penningkabinet", *Oud-Holland*, 1951, pp. 191-211.

MODERN MAPS AND CHARTS

Army Maps:
    Ajana: No. 1194. G50/13. Zone I. 4 m. to in. 1943.
    Bowes: No. 292. Zone I. 1 in. Series. 1943.
    Geraldton: Second Edition H49/4 and H50/1. Zone I. 4 m. to in. 1942.
    Lesueur and Green Head: Nos. 249, 350. Zone I. 1953.
    Lynton: No. 1537. Emergency Ed. 1 in. Series. 1944.
    Minilya: No. 1261. F50/13 and F49/6. 4 m. to in. 1944.
    Point Cloates: F49/12 and 16. Zone I. 8 m. to in. 1942.
    Yanrey: No. 1237. F50/9 and 12. Zone I. 4 m. to in. 1944.
Australian Aeronautical Map: H. 3—Geraldton. Dec. 1949.
Admiralty Charts:
    Bedout Island to Cape Cuvier. No. 1055.
    Cape Cuvier to Champion Bay. No. 1056.
    The Houtman Rocks and Adjacent Coast. No. 1723.

PRINTED WORKS OF GENERAL REFERENCE

Ashley, Maurice, *England in the Seventeenth Century* (1603-1714). London, 1952.
Bontekoe, Willem Ysbrantsz, *Memorable Description of the East Indian Voyage, 1618-25*. Translated from the Dutch by Mrs C. B. Bodde-Hodgkinson and Pieter Geyl, Litt. D., with Introduction and notes by P. Geyl. London, 1929.
Brendon, J. A., B.A., F.R.Hist.Soc., *Great Navigators and Discoverers*. London, 1929.
Burckhardt, Jacob, *Recollections of Rubens*. Ed. H. Gerson. London, 1950.
Carrington, C. E., *The British Overseas*. Cambridge, 1950.
Chambers's Encyclopaedia. London, 1901 edition.
Clark, G. N., M.A., *The Seventeenth Century*. Oxford, 1931.
Colenbrander, H. T., *Jan Pietersz. Coen, Levensbeschrijving*. The Hague, 1934.
Du Bois, J. P. I., *Vies des Gouverneurs Généraux, avec l'abrégé de l'histoire des etablissemens Hollandois aux Indes Orientales*. The Hague, 1763.
Encyclopaedia Britannica. London, 1947.
Encyclopaedia of Religion and Religions. Ed. E. Royston Pike. London, 1951.
Geyl, P. *See under* Bontekoe, Willem Ysbrantsz.
Hunter, Sir William Wilson, K.C.S.I., M.A., LL.D., *A History of British India*, vol. i. London, 1899.
Kett, Charles W., M.A., *Sir Peter Paul Rubens*. London, 1882.
Moreland, W. H., C.S.I., and Chatterjee, Atul Chandra, C.I.E., K.C.S.I., *A Short History of India*. London, 1944.
Motley, John Lothrop, D.C.L., LL.D., *Life and Death of John of Barneveld, Advocate of Holland*. 2 vols. London, 1875.

Mumford, Lewis, *The Condition of Man*. London, 1944.
Murray, Sir James, *Murray's English Dictionary on Historical Principles*. Oxford, 1919.
Mutch, T. D., "The First Discovery of Australia, with an Account of the Voyage of the 'Dufken' etc.", *Journal of the Royal Australian Historical Society*, vol. xxviii, 1942, part 5.
Nieuw Volledig Engelsch-Nederlandsche, Nederlandsche-Engelsch Woordenboek. Ed. I. M. Calisch. Tiel, 1892.
Purchas, Samuel, B. D., *Hakluytus Posthumus, or Purchas His Pilgrimes*, vols. iv, ix. Glasgow, 1957.
Scott, Ernest, *A Short History of Australia*, 8th ed. Revised by Herbert Burton, M.A.Oxon. Oxford University Press, Melbourne, 1950.
Sherrington, Sir Charles, O. M., *Man on His Nature*. The Gifford Lectures, Edinburgh, 1937-8. Cambridge, 1946.
The Netherlands. Ed. Bartholomew Landheer, Ph.D. Berkeley, 1943.
Trevelyan, George Macaulay, *England Under the Stuarts*. 16th ed., London, 1933.
Vlekke, Bernard H. M., *Nusantara, A History of the East Indian Archipelago*. Cambridge, Mass., 1945.
Waters, David W., *The Art of Navigation in England in Elizabethan and Early Stuart Times*. London, 1958.
Witsen, Nicolaus, *Aeloude en Hedendaegsche Scheepsbouw en Bestier (Old and Present-day Ship Building and Management)*. Amsterdam, 1671.

INDEX*

Aborigines, Pelsaert's instructions concerning, 12, 48-9; sighted from *Batavia's* boat, 113, 300, 302
Abri vossos olhos, Portuguese phrase, 277-8
Abrolhos Islands *see* Houtman's Abrolhos
Adamite sect, 73, 74, 76
Admiralty charts, 3, 12, 278n
Agra, 3, 13, 16, 17, 18, 19, 21, 22-3, 24, 26, 27, 56, 59, 84, 87, 262, 274
Agulhas, 40
Ahamadabad, 21
Akbar, Emperor, 3, 16, 23, 24
Aldersz, Cornelis, 116
Almaric, 74
Amboina, 15, 37, 81, 92, 99, 101
Amsterdam, 3, 6, 8, 11, 26, 27, 32, 35, 37, 38n, 45, 49, 52, 56, 57, 58, 61, 63, 64, 65, 66, 67, 71, 73, 74, 88n, 91, 99, 122n
Anabaptist sect, 74
Antwerp, 14, 15, 35n, 36, 88, 90, 92
Arakan, 65n
Arminius, Jacobus, 76, 77
Ashburton River, 302
Assendelft, ship, 38
Australia Pilot, 289, 291, 297
Australian continent, landings on, 12, 48, 295 *et seq.*; first mention of birds of, 236n; first mention of marsupials of, 47, 235n; Pelsaert's probable time on, 304

Banda, 15, 79
Bastiaensz, Gijsbert, 77 *et seq.*, 115, 116, 117, 148n, 202n, 290; his letter concerning the wreck and its aftermath, 4n, 37, 39, 69, 77, 78, 79, 98, 224n, 263-9, 284, 292; family of, 77, 115, 294; appointment as Predikant, 77; embarks on *Batavia*, 77; remarriage, 79; death, 79; and Wurffbain, 80; and the carrying out of lesser sentences, 102
Bastiaensz, Gijsbert (son of Predikant), 77
Bastiaensz, Judith (or Judick), 70, 77, 80, 81, 115
Bastiaensz, Roelant, 77, 115
Bastiaensz, Willemyntgie, 77, 115

Batavia, city, 10, 25n, 27, 31, 33, 36, 37, 38, 39, 40n, 42, 43, 44, 45, 46, 47, 49, 50, 51, 52, 53, 54, 55, 57, 58, 59, 61, 62, 64, 65, 70, 71, 72, 73, 80n, 99, 100, 224n. *See also* V. O. C.
Batavia, ship, 34, 36, 38; wreck of, 3, 17, 19, 41, 42-3, 53-4, 62, 112, 122 *et seq.*, 275-93; leaves the Texel, 12, 37-8; plan to seize, 34, 40; description of, 38, 38n; officers, crew and others aboard, 38, 51, 107 *et seq.*; runs into storm, 39, 40; records of voyage from Holland missing, 43; treasure and goods carried by, 42, 43, 44, 47, 49, 50, 51, 52, 53, 57, 62n, 81, 82, 86, 88-9, 90, 97, 98, 117, 118, 120, 257, 258, 294; deaths listed, 50; fate of survivors, 50, 81; Pelsaert's journals concerning, 43, 94 *et seq.*, 122 *et seq.*; women and children aboard, 110-11; summary of events following wreck, 112-21; relics of, 294. *See also Ongeluckige Voyagie van't Schip Batavia*.
Batavia's Graveyard, 41n, 43n, 68, 70n, 76, 79, 95, 96, 113, 117, 118, 119, 120, 175n, 224n, 280, 285, 290 291, 292, 294
Battye, J. S., 277n
Beacon Island, 290, 292, 293. *See also Batavia's* Graveyard.
Beckford, William, and the Rubens Vase, 93
Beecke, Johannes Torrentius van der, 50, 73-4, 75
Beejoo Well, 301
Beer, Mattys, 116; tried and sentenced, 154, 189-94
Benkulen, 134n
Bennett, A. J., 303
Berger-Boot, ship, 61
Birds of Australia, first mention of, 236n
Bluff Point, 299
Bodde-Hodgkinson, Mrs C. B., 39n
Bontekoe, Willem Ysbrantsz, 39, 61
Both, Pieter, 15
Boudaen, Gaspar, great jewel of, 4, 50, 56, 57, 58, 84, 85-6, 87-8, 89
Brethren of the Free Spirit, 74
Broadhurst, F. C., 279

* This includes no detailed index to the Journals.

Brockman, G. J., 301, 303
Broecke, Pieter van den, 17, 18, 21n, 22, 32, 33n, 45, 72
Brouwer, Geertruid, 49
Brouwer, Hendrik, 6-7, 13, 14, 35-6, 60n, 88n, 277; becomes Pelsaert's brother-in-law, 7, 13, 14; and Pelsaert's estate, 15, 59; Governor-General at Batavia, 27, 49; and appointment of Pelsaert to Council of India, 36n; wife of, 13-14, 49; Route of, 41n; and the Indian "toy" trade, 86
"Brouwer's Route", 41n
Brouwershaven, ship, 65n
Brush Bronzewing, 236n
Bruyn, Andries de, 115
Burch, Jan van der, 52, 72
Burckhardt, Jacob, 91
Buren or *Bueren*, ship, 38
Burkitt, Professor Neville, 94
Burton, Dick, 290n

Calvert, A. F., 302
Calvin, doctrines of, 76, 101
Cameo, Great, 4, 50, 57, 58, 84, 85, 86, 87-8, 89
Cape of Good Hope, 8, 39, 40, 41n, 54, 62, 100, 287
Carlton, Sir Dudley, 74
Carnarvon, 301
Carpentier, Pieter de, 42, 43, 88n, 121
Carrington, C. E., 84n
Carstensz, Jan, 68, 189n
Celebar, 134n
Chapman River, 219n
Charles I of England, 4, 74
Chisholm, A. H., 47n, 236n
Claasz, Wybrecht, 68, 69, 78
Clark, G. N., 6n, 7n
Cleenen Davidt, ship, 38
Cnijf, Maria, 79
Cocos Islands, 120, 121, 300
Coen, Jan Pieterszoon, 7, 36n, 39, 43, 44, 45, 61, 71, 277, 286, 287, 288, 297; appointed Governor-General, 7, 15, 286; and Dutch trading activities, 12, 15, 17, 18, 27, 40n, 85, 99; use of term "mile" in his dispatches, 19; Pelsaert recommended to, 36-9, 52; order to Pelsaert following wreck of *Batavia*, 43, 46, 47, 99, 100, 114, 115, 257-8; his reputation for sternness, 45, 46, 99-100; death and funeral of, 49, 72, 118; interview with Pelsaert, 114
Cohen, B. C., 73n
Colenbrander, H. T., 37n, 38n, 39n, 40n, 44n, 45n, 46n, 56n, 57n, 61n, 71n, 81n, 85n, 86n, 88n, 257n, 262n

Collingridge, George, 80n
Commandeur, title of, 3, 5, 11, 12, 96
Commonwealth Bureau of Mineral Resources, 300
Constantine the Great, 86
Coolhaas, Dr W. Ph., 18n, 21n, 33n, 45n, 52n, 58n, 65n
Cooper, Commander A. H., 293, 294n
Cornelisz, Jeronimus, 61, 80n, 113, 119, 213, 223n, 291, 293; on relations between Pelsaert and Jacobsz, 33, 34; crimes of, 34, 40, 60, 67, 68, 113, 114, 115, 116, 172-7, 248-54, 259; and Lucretia Jansz, 64, 67, 68, 70; note in *Ongeluckige Voyagie* re, 67-8; tried and sentenced, 73, 79, 95, 96, 97, 100, 101, 102, 118, 154, 158-62, 163-5, 166, 167, 168-9, 176-7; his early life, 73; character of, 73, 75-6; beliefs preached by, 73-5; attempts suicide, 75, 118; and the Great Cameo and other jewels, 88-9; and the search for water, 113; elects own "council", 114; pacts with other mutineers, 115; letter to French soldiers, 115; oaths of allegiance to, 116; captured at Abrolhos, 117; public reading of his examination and confessions, 118, 211-12; Pelsaert's "declaration in short" of his intent to murder, 248-54; attempt to discredit Pelsaert, 290
Cornelisz, Daniel, 115; sentenced, 240
Cornelisz, Jacob, 71
Coromandel Coast, 17, 27, 38
Coryat, Thomas, 21n
Council of India, 10-11, 12, 52, 93, 121; appointment of Pelsaert to, 12, 27, 36n, 37, 52, 116; Pelsaert's report to, 43-4; record of wreck, etc., 44; order to arrest Ariaen Jacobsz, 46, 56; criticism of Pelsaert, 52; minutes re death of Pelsaert, 55. *See also* V. O. C.
Cox, G. A., 10n, 38n
Crijnen, Dirk, 66n, 273
Cuick, Jacob Cornelisz, 64n, 70, 71
Cuyck, Pieter Willemsz, 70

Dam, Pieter van, 41n
Decker, Rogier, 116; sentenced, 231-2
Delabeeque, Louis, 37n
Denys, Hendrick, 115
Deschamps, Salomon, 115, 247n; his signature, 94; takes seat on trial council, 96; signs documentary evidence, 96-7, 192n, 226n; sentenced, 98, 223, 224n, 231, 234n
Deventer, ship, 58
Dick's Island, 290, 291, 292, 293

INDEX 319

Diemen, Antonio van, 45, 49, 58, 71, 81, 89n; on the wreck and subsequent events, 42-3, 49-50, 52, 62-3, 121; attitude to Pelsaert, 43, 51, 52, 58; lists goods salvaged from *Batavia*, 51; on Pelsaert's death and on appointment of new councillor, 52; on Ariaen Jacobsz, 58; on Pelsaert's jewels, 57-8
"Dilettante, A", 4, 13, 78
Dircksen, Jeronimus, *see* Cornelisz, Jeronimus
Dircx, Weijntgen, 66n, 67, 71
Dircx, Willempje, 70
Dobbelworst, Johannes, 55, 56
Dordrecht, 77
Dordrecht, ship, 32, 33, 36, 38, 61n, 79, 133n, 163n
Drake, Sir Francis, 8, 15
Drake-Brockman, H., 303n; *The Wicked and the Fair*, 5n, 290n; paper on Pelsaert, 219n; article on the wreck of the *Batavia*, 281n, 290n, 295
Drok, E. D., 21n, 22n, 33n, 52n, 59, 72n, 257n, 259n, 262n, 263n, 270n, 285n, 295n, 299
Dutch East India Company *see* V. O. C.
Dyke, Sir Anthony van, 87

Early Days (Journal and Proceedings, W.A. Historical Society), 219n, 278n
East Wallabi, 127n, 214n, 215n, 281, 282, 284, 288, 290, 291, 292, 293
Easter Group, Houtman's Abrolhos, 139n, 140n, 278, 281, 283, 284, 286
Eeghen, Dr I. H. van, 273
Eendracht, ship, 44n, 277n
Eendracht Land, 44n, 82, 277n, 278, 286, 287
Elizabeth I of England, 8, 67
Ende, Passchier van den, 115, 183n
English East India Company, 6, 8, 9, 12, 15-16, 17, 18, 22n, 28, 32, 34
Epicurus, 203n
Eugene, Prince, 281n
Eupen, 14, 36
Evening Reef, 286
Evertsz, Jan, 42n, 63, 114
Exmouth Gulf, 302

Fairbridge, Rhodes, 275, 280n, 288, 289
Flagstaff Hill, East Wallabi, 291, 293
Fleet President, office of, 11, 12
Fonthill Abbey, and the Rubens Vase, 93
Forsyth, John, 277n, 278
Foster, William, 21n, 32n
Fourment, Daniel, 88, 92
Fransz, Gillis, 112
Fraser Island, 301
Frederick Henry, Prince, 242n

Fredrick, Hans, sentenced, 244-5
Fredrick Hendrick, ship, 42
Fredricxsz, Rutger, tried and sentenced, 155-6, 205-7

Galias or *Gailliasse*, ship, 38, 51, 286
Gandevia, B., 73
Gantheaume Bay, 298, 299
Garden Island, 282n
Gellisz, Lucas, 169; sentenced, 223, 232-3
Geraldton, 122n, 219n, 282, 289n
Gerritsz, Abraham, 166n, 223n; sentenced, 232
Gerritsz, Claas, 46, 47, 96, 217n, 283n, 285, 286, 287, 288, 300
Gerritsz (or Gerritszoon), Hessel, maps, 277, 295, 302
Geyl, Professor P., 5, 22n, 39n
Gheleijnsen, Wollebrand, 33
Gilbert, John, 290
Glauert, L., 282n
Goldsmith, Frank H., 279
Gomarus, Franz, 76
Goss Island, 290n
Goss Passage, 294
Gouden Leeuw, ship, 37n, 55
Gould, John, 281n
Grasleen, Pelsaert family property, 13, 14
Green Head, 282
Gregorian Calender, 3, 122n
Grey, Sir George, 298, 299
Grijph, Commandeur, 33
Grootenbroeck, yacht, 278n
Grotius, Hugo, 6, 7, 77
Guano deposits, Abrolhos Islands, 279
Guillaume River, 303
Gujarat, 44n, 150n, 257
Gun Island, 279
Gupta, Das, 13n
Gysels, —, 37

Haarlem, 40, 73
Half Moon Reef, 279n, 281, 283, 288
Hardens, Anneken, 114, 116, 189n
Hardens, Hans, 114
Hardens, Hilletje, 114
Harmansz, Claas, sentenced, 223, 233-4
Hartger(t)s, Joost, 4n, 69, 78
Hartog, Dirk, 44n, 277n
Hawkins, Captain William, 16
Hayes, Wiebbe, 68, 95, 96, 116, 119, 127n, 175n, 240n, 245n, 254n, 284, 291, 292
Heer, C. de, 10n, 59, 91
Heeres, Professor J. E., 49n, 72n, 81n, 82n, 139n, 141n, 235n, 275, 277n, 278n, 279, 280, 283n, 285n, 287n, 291, 295, 299, 302n, 303

Heiljlweck, Hans Jacob, sentenced, 240-1
Helmichii, Helmichius, 80, 81
Hendricx, Abraham, 223n
Hendricxsz, Jacop, 183n
Hendricxsz, Jan, 114, 115, 116; tried and sentenced, 154, 162-3, 177-85
Hendrix, Zwaantie, 40, 62, 63, 64, 112
Heuten, Walter van, 18, 21
High and Mighty Seventeen, 8n, 9n, 13, 35-6, 58, 77, 90; recommendation of Pelsaert, 36-7; grant to Judith Bastiaensz, 81; and the great jewel, 86, 88n. See also V. O. C.
Hilkes, Johannes, 71
Hoeven, Pieter van der, 80-1
Holland mile, 18, 19, 20, 23n, 122n, 131n, 230n, 277
Hollandia, ship, 39n, 49, 72
Hope, J., 303
Hopkinson, Joseph, 21n
Houtman, Cornelis de, 8
Houtman, Frederik de, 8, 33, 61n, 277, 297
Houtman Rocks, *see* Houtman's Abrolhos
Houtman's Abrolhos, 3, 6, 8, 12, 33, 41, 42, 43, 44, 47, 53, 54, 61n, 62, 65, 67, 69, 73, 77, 82, 97, 98, 100, 101, 112 *et seq.*, 219n, 257, 259, 275 *et seq.*, 295 *et seq. See also under names of specific islands.*
Houtten, Cornelis van, 65n
Humayan, 22
Hummock Island, 139n, 282
Hunter, Sir William Wilson, 15n, 16n, 35n, 97n, 100n, 101n, 102n
Hutt Lagoon, 297, 299
Hutt River, 297, 298, 299, 300
Huygens, Christian, 6
Huyssen, Coenraat van, 80, 114, 115, 117, 244n

Ile de Ferro, 135n, 297
Indigo trade, 16, 17, 22n, 25, 26, 27
Inquirer, The, 290n
Isbrantsen, Isbrant, sentenced, 246

"Jac. Rommer River", 302
Jacobs, Jacob, 66
Jacobsen, Captain Dines, 291
Jacobsz, Ariaen, 61-3, 287, 289; his relations with Pelsaert, 20, 33, 34, 40, 41, 42, 46, 59; on ship *Dordrecht*, 33n; arrested and in prison, 33, 46, 56, 62, 63, 65, 79, 115, 287, 288; given command of *Batavia*, 34, 61, 62; his part in mutiny plans, 34, 40, 41, 62; and Zwaantie Hendrix, 40, 62, 63, 64, 112; and Lucretia Jansz, 40, 43n, 62, 64, 67; open-boat journey after the wreck, 42, 61, 112, 287, 288,

Jacobsz, Ariaen—*continued*
295, 300, 302; plan to kill Pelsaert, 42, 62; accused by Pelsaert, 46; career, 61; and the position of the wreck, 285, 286n, 287, 298
Jacobsz, Jacop, 223n, 251, 287; commands *Sardam* on rescue voyage, 46; lost in storm, 47, 54, 281, 286; on *Sardam* council, 96; and the position of the wreck, 285, 288
Jahan, Shah, 57
Jahangir, Emperor, 3, 16, 17, 18, 21, 24, 26, 28, 29, 32, 57, 84. *See also under* Moreland, W. H. (*Jahangir's India*).
Jambi, 55, 121
James I, 9n
Jansz, Allert, 41n, 68; tried and sentenced, 154-5, 194-200
Jansz, Anneken, 189n
Jansz, Aris, 115, 118, 196-7
Jansz, Claas, 68
Jansz, Cornelis, sentenced, 241-3
Jansz, Frans, 73n, 116, 241n
Jansz, Hendrick, 116
Jansz, Jacop, 46, 96, 223n, 283n, 285, 286, 287, 288, 300
Jansz, Jan, 4n, 5, 78, 79n, 89, 279n
Jansz, Lucretia, 63-5, 69, 78, 115, 273; and Ariaen Jacobsz, 40, 43n, 62, 64, 70; and Jan Evertsz, 42-3, 63; assault on, 46, 63, 65, 70n, 114; death of husband, 46, 65; remarriage, 64, 70; and Jeronimus Cornelisz, 64, 67, 68, 70; first marriage, 65-6, 67; embarks on *Batavia*, 67; statement re, 68; character of, 70; named godmother, 70, 71; return to Netherlands, 70; tomb of, 71n
Jansz, Pieter, provost, 114
Jansz, Sara, 66, 67
Jansz, Willem, 302
Japan, 11
Java, 15, 18, 38, 39, 40n, 42, 47, 53, 302. *See also* Batavia.
Java Head, 98
Johnstone, Murray, 302, 303
Jonas, Andries, tried and sentenced, 155, 200-4
Joosten, Steffanie, 66, 67, 273
Journal of Royal Society of Western Australia, 275n
Jumna, fort, 23
Juriaen, Captain Hans, 70, 71

Kastensen, Jan, *see* Carstensz, Jan
Keppler's map, 302
Kett, C. W., 51n
Krijnen, Dirk, 67
Kuyk, Jacob van, 67

Laet, John de, 22
Lands and Surveys Department, W.A., 300, 301n, 303
Leupe, P. A., 302, 303n
Leur, Gerrit de, 67
Leur, Nicolaes van der, 66
Leyden, 70, 71
Leyden, ship, 134n, 166n, 223n, 232n
Liebent, Andries, 114; sentenced, 243-4
Linschoten, Jan Huyghen de, 8
Lisbon, 17
L'Isle, Guillaume de, Maps of the World, 12, 61, 278
Little North Island, 139n
Long Island, *see* Seals Island
Loos, Wouter, 48, 49, 70, 81, 82, 98, 117, 224n, 300; tried and sentenced, 98, 119, 222-3, 224-8, 229-30
Lucasz, Philips, 37
Lynden—de Clerq, Baroness van, 273

Maagd van Dordrecht, ship, see *Dordrecht*
Macco, H. F., 13
McMahon, Hon. W., 292
Major, R. H., 82n
Malacca, 62
Marsupials, 47, 98, 119, 120, 127n, 214n, 235n, 281-2, 291
Masulipatam, 17, 18, 27, 65
Mataram, war with ruler of, 38, 71, 100, 119, 239n
Maurice, Prince of Orange, 6n
Mauritius, ship, 45, 302, 303
Medical Journal of Australia, 73n
Meenarra Hill, 298
Meilink-Roelofsz, Mrs, 65n
Mercantile Marine Atlas, 18n, 22n
Meynertsz, Hans, 66, 67, 273
Michielsen, L. J. J., 80
Michielsz van Os, Leenert, 43n, 115, 263n; tried and sentenced, 154, 185-9
Middle Channel, Houtman's Abrolhos, 286
Middle Island, 280
Mijlen, Boudewijn van der, 40, 46, 64, 65, 66, 67, 242n
Mint, at Surat, 17
Mollema, J. C., 65n
Moluccas, 15
Mooy, J., 25n
Moreland, W. H., 60n, 96; on the Amboina trials, 99; *Jahangir's India*, 5, 13, 14n, 15, 18, 19, 20, 22n, 23n, 24n, 25n, 26n, 27n, 28n, 29n, 30n, 31n, 32n, 35n, 52n, 84-5, 96n, 122n, 236, 274n (see also *Remonstrantie*); *From Akbar to Aurangzeb*, 8n, 9n, 17n, 27n, 38n, 99n, 100n; opinion of Pelsaert's literary talent, 21; on the

Moreland, W. H.—*continued*
spice trade, 27; on the "Holland mile", 19, 23n; and Pelsaert's Mogul history, 22; and Pelsaert's appointment to Council of India, 52; assesses Pelsaert's character, 274
Morning Reef, Houtman's Abrolhos, 275, 286, 288, 290, 293, 294
Motley, J. L., 76, 77
Mount Albert, 299
Mount Victoria, 299
Murchison River, 299
Mutch, T. D., 302n
Mutineers, oaths of, 95, 116, 117, 146, 147, 148, 165, 166; women kept by, 146-7

Napoleon, and the Great Cameo, 87
New Hoorn, ship, 61n
Noon Reef, Houtman's Abrolhos, 131n, 275, 286, 288, 289, 290, 293, 294n
Norris, Mrs Constance, 219n
North Head, 282
North Island, 127n, 217n, 278, 281, 284, 285, 286
Nusa Kambangan, 302

Ongeluckige Voyagie van't Schip Batavia, 4, 5, 64, 67, 68n, 69, 78, 79n, 89, 263n, 279, 280, 291; reference to illustrations in, 95, 101, 102, 290
Os, Leenert van, *see* Michielsz van Os, Leenert
Oud-Holland, 13n, 14n, 86n

Pabst van Bingerden, van, 87
Papal Bull of 1493, 8
Pasco, J. Crawford, 278
Peiresc, Fabri de, 87, 90, 91, 92, 272
Pelgrom de Bye, Jan, 48, 49, 73, 81, 82, 98, 119, 165n, 300; tried and sentenced, 155, 207-11, 229-30
Pelsaert, Francisco, 3, 13-14, 15, 46n, 59; *Remonstrantie* or Indian Report, 3, 5, 14-15, 18, 19, 21-32; his title of Commandeur, 3, 5, 11, 12, 96; joins V. O. C., 5, 9, 14, 15; and the Great Cameo and other jewels, 4, 55, 56, 57, 58, 84, 85, 86, 87, 88, 89; death of, 4, 14, 36, 52, 58, 89, 92, 121; Journals of, 3, 4, 5, 19, 20, 33, 43, 46, 47, 48, 53, 59, 60, 64, 67, 68, 69, 94-103, 122-254, 295; *Ongeluckige Voyagie*, 4, 5, 64, 67, 68n, 69, 78, 79n, 95, 101, 102, 279, 280, 290, 291; appointed to Council of India, 12, 27, 36n, 37, 52, 116; as Fleet President on *Batavia*, 12, 34, 36, 38-9, 40, 52, 56, 79; his notable career, 12, 34, 37; suggests trading

Pelsaert, Francisco—*continued*
improvements, 12, 26, 27, 28, 59; signature of, 12-13; spelling of name, 12-13; family of, 13, 14; etching of, 13; posted to Surat, 16, 21n; posted to Agra, 18, 21; describes Surat, 18; and van den Broecke's report, 18n; his use of term "mile", 18, 19, 20, 122n, 131n, 230n, 277; describes Agra, 22-3; on trade in Sikandra, 23-4; reported to Church Council, 25n; on indigo trade, 25, 26; and the spice trade, 26, 27; on English articles of trade, 28; describes Kashmir and its people, 28; on "rarities" or curios, 28; on government and the ruling classes, 28, 29, 30-1; and the Emperor Jahangir, 29, 32, 57; his pride in Dutch justice and administration, 29-30; his relations with Ariaen Jacobsz, 20, 33, 34, 40, 41, 46, 59, 112; history of Mogul Empire, 22; on the climate of India, 32; religion, 30; on social customs of India, 30; character and qualities, 31, 36, 54-5, 59, 77, 97, 99, 102, 274; health, 31, 32, 40-1, 53, 54, 55, 58, 260; termination of Indian appointment, 32; returns to Amsterdam, 35; orders *objets d'art* for Mogul Court, 32, 36; privately engaged in jewel trade, 36; recommended to J. P. Coen by V. O. C., 36-7, 42; and the wreck of the *Batavia*, 41, 43-4, 47, 53-4, 58, 84, 112, 259-61, 275, 278, 279n, 283, 284, 285, 286, 287, 289, 293; voyage to Java from the wreck, 42, 46, 53, 54, 62, 65, 112-14, 295, 300; returns to Abrolhos, 42, 46, 47, 71, 73, 95, 115, 134 *et seq.*, 232n, 281, 285, 297; van Diemen's attitude to, 43, 51, 58; Coen's opinion of, 43; Coen's order to, 43, 46, 47, 99, 100, 114, 257-8; and the search for water, 44, 112, 118, 119, 259, 279, 284, 291-2, 302; and the trial and punishment of offenders, 47, 53, 73, 95 *et seq.*; describes wallabies, 47, 98, 120, 281; returns from Abrolhos, 47, 49, 53, 98, 120-1, 300; records sighting of land birds, 47n; and the aboriginals, 48-9; and the landings on the continent, 48, 295 *et seq.*; instructions to men to be marooned, 48-9, 98; criticism of, 52; writes to V. O. C., 53-5, 62n, 78, 121, 259-61, 286n; only official letter in existence, 53-4; mother applies to have will cleared, 59; reference to in Batavia Day Book, 59-60; expedition to Jambi, 55, 121; and the attack on

Pelsaert, Francisco—*continued*
Lucretia Jansz, 70n, 241n; and Jeronimus Cornelisz, 73, 76, 97, 248-54, 259, 290; and the Rubens Vase, 92; member of *Sardam* council, 96; and Salomon Deschamps, 96; "declaration in short", 97, 98, 248-54; and Dutch ordinances regarding torture, 101; interview with Coen, 114; paper on read before W.A. Historical Society, 219n; Moreland's assessment of, 274; last letter of, 259-61, 286n.
Pelsart Group, Houtman's Abrolhos, 139n, 159n, 278, 279, 280, 281, 282, 284, 285
Pepper trade, 16, 18, 55
Persia, 11, 27, 89
Perth Gazette, 280n
Pietersen, Barent, 262
Pietersz, Jacop, 114, 117
Pigeon Island, 215n
Pinten, Jan, 115, 183n
Playford, P. E., 298, 299
Ploeis, Niclas de, 66
Point Cloates, 301, 304
Point Maud, 300
Point Moore, 282
Pontius, Paulus, 87, 89, 90
Port Gregory, 283
Portugal, 15, 16, 17, 55, 62
Predikant, the, *see* Bastiaensz, Gijsbert
Princen Islands, 98, 113, 115, 121
Proceedings of the Linnean Society of N.S.W., 275n

Raemburch, Hon. Crijn, 37, 42, 114
Rastell, President, 21n
Raye, Maria, mother of Francisco Pelsaert, 13
Rat Island, 281
Rechteren, Seyger van, 80n
Red Bluff, 298
Red Sea, 16, 17, 18
Religion, influence of, 7, 73-5, 76-7
Rembrandt, 6
Remmessens, Jacob, 302, 303, 304
Remmessens River, 302
Remmetszoon, Jan, 303
Remmetz, Jacob, 303
Remonstrantie (Pelsaert's Indian Report to V. O. C.), 3, 4, 5, 13, 14-15, 18, 19, 21-32, 43, 59, 60, 84-5, 96, 99
Renou, Jean, sentenced, 245-6
Rijkaert, Andries, 37n
Roe, Sir Thomas, 16, 17, 18, 21n, 28, 84
Rogiers, Theodore, 87
Rosicrucians, 75
Ross, Marvin C., 90, 91, 92n, 93, 272n
Rottnest Island, 219n, 282n
"Route de Pelsart", 12, 61, 278

Royal Australian Air Force, 300
Rubens, Peter Paul, 3-4, 6, 35, 36; and the Great Cameo, 4, 87-8, 89; and the Rubens Vase, 89-93, 272; letter to Peiresc, 90-1, 92, 272

Saeghman, Gilles Joosten, 4n, 69n
Sardam, yacht, 38, 48n, 114, 117, 118, 120, 224n, 270-1; picks up Pelsaert and Jacobsz, 42, 45, 114; sails for Abrolhos on rescue voyage, 42, 44, 46-7, 115, 232n; and the *Batavia's* treasure, 42, 44, 82, 89n, 117, 118, 119, 120, 257, 258; returns to Batavia with survivors, 43, 49, 73, 79, 261, 295, 300; loss of skipper, 47, 54, 281, 286; and the carrying out of lesser sentences, 79, 98, 102; Pelsaert's journal of voyage, 94, 95, 96, 97, 98, 134 *et seq.*; and the holding of the trials, 95, 96, 97, 98, 234n; council of, 96, 97, 98; crew of, on rescue voyage, 98, 153n; and Coen's order to Pelsaert, 100, 257; and ships' punishment methods, 101; course followed on rescue voyage, 115-17, 280-1, 282-5, 287, 288; and the site of the wreck, 235n, 280-1, 282-5, 287, 288, 290, 295; and the search for water, 119, 284, 292; and the landings on the Australian continent, 297, 298, 300
Sati, 24
Schepens, Maria, wife of Predikant, 77, 174n, 294
Scheldt, River, 35
Schilder, Pieter de, 37n
Schoonhoven, Simon Jacobsz, 37n
Seals Island, 73, 95, 97, 113, 115, 116, 117-18, 119, 159n, 290, 291, 294
Sebastiaensz, G., *see* Bastiaensz, Gijsbert
Seevanck, David van, *see* Zeevanck, David van
"Seventeen, the", *see* High and Mighty Seventeen
's Gravenhage, ship, 39
Shakespeare, William, 7
Ships' councils, constitution of, 11-12
Siam, 89
Siebenhaar, William, 5, 64, 68n, 279
Sierra Leone, 39, 134n, 166n, 223n
Sikandra, 23-4
Snellius mile, 19, 122n
Spain, 6, 8, 35
Specx, Jacques, 36n, 37, 45, 53, 76-7, 80n, 121, 134n, 260; and the records of the inquiry at Batavia, 33; elected provisional Governor-General, 49, 72, 118; and Pelsaert's promotion, 52; note re salvaged jewels, 57; on the

Specx, Jacques—*continued*
jewel trade, 57, 85, 86; his daughter Sara and Cortenhoeff, 45
Spice Islands, 9n, 11, 15, 27, 99
Spice trade, 11, 15, 18, 26, 27
Stapel, F. W., 41n
Steijns, Jan, 279n
Stoffelsz, Stoffel, 116
Stokes, J. Lort, 278, 279, 280n, 281, 283, 284, 288, 291
Stortenbeker, W., 80n
Sumatra, 55, 88, 89
Sunda, Straits of, 33n, 42, 61, 113
Surat, 11, 16, 17, 18, 20, 21, 22n, 26, 27, 32, 34, 36, 44n, 45, 57, 86, 133n, 163n
Swaenswijk, IJsbrand van, 79
Swally, 18, 32, 33, 40
Sweers, Aernolt, 37n

Table Bay, 40
Tasman, Abel Janszoon, 81, 82-3, 283n, 294, 295, 296, 297, 302, 303
Teichert, Curt, 275, 277n, 278n, 280n, 282, 289, 291
Texel, 12, 37, 39, 85
Thévenot, M., 4, 13, 278
Thiriou, Jean, 221n; sentenced, 243
Thirty Years' War, 35
Thwartway Island, 113
Topper's Hat Island, 113
Torrentius van der Beecke, Johannes, 50, 73-4, 75
Torture, 99, 100-2
"Toys", trade in, 17, 84, 85, 86, 230n
Traitors Island, 114, 290, 292
Troostenburg de Bruijn, C. A. L. van, 77n, 79n, 81n, 174n
Twelve Years' Truce, 35

United East India Company of the Netherlands (Vereenigde Oost-Indische Compagnie), *see* V. O. C.
Uren, Malcolm, 279
Utrecht, 58n
Uytrecht or *Utrecht*, ship, 45, 133n

Vase, Rubens, 89-93, 272
Visch, Jan Willemsz, 96
Vlack, Dr Pieter, 44n, 45, 49, 55
Vlekke, B. H. M., 6n, 45n
V. O. C., 3-18, 21, 46n, 47, 55, 59-60, 65, 67, 77, 80n, 100, 142n, 143n, 249n, 259n, 262n, 270n, 279n; Pelsaert's letters and reports to, 3, 21 *et seq.*, 47, 53-5, 62n, 121, 134n, 259-61, 286n (see also *Remonstrantie*); and the title of Commandeur, 3, 5; rules for ships and their crews, 6, 10, 11-12, 41n; Day Books of, 7, 49n,

V. O. C.—*continued*
59-60, 63, 71-2, 72-3, 81n, 93, 262; formation and administration of, 8, 15-18; High and Mighty Seventeen, 9n, 13, 35-6, 37-8, 58, 77, 81, 86, 88n, 90; Pelsaert's appointments with, 9, 12, 15, 18, 26, 31, 32, 36, 37, 52, 55; and the spice trade, 15, 16, 18, 26, 27, 55; and the indigo trade, 16, 17, 26, 27; records missing, 33, 43, 63, 72-3, 93; attitude to private trading, 34, 56, 88; and the States-General, 36, 100; letter to Coen recommending Pelsaert, 36-7, 52; trading ships of, 38; V. O. C. skipper describes voyage to Indies, 39-40; de Carpentier's influence in, 43; elects Governor-General to succeed Coen, 49; value of assets, 51; van Diemen's report to Directors of, 52; provide rescue yacht, 63; record of Pelsaert's death, 55; and the jewel trade, 55, 56-7, 58, 84 *et seq.*; and the jewels bought by Pelsaert, 56-8; attitude to Pelsaert, 58, 59, 60, 77; and Pelsaert's will, 59; and Ariaen Jacobsz, 61, 62, 63; and religious conformity, 76, 77; and the *Batavia's* money chest, 81; and Tasman's voyage of discovery, 81-3; and the "toy" trade, 84, 85, 86; record of the Great Cameo, 87-8; and the Rubens Vase, 92, 93; and the Amboina trials, 99; policy concerning evildoers, 99; and ships' torture instruments, 101; officers of on *Batavia*, 107; and the position of the wreck, 275; and Houtman's discovery of the archipelago, 277; J. P. Coen writes to, 286. *See also* Batavia; Council of India.
Vrede, ship, 303
Vries, Andries de, 114, 115
Vries, Lucas de, 4n, 69n, 78, 79n, 263n

Vry, Cornelis de, 37

Waddell, Helen, 103n
Walkabout magazine, 281n, 290n, 295
Wallabi Islands, 79, 127n, 214n, 235n, 236n, 257n, 275, 273, 281, 282, 284, 285, 286, 288, 289, 290, 291, 292, 293, 294. *See also under names of specific islands.*
Wallabies, 47, 98, 119, 120, 127n, 214n, 235n, 281-2, 291
Wallace-Crabbe, K., 13n
Wapen van Enckhuysen, ship, 134n
Wapen van Zeelant, ship, 15
Warrego, survey sloop, 293
Welderen, Olivier van, sentenced, 245
West Wallabi, 127n, 214n, 281, 282, 284, 288, 291, 292, 293
Western Mail, 5, 68n, 279
Whaleback Hill, 301
"White Angel", house, 66, 67, 273
White Cliffs, 297
Wickham, Commander John, 278, 281
"Willems Rivier", 302
William I of the Netherlands, 86-7
Witsen, Nicolaus, 12n
Wittecarra Gully, 298, 299
Wreck Point, Pelsart Island, 139n, 278, 281, 283
Wright, Joseph, 219n
Women, and the Abrolhos trials, 69-70; kept by mutineers, 146-7; aboard the *Batavia*, and their children, 110-11
Wurffbain, Jean-Sigismond, 80, 81

Yardie Creek, 131n, 301, 303
Yopson (or Yopzoon), Symon, 96, 217n

Zadoks-Josephus Jitta, Mrs, 86n, 87n, 89
Zeevanck, David van, 68, 69, 114, 116, 117, 201n
Zeewyck, ship, 159n, 279, 280
Zuytdorp, ship, 298n